A GRAMMATICAL VIEW OF
LOGIC PROGRAMMING

A GRAMMATICAL VIEW OF LOGIC PROGRAMMING

Pierre Deransart and Jan Małuszyński

The MIT Press
Cambridge, Massachusetts
London, England

This book was printed and bound in the United States of America.

Frontispiece illustration by José-Luis Deransart.

Library of Congress Cataloging-in-Publication Data

Deransart, Pierre.
  A grammatical view of logic programming / Pierre Deransart and Jan Małuszyński.
    p.   cm. — (Logic programming)
  Includes bibliographical references and indexes.
  ISBN 0-262-04140-5
  1. Logic programming.   I. Małuszyński, J. (Jan), 1941– . II. Title. III. Series.
QA76.63.D47   1993
005.13'1—dc20   93-25103
                                                                       CIP

Contents

List of Figures

List of Tables

Series Foreword

The logic programming approach to computing investigates the use of logic as a programming language and explores computational models based on controlled deduction.

The field of logic programming has seen a tremendous growth in the last several years, both in depth and in scope. This growth is reflected in the number of articles, journals, theses, books, workshops, and conferences devoted to the subject. The MIT Press series in logic programming was created to accommodate this development and to nurture it. It is dedicated to the publication of high-quality textbooks, monographs, collections, and proceedings in logic programming.

Ehud Shapiro
The Weizmann Institute of Science
Rehovot, Israel

Foreword by J.H. Gallier

Writing computer programs, as rewarding as it may be, is also a very demanding and difficult task. The main reason why it is so difficult to write (correct) programs is that we have to convert the logical specification of the algorithm that we have in our head into an explicit set of instructions written in some programming language. Unfortunately, programming languages do not permit the direct writing of "logical specifications", and we have to work out the translation and implementation of the logical specification that we have in mind into a programming language. Also, typically, a programming language is more friendly to a machine than to a human.

In the seventies, the idea that one could perhaps write a computer program as a form of logical specification arose (idea developed by Colmerauer and Kowalski). An important ingredient that made this idea actually viable was the invention by Alan Robinson of the resolution method and of a practical unification algorithm, in the early sixties. It was observed that when the resolution method is applied to certain restricted clauses known as Horn clauses, then it can be constrained to work in a certain canonical manner, and thus it is more efficient. Horn clauses are typically classified in three categories: atomic clauses of the form $q(t_1, \ldots, t_k)$, also called *facts*, clauses of the form $(A_1 \wedge \ldots \wedge A_m) \supset B$, called *definite clauses*, and clauses of the form $\neg A_1 \vee \ldots \vee \neg A_m$, called *goals* (where A_i, B are atomic formulae). Basically, the resolution method for Horn clauses only forms resolvents involving a (single) goal, facts, and definite clauses. A major insight to the idea that the resolution method can be used as an evaluation procedure is that a definite clause $(A_1 \wedge \ldots \wedge A_m) \supset B$, if written as $B \leftarrow A_1, \ldots, A_m$, can be thought of as a procedure definition, where the "head" $B = q(t_1, \ldots, t_k)$ is defined (perhaps recursively) in terms of the "body" $A_1, \ldots, A_m$. A definite program P is then just a finite set of definite clauses and facts. Given a definite program P, computing "answers" to a query $q(t_1, \ldots, t_k)$ amounts to applying the resolution method to the set of clauses $P \cup \{\neg q(t_1, \ldots, t_k)\}$. This process involves crucially the computation of certain substitutions known as most general unifiers (or mgu's). However, unlike in automated theorem proving, we are not just interested in the fact that $P \cup \{\neg q(t_1, \ldots, t_k)\}$ is unsatisfiable (i.e., that the resolution method terminates with the empty clause). We also want *answer substitutions*, that is, one (or all) substitution(s) for the variables occurring in $q(t_1, \ldots, t_k)$ involved in showing that $P \cup \{\neg q(t_1, \ldots, t_k)\}$ is unsatisfiable. Thus, in the paradigm of logic programming just sketched, computing substitutions plays a major role.

The semantics of definite programs can be neatly explained in terms of certain kinds of trees, called proof trees. A very fruitful observation is that, given a definite clause $B \leftarrow A_1, \ldots, A_m$, stripping the arguments of the atomic formulae $B, A_1, \ldots, A_m$ (for example, if $B = q(t_1, \ldots, t_k)$ and $A_i = q_i(t_1^i, \ldots, t_{k_i}^i)$), yields a context-free rule $q \rightarrow q_1 \ldots q_m$. Thus, given a definite program P, by stripping the arguments of the predicate symbols, we obtain a context-free grammar G_P. Of course, we have lost a lot of information in the process. However, it turns out that people interested in compiler construction (Knuth being one of the major contributors) defined and investigated a generalization of the concept of a context-free grammar known as *attribute grammar*. Remarkably, as observed by the authors of this book (and others), there is an intimate relationship between the notion of a definite program and the notion of an attribute grammar. Furthermore, various evaluation schemes were developed for attribute grammars, and it turns out that some of these evaluation schemes can be adapted fruitfully for evaluating (certain) definite programs. Another benefit of "transferring technology" from the area of attribute grammars to the area of logic programming (at least the approach in terms of Horn clauses) is that methods for proving the correctness of attribute grammars yield methods for proving the correctness of definite programs.

Thus, the analogy between attribute grammars and definite programs that we briefly sketched sets the stage for the contents of the present book and explains its title **A grammatical view of logic programming**. The authors develop an original and unified theory of logic programming exploiting the intimate relationship between attribute grammars (suitably generalized) and definite programs mentioned earlier. Among the main novelties, we would like to stress the comparison with other kinds of grammars such as DCG's and Van Wijngaarden grammars, the systematic development of proof techniques for definite programs, and an investigation of the occur-check problem. The authors start basically from scratch, but they lead the reader to the frontiers of research. In this respect, this book should be of interest to beginning students and to more experienced researchers as well. We believe that it will be a source of inspiration to many, researchers and practitioners alike.

Philadelphia, May 1993.

Preface

The field of logic programming has its origins in logic and automatic theorem proving. Over more than one decade the research on foundations of logic programming introduced a number of important concepts which were presented in the perspective of first-order logic. On the application side logic programming has been often claimed useful for natural language processing and for compiler construction. Traditionally, the research in these fields uses some notions of grammars. This motivated many attempts to transform grammars of interest into logic programs.

This book presents a complementary approach of putting logic programs into a grammatical perspective, i.e. viewing logic programs as grammars. The motivation is to enrich the field of logic programming by some concepts and techniques developed in the theory of formal grammars and to show their usefulness in this field.

The class of logic programs considered is restricted to definite programs. The "grammatical view" of such programs is given by the well-known semantics associating with a program a class of its proof trees. This allows for relating logic programs to the grammars having a notion of parse tree which is rich enough to represent proof trees of definite programs. As the proof tree semantics is known to be equivalent to the other well-established kinds of declarative semantics of definite programs the "grammatical view" does not lead us away from logic. In the same time the grammars considered become natural extensions of logic programs with the same kind of declarative semantics.

The book relates definite programs to the well-known kinds of grammars: Van Wijngaarden grammars and attribute grammars. This is achieved by showing that a proof tree of a definite program can be seen as a parse tree of each of the grammars. This makes possible a formal comparison of these grammars and definite programs. The comparison shows the following important differences:

- Definite programs have no concept of the terminal alphabet and of the language generated by a program.

- The grammars considered use a many-sorted type discipline, while definite programs use one-sorted terms.

- The attribute grammars have an explicit notion of (data) dependency
  which is not present in definite programs. This has been one of the
  fundamental notions of the formalism. It gave rise to classification of
  attribute grammars and inspired development of efficient operational
  semantics applicable to subclasses of attribute grammars. In these developments the dependency relation has been used to infer properties of
  the computations.

- The attribute grammars allow for use of specific algebraic structures as
  semantic domains, while definite programs have no predefined interpretation.

- The operational semantics of attribute grammars is based on evaluation
  of ground terms while the operational semantics of definite programs
  is based on unification. The attribute grammars conceptually separate
  the computation process into two phases: construction of a parse tree
  and decoration of the tree. No such separation is defined for definite
  programs; the resolution procedure constructs a proof tree; the labels of
  the tree may include uninstantiated variables which may be updated as
  a result of subsequent unification steps.

Thus, definite programs considered as grammars are rather restricted
in comparison to the above mentioned grammatical formalisms. The
differences may be a source of inspiration for defining extensions of definite programs. As a matter of fact some extensions of definite programs proposed in the literature attempt to incorporate grammatical
features discussed above, sometimes without direct reference to the existing grammatical formalisms. A grammatical view of logic programming gives a uniform perspective of such extensions. For justifying this
claim we mention some of the existing proposals which can be related
to the above comparison.

- The notion of definite clause grammar (DCG) [PW80] has been introduced as a grammatical extension of definite programs to deal with languages. It is usually understood as a "syntactic sugar" for a special type
  of Prolog program. A grammatical view of logic programming allows one
  to consider DCG's as a special class of Van Wijngaarden grammars, obtained by introducing terminal symbols to definite programs. With this
  view the usual transformation of DCG's to Prolog program is an implementation of DCG's in Prolog. Other implementations, like [Nil86],

may be developed and proved correct with respect to the grammatical semantics. On the other hand, any definite program can be seen as a special case of a DCG, due to its grammatical reading.

- There have been attempts to introduce explicit many-sorted type discipline to logic programming. A commercial product using this idea was the Turbo Prolog system [Bor86]. The concepts of Turbo Prolog can be directly linked to Van Wijngaarden grammars.

- The notion of dependency relation originating from attribute grammars has been used for static analysis of logic programs and their extensions. Several papers report on its usefulness for groundness analysis (e.g. [Dra87]), termination (e.g.[Plü91]) and occur check analysis (e.g. [DM85b, AP92b]).

- The idea of logic programming on predefined algebraic structures has recently gained a lot of attention under the name of constraint logic programming (e.g. [JL87, Hen89]). An approach aiming at declarative integration of Prolog with procedures written in other programming languages presented in [BM88, MBB+93] is another extension incorporating algebraic structures in logic programming. At least declarative semantics of such extensions can be discussed in the framework presented in this book. It is, however, very likely that some concepts, like dependency relation, may also be useful.

- There have been many attempts to integrate unification with term reduction. They necessarily lead to a concept of delayed evaluation of insufficiently instantiated terms. Similar delays are also used in constraint logic programming. The concept of delay seems to bridge a gap between dependency-controlled operational semantics of attribute grammars and resolution-based operational semantics of definite programs. A study of the operational semantics with a grammatical perspective allows one to find a common denominator which reduces the problem of construction of a proof tree (or of a parse tree) to finding a solution of a set of equations. Different control strategies imposed on the process of equation solving, and different algebraic structures on which the equations are solved, cause differences in the operational semantics. This book presents a general equational framework, which on one hand includes as special cases the operational semantics of both formalisms, and on the other hand provides inspiration for defining new kinds of operational semantics.

The grammatical view of logic programming presented in this book gives a natural unifying framework for studying of these and other extensions of logic programming proposed in the literature, and possibly for defining new ones, like new kinds of operational semantics based within the presented framework.

Another gain of taking the grammatical view is a possibility of applying to logic programs methods defined for grammars. Two chapters of this book are devoted to proof methods for logic programs. The proof methods for definite programs are being derived from methods developed for attribute grammars [Der84, CD88]. Grammars as well as logic programs are often considered to be axiomatic specifications. With this view the problem of their validation has been often neglected in the early days of logic programming. However, logic programs, like other kinds of programs, should properly reflect intentions of the users and may be subject to validation with respect to specifications describing these intentions. The need for verification methods grows with the growing size of logic programs used in a growing number of applications in software and knowledge engineering. Verification of logic programs is one of the important topics of this book. The nature of logic programs may make verification relatively simple. Attribute grammars provide a uniform framework for presentation of many of the known proof methods. This presentation may facilitate new developments.

Other examples of the transfer of methods are the above mentioned alternative parsers for the DCG's employing look-ahead techniques and the applications of the dependency techniques for static analysis of logic programs.

The book consists of:

- A new presentation of the foundations of logic programming, based on the notion of proof tree. The presentation facilitates discussion of grammatical aspects of definite programs and introduces new kinds of semantics for definite programs. The relations between various kinds of semantics are discussed.

- A survey of some relevant grammatical formalisms, with a comprehensive introduction to attribute grammars and Van Wijngaarden grammars, addressed to the people working in logic programming.

- A formal comparison of definite programs and the above mentioned grammars. The comparison identifies the grammatical concepts of interest for logic programming.

- A presentation of the verification methods for definite programs derived from verification methods for attribute grammars.

- Analysis of the occur-check problem as an example of the application of the grammatical view of logic programming.

The material is organized in 8 chapters.

Chapter 1 presents preliminaries. It is thought more as a survey of some relevant notions than as a tutorial exposition and can probably be skipped by most readers. It is however recommended to have a look at the concept of parse tree of a context-free grammar which is presented in algebraic setting. (Section 1.5)

Chapter 2 discusses foundations of logic programming using the concept of proof tree [Cla79] as a basic notion. A general framework for construction of proof trees is discussed, which reduces the problem to equation solving. This framework subsumes as special cases the operational semantics of both attribute grammars and definite programs. The declarative semantics of a definite program is defined as the set of the proof trees which can be constructed for a given program. The semantics is parameterized by the interpretation of the functors of the language, which in the classical case are interpreted as term constructors. Interpretations on other algebraic structures may also be considered in this framework. This semantics gives a foundation of the grammatical view of logic programming since the proof trees can be seen as the parse trees of the grammars defined in the following chapters. The proof tree semantics is then related to other kinds of semantics, such as the model-theoretic semantics, the fixpoint semantics and a semantics describing the observational behaviour of definite programs. The classical operational semantics based on the SLD resolution is also discussed as a special case of the general framework. A brief presentation of the notion of completion concludes the chapter.

Chapter 3 gives an introduction to Van Wijngaarden grammars and to definite clause grammars defined as a subclass of Colmerauer's metamorphosis grammars. A comparison of parse trees of these grammars with proof trees of definite programs shows that the latter can be seen as the special class of both Van Wijngaarden grammars and DCG's.

The relation between DCG's and Van Wijngaarden grammars is also discussed. The commonly used compilation of DCG's into definite programs is presented.

Chapter 4 gives an introduction to attribute grammars. The notion of attribute grammar is presented as a specification of a class of context-free parse trees with nodes labeled by tuples of semantic values. This declarative view gives a basis for subsequent comparison with definite programs. The notion of attribute grammar originating from Knuth [Knu68a] is obtained by putting certain restrictions on this general definition. A special attention is devoted to the notion of dependency relation which is studied in the abstract setting of attribute dependency schemes. The approaches to attribute evaluation are briefly discussed together with the classification of attribute dependency schemes. The remaining part of the chapter discusses the notions of partial correctness and completeness of an attribute grammar with respect to a specification and surveys methods for proving partial correctness and completeness.

Chapter 5 relates logic programs and attribute grammars. It shows a number of formal constructions which allow for identifying subclasses of attribute grammars and definite programs which are equivalent in some well-defined sense. The constructions allow for modelling semantics of definite programs by attribute grammars. Different constructions are defined for modelling different kind of semantics. The chapter discusses also a concept of directionality for logic programs and illustrates a possibility of using the notion of dependency relation for static analysis of definite programs.

Chapter 6 derives proof techniques for definite programs from proof techniques for attribute grammars. This is done by applying the proof methods of Chapter 4 to the attribute grammars modelling different kinds of semantics of definite programs. It gives a general survey of the techniques obtained in that way.

The objective of Chapter 7 is to give an independent presentation of two proof methods for partial correctness of definite programs. The methods have been derived in Chapter 6 but the intention of Chapter 7 is to define them without reference to the constructions of Chapter 5. Thus, Chapter 7 may be read independently of Chapter 5 and Chapter 6. Additionally it presents a larger example.

Chapter 8 discusses the notion of a definite program not subject to occur-check (NSTO). The occur-check problem is an interesting unde-

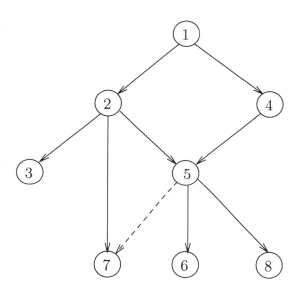

Figure 0.1
Dependency structure of the chapters

cidable problem with practical importance for correct implementation of
logic programming systems. The concepts presented in this book allow
us to define a number of non-trivial sufficient conditions for checking
that a program has the NSTO property.

We did not intend to set an exhaustive bibliography related to all
the topics considered in the book: the different fields which we try to
connect have given rise to a large amount of publications impossible to
cite exhaustively. Sometimes we quote the basic sources of references.

The dependency structure of the chapters is shown in Fig. 0.1. Chapter 5 is the central chapter of the book. It combines the concepts originating from attribute grammars (Chapter 4) with the concepts originating from logic programming (Chapter 2). Chapter 7 has been made
independent of Chapter 6, although both discuss verification issues. This
introduces some redundancy, but the objective is to allow for studying
verification methods for partial correctness without reading Chapter 5.
Nevertheless a few definitions of Chapter 4 and of Chapter 5 are needed
in Chapter 7.

The idea of the book originated from the paper on relations between logic programs and attribute grammars published by the authors in 1985 [DM85b]. Since then many results related to this topic have been obtained by different people and the ideas found some applications. The book was intended to be a synthesis of most of these results, including some unpublished ones. Starting from a "short" paper, we have been surprised by the growth of the draft when trying to discuss existing and potential applications of the grammatical view. To keep the reasonable size of the book we limited the study to "pure" logic programming, namely to definite clauses extended with goals. Extensions of the grammatical view to logic programming with negation, to constraint logic programming, to amalgamations of logic programming with functional programming and to concurrent logic programming are not discussed, although many of the concepts presented in this book have already shown usefulness in the study of properties of such extensions.

We hope that the material presented will contribute to better understanding of the nature of logic programming and of the methodology of programming with axioms.

Acknowledgments   The authors are very grateful to many people who contributed to this book in different ways:

- to Gérard Ferrand who constantly participated in the development of many of the presented ideas;
- to Jean-François Boulicaut, Jean-Louis Bouquard, Pascal Chambre, Włodek Drabent, Bruno Dumant, Nissim Francez, Laurent Fribourg, Jukka Paakki, Vasco Pedro, Sophie Renault, students and anonymous referees of related papers for their critical comments on previous manuscripts;
- to François Barthélémy, Staffan Bonnier, Johan Boye, Marc-Michel Corsini, Bruno Courcelle, Jean-Paul Delahaye, Gilberto Filé, Martin Jourdan, Bernard Lorho, Ulf Nilsson, Claude Pair, Michel Téguia, for stimulating discussions on the topics related to the contents of this book.

Thanks are due to Teresa Ehling and Bob Prior of the MIT Press for their encouragement and patience concerning the deadlines. Special thanks are due to the people who helped us with typesetting and editorial matters, especially Florence Bridon, Olivier Durin, Agnès Frapy at INRIA and Jenya Weinreb at the MIT Press. Last but not least, our particular thanks go to our families for their support and patience during this long march. Many thanks, José-Luis, for your drawings.

Linköping University and INRIA–Rocquencourt provided excellent environments for this work. The work of the second author was supported in the initial phase by the W. W. Clyde Visiting Professorship at the University of Utah College of Engineering. Parts of this work have been supported by EEC Esprit Basic Research Action "Integration", by the Swedish Research Council for Engineering Science (TFR) and by the projects ATTRISEM and METHEOL of the CNRS "GRECO de Programmation".

1 Preliminaries

This chapter is a survey of basic mathematical concepts to be used in the book. It is thought more as a reference than as a tutorial presentation.

1.1 Relations

Let $\mathcal{D}$ be a finite family $D_1, ..., D_n$ of not necessarily distinct sets, where $n \geq 1$. A *relation* on $\mathcal{D}$ is a set of tuples $\langle a_1, ..., a_n \rangle$ where $a_i \in D_i$ for $i = 1, ..., n$. The set of all such tuples is called the *full n-ary relation* or the *Cartesian product* of the sets. The set may be empty and is then called the *empty relation* and it is denoted λ. If all sets D_i are identical with a set D the relation is called an n-ary relation on D.

An $n+1$-ary relation R on D such that for any n tuple $\langle a_1, ..., a_n \rangle$ there exists at most one element b in D such that $\langle a_1, ..., a, b \rangle$ is in R is called an n-ary function on D. A function is *partial* iff for some tuple $\langle a_1, ..., a_n \rangle$ there is no b such that the tuple $\langle a_1, ..., a_n, b \rangle$ is in R. Otherwise the function is *total*.

Let R be a binary relation on a set D. The notation aRb is often used instead of $\langle a, b \rangle \in R$. R is said to be

- *reflexive* iff aRa for every a in D,
- *transitive* iff for every a, b, c in D if aRb and bRc then aRc,
- *symmetric* iff for every a, b in D if aRb then bRa,
- *antisymmetric* iff for every a, b in D if aRb and bRa then $a = b$.

A binary relation R on D which is reflexive, transitive and symmetric is called an *equivalence* relation on D. An equivalence relation R induces partition of D into disjoint subsets called *equivalence classes* of R. For a given a in D the equivalence class of a denoted $[a]_R$ is the subset of D consisting of all b such that aRb.

A binary relation R on D which is reflexive, transitive and antisymmetric is called an *ordering* relation on D. Let $\leq$ be an ordering relation on D. An element a of D is called:

- a *maximal* element of D iff there is no b in D distinct from a such that $a \leq b$.
- a *minimal* element of D iff there is no b in D distinct from a such that $b \leq a$.
- the *greatest element* of D iff for every b in D $b \leq a$.

- the *least element* of D iff for every b in D $a \leq b$.

  Notice that the set inclusion relation on a family of sets is an ordering relation. It will often be used for comparing sets, as for example in the following definition.

  A transitive and reflexive *closure* R^* of R is the least transitive and reflexive relation including R. The least transitive relation including R is called the *transitive closure* of R and it is denoted R^+.

  Let $\leq$ be an ordering relation. Elements a, b of the domain are called *comparable* iff either $a \leq b$ or $b \leq a$, otherwise they are said to be *incomparable*. An ordering $\leq$ is called *total* iff for every a, b in its domain $a \leq b$ or $b \leq a$.

  Let $\leq$ be an ordering on a set D.

- An element a of D is an *upper bound* of a subset S of D iff $b \leq a$ for every b in S.

- An element a of D is a *lower bound* of a subset S of D iff $a \leq b$ for every b in S.

- $\langle D, \leq \rangle$ is a *lattice* iff for every a, b in D there exist the least upper bound and the greatest lower bound of the set $\{a, b\}$.

- A lattice $\langle D, \leq \rangle$ is *complete* iff there exist the least upper bound and the greatest lower bound of every nonempty subset S of D.

  It follows by the definition that every finite lattice is complete. This need not be true for infinite lattices. An example of infinite complete lattice is the set of all subsets of a given infinite set ordered by set inclusion. The least upper bound of an infinite family of subsets is the union of these subsets.

  An element a will be called a *direct predecessor* of an element b in an ordering $\leq$ iff $a \leq b$, a and b are distinct, and if $a \leq c \leq b$ then $c = a$ or $c = b$.

  A *tree ordering* or a *tree* on a set T of *nodes* is an ordering such that:

1. There exists the least element, called the *root* of T,

2. Every node different from the root has exactly one direct predecessor called its *parent*.

  A node b will be called a *child* of a iff a is a parent of b. The maximal nodes of a tree are called *leaves*.

An *ordered* tree is a tree $\langle T, \leq \rangle$ with an additional ordering $\sqsubseteq$ on T such that:

1. For every node of T, $\sqsubseteq$ is a total ordering on the set of its children,
2. For every nodes a, a', b, b' if $a \sqsubseteq b$, $a \leq a'$ and $b \leq b'$, then $a' \sqsubseteq b'$.

Notice that distinct nodes a, b of an ordered tree are comparable in $\sqsubseteq$ iff they are incomparable in $\leq$.

A *labeled* tree is a tree with a function from its nodes into a set disjoint with the domain, whose elements are called *labels*.

1.2   Formal languages and context-free grammars

An *alphabet* is a finite or infinite set. The elements of an alphabet are called *symbols*. A *string* over an alphabet Σ is a finite, possibly empty, sequence of symbols. The *empty string* will be denoted ε. The set of all strings over Σ will be denoted Σ^*. A *language* over Σ is a subset of Σ^* i.e. it is a set of strings over Σ.

Example 1.1
Let $\Sigma = \{0, 1, 2, 3, 4, 5, 6, 7, 8, 9, -\}$. An integer numeral is 0 or a nonempty string of digits that does not begin with 0 or such a string preceded by $-$. Thus 1989 and -120 are integer numerals but 025 is not. The language of integer numerals consists of all integer numerals. □

The language of Example 1.1 is infinite. It has been specified by a finite definition. The definition uses auxiliary notions, like integer numeral, string of digits, etc. Each of them refers to a certain kind of strings. Thus, the example defines not only the language of integer numerals but a finite family of languages indexed by the auxiliary notions. These notions will be called *nonterminal symbols*, or *nonterminals*. The alphabet of nonterminals will be called the *nonterminal alphabet*. We now reformulate the language definition of Example 1.1 with explicit use of nonterminals.

Example 1.2
For the definition of Example 1.1 we introduce the nonterminal alphabet

$$N = \{\langle integer\ numeral\rangle, \langle natural\ numeral\rangle, \langle sign\rangle,$$
$$\langle digit\rangle, \langle non\ zero\rangle, \langle string\ of\ digits\rangle\}.$$

Now the integer numerals can be defined as follows:

- Every $\langle integer\ numeral\rangle$ consists of a $\langle sign\rangle$ and $\langle natural\ numeral\rangle$.

- A $\langle sign\rangle$ is either $-$ or ε.

- A $\langle natural\ numeral\rangle$ is either a $\langle digit\rangle$ or it consists of a $\langle non\ zero\rangle$ digit and a $\langle string\ of\ digits\rangle$.

- A $\langle digit\rangle$ is either 0 or a $\langle non\ zero\rangle$ digit.

- A $\langle non\ zero\rangle$ digit is 1 or 2 or 3 or 4 or 5 or 6 or 7 or 8 or 9.

- A $\langle string\ of\ digits\rangle$ is either a $\langle digit\rangle$ or it consists of a $\langle digit\rangle$ and a $\langle string\ of\ digits\rangle$.

The above definitions describe the structure of the strings in the languages associated with the nonterminals. A commonly used notation for writing such definitions is called *Backus-Naur* notation or *BNF*. In this notation our definitions can be expressed as the following BNF *rules*.

$$
\begin{aligned}
\langle integer\ numeral\rangle &::= \langle sign\rangle\langle natural\ numeral\rangle \\
\langle sign\rangle &::= - \mid \varepsilon \\
\langle natural\ numeral\rangle &::= \langle digit\rangle \mid \langle non\ zero\rangle\langle string\ of\ digits\rangle \\
\langle digit\rangle &::= 0 \mid \langle non\ zero\rangle \\
\langle non\ zero\rangle &::= 1\mid2\mid3\mid4\mid5\mid6\mid7\mid8\mid9 \\
\langle string\ of\ digits\rangle &::= \langle digit\rangle \mid \langle digit\rangle\langle string\ of\ digits\rangle
\end{aligned}
$$

The rules can be used to construct the strings of the language. For example, the first rule says that to obtain an integer numeral one has to construct a sign and a natural numeral. By the second rule, the symbol $-$ can be used as a sign. The third rule defines two different ways of construction of natural numerals. One of them is to take a digit. The following rules show that 2 is a digit. Hence the terminal string -2 is an integer numeral. Thus, the construction process consists in rewriting of the original nonterminal $\langle integer\ numeral\rangle$ by the BNF rules until a terminal string -2 is obtained. During the rewriting some choices are made. Systematic exploration of all of them would lead to enumeration of all elements of the language defined.

□

The ideas illustrated by the example are now formalized by the following definitions.

Definition 1.1

A *context-free grammar* is a triple $\langle N, \Sigma, P \rangle$, where N is a finite set of *nonterminal symbols,* Σ is a finite set of *terminal symbols* disjoint with N, P is a finite set of pairs $X \rightarrow \alpha$, where $X \in N$, $\alpha \in (N \bigcup \Sigma)^*$.
□

The strings over the alphabet Σ are called *terminal* strings. The elements of P are called *production rules* (or briefly *productions* of the grammar. Notice the assumption about finiteness of the terminal alphabet. If a language is to be defined over an infinite alphabet, the symbols of the alphabet may be represented as strings over another, finite, alphabet. In this case the grammar of the language should also define the representation. For example, it is often assumed that the alphabet of a programming language includes an infinite number of variables. A common practice is to represent variables by identifiers, which are sequences of digits and letters beginning with a letter. This representation can be easily expressed by production rules of a context-free grammar.

For each of its nonterminal symbols the grammar defines a language over Σ. This language is defined using the following auxiliary notions.

Definition 1.2

Let $G = \langle N, \Sigma, P \rangle$ be a context-free grammar. A string α over $N \cup \Sigma$ is said to *directly derive* in G a string β iff

1. α is of the form $\alpha_1 X \alpha_2$,

2. β is of the form $\alpha_1 \gamma \alpha_2$,

3. $X \rightarrow \gamma$ is a production rule of G.

□

The binary relation on strings defined above is called *direct derivability* and it is denoted $\Rightarrow_G$. Whenever it causes no confusion the subscript G will be omitted. The transitive and reflexive closure of this relation is called the *derivability relation.* A sequence $\alpha_1, ..., \alpha_n$ of strings such that $\alpha_i \Rightarrow_G \alpha_{i+1}$ for each $i = 1, ..., n - 1$ is called a *derivation* in G. For a nonterminal X of G the strings derivable from X are called X-*sentential forms* of G. A *sentential form* of G is an X-sentential form for some nonterminal X.

Definition 1.3

Let $G = \langle N, \Sigma, P \rangle$ be a context-free grammar and let X be a nonterminal symbol of G. By the *language* defined by G and X we mean the set $L(G, X)$ of all terminal strings α such that $X \Rightarrow_G^+ \alpha$.
□

A language L is called a *context-free language* iff it can be defined by a context-free grammar. A standard example of a non-context-free language is the set $\{a^n b^n c^n | n = 1, 2, ...\}$, where a, b and c are symbols and x^n denotes the string consisting of n repetitions of the symbol x.

1.3   Algebras and terms

An *algebra* $\mathcal{A}$ (or a *one-sorted algebra*) is a pair $\langle A, \mathcal{F} \rangle$, where A is called the *carrier* of $\mathcal{A}$ and $\mathcal{F}$ is a family of functions on A, which are called the *operations* of $\mathcal{A}$. An example is the algebra of strings over an alphabet Σ. Its carrier is the set Σ^*. Its operations are: the binary *concatenation* (which for the strings $a_1...a_n$ and $b_1...b_m$, where $a_1, ..., a_n$ and $b_1, ..., b_m$ are symbols and $m, n \geq 0$, gives the result $a_1...a_n b_1...b_m$) and the nullary operations ε and x_s for every $s \in \Sigma$ (which give as the results, respectively, the empty string and the one-element string s).

We now survey a standard way for representing carrier elements of an algebra in a formal language whose elements are called *ground terms*. The alphabet of the language includes symbols representing the operations of the algebra. The symbols are called *function symbols* or *functors*. Each functor has associated a natural number, called its *arity*, which corresponds to the arity of the represented operation. The functors of arity 0 are called *constants*. They represent fixed elements of the carrier. Additional elements of the alphabet are the auxiliary symbols: left parenthesis, right parenthesis and comma.

The language of ground terms is defined as the least set L including all constants and such that if f is an n-ary functor, for some $n > 0$ and $t_1, ..., t_n$ are in L then the string $f(t_1, ..., t_n)$ is in L.

Notice that this definition can easily be reformulated as a context-free grammar.

It is often convenient to consider terms as labeled ordered trees. For a term which is a constant the corresponding tree is a single node labeled

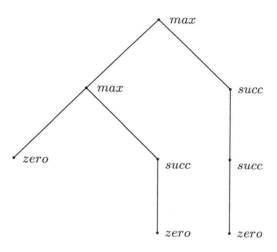

Figure 1.1
The tree representation of a term

by this symbol. A term of the form $f(t_1, ..., t_n)$ corresponds to the tree obtained from the trees corresponding to the terms $t_1, ..., t_n$ by making a node labeled f into the parent of their roots. For example, if the language includes the constant *zero*, the unary functor *succ* and the binary functor *max*, then the ground term

$max(max(zero, succ(zero)), succ(succ(zero)))$

can be represented by the tree in Figure 1.1.

What are the carrier elements represented by ground terms? The correspondence between the functors of the language and the operations of the algebra can be formally defined as a mapping $\mathcal{J}$, called *preinterpretation*. For every functor f we denote by $f_\mathcal{J}$ the corresponding operation. We extend $\mathcal{J}$ into a function that maps every ground term t into an element of the carrier of $\mathcal{A}$, denoted $[t]_\mathcal{J}$. The carrier will be called the *domain* of the preinterpretation. Every ground term is either a constant or it has components, which are themselves compound terms or constants. Clearly, the preinterpretation maps the constants of the language into fixed elements of the domain. For a compound term $f(t_1, ..., t_n)$ the represented domain element $[f(t_1, ..., t_n)]_\mathcal{J}$ is defined as the result of application of the operation $f_\mathcal{J}$ to the arguments $[t_1]_\mathcal{J}, ..., [t_n]_\mathcal{J}$. For the term represented in Figure 1.1 a natural preinterpretation would be on the domain of natural numbers with *zero* denoting the number 0, *succ* denoting the successor function and *max* denoting the function selecting maximal of its arguments. In this preinterpretation the term represents the natural number 2.

The notion of ground term is a special case of a more general notion of *term*. The alphabet of the language of terms includes *variables*, which constitute another kind of elementary terms, in addition to the constants.

The *language of terms* is defined as the least set L including all variables and all constants and such that if f is an n-ary functor and $t_1, ..., t_n$ are in L then the string $f(t_1, ..., t_n)$ is in L. The language of terms for given set of functors $\mathcal{F}$ and set of variables V will be denoted $T(\mathcal{F}, V)$, or $TERM$ if $\mathcal{F}$ and V are clear in the context.

For a given term t we denote by $Var(t)$ the set of all variables that occur in t.

The terms represent functions over the carrier: the variables are assumed to range over the carrier. A *valuation* ν is a function from variables to the carrier. For a given preinterpretation $\mathcal{J}$ and valuation ν a term t represents the carrier element $[t]_{\mathcal{J},\nu}$ defined as follows. For a variable X it is the element $\nu(X)$ defined by the valuation. For a constant c it is the element defined by the preinterpretation $\mathcal{J}$. For a compound term $f(t_1, ..., t_n)$ the represented carrier element $[f(t_1, ..., t_n)]_{\mathcal{J},\nu}$ is defined as the result of application of the operation $f_{\mathcal{J}}$ to the arguments $[t_1]_{\mathcal{J},\nu}, ..., [t_n]_{\mathcal{J},\nu}$.

1.4   Many-sorted algebras

It is often convenient to extend the notion of algebra for the case where the operations take arguments and produce results belonging to various carriers. For example the binary operation of comparison of integers produces boolean results. The carriers of such an algebra are given names called *sorts* and the algebra is called a *many-sorted algebra*. The extension can be formally defined as follows.

Let S be a finite set of sorts. An *S-sorted functional signature* $\mathcal{F}$ (or simply an *S-signature*) is a finite set F of functors with a mapping π on F which associates with each functor f a pair $\langle w_f, s_f \rangle$, where $w_f \in S^*$

and $s_f \in S$, called the *profile* of f. Intuitively, the string of sorts w_f characterizes the argument sorts of the operation represented by f while s_f characterizes the sort of its results. Thus, if S is a singleton (one-sorted case) the signature can be seen as the arity of the functors since the only relevant information it provides is the number of arguments. A function symbol f such that w_f is the empty string is a constant. Notice that there may be constants of different sorts.

Definition 1.4

Let S be a set of sorts and let $\mathcal{F}$ be an S-sorted functional signature. An S-sorted $\mathcal{F}$-algebra $\mathcal{A}$ is a pair $\langle \{A_s\}_{s \in S}, \{f_\mathcal{A}\}_{f \in \mathcal{F}} \rangle$, where
$\{A_s\}$ is a family of sets indexed by S, called the carriers of $\mathcal{A}$,
$f_\mathcal{A}$ is an operation from $A_{s_1} \times \ldots \times A_{s_n}$ to A_s where $\langle s_1 \ldots s_n, s \rangle$ is the profile of f defined by $\mathcal{F}$.
□

The elements of the carriers of a many-sorted algebra can be represented by *many-sorted terms*. Syntactic definition of a many-sorted term relies on the concept of many-sorted signature. A term has a sort, which gives the information about the carrier of the element represented by the term. In particular every variable x has a sort.

Definition 1.5

Let S be a set of sorts and let $\mathcal{F}$ be an S-sorted signature. The family of $\mathcal{F}$-terms of sort s for $s \in S$ consists of the least sets such that:

- A variable x of sort s is an $\mathcal{F}$-term of sort s,

- A constant f in $\mathcal{F}$ of sort s is an $\mathcal{F}$-term of sort s,

- If $t_1, \ldots, t_n$ are $\mathcal{F}$-terms of sorts $s_1, \ldots, s_n$, respectively, and f is a functor in $\mathcal{F}$ of profile $\langle s_1 \ldots s_n, s \rangle$ then the string $f(t_1, \ldots, t_n)$ is an $\mathcal{F}$-term of sort s.

□

Whenever this causes no ambiguity S-sorted $\mathcal{F}$-terms will be simply called terms or many-sorted terms.

A many-sorted term not including variables is called a *ground* term.

The notions of preinterpretation and valuation defined for one-sorted case extend naturally for many-sorted signatures and many-sorted variables.

1.5   Context-free grammars seen as algebras

A context-free grammar defines a finite family of languages: a language
is associated with every nonterminal of the grammar. Let $G = \langle N, P, \Sigma \rangle$
be a context-free grammar and let $X \to \alpha_1 X_1 ... X_n \alpha_{n+1}$ be a production
rule of G, where $X, X_1, ..., X_n$ are nonterminal symbols and $\alpha_1, ..., \alpha_{n+1}$
are terminal strings. One can consider the rule as an N-sorted operation
on languages: given strings $s_1 \in L(G, X_1), ..., s_n \in L(G, X_n)$ it produces
the string $\alpha_1 s_1 .... s_n \alpha_{n+1}$ in $L(G, X)$. The profile of the production rule
is thus $\langle X_1 ... X_n, X \rangle$. Consequently, the grammar G can be seen as an
N-sorted P-algebra $\mathcal{M}$ with the carriers $\{ M_s = L(G, s) \}_{s \in N}$ and with
the production rules defining operations on the carriers as described
above. It follows by the definition that any rule without nonterminals
in the right-hand side is a nullary operation. For every nonterminal X
of G any string x of $L(G, X)$ is constructed by composition of a finite
number of operations of the algebra. This composition of operations can
be described by a ground term. Each ground term of sort X gives rise
to a string in $L(G, X)$. However, different terms may define the same
string. In this case the grammar is said to be *ambiguous*.

Example 1.3
   Consider the context-free grammar with the following production
rules, where the nonterminal symbols are indicated by the angle brackets:
   $p_1 : \langle expr \rangle \to a$
   $p_2 : \langle expr \rangle \to \langle expr \rangle + \langle expr \rangle$
   $p_3 : \langle expr \rangle \to \langle expr \rangle * \langle expr \rangle$
   The ground term $p_2(p_3(p_1, p_1), p_1)$ defines the string $a * a + a$. The
same string is defined by the term $p_3(p_1, p_2(p_1, p_1))$
$\square$

   An important concept related to context-free grammars is the notion
of *parse tree*. The motivation behind it is to make explicit the structure
of sentential forms of the grammar. We introduce here a notion of parse
tree motivated by the algebraic view of context-free grammars. This
will simplify its extensions for non-context-free grammars discussed in
Chapter 3 and its comparisons with the proof trees of logic programs
discussed in Chapter 2. A link to a traditional understanding of a parse
tree will be given by a notational convention used in most examples.

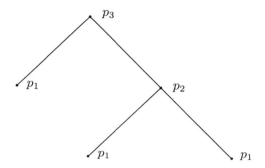

Figure 1.2
A complete parse tree of the context-free grammar of Example 1.3

Definition 1.6

A *parse tree* of a context-free grammar G is any labeled ordered tree such that:

- The root is labeled by a production of G,
- Any node labeled by a production p of the profile $\langle X_1 \ldots X_n, X \rangle$ has n children; for $i = 1, \ldots, n$ the label of the i-th child is either a production of sort X_i or the empty label $\bot$.

□

A parse tree is called *complete* if none of its nodes is labeled by the empty label. Such a tree can be seen as a ground term of the many-sorted term algebra defined by G.

An example of a complete parse tree of the grammar of Example 1.3 is shown in Figure 1.2. An incomplete parse tree for this grammar is shown in Figure 1.3.

In the algebra corresponding to a context-free grammar the sorts are nonterminals of the grammar, their domains are the context-free languages generated by the nonterminals and each production rule defines an operation on strings. Thus, any complete parse tree represents a terminal string. On the other hand, incomplete parse trees represent sentential forms. To make this more explicit we allow each node of the tree to be additionally (and redundantly) labeled by its sort and to have an indication of the terminal strings that appear in the right-hand side of

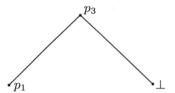

Figure 1.3
An incomplete parse tree of the context-free grammar of Example 1.3

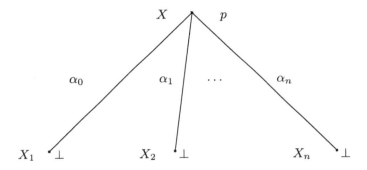

Figure 1.4
A convention for graphical representation of parse trees with indication of the terminal strings

the corresponding production rule. More precisely, for a node of a parse tree labeled by a production rule p of the form $X \to \alpha_0 X_1 \alpha_1 \dots X_n \alpha_n$, where $X_1, \dots X_n$ are nonterminals and $\alpha_0, \dots, \alpha_n$ are terminal strings the graphical representation will include the string α_{i-1} placed to the left of the i-th outgoing arc, for $i = 1, \dots, n$, and the string α_n placed to the right of the n-th outgoing arc, as illustrated in Figure 1.4. If $n = 0$ the only terminal string α_0 is placed directly under the node. This convention used in Figure 1.5 shows that the incomplete parse tree of Figure 1.3 represents the structure of the sentential form $a + \langle expr \rangle$.

According to the definition of the notion of context-free grammar a production rule can be identified by its profile and by the terminal strings occurring in its right-hand side. Hence, the names of the production rules need not appear in graphical representations of parse trees.

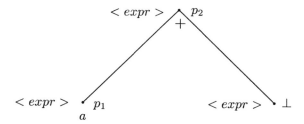

Figure 1.5
An incomplete parse tree with indication of the terminal strings (the context-free grammar of Example 1.3)

For example, the tree of Figure 1.2 may alternatively be represented as shown in Figure 1.6.

1.6 Equations and substitutions

1.6.1 Equations

For a given alphabet of variables and functors an *equation* is a pair of terms $\langle t_1, t_2 \rangle$, to be denoted as $t_1 = t_2$. For a given preinterpretation $\mathcal{J}$ a *solution* of an equation $t_1 = t_2$ is any valuation ν such that $[t_1]_{\mathcal{J},\nu}$ and $[t_2]_{\mathcal{J},\nu}$ are identical. A solution of a set of equations E is any valuation ν which is a solution of every equation in E.

1.6.2 Substitutions

Solutions of equations should be expressed in the language. A relevant concept for that purpose is the notion of *substitution*. A substitution is a mapping from variables to terms. (In the case of many-sorted substitutions the variable and the term assigned to it by a substitution must be of the same sort).

It is usually assumed that a substitution is the identity mapping with except of a finite number of variables. For representing such substitutions the notation $\{x_1/t_1, ..., x_n/t_n\}$ is used, to denote that all variables with except of $x_1, ..., x_n$ are mapped to itself, and each variable x_i is mapped to a term t_i different from x_i, for $i = 1, ..., n$. The set $\{x_1, ..., x_n\}$ is called the *domain* of the substitution. The set $\{t | t = t_i$

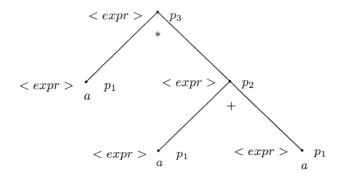

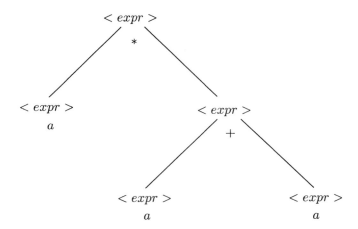

Figure 1.6
Alternative representations of the parse tree of Figure 1.2

for some $i = 1, \ldots n\}$ is called the *range* of the substitution. For a given substitution σ we denote by $Var(\sigma)$ the set of all variables which appear in the domain and in the range of σ

The *identity substitution* is denoted ϵ. In the notation defined above, ϵ is represented as $\{\}$. Therefore it is sometimes called the *empty substitution*.

A substitution such that all terms in its range are ground is called a *ground substitution*. For a given preinterpretation $\mathcal{J}$ a ground substitution $\{x_1/t_1, \ldots, x_n/t_n\}$ denotes a class of valuations which assign $t_{i_{\mathcal{J}}}$ to x_i for $i = 1, \ldots, n$ and arbitrary elements of the domain to the other variables. The valuations denoted by a non-ground substitution are those obtained by arbitrary valuation of the range terms.

A substitution σ is naturally extended to a function on terms by defining $\sigma(f(t_1, \ldots, t_n))$ to be $f(\sigma(t_1), \ldots, \sigma(t_n))$. In particular for any constant c, $\sigma(c)$ is defined to be c. For representing application of a substitution σ to a term t the postfix notation $t\sigma$ will be used.

As substitutions are mapping they can be composed. Let θ and σ be the substitutions represented, respectively, by $\{x_1/s_1, \ldots, x_n/s_n\}$ and by $\{y_1/t_1, \ldots, y_m/t_m\}$. The representation of their composition can be obtained from the set $\{x_1/s_1\sigma, \ldots x_n/s_n\sigma, y_1/t_1, \ldots, y_m/t_m\}$ by removing all bindings $x_i/s_i\sigma$ for which $x_i = s_i\sigma$ and all bindings y_j/t_j such that $y_j \in \{x_1, \ldots, x_n\}$. A substitution σ is idempotent (i.e. $\sigma\sigma = \sigma$) iff its domain is disjoint with the set of the variables of its range.

The following properties of substitutions follow from the definitions. Let θ, σ and γ be substitutions and let t be a term, then

- $(\theta\sigma)\gamma = \theta(\sigma\gamma)$,
- $t(\theta\sigma) = (t\theta)\sigma$,
- $\epsilon\theta = \theta\epsilon = \theta$,

where $=$ denotes the identity of, respectively, substitutions and terms.

A substitution σ is called a *renaming* of a set of variables V iff the domain of σ is a subset of V, the range of σ is a set of variables and for every distinct $x, y \in V$, $x\sigma$ is distinct from $y\sigma$.

A term t is called a *variant* of a term s iff there exists a renaming σ on variables of s such that $s\sigma = t$. "Being a variant of" is an equivalence relation on terms.

Substitutions σ and δ are said to be unique up to renaming iff there
exists a renaming θ on $Var(\sigma)$ such that $\sigma\theta = \delta$. This is an equivalence
relation on substitutions.

A substitution θ is said to be *more general* than a substitution σ
iff there exists a substitution γ such that $\sigma = \theta\gamma$. This relation on
substitutions is reflexive and transitive but it is neither symmetric nor
antisymmetric. The reason why it is not antisymmetric is the existence
of renaming substitutions: the composition of renamings may give the
identity substitutions. Substitutions σ and δ have the property that σ
is more general than δ and δ is more general than σ iff there exists a
renaming α of $Var(\delta)$ such that $\delta\alpha = \sigma$.

By abuse of terminology a substitution σ is said to be a *solution of
a set of equations* $E = \{t_1 = s_1, ..., t_n = s_n\}$ in preinterpretation $\mathcal{J}$ iff
for every valuation ν $[t_i\sigma]_{\mathcal{J},\nu}$ and $[s_i\sigma]_{\mathcal{J},\nu}$ are identical for $i = 1, ..., n$.
Thus, σ is a solution of E if every valuation in $\mathcal{J}$ denoted by σ is a
solution of E.

For a substitution $\sigma = \{x_1/t_1, \ldots x_n/t_n\}$ the set of equations $\{x_1 = t_1, \ldots, x_n = t_n\}$ will be called the *equational representation* of σ and
will be denoted $eq(\sigma)$. Notice that an idempotent σ is a solution of its
equational representation in every preinterpretation. This is not true if
σ is not idempotent.

A set of equations is said to be in a *solved form* iff it is an equational
representation of an idempotent substitution, i.e. iff the left-hand sides
of the equations are distinct variables which do not occur in any of the
right-hand sides.

1.6.3   Unifiers

A substitution θ is a *unifier* of terms t_1 and t_2, or of the equation $t_1 = t_2$
iff $t_1\theta$ and $t_2\theta$ are identical. Thus, a unifier is a solution of the equation
in every preinterpretation. A most general unifier θ of the equation
$t_1 = t_2$ is a unifier that is more general than any other unifier. It follows
by the definition that θ is unique up to renamings on $Var(\theta)$. For a
given set of equations E we will denote by $mgu(E)$ a substitution in the
equivalence class of the most general unifiers of E.

A substitution is a *unifier of a set of equations* iff it is a unifier
of every equation in this set. A substitiution is a *unifier of a set of
terms* $\{t_1, t_2, \ldots, t_n\}$ iff it is a unifier of every equation $t_i = t_j$ for
$i, j = 1, 2, \ldots, n$. A set of equations or a set of terms E is said to

be *unifiable* iff there exists a unifier of E.

We now present an algorithm that for a given set of equations E produces a most general idempotent unifier or reports non-existence of a unifier. The algorithm is nondeterministic and is described below by four equation transformation rules and by two failure conditions. At every step the state of the computation is characterized by a set of equations. The initial set is E. The step consists in application of a transformation rule to one of the equations or in checking that an equation satisfies a failure condition. The computation terminates if an equation in the current set of equations satisfies a failure condition or if none of the rules is applicable to any equation.

- The transformation rules

1. *Splitting*: Replace an equation of the form $f(s_1, \ldots, s_n) = f(t_1, \ldots t_n)$, where $n \geq 0$ by the equations $s_1 = t_1, \ldots, s_n = t_n$.

2. *Identity removal*: Remove an equation of the form $x = x$, where x is a variable.

3. *Swapping*: Replace an equation of the form $t = x$ where x is a variable and t is not a variable by the equation $x = t$.

4. *Variable elimination*: If there is an equation of the form $x = u$, where x is a variable, such that x does not appear in u but x appears in some other equation then replace any other equation $s = t$ by the equation $s\{x/u\} = t\{x/u\}$.

- The failure tests: halt and report failure if the set includes an equation in one of the following forms:

1. *Disagreement*: $f(s_1, \ldots, s_n) = g(t_1, \ldots t_m)$ where $f \neq g$, $n, m \geq 0$.

2. *Occur check* : $x = t$ where x is a variable and t is a non-variable term including x.

The following observations justify correctness of the algorithm.

- The algorithm terminates for every input. Application of rule (1) or (2) reduces the total size of the equations, rule (3) reduces the total size of the left-hand sides of the equations. Hence, if there exists an infinite computation it must include infinite number of applications of rule (4). But after the application of rule (4) to an equation having a variable x

as the left-hand side the number of occurrences of x in any subsequent set equals 1 and rule (4) is no longer applicable to such an equation. As no transformation introduces new variables the number of applications of rule (4) in any computation must be finite.

- The transformations of the algorithm do not affect unifiers; let E' be the set of equations obtained from a set E by application of a transformation rule. Then σ is a unifier of E' iff it is a unifier of E. This follows directly by the definitions of the transformations.

- If a failure test succeeds for an equation in a set E then no unifier of E exists. This follows directly by the definition of unifier.

- If the algorithm terminates without failure then the final set of equations is in solved form. This follows directly by the definitions of the transformations.

- If E is in solved form, i.e. if $E = eq(\sigma)$ for some idempotent substitution σ then σ is a most general unifier of E. This follows directly by the definitions of solved form and of mgu.

Thus, the unification algorithm is correct: for a given set of equations E it either halts with failure iff E is not unifiable or it terminates with a solved set of equations representing a most general idempotent unifier of E.

The unification algorithm is nondeterministic but the most general unifier of a given set of equations is unique up to renaming. The order of application of the rules influences the result only up to renaming. For example for the set of equations $\{f(x) = f(y), f(y) = f(x)\}$, where x and y are variables, the result obtained may be either $\{x/y\}$ or $\{y/x\}$. This allows for defining various strategies of computations. In particular, it may be interesting to consider how splitting of a set of equations E into subsets may influence computations of an mgu of E. When discussing this issue we will use the notation $E\sigma$ to denote the set of equations obtained from a set E by application of a substitution σ to both sides of every equation in E.

Let E be a set of equations which is the union of some sets E_1 and E_2. The following strategies of computing $mgu(E_1 \bigcup E_2)$ are possible:

- A *sequential* strategy: compute first $mgu(E_1)$ and use the result for computing $mgu(E_1 \bigcup E_2)$. If E_1 is unifiable then the equations of the resulting E_1' in solved form may be used for variable elimination in E_2. This results in transformation of E_2 into $E_2' = E_2 mgu(E_1)$. Clearly, no left-hand side of E_1' appears in E_2'. Compute $mgu(E_2')$; if the computation succeeds then the left-hand sides of the resulting set of equations can only appear in the right-hand sides of E_1'. Hence $mgu(E_1)mgu(E_2 mgu(E_1))$ is an mgu of E.

- A *parallel* strategy: compute independently $mgu(E_1)$ and $mgu(E_2)$ and use the results for computing $mgu(E_1 \bigcup E_2)$.
  Thus, $mgu(eq(mgu(E_1)) \cup eq(mgu(E_2)))$ is an mgu of E. This strategy is applicable if both $mgu(E_1)$ and $mgu(E_2)$ are idempotent.

These strategies of unification are based on the following general properties of mgu's of a set of equations, which are independent of the unification algorithm.

Proposition 1.1

Let E_1 and E_2 be sets of equations, let σ_1 be an mgu of E_1 and let σ_2 be an mgu of $E_2\sigma_1$. Then $\sigma_1\sigma_2$ is an mgu of $E_1 \bigcup E_2$.
□

Proposition 1.2

Let E_1 and E_2 be set of equations, let σ_1 be an idempotent mgu of E_1 and let σ_2 be an idempotent mgu of E_2. Then an mgu of $eq(\sigma_1) \cup eq(\sigma_2)$ is an mgu of $E_1 \bigcup E_2$.
□

1.7 Algebraic structures and logical formulae

1.7.1 Many-sorted structures

The notion of *algebraic structure* extends the notion of algebra: an algebraic structure is a domain with a number of functions and relations on it. To represent elements of the relations of an algebraic structure a language of formulae is constructed. In the many-sorted case this construction uses the following generalizations of the definitions of Section 1.4.

Let S be a finite set of sorts. An *S-sorted signature* $\mathcal{R}$ (or simply an *S*-signature) is a tuple $\langle F, P, \pi \rangle$ where F is a finite set of functors, P is a finite set of *predicates* and π is a mapping π on $F \bigcup P$ such that for each predicate p, $\pi(p) \in S^*$ and for each functor f, $\pi(f)$ is a pair $\langle w_f, s_f \rangle$, where $w_f \in S^*$ and $s_f \in S$. For every symbol $q \in F \bigcup P$ $\pi(q)$ is called the *profile* of q. Thus, an S-sorted signature $\mathcal{R}$ restricted to its set of functors is a functional S-signature in the sense of Section 1.4. Consequently, the notion of $\mathcal{R}$-term will be used for the terms obtained by this restriction.

A formal definition of the notion of algebraic structure extends Definition 1.4 .

Definition 1.7

Let S be a set of sorts and let $\mathcal{R} = \langle F, P, \pi \rangle$ be a S-sorted signature. An *S-sorted $\mathcal{R}$-structure* $\mathcal{A}$ is a triple $\langle \{A_s\}_{s \in S}, \{f_\mathcal{A}\}_{f \in F}, \{p_\mathcal{A}\}_{p \in P} \rangle$, where:

- $\{A_s\}$ is a family of sets indexed by S, called the *carriers* of $\mathcal{A}$,
- $f_\mathcal{A}$ is an operation from $A_{s_1} \times \dots \times A_{s_n}$ to A_s where $\langle s_1 \dots s_n, s \rangle$ is the profile of f defined by $\mathcal{R}$,
- $p_\mathcal{A}$ is a subset of $A_{s_1} \times \dots \times A_{s_k}$ where $s_1 \dots s_k$ is the profile of p defined by $\mathcal{R}$.

□

Whenever it causes no ambiguity an S-sorted $\mathcal{R}$-structure will be simply called an *algebraic structure*.

1.7.2   Formulae

Elements of the relations of an algebraic structure are often represented by formulae. The language of formulae is defined for a given set S of sorts and for a given S-sorted signature. Its alphabet consists of the following subsets:

- For every $s \in S$ a denumerable set of variables of sort s. In the examples the variables will be represented by identifiers beginning with capital letters. The sort of each variable will be given explicitly unless clear from its context.
- The functors of the signature.
- The predicates of the signature.
- The *logical connectives*: $\wedge$ (conjunction), $\vee$ (disjunction), $\rightarrow$ (implication) and $\neg$ (negation).

- The *quantifiers*: ∀ (universal quantifier) and ∃ (existential quantifier).
- The auxiliary symbols: parentheses and commas.

Definition 1.8

Let S be a set of sorts and let $\mathcal{R}$ be an S-sorted signature. The language of $\mathcal{R}$-*formulae* or a *first-order logical language* is the least set L such that:

- If p is a predicate of $\mathcal{R}$ of the profile $s_1...s_n$ and $t_1, ..., t_n$ are $\mathcal{R}$-terms of the sorts, respectively $s_1, ..., s_n$ then the string $p(t_1, ..., t_n)$ is in L; such a string is called an *atomic* $\mathcal{R}$-formula.
- if α and β are strings in L then also the strings $(\alpha \wedge \beta)$, $(\alpha \vee \beta)$, $(\alpha \rightarrow \beta)$ and $(\neg\alpha)$ are in L.
- if α is a string in L and x is a variable then also the strings $(\forall x\alpha)$ and $(\exists x\alpha)$ are in L.

□

If the signature $\mathcal{R}$ is clear from the context, the $\mathcal{R}$-formulae will simply be called *logical formulae*, or formulae. It is worth noticing that for a finite alphabet of function symbols and predicate symbols the language of formulae is a context-free language.

The syntax of formulae as defined above uses many parentheses. To minimize the number of parentheses it is assumed that the connective ¬ and the quantifiers ∀ and ∃ bind stronger than ∧, which in turn binds stronger than ∨. The weakest connective in the sense of bindings is →. The connectives are also assumed to be left-associative.

For a formula of the form $\forall x\alpha$, or $\exists x\alpha$, the string $\forall x$, or $\exists x$ will be called a *quantifier of x*, and the component formula α will be called the *scope* of the quantifier of x. A variable y is said to be *free* in a formula ϕ if some occurrence of y in ϕ is neither in a quantifier of y nor in the scope of a quantifier of y. A formula without free variables is said to be *closed*.

Let ϕ be a formula and let $\{x_1, \ldots, x_n\}$ for some $n \geq 0$ be the set of all variables free in ϕ. The formula $\forall x_1 \ldots \forall x_n \phi$ will be called the *universal closure* of ϕ and will be denoted $\forall\phi$. Similarly, the formula $\exists x_1 \ldots \exists x_n \phi$ will be called the *existential closure* of ϕ and will be denoted $\exists\phi$. The universal closure and the existential closure of a closed formula ϕ is ϕ.

1.7.3   The semantics of formulae

The meaning of an $\mathcal{R}$-formula is defined by relating the signature $\mathcal{R}$ to an $\mathcal{R}$-structure. This is described by the following formal notion. An *interpretation* of a signature $\mathcal{R}$ is a mapping $\mathcal{I}$ that associates each symbol of the signature with, respectively, operation or relation of the same profile of a given $\mathcal{R}$-structure. Notice that $\mathcal{I}$ restricted to the functors is a preinterpretation. Following the notation of Section 1.3 the operation associated by $\mathcal{I}$ with a functor f will be denoted by $f_{\mathcal{I}}$. Similarly the relation associated by $\mathcal{I}$ with a predicate p will be denoted by $p_{\mathcal{I}}$.

Now the meaning $\psi_{\mathcal{I},\nu}$ of a formula ψ in a given interpretation $\mathcal{I}$ and valuation ν will be defined as a *truth* values *true* or *false*.

- For an atomic formula $p(t_1, \ldots, t_n)$

  $p(t_1, ..., t_n)_{\mathcal{I},\nu}$ is true iff $\langle [t_1]_{\mathcal{I},\nu}, \ldots, [t_n]_{\mathcal{I},\nu} \rangle \in p_{\mathcal{I}}$
- If α and β are formulae then:

  - $(\alpha \wedge \beta)_{\mathcal{I},\nu}$ is true iff both $\alpha_{\mathcal{I},\nu}$ and $\beta_{\mathcal{I},\nu}$ are true,
  - $(\alpha \vee \beta)_{\mathcal{I},\nu}$ is true iff at least one of the values $\alpha_{\mathcal{I},\nu}$ and $\beta_{\mathcal{I},\nu}$ is true,
  - $(\alpha \rightarrow \beta)_{\mathcal{I},\nu}$ is true iff $\alpha_{\mathcal{I},\nu}$ is false or $\beta_{\mathcal{I},\nu}$ is true,
  - $(\neg \alpha)_{\mathcal{I},\nu}$ is true iff $\alpha_{\mathcal{I},\nu}$ is false,
  - $(\forall x \alpha)_{\mathcal{I},\nu}$ is true iff $\alpha_{\mathcal{I},\nu'}$ is true for any valuation ν' such that $\nu'(y) = \nu(y)$ for all variables y different from x,
  - $(\exists X \alpha)_{\mathcal{I},\nu}$ is true iff $\alpha_{\mathcal{I},\nu'}$ is true for some valuation ν' such that $\nu'(y) = \nu(y)$ for all variables y different from y.

Formulae are often written to "describe" some given structure. In other words, given a signature interpreted on a given structure one wants to write formulae which are true in this interpretation for every valuation. On the other hand, given a formula one may search for an interpretation under which the formula is true for every valuation. Such an interpretation is called a *model* of the formula. An interpretation is a model of a set of formulae iff it is a model of each formula in the set. A formula is said to be

- *satisfiable* if it has a model.
- *unsatisfiable* if it has no model.

- *valid* if every interpretation is its model. Valid formulae are sometimes called *tautologies*.

  Let ϕ be a formula of a logical language and let $\mathcal{I}$ be an interpretation. Given a valuation ν we write $(\mathcal{I}, \nu) \models \phi$ if $\phi_{\mathcal{I}, \nu}$ is true. The notation $\mathcal{I} \models \phi$ means "$\mathcal{I}$ is a model of ϕ".

  The notation $\models \psi$ is used to denote that ψ is a tautology.

  The truth values of formulae may be related in every interpretation and valuation. An important case of such a relationship is described by the following definition.

Definition 1.9

  A formula ψ is called a *logical consequence* of a set Φ of formulae iff every model of Φ is also a model of ψ. The notation $\Phi \models \psi$ is used to denote that ψ is a logical consequence of Φ.

  □

  The notion of logical consequence reflects the intuition of correct reasoning: conclusions drawn from a set of premises should be true whenever the premises are true. Notice that any formula is a logical consequence of an unsatisfiable set Φ. On the other hand if Φ is a (possibly empty) set of tautologies then all its logical consequences are also tautologies.

2 Foundations of Logic Programming

This chapter gives an introduction to foundations of logic programming in definite clauses. The syntax and various kinds of semantics of definite logic programs are presented. The presentation focuses on the syntactic concept of proof tree which later makes it possible to relate logic programs and formal grammars. This way of presentation also facilitates proofs of some classical results.

2.1 Syntactic notions

2.1.1 Definite programs

The idea of logic programming is to describe structures of interest by sets of logic formulae and to infer the information about the described structures from their descriptions. Thus, logic programs are finite sets of logic formulae. We focus our attention on a special class of logic programs, called definite programs. To define programs we refer to the notions of Section 1.7.2. The language is one-sorted. Its alphabet consists of

- A denumerable set V of variables,
- A finite set F of function symbols with associated arities,
- A finite set P of predicate symbols with associated arities,
- Logical connectives $\neg, \vee, \wedge$ and $\rightarrow$,
- The universal quantifier $\forall$,
- Auxiliary symbols: parentheses and commas.

The atomic formulae are constructed as in Section 1.7.2. In the sequel they will be sometimes called *atoms*. A *literal* is an atomic formula or a negated atomic formula. A literal which is an atomic formula is called a *positive* literal. A literal which is a negated atomic formula is called a *negative* literal. According to notational convention used in logic programming.

- a formula of the form $A \rightarrow B$, where A and B are component formulae is written in the form $B \leftarrow A$,
- the connective $\wedge$ is represented by comma,

- the variables are represented by identifiers beginning with capitals.

To define the syntax of definite programs the following auxiliary concepts are used.

Definition 2.1
Let $h, a_1 \ldots a_m$ be atomic formulae for some $m \geq 0$ and let $x_1, \ldots x_l$ be all variables occurring in these formulae.

Then the formula $\forall (h \leftarrow a_1, \ldots, a_m)$ is called a *definite clause*. If $m = 0$ the formula is called a *unit clause*.
□

The atomic formula h is called the *head* of the clause, while $a_1, \ldots, a_m$ is called its *body*. Unit clauses are sometimes called *facts* as opposed to non-unit clauses that are called *rules*. Since all variables of a definite clause are universally quantified we adopt the notational convention to omit the quantifiers.

The set of all variables occurring in a clause c is denoted $Var(c)$. The clause c' obtained from a clause c by application of a substitution to all terms occurring in c is called an *instance* of c. The instance is called a *variant* of c if it can be obtained by application of a renaming substitution on $Var(c)$. It is called a *ground* instance iff it is variable-free.

Definition 2.2
A *definite program* is a finite set of definite clauses.
□

The example programs will be presented without explicit definition of the alphabet. It should be then assumed that the alphabet includes the symbols appearing in the program.

Example 2.1
We illustrate the notion of definite program by the following example.

$c_1 : rev(nil, nil) \leftarrow$
$c_2 : rev(l(X, Y), Z) \leftarrow rev(Y, V), app(V, l(X, nil), Z)$
$c_3 : app(nil, X, X) \leftarrow$
$c_4 : app(l(X, Y), U, l(X, W)) \leftarrow app(Y, U, W)$
□

Since this section is devoted to the syntax we do not comment on the meaning or possible use of the example program.

The definite programs constitute an important subset of the programming language Prolog. For more information on Prolog the reader is referred to the literature, e.g. to the textbooks [NM90, SS86].

2.1.2   Proof trees

We now introduce a syntactic concept of proof tree which will be used also for defining semantics of definite programs. The intuition is that the clauses of a program are building blocks for objects called *derivation trees*. This resembles the use of grammatical rules for construction of parse trees. The *proof trees* will then be defined as a special class of derivation trees.

A pair $\langle c, \sigma \rangle$ where c is a clause and σ is a substitution will be called an *instance name* of the clause c. Clearly every instance name $\langle c, \sigma \rangle$ determines the unique instance $c\sigma$ of the clause c. Now the concept of derivation tree is defined in terms of instance names.

Definition 2.3

For a definite program P a *derivation tree* is any labeled ordered tree T such that

1. Every leaf node is labeled by the "empty label" $\bot$ or by an instance name of a clause of P.

2. Every non-leaf node of T is labeled by an instance name of a clause of P.

3. Let n be a node labeled by an instance name $\langle c, \sigma \rangle$, where c is the clause $h \leftarrow a_1, \ldots, a_m$ and $m \geq 0$. Then n has m children and for $i = 1, \ldots, m$ the i-th child of n is labeled either

   - $\langle c', \sigma' \rangle$, where c' is a clause with the head h' such that $a_i\sigma = h'\sigma'$, or
   - $\bot$

□

The intuition behind this definition is that a derivation tree is obtained by combining appropriate instances of program clauses. The precise meaning of "appropriate instances" is expressed by condition 3. The empty label $\bot$ indicates nodes where the derivation tree may be

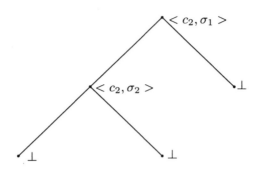

$$\sigma_1 = \{X/1, Y/l(2, nil), V/Z^1, Z/V^1\}$$
$$\sigma_2 = \{X/2, Y/nil, V/V^2, Z/Z^1\}$$

Figure 2.1
An example incomplete derivation tree of Example 2.1

extended, if there exists an appropriate instance of a clause. A node
with the empty label will be therefore called an *incomplete node* of the
tree. The other nodes will be called the *complete nodes*.

Definition 2.4
    A derivation tree without incomplete nodes is called a *proof tree*. It
is also a *complete* derivation tree. A derivation tree which is not a proof
tree is said to be *incomplete*. A derivation tree incomplete or not is also
said *partial*.
□
    A definite program defines a set of proof trees. This can be seen as
a semantics of definite programs. The next section shows the relation
between this and other approaches to defining semantics of definite programs.
    For the program of Example 2.1 an example derivation tree is shown
in Figure 2.1. It is then extended to the proof tree shown in Figure 2.2.
    The notion of proof tree can be related to the concepts of proof de-
fined in symbolic logic. There are several such concepts, but the proof is

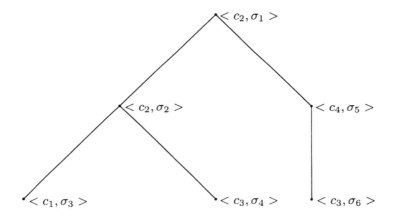

$$\sigma_1 = \{X/1, Y/l(2, nil), V/l(2, nil), Z/l(2, l(1, nil))\}$$
$$\sigma_2 = \{X/2, Y/nil, V/nil, Z/l(2, nil)\}$$
$$\sigma_3 = \{\ \}$$
$$\sigma_4 = \{X/l(2, nil)\}$$
$$\sigma_5 = \{X/2, Y/nil, U/l(1, nil), W/l(1, nil)\}$$
$$\sigma_6 = \{X/l(1, nil)\}$$

Figure 2.2
An example proof tree of Example 2.1

always a syntactic object which is constructed by syntactic transformations from a set of formulae (sometimes called the *premises*) and yields
a formula (sometimes called the *conclusion*). The transformations are
defined by *inference rules*. The following inference rules allow us to link
our concept of proof tree to proofs in logic:

- *Elimination of the universal quantifier.* For our discussion it is sufficient
  to consider the following special case of a more general rule (discussed
  e.g. in [Dal83]). A formula of the form $\forall x(\phi)$, where ϕ is a quantifier-
  free formula rewrites to the formula $\phi\{x/t\}$ where t is an arbitrary term.
  This is schematically represented as:

$$(\forall E) \ \frac{\forall x \phi}{\phi\{x/t\}}$$

- *Introduction of conjunction.* A set of formulae $\{\phi, \psi\}$ rewrites to the
  formula $\phi \wedge \psi$. This is schematically represented as:

$$(\wedge I) \ \frac{\phi \ \psi}{\phi \wedge \psi}$$

- *Elimination of implication.* A set of formulae of the form $\{\phi, \phi \rightarrow \psi\}$
  rewrites to the formula ψ. This is schematically represented as:

$$(\rightarrow E) \ \frac{\phi \ \phi \rightarrow \psi}{\phi \wedge \psi}$$

An application of an inference rule to appropriate premises yields a
conclusion. The conclusions obtained from different applications may be
again used as premises. In this way applications can be composed. The
composition can be represented by a tree, called an *inference tree*. Every
node of such a tree is labeled by a formula. The formula labelling the
root will be called the *conclusion* while the formulae labelling the leaves
will be called the *premises* of the inference tree. The usual graphical
representation of inference trees extends that used for the inference rules:
the children of a node are graphically represented over their parent. Thus
the representation of the root is placed at the bottom. This is illustrated
by the following example.

$$(\forall\ E)\ \dfrac{\forall\ X\ c_3}{c_3\{X/nil\}}$$

$$(\rightarrow\ E)\ \dfrac{}{app(l(2,nil),nil,l(2,nil))}$$

$$(\forall\ E)\ \dfrac{\forall\ X,Y,U,W c_4}{c_4\{X/2,Y/nil,U/nil,W/nil\}}$$

$$(\forall\ E)\ \dfrac{\forall\ X,Y,U,W c_4}{}$$

$$app(l(2,nil),nil,l(2,nil))\ \ c_4\{X/1,Y/1(2,nil),U/nil,W/l(2,nil)\}$$

$$(\rightarrow\ E)\ \dfrac{}{app(l(1,l(2,nil)),nil,l(1,l(2,nil)))}$$

Figure 2.3
An inference tree

Consider the append program of Example 2.1 :

$(c_3)\ app(nil,X,X) \leftarrow$
$(c_4)\ app(l(X,Y),U,l(X,W)) \leftarrow app(Y,U,W)$

Figure 2.3 shows construction of an inference tree, whose premises are the clauses of the program (with explicitly added universal quantifiers). The tree is constructed from two other inference trees by taking the conclusion of one of them as the premise of the other.

Let A be a set of formulae, to be called *axioms*. An inference tree is called a proof with respect to A iff all its premises are in A.

Figure 2.4 illustrates the fact that there is a correspondence between proof trees of a definite program P and proofs with respect to P, where clauses are considered as (universally quantified) axioms. A node of a proof tree together with all its children represents an application of the $(\rightarrow E)$ rule together with $n-1$ applications of the $(\wedge I)$ rule, where n is the number of the body atoms of the clause labelling the node. The $(\forall E)$ rules of the proof are implicitly represented in the proof tree by the appropriate instance names. Figure 2.4 shows a proof tree of the example program and the corresponding proof. The formulae of the proof distinguished by the frames, are obtained from the node labels of

Proof tree :

1    $< c_4, \{X/1, Y/l(2, nil), U/nil, W/l(2, nil)\} >$
|
2    $< c_4, \{X/2, Y/nil, U/nil, W/nil\} >$
|
3    $< c_3, \{X/nil\} >$

corresponding proof :

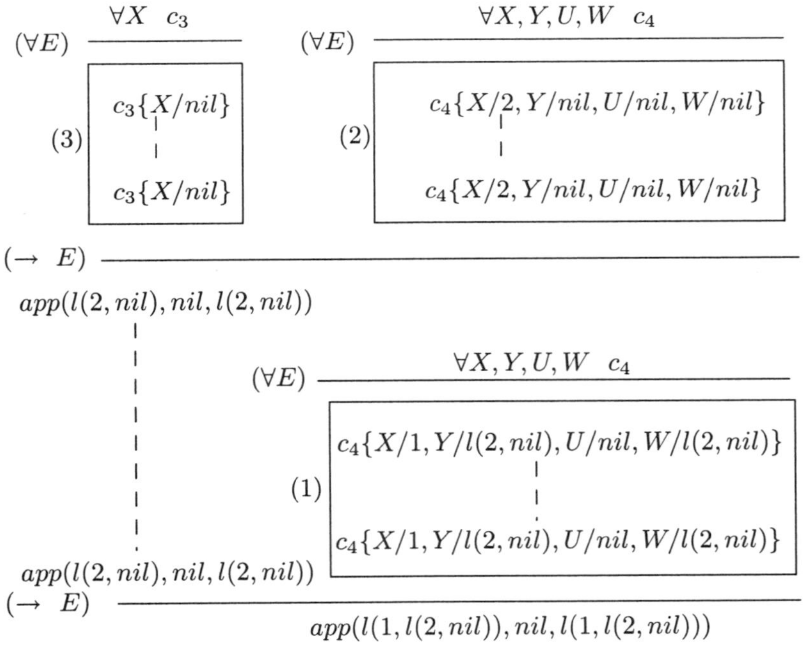

$$(\forall E) \quad \dfrac{\forall X \quad c_3}{\boxed{\begin{array}{c} c_3\{X/nil\} \\ | \\ | \\ c_3\{X/nil\} \end{array}}} \quad (3)$$

$$(\forall E) \quad \dfrac{\forall X, Y, U, W \quad c_4}{\boxed{\begin{array}{c} c_4\{X/2, Y/nil, U/nil, W/nil\} \\ | \\ | \\ c_4\{X/2, Y/nil, U/nil, W/nil\} \end{array}}} \quad (2)$$

$$(\to E) \quad \overline{\begin{array}{c} app(l(2, nil), nil, l(2, nil)) \\ | \\ | \\ | \\ | \\ | \\ | \\ | \\ | \\ | \\ app(l(2, nil), nil, l(2, nil)) \end{array}}$$

$$(\forall E) \quad \dfrac{\forall X, Y, U, W \quad c_4}{\boxed{\begin{array}{c} c_4\{X/1, Y/l(2, nil), U/nil, W/l(2, nil)\} \\ | \\ | \\ c_4\{X/1, Y/l(2, nil), U/nil, W/l(2, nil)\} \end{array}}} \quad (1)$$

$$(\to E) \quad \overline{app(l(1, l(2, nil)), nil, l(1, l(2, nil)))}$$

Figure 2.4
A proof tree and the corresponding proof

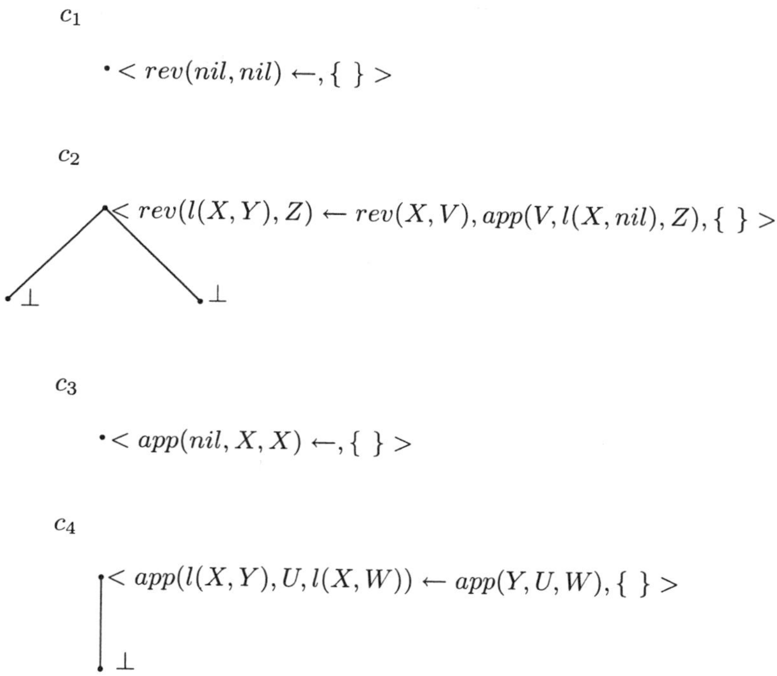

c_1

$\bullet < rev(nil, nil) \leftarrow, \{ \ \} >$

c_2

$< rev(l(X,Y), Z) \leftarrow rev(X,V), app(V, l(X, nil), Z), \{ \ \} >$

$\perp$ $\perp$

c_3

$\bullet < app(nil, X, X) \leftarrow, \{ \ \} >$

c_4

$< app(l(X,Y), U, l(X, W)) \leftarrow app(Y, U, W), \{ \ \} >$

$\perp$

Figure 2.5
Representation of clauses as derivation trees (Example 2.1 p. 26)

the proof tree.

It is worth noticing that a clause c of a definite program may be seen as a derivation tree with the root labeled by the instance name $\langle c, \{\} \rangle$. The other nodes of the tree are the children of the root. Each of them is an incomplete node. The number of the children equals the number of the body atoms of c. Thus there is a one-one correspondence between the incomplete nodes of the tree and the body atoms of c. A unit clause corresponds to a one-node proof tree.

Figure 2.5 shows the clauses of the example program represented as derivation trees.

A derivation tree is constructed from instances of clauses. By analogy to the clauses we introduce a notion of the head of a derivation tree. It will be used then to define a semantics of definite programs.

Definition 2.5 Head of a derivation tree

Let T be a derivation tree with the root labeled by an instance name $\langle c, \theta \rangle$ where c is the clause $h \leftarrow a_1, \ldots, a_m$. Then the atom $h\theta$ will be called the *head* of T.
□

Similarly, we introduce a notion of the atom corresponding to an incomplete node of a derivation tree.

Definition 2.6 Node atom

Let n be an incomplete node of a derivation tree and let i be the number such that n is the i-th child of its parent. Let $\langle h \leftarrow a_1, \ldots, a_m, \sigma \rangle$ be the label of the parent node of n. The atom $a_i\sigma$ is called the *node atom* of n and it is denoted $atom(n)$.
□

Example 2.2

The head of the derivation tree of Figure 2.1 is

$$rev(l(1, l(2, nil)), V^1)$$

and the node atoms of its incomplete nodes are

$$rev(nil, V^2),$$
$$app(V^2, l(2, nil), Z^1),$$
$$app(Z^1, l(1, nil), V^1).$$

□

The substitutions in the nodes of a derivation tree need not be ground. Thus, any derivation tree consists of finite number of not necessarily ground instances of the clauses of the program.

A derivation tree is called a *ground* derivation tree iff for every node label $\langle c, \sigma \rangle$ the clause instance $c\sigma$ is ground. The ground derivation tree in Figure 2.6 is an instance of the tree in Figure 2.1 under the substitution $\{Z^1/nil, V^1/nil, V^2/nil\}$.

In practice definite programs are often augmented with goal clauses, which may be used to control computations. The syntax of such programs is defined as follows.

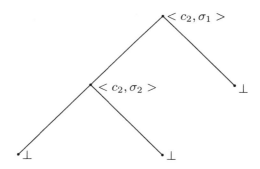

$$\sigma_1 = \{X/1, Y/l(2, nil), V/nil, Z/nil\}$$
$$\sigma_2 = \{X/2, Y/nil, V/nil, Z/nil\}$$

Figure 2.6
An example of ground derivation tree, instance of the tree in Figure 2.1

Definition 2.7

A *definite goal clause* (or a *definite goal*) is a formula of the form $\leftarrow a_1 \ldots a_m$, where $a_1, \ldots a_m$ are atomic formulae and $m \geq 1$. A *Horn clause* is a definite clause or a definite goal clause. A *Horn program* is a finite set of Horn clauses.
□

The notion of derivation tree given by Definition 2.3 p.27 extends without change for Horn programs. The only difference is that any goal clause has no head. Thus it can only label the root of a derivation tree.

Figure 2.7 shows a complete derivation tree for the program of Example 2.1 p. 26 augmented with the goal clause g:

$\leftarrow app(X, Y, l(1, l(2, nil))), app(Y, X, W)$

This illustrates the use of goal clauses with several body atoms. They allow one to construct tuples of interrelated proof trees: the goal clause combines the tuple into one tree. In this way the proof tree construction techniques are used for construction of tuples of trees.

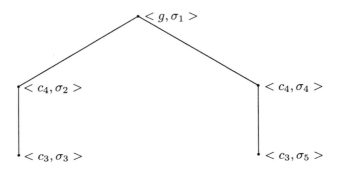

$$g = \leftarrow app(X, Y, l(1, l(2, nil))), app(Y, X, W)$$
$$\sigma_1 = \{X/l(1, nil), Y/l(2, nil), W/l(2, l(1, nil))\}$$
$$\sigma_2 = \{X/1, Y/nil, U/l(2, nil), W/l(2, nil)\}$$
$$\sigma_3 = \{X/l(2, nil)\}$$
$$\sigma_4 = \{X/2, Y/nil, U/l(1, nil), W/l(1, nil)\}$$
$$\sigma_5 = \{X/l(1, nil)\}$$

Figure 2.7
An example derivation tree of Horn program (Example 2.1 p. 26 augmented with the goal clause g)

2.1.3   Equational characterization of derivation trees

A derivation tree can be obtained by grafting instances of clauses of the program. We want to develop a nondeterministic construction algorithm based on this observation. The difficulty is in finding appropriate instances of clauses to be grafted. The solution suggested is to distinguish conceptually between the selection of clauses which are to be used for construction of a derivation tree and the search for matching instances of the selected clauses. This idea is reflected by introducing the concept of skeleton and by associating with a skeleton a set of equations, whose solutions added to the skeleton make it into a derivation tree.

Definition 2.8

For a Horn program P a *skeleton tree*, or briefly a *skeleton*, is any labeled ordered tree T such that

1. Every leaf node of T is labeled by $\perp$ or by a clause of P.

2. Every non-leaf node of T is labeled by a clause of P.

3. Let n be a node labeled by a clause with the body $a_1, \ldots, a_m$, where $m \geq 0$. Then n has m children and for $i = 1, \ldots, m$ the label of the i-th child of n is either

   - a clause with the head h' such that a_i and h' have the same predicate, or
   - $\perp$

   □

A leaf of the skeleton labeled by $\perp$ is called an *incomplete* node. The other nodes are called *complete* nodes. The skeleton without incomplete nodes is called a *complete* skeleton, otherwise it is *incomplete*. A complete or incomplete skeleton is also said *partial*.

By analogy to derivation trees we also define the notions of the head of a skeleton and of the atom of an incomplete node.

Definition 2.9

Let S be a skeleton with the root labeled by the clause
$h \leftarrow a_1, \ldots, a_m$.
Then the atom h will be called the *head* of S.
□

Definition 2.10

Let n be an incomplete node of a skeleton and let i be the number such that n is the i-th child of its parent. Let $\langle h \leftarrow a_1, \ldots, a_m \rangle$ be the label of the parent node of n. The atom a_i is called the *node atom* of n and it is denoted $atom(n)$.

□

A skeleton can be viewed as a plan for combining clauses into a derivation tree. The clauses to be combined appear as the node labels. To transform a given skeleton into a derivation tree the labels should be augmented with substitutions such that condition 3 of Definition 2.3 p. 27 is satisfied for each node. As illustrated in Figure 2.9 some skeletons cannot be transformed into derivation trees. On the other hand any derivation tree can be transformed into a skeleton.

Let T be a derivation tree of a program P. Let $Sk(T)$ be the labeled ordered tree obtained from T by replacing each node label of T of the form $\langle c, \sigma \rangle$ by the label c. It is easy to see that $Sk(T)$ is a skeleton tree of P. It will be called the *skeleton of T*. If S is the skeleton of T then T is called a derivation tree *based on S*.

The notions of instance and variant (obtained by renaming), defined for terms, atoms and clauses extend to derivation trees as follows.

Let T and T' be derivation trees based on the same skeleton S. Let n be a node of S; denote the label of the node by c_n. Denote by σ_n and σ'_n the substitutions augmenting c_n in the trees T and T'. The tree T is said to be *more general* than T' iff for every node n of S $c_n \sigma'_n$ is an instance of $c_n \sigma_n$.

For the program of Example 2.1 p. 26 the skeleton shown in Figure 2.8 can be augmented to the derivation tree shown in Figure 2.2. Thus, the skeleton of Figure 2.8, which is complete, is the skeleton of the proof tree of Figure 2.2.

The question arises how to find a derivation tree extending a given skeleton. The problem reduces to finding for each complete node n of the skeleton a substitution σ_n such that for the node n condition 3 of Definition 2.3 p. 27 is satisfied. The condition is of the form $a_i \sigma = h' \sigma'$ where σ' and σ are the substitutions to be associated with node n and its parent, respectively. If a_i and h' share no variable the problem can be solved by finding a most general unifier (mgu) μ of the equation $a_i = h'$. In this case the restrictions of σ (resp. σ') to the variables of a_i (resp.

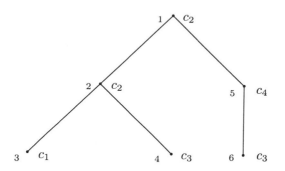

Figure 2.8
An example complete skeleton which can be augmented to a derivation tree (the skeleton of the tree of Figure 2.2)

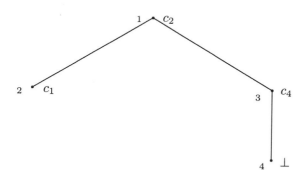

Figure 2.9
An example complete skeleton which cannot be augmented to a derivation tree (Example 2.1 p. 26)

h') is the restriction of μ to the variables of a_i (resp. h'). Otherwise, let δ and η be the renaming substitutions such that $a_i\delta$ and $h'\eta$ share no variable. Let μ' be a mgu of $a_i\delta$ and $h'\eta$. Now the restrictions of σ (resp. σ') to the variables of a_i (resp. h') is the restriction of $\delta\mu'$ (resp. $\eta\mu'$) to the variables of a_i (resp. h').

Notice that the restrictions of $\delta\mu$ and $\eta\mu'$ are not the only substitutions solving our problem. However, they are more general than any other substitutions solving the problem.

Generally the problem of extending a given skeleton S can be reduced to the problem of finding mgu of a set of equations associated with S. For this we need the following auxiliary concept:

Definition 2.11

Let S be a skeleton (or a derivation tree). For every node n of S denote by c_n the clause labelling n in S. Let $\{\rho_{n,S}\}$ be a family of renaming substitutions indexed by the nodes of S and such that for every node $n' \neq n$ the images of $\rho_{n,S}(Var(c_n))$ and $\rho_{n',S}(Var(c_{n'}))$ are disjoint. Every substitution $\rho_{n,S}$ is called a *standardizing substitution* for n in S.

A set of skeletons (or derivation trees) is said *standardized* if there is an associated family of standardizing substitutions for all the different nodes in the sets.
□

Let n' be the j-th child of n labeled by a clause $c_{n'}$ and let h' be the head of this clause. Denote by $eq(n,n')$ the equation $a_j\rho_{n,S} = h'\rho_{n',S}$, where $\rho_{n,S}$ and $\rho_{n',S}$ are standardizing substitutions. Denote by $Eq(S)$ the set of all equations $eq(n,p)$ where n and p are adjacent complete nodes of the skeleton S. Notice that different equations may share variables (but no equation has a variable shared by its left-hand side and right-hand side). Notice also that the standardizing substitutions are not unique but the only possible effect of changing them is renaming of the variables in the resulting set of equations.

By our construction and by definition of the derivation tree we have:

Proposition 2.1

Let S be a skeleton. A derivation tree based on S exists iff $Eq(S)$ has a unifier.
□

We now have the following method for construction of derivation trees based on a given skeleton S.

Theorem 2.1

Let S be a skeleton and let σ be an mgu of $Eq(S)$. Let $D(S)$ be the tree obtained from S by replacing each node label c_n, such that c_n is a clause, by the pair $\langle c_n, \sigma_n \rangle$, where $\sigma_n = (\rho_{n,S}\sigma)$ and $\rho_{n,S}$ is the standardizing substitution for n in S used to build $Eq(S)$. Then $D(S)$ is a derivation tree of the program more general than every other derivation tree based on S.

$\square$

Proof. Every pair of the adjacent nodes of the tree $D(S)$ satisfies condition 3 of Definition 2.3 p. 27, hence $D(S)$ is a derivation tree.

Let T be a derivation tree based on S. We show that T determines a unifier of $Eq(S)$, hence the mgu of $Eq(S)$ exists and $D(S)$ is more general than T.

Let n and p be complete nodes of T such that p is the i-th child of n for some $i > 0$. The label of n is of the form $\langle c_n, \sigma_n \rangle$, where σ_n is a substitution. Similarly the label of p is of the form $\langle c_p, \sigma_p \rangle$. By the definition of derivation tree $a_i \sigma_n = h' \sigma_p$, where a_i is the i-th body atom of c_n and h' is the head of c_p. Let $\rho_{n,T}$ and $\rho_{p,T}$ be the standardizing substitutions for n and p in T. Since S is a skeleton of T then they are also standardizing substitutions for the corresponding nodes of S.

Let us restrict our attention to the variables of the clauses named in the instance names in T. By a general property of renaming substitutions there exist substitutions δ_n and δ_p whose domains are respectively the variables of $c_n \rho_{n,T}$ and $c_p \rho_{p,T}$ such that $\sigma_n|_{Var(c_n)} = \rho_{n,T}|_{Var(c_n)}\delta_n$ and $\sigma_p|_{Var(c_p)} = \rho_{p,T}|_{Var(c_p)}\delta_p$. By definition of the standardizing substitutions the domains of the δ_k's in T are all disjoint.

Thus $a_i \sigma_n = a_i \rho_{n,T}\delta_n = a_i \rho_{p,T}\delta_p = h'\sigma_p$. But $a_i \rho_{n,T} = h'\rho_{p,T}$ is the equation $eq(n,p)$ in $Eq(S)$. But as for every complete node k in T the substitution δ_k has a unique domain, the union of δ_n and δ_p is a substitution and it is a unifier of the equation $eq(n,p)$. Consequently, the union of the substitutions δ_k of all complete nodes of T is a unifier of $Eq(S)$. Denote it δ. Then there exists an mgu γ of $Eq(S)$, i.e $\delta = \gamma\psi$

for some substitution ψ. Hence $D(S)$ exists and is more general than T.

$\square$

The tree $D(S)$ exists iff $Eq(S)$ has a unifier and in this case it is unique up to renaming of variables in the range of the substitutions. A skeleton S such that $Eq(S)$ has a unifier will be called a *proper* skeleton. The theorem shows that the derivation tree $D(S)$ for a given skeleton S is a most general one among those based on S. In particular, for a given derivation tree one can find a most general derivation tree based on the same skeleton.

We now illustrate the method by an example.

Example 2.3

For the skeleton S of Figure 2.8 we construct the set $Eq(S)$. The renaming substitutions are constructed by indexing the variables by the indices of the nodes of the skeleton.

$$rev(Y^1, V^1) = rev(l(X^2, Y^2), Z^2))$$

$$app(V^1, l(X^1, nil), Z^1) = app(l(X^5, Y^5), U^5, l(X^5, W^5))$$

$$rev(Y^2, V^2) = rev(nil, nil)$$

$$app(V^2, l(X^2, nil), Z^2) = app(nil, X^4, X^4)$$

$$app(Y^5, U^5, W^5) = app(nil, X^6, X^6)$$

This set has the following mgu:

$$\sigma = \{Y^1/l(X^5, nil), V^1/l(X^5, nil), Z^1/l(X^5, l(X^1, nil)), X^2/X^5$$
$$Y^2/nil, V^2/nil, Z^2/l(X^5, nil), X^4/l(X^5, nil), Y^5/nil, U^5/l(X^1, nil),$$
$$W^5/l(X^1, nil), X^6/l(X^1, nil)\}$$

The tree $D(S)$ is shown in Figure 2.10.

For the skeleton in Figure 2.9 we obtain the following set of equations:

$$rev(Y^1, V^1) = rev(nil, nil)$$
$$app(V^1, l(X^1, nil), Z^1) = app(l(X^3, Y^3), U^3, l(X^3, W^3))$$

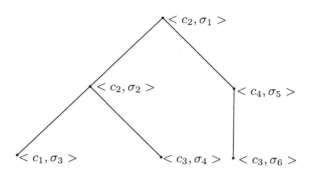

$$\sigma_1 = \{X/X^1, Y/l(X^5, nil), V/l(X^5, nil), Z/l(X^5, l(X^1, nil))\}$$
$$\sigma_2 = \{X/X^5, Y/nil, V/nil, Z/l(X^5, nil)\}$$
$$\sigma_3 = \{\}$$
$$\sigma_4 = \{X/l(X^5, nil)\}$$
$$\sigma_5 = \{X/X^5, Y/nil, U/l(X^1, nil), W/l(X^1, nil)\}$$
$$\sigma_6 = \{X/l(X^1, nil)\}$$

Figure 2.10
The derivation tree obtained for the skeleton of Figure 2.8 (a most general proof tree)

This set has no unifier: the attempt to find a unifier would produce the equations $V^1 = nil = l(X^3, Y^3)$ which have no unifier.
□

The construction described above produces the set of equations $Eq(S)$ for a given skeleton S. The mgu of this set determines a derivation tree based on S. The construction may be extended to finite sets of skeletons. For this the standardizing substitutions should give a unique renaming for each complete node of every skeleton. Thus, for a set S of skeletons and for a complete node n in one of them we have a standardizing substitution ρ_n which renames every variable of c_n into a unique new variable. In this case the technique described above produces one set of equations for all skeletons. The mgu of this set determines a derivation tree for every skeleton in the set.

2.1.4   Construction of derivation trees

Theorem 2.1   p. 41 shows that a derivation tree is fully characterized by a skeleton and by a solution of the equations associated with it. To construct a derivation tree it is sufficient to construct a skeleton and to solve the associated set of equations. This section presents a general scheme where derivation trees are built by interleaving a process of skeleton construction with a process of equation solving. The well-known notion of SLD-resolution, a fundamental concept which made it possible to develop Prolog, is presented as a particular instance of the scheme.

Skeleton construction

We first outline some possible approaches to the construction of the skeletons. The definition of a skeleton (Definition 2.8   p. 37) relies on the clauses of the program. The number of children of each node is determined by its label. Thus, for each clause c of the form $h \leftarrow a_1, ..., a_m$ where $m \geq 0$ (there may be no head), one can consider a corresponding elementary skeleton which consists of the root labeled by c and m children. Each of the children is labeled $\perp$. The skeletons corresponding to unit clauses have no children and are complete. The skeleton corresponding to a clause c will be called the *clause skeleton* of c and will be denoted $Csk(c)$. The set of all clause skeletons of a Horn program P will be denoted $Csk(P)$. Now each skeleton of P can be seen as a combination of a number of copies of clause skeletons in $Csk(P)$. Each of the copies is itself a skeleton. Construction of a skeleton may be defined as a process with *states* being sets of skeletons and the *initial state* being some subset of $Csk(P)$. A new state is obtained by combining copies of some skeletons of the old state and copies of some skeletons in $Csk(P)$, adding the resulting skeletons to the state and removing some old elements. The final state, if any, is a set of skeletons satisfying certain condition. Let us denote the state by $\mathcal{C}$ and the state transition by $comp(\mathcal{C}, Csk(P))$. Using this notation we may present a general nondeterministic skeleton construction scheme. The idea is to repeat the construction step until some condition on the state $\mathcal{C}$ is satisfied.

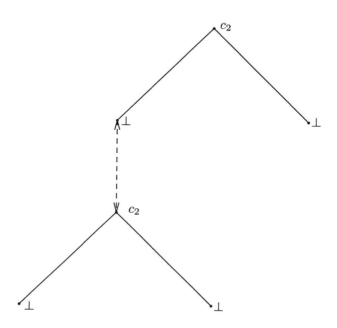

Figure 2.11
An example of composition of skeletons rules of Example 2.1 p. 26

The scheme is shown in Table 2.1. This scheme is too general to be of practical interest. It is however a good starting point for developing and classifying algorithms for skeleton construction.

To refine the scheme one has to define the notion of combination of two skeletons. Let $S1$ and $S2$ be skeletons, and let n be an incomplete leaf of $S1$. The skeleton $S2$ is said to *fit* $S1$ at n iff $atom(n)$ and $head(S2)$ have the same predicate symbol. If $S2$ fits $S1$ at n then the skeleton obtained by grafting $S2$ at the node n of $S1$ is called n-*composition* of $S1$ and $S2$. A skeleton S is said to be a *composition* of $S1$ and $S2$ iff it is their n-composition for some leaf n such that $S2$ fits $S1$ at n. Figure 2.11 shows clause skeletons of the program of Example 2.1 p. 26 and illustrates composition of skeletons.

In practical cases one may be interested in "top-down" skeleton construction where the state is always a singleton. The initial state skeleton is given. The new state is obtained by composing the *actual state* using

Table 2.1
General skeleton construction scheme (GSCS)

begin
$\quad\quad \mathcal{C} := \mathcal{C}_I;\ (\mathcal{C}_I \subseteq Csk(P))$
$\quad\quad$ **while** condition($\mathcal{C}$)
$\quad\quad\quad\quad$ **do**
$\quad\quad\quad\quad \mathcal{C} := \mathrm{comp}(\mathcal{C}, Csk(P))$
$\quad\quad\quad\quad$ **od**
end

Table 2.2
A top-down skeleton construction scheme (TSCS)

begin
$\quad\quad \mathcal{C} := \{S_0\};\ (S_0 \in Csk(P))$
$\quad\quad$ **while** condition($\mathcal{C}$)
$\quad\quad\quad\quad$ **do**
$\quad\quad\quad\quad$ select a copy T in $Csk(P)$
$\quad\quad\quad\quad\quad\quad$ which fits some S in $\mathcal{C}$ at some leaf n ;
$\quad\quad\quad\quad \mathcal{C} := (\mathcal{C} - \{S\}) \cup \{n\text{-composition}(S,T)\}$
$\quad\quad\quad\quad$ **od**
end

some unique clause skeleton. This idea may be described by the scheme in Table 2.2.

Figure 2.12 gives an example of a finite sequence of steps of a top-down skeleton construction process.

Another approach is to construct complete skeletons only. Now the state is a set of complete skeletons. The initial state consists of the set $Usk(P)$ of all unit clause skeletons of the program P. The scheme is presented in Table 2.3.

Figure 2.13 gives an example of a finite sequence of steps of a bottom-up skeleton construction process.

Notice that the schemes are nondeterministic and may perform repetitive construction of the same skeleton. For development of realistic

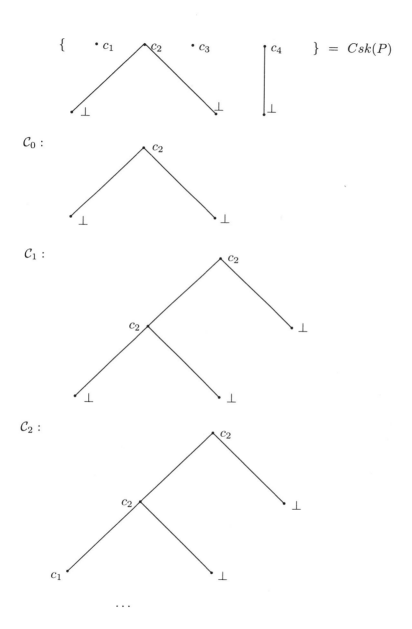

Figure 2.12
Top-down skeleton construction (Example 2.1 p. 26)

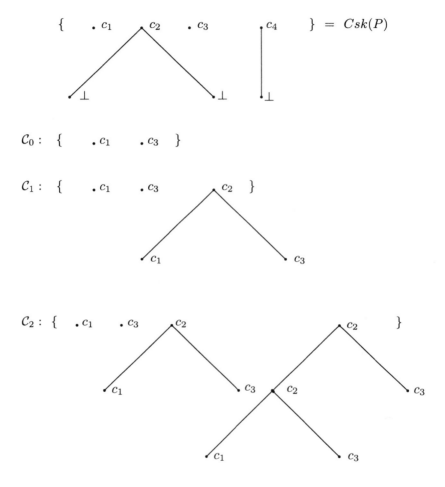

Figure 2.13
Bottom-up skeleton construction (Example 2.1 p. 26)

Table 2.3
A bottom-up skeleton construction scheme (BSCS)

begin
  $\mathcal{C} := Usk(P)$;
  while condition($\mathcal{C}$)
    do
      select a copy T in $Csk(P)$ with leaves $n_1, ..., n_k$
        such that for $i = 1, ...k$
         there is a copy S_i in $\mathcal{C}$ which fits T at n_i;
      $\mathcal{C} := \mathcal{C} \cup n_1\text{-composition}(S_1, ..., n_k\text{-composition}(S_k, T) ...)$
    od
end

algorithms which enumerate all complete skeletons further restrictions should be imposed on the schemes.

Solving equations associated with skeletons

Every skeleton S determines the set $Eq(S)$ of equations defined in Section 2.1.3. This set is unique up to renaming of variables. Some of the skeleton construction schemes discussed above produce sets of skeletons. Given a set $\mathcal{S}$ of skeletons one can assume that for every S and $S' \in \mathcal{S}$ the equations of $Eq(S)$ share no variables with the equations of $Eq(S')$. In this case we denote by $Eq(\mathcal{S})$ the union of all sets of equations $Eq(S)$ for $S \in \mathcal{S}$. Now every state of a skeleton construction process can be associated with a set of equations. A new state is obtained during a state transition by composition of some skeletons of the old state.

We now show how to construct the set of equations associated with a composition of skeletons. Let S and S' be skeletons such that S' fits S at some node n. We assume without loss of generality that the equation sets $Eq(S)$ and $Eq(S')$ share no variables. This can be achieved by standardization on the set of skeletons rather than on one skeleton. Clearly n is an incomplete node of S and must be labeled by $\perp$. Let n' be the root of S' and let n'' be the parent node of n. The set of equations associated with n-composition of S and S' consists of $Eq(S)$, $Eq(S')$ and of the additional equation $atom(n)\rho_{n'',\{S,S'\}} = head(S')\rho_{n',\{S,S'\}}$ (to recall the notational conventions see Definition 2.5 and Definition 2.6

on page 34). Notice that the standardization is done on the set of skeletons.

Example 2.4

Figure 2.14 shows two fitting skeletons of the program of Example 2.1 p. 26. We construct first the corresponding sets of equations standardized in such a way that they do not share equations.

$$Eq(S) = \{rev(Y^1, V^1) = rev(l(X^2, Y^2), Z^2)\}$$
$$Eq(T) = \{app(Y^6, U^6, W^6) = app(nil, X^7, X^7)\}$$

Their mgu's are

$$mgu(Eq(S)) = \{Y^1/l(X^2, Y^2), V^1/Z^2\}$$
$$mgu(Eq(T)) = \{Y^6/nil, U^6/X^7, W^6/X^7\}$$

The new equation describing composition of S and T at node 5 is

$$app(V, l(X, nil), Z)\{X/X^1, Y/Y^1, V/V^1, Z/Z^1\} =$$
$$app(l(X, Y), U, l(X, W))\{X/X^6, Y/Y^6, U/U^6, W/W^6\}$$

thus it is of the form

$$app(V^1, l(X^1, nil), Z^1) = app(l(X^6, Y^6), U^6, l(X^6, W^6))$$

□

We now consider the problem whether the mgu of a set of equations can be computed incrementally by combining the mgu's of subsets. In this case the process of constructing skeletons could be interleaved with unification steps consisting in computing and combining the mgu's of selected subsets of equations.

Let E and F be sets of equations. The problem is to express the mgu of $E \bigcup F$ in terms of the mgu's of E and F. Two solutions of this problem follow by the properties of mgu's discussed in Section 1.6.3.

The first solution suggests a sequential approach to incremental computation of mgu's. To compute a mgu of $E \cup F$ first find a mgu of E, then a mgu of $Fmgu(E)$ and finally compose the results. More formally, let σ be a mgu of E and let γ be a mgu of $F\sigma$. Then $\sigma\gamma$ is a mgu of $E \cup F$. This can be stated as the following formula:

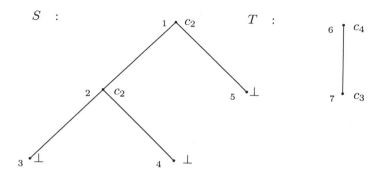

Figure 2.14
Skeletons in Example 2.4

$$mgu(E \cup F) = mgu(E)mgu(Fmgu(E))$$

Example 2.5

We apply the sequential approach to the equations of Example 2.4 . We have to compute an mgu of the set of equations obtained by putting together the sets $Eq(S)$, $Eq(T)$ and the new equation e. We begin with $E = Eq(S) \bigcup e$.

$$mgu(Eq(S)) = \{Y^1/l(X^2, Y^2), V^1/Z^2\}.$$

Denote this substitution by σ_1. Now $e\sigma_1$ is:

$$app(Z^2, l(X^1, nil), Z^1) = app(l(X^6, Y^6), U^6, l(X^6, W^6)).$$

An mgu of this equation is

$$\sigma_2 = \{Z^2/l(X^6, Y^6), U^6/l(X^1, nil), Z^1/l(X^6, W^6).$$

Using the sequential method we obtain:
$mgu(E) = \sigma_1\sigma_2 =$
$\{Y^1/l(X^2, Y^2), V^1/l(X^6, Y^6), Z^1/l(X^6, W^6),$
$$Z^2/l(X^6, Y^6), U^6/l(X^1, nil)\}.$$
Denote this substitution by σ. Now the sequential method can be applied to compute $Eq(T) \bigcup E$. $Eq(T)$ is the singleton

$$\{app(Y^6, U^6, W^6) = app(nil, X^7, X^7)\}.$$

Hence $Eq(T)\sigma$ is the singleton

$$\{app(Y^6, l(X^1, nil), W^6) = app(nil, X^7, X^7)\}$$

and finally we obtain $mgu(Eq(T)\bigcup E) =$

$$\{Y^1/l(X^2, Y^2), V^1/l(X^6, nil), Z^1/l(X^6, l(X^1, nil)), Z^2/l(X^6, nil),$$
$$U^6/l(X^1, nil), Y^6/nil, W^6/l(X^1, nil), X^7/l(X^1, nil)\}.$$

□

The other solution is based on the parallel approach of Section 1.6.3. The idea is to compute independently the mgu of E and the mgu of F. We assume that both mgu's are idempotent. (For example the unification algorithm of Section 1.6.3 computes an idempotent mgu of a unifiable set of equations). The results are to be combined into the mgu of $E \cup F$. To achieve this the mgu of each component is to be transformed into the corresponding set of equations.[1] The mgu of the set of equations $eq(mgu(E)) \cup eq(mgu(F))$ is the mgu of the set $E \cup F$. This can be summarized by the following formula:

$$mgu(E \cup F) = mgu(eq(mgu(E)) \cup eq(mgu(F))).$$

The formula suggests a parallel approach to computation of the mgu's. To compute the mgu of a set of equation compute separately the mgu's of its components. To obtain the final result compute the mgu of the component results. It is worth noticing that this strategy generalizes for arbitrary number of components :

$$mgu(E_1 \cup \ldots \cup E_n) = mgu(eq(mgu(E_1)) \cup \ldots \cup eq(mgu(E_n)))$$

Example 2.6

Consider the set of equations of Example 2.4 p. 50.
$mgu(Eq(S) \cup \{e\}) = (mgu(E)$ in Example 2.5)

$$\{Y^1/l(X^2, Y^2), V^1/l(X^6, Y^6), Z^1/l(X^6, W^6),$$
$$Z^2/l(X^6, Y^6), U^6/l(X^1, nil)\},$$

---

[1] As defined in Section 1.6.3 for a substitution $\sigma = \{X_1/t_1, \ldots X_n/t_n\}$ the corresponding set of equations $eq(\sigma)$ is $\{X_1 = t_1, \ldots X_n = t_n\}$.

$$mgu(Eq(T)) = \{Y^6/nil, U^6/X^7, W^6/X^7\}.$$

The set of equations resulting from these mgu's is

$$\{Y^1 = l(X^2, Y^2), V^1 = l(X^6, Y^6), Z^1 = l(X^6, W^6), Z^2 = l(X^6, Y^6),$$
$$U^6 = l(X^1, nil), Y^6 = nil, W^6 = X^7, U^6 = X^7\}.$$

Its mgu is the same as that obtained in Example 2.5

$\square$

General resolution scheme

We now address the problem of construction of derivation trees of a given Horn program. In a most general setting such trees may be constructed by a nondeterministic process that interleaves construction of a skeleton and solution of selected equations associated to the constructed parts of the skeleton. Our objective is to define a scheme describing such processes, called *general resolution scheme* (GRS), which can be then specialized to obtain specific resolution schemes and algorithms. In particular it should be possible to specialize GRS to the classical SLD-resolution scheme.

The processes we want to describe include two kinds of computational steps: skeleton construction steps and equation solving steps. The effect of these steps at every stage of a process is characterized by a *state*, which is a pair $\langle S, \sigma \rangle$ where S is a finite set of skeletons and σ is a substitution resulting from all previous equation solving steps.

A construction step changes S by combining some of its fitting skeletons or by combining some of its elements with fitting clause skeletons. The combined skeletons may or may not be removed from S. The construction step results in a new set S of skeletons. As discussed above the set S determines a unique set of equations.

An equation solving step constructs the mgu of some equations in $Eq(S)$, i.e. some of the equations defined by the set of skeletons already constructed in the current state. The component σ of the state is the mgu of all equations which have been selected at all preceding equation solving steps. The incremental techniques described above may be used to combine the mgu's of previously selected equations with the mgu's of the equations selected at the current step of the process.

We define the *resolution process* as a sequence of states where the transition between the consecutive states is defined by a construction

Table 2.4
General resolution scheme (GRS)

begin
       $\sigma := \{\}$;
       $\mathcal{S} := \mathcal{S}_0$;
       while condition$(\mathcal{S}, \sigma)$
           do
               skeleton construction step
           or
               equation solving step
           od
end

step or by an equation solving step. We have to be more specific about the initial state of the process. We assume that the construction goes from scratch. This means that the components of the initial state are:

- a set $\mathcal{S}_0$ of skeletons including at most the clause skeletons of the program, and
- the identity substitution.

The resolution process will be controlled by some termination condition on the states. For example, one may want to stop it as soon as a proof tree is constructed. This may be understood as reaching a state $\langle \{S\}, \sigma \rangle$ where S is a complete skeleton and σ is the mgu of $Eq(S)$. The states satisfying the termination condition will be called the *final* states. If a final state of a resolution process corresponds to a derivation tree then we say the tree is *constructed* by resolution.

To summarize the discussion we describe the resolution process by the general scheme shown in Table 2.4, where **"or"** means that at least one of the steps is performed during each iteration.

The scheme has a Horn program as input parameter. The step chosen for execution by the **or** construct may cause abnormal termination of the process, called *failure*. This happens, for example, if the equation solver discovers that the set of equations constructed has no solution. The scheme gives a framework for specifying concrete algorithms. In particular one has to be specific about

- the initial set S_0 of clause skeletons,
- the termination condition,
- the skeleton construction step,
- the equation solving step,
- the way of interleaving of the construction steps with the equation solving steps.

A scheme obtained from the GRS by providing this information will be called a *resolution scheme* (RS). A resolution scheme defines a class of *resolution processes*, called also *computations*.

Definition 2.12

A *$\mathcal{R}$-computation* of given RS $\mathcal{R}$ and Horn program P is a finite or infinite sequence of states $\langle S_0, \{\} \rangle, \ldots \langle S_n, \sigma_n \rangle, \ldots$ such that for each $i \geq 0$ the state $\langle S_{i+1}, \sigma_{i+1} \rangle$ is obtained from the state $\langle S_i, \sigma_i \rangle$ by a single skeleton construction step and/or by a single equation solving step. If the last state of a finite computation satisfies the termination condition then the computation is called (*successfully*) *terminated*. For a terminated computation the substitution σ_n of its last element will be called a *computed substitution* for P.
□

One would expect that a resolution scheme should be able to construct for any program P and goal clause g a proof tree of P with the root labeled by an instance name of g, if such a tree exists. In other words, it should be able to construct a skeleton S with the root label g and to compute an mgu σ of $Eq(S)$. Sometimes we may be interested only in the restriction of the substitution to the variables of the goal. The restriction of σ to the variables of g will be called an *answer substitution* for $P \cup \{g\}$.

Furthermore one is interested in resolution schemes which are also complete in the sense that they compute all possible proper skeletons with the root labeled by an instance name of the goal clause. Schemes satisfying these expectations can be described by the following definition.

Definition 2.13 Full resolution scheme

Let P be a definite program and g be a definite goal clause. A resolution scheme $\mathcal{R}$ such that σ is a computed substitution for $P \cup \{g\}$ iff

$\sigma = mgu(Eq(S))$ for some complete skeleton S of $P \cup \{g\}$ with the root labeled by g is called a *full* RS.
□

Remark that the main characteristics of a full RS is to compute all the most general proof trees based on proper skeletons.

As an example of a full resolution scheme we derive the scheme of SLD-resolution. Generally, the SLD-resolution combines a restricted version of top-down skeleton construction scheme with the sequential equation solving. We start with a scheme similar to SLD-resolution, which we call SLDT-resolution (SLD-resolution on Trees).

We want SLDT-resolution to have the following properties:

- The computation starts with a Horn program including one goal clause g. The initial set S_0 is the singleton whose only element is the skeleton of g. At every step of computation the *actual set of skeletons* is a singleton $\{S\}$.

- The process terminates with success iff it reaches a state $\langle \{S\}, \sigma \rangle$ such that S is a complete skeleton and σ is the mgu of $Eq(S)$. The process may also abort by failure.

To achieve this goal we make the following design decisions:

- The skeleton construction step is as in the top-down skeleton construction scheme: if S is an incomplete skeleton then an incomplete leaf l of S is selected; if there is a clause skeleton c that fits S at l then S and c are combined at l. Otherwise the process fails.

- The equation solving is done immediately for the new skeleton S constructed at each step of the process. Combination of S with c at l results in a new equation $atom(l)\sigma = h\rho_{l,\{S,c\}}$ where h is the head of c and $\rho_{l,\{S,c\}}$ is the standardizing substitution for S and c at the node l. (see Definition 2.11 p. 40). The mgu of the equations associated with the new skeleton is obtained by composition of σ with the mgu of the new equation.

Table 2.5 shows that the SLDT-resolution scheme is a specialization of the GRS of Table 2.4, which applies to arbitrary definite program P with goal g.

The scheme is nondeterministic. The sources of the nondeterminism are: the choice of the leaf l and the choice of the clause skeleton c.

Table 2.5
SLDT-resolution

begin
 $S := Csk(g)$
 $\sigma := \{\};$
 while S is incomplete
  do
    choose an incomplete leaf l in S;
    create a copy C of some clause skeleton in $Csk(P)$
      with head h that fits S at l;
    if $atom(l)\sigma$ unifies with $h\rho_{l,\{S,C\}}$
    then $\sigma := \sigma mgu(atom(l)\sigma, h\rho_{l,\{S,C\}})$
    $S:= l\text{-composition}(S,C)$
    else fail
  od
end

There are no restrictions on the choices. Each step of the computation includes a skeleton construction step followed by an equation solving step. A computation described by the scheme may terminate with a proof tree presented as a complete skeleton and the mgu of the set of equations associated with this skeleton. Otherwise it may fail or loop.

Example 2.7
 We illustrate the SLDT-resolution by an example SLDT-computation for the program of Example 2.1 p. 26 and goal clause
 $g = \leftarrow rev(X,Y).$
The computation is shown in Figure 2.15.
□
 We now prove that SLDT-resolution is a full resolution scheme. We prove first two auxiliary properties.

Proposition 2.2
 Let P be a definite program and let g be a goal. If $\langle Csk(g), \{\}\rangle,$
 $\langle S_1, \sigma_1\rangle, \ldots, \langle S_l, \sigma_l\rangle$, where $l \geq 0$ is an SLDT-computation then σ_l is the

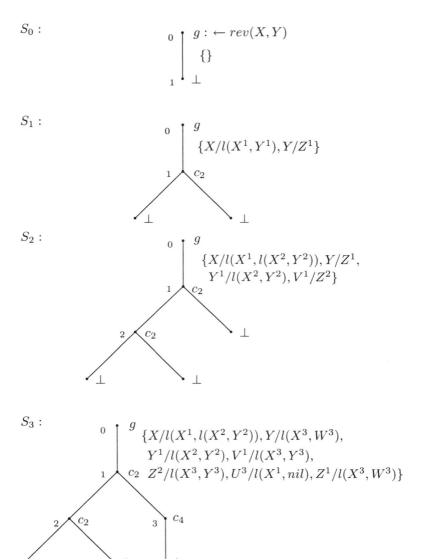

Figure 2.15
Example SLDT-computation

mgu of $Eq(S_l)$.
□

Proof. We prove the result by induction on the length l of the computation. For $l = 0$ the skeleton S_0 is $Csk(g)$. It has no internal nodes, hence $Eq(S_0)$ is the empty set of equations and $\sigma_0 = \{\}$ is its mgu.

Consider a computation of length k for some $k > 0$ Assume that the result holds for its subcomputation of length $k-1$ obtained by removing the last state. By this assumption the substitution σ_{k-1} is the mgu of $Eq(S_{k-1})$. The skeleton S_k is obtained by combining S_{k-1} with the skeleton of the clause c selected at the step $k-1$ of the computation. Let n be the selected node of S_{k-1} and let c be the clause whose skeleton $Csk(c)$ is attached at n to obtain S_k. The set $Eq(S_k)$ consists of the equations of $Eq(S_{k-1})$ and of the additional equation e_k of the form $atom(n) = h\rho$ where h is the head of $Csk(c)$ and ρ is $\rho_{n,\{S,Csk(c)\}}$, the standardizing substitution for S and $Csk(c)$ at n. Using the sequential scheme the mgu of $Eq(S_k)$ can be computed as follows $mgu(Eq(S_k)) = mgu(Eq(S_{k-1}))mgu(e_k mgu(Eq(S_{k-1})))$.

By the induction hypothesis $mgu(Eq(S_{k-1})) = \sigma_{k-1}$.

Hence $mgu(Eq(S_k)) = \sigma_{k-1}mgu(atom(n)\sigma_{k-1} = h\rho\sigma_{k-1})$.

It follows by the definition of ρ that $h\rho\sigma_{k-1} = h\rho$.

Hence $mgu(Eq(S_k)) = \sigma_{k-1}mgu(atom(l)\sigma_{k-1}, h\rho)$.

But by the definition of SLDT-resolution

$\sigma_{k-1}mgu(atom(l)\sigma_{k-1}, h\rho) = \sigma_k$.

Hence $\sigma_k = mgu(Eq(S_k))$.
□

It follows by Proposition 2.2 that for a skeleton S constructed by an SLDT-computation the set of equations $Eq(S)$ has an mgu. We now show that the SLDT-resolution allows to construct all skeletons which have this property.

Proposition 2.3

Let P be a definite program and let g be a goal. For every proper skeleton S of P with the root labeled by g there exists a finite SLDT-computation with the last state of the form $\langle S, \sigma \rangle$, where σ is a most

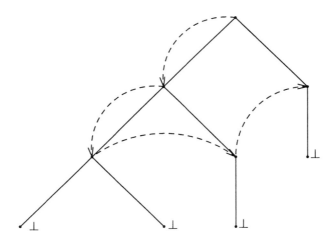

Figure 2.16
The traversal order on the complete nodes of a skeleton

general unifier of $Eq(S)$.
□

Proof. Consider the depth-first traversal order on the complete nodes of S, illustrated in Figure 2.16.

Enumerate the nodes in this order. Denote by c_i the clause labelling each node i. Define S_i to be the skeleton obtained from S by removing all subtrees of S rooted at the nodes $j > i$; some internal nodes of S are transformed by this operation into incomplete leaves of S_i. Notice that $Eq(S_i)$ is a subset of $Eq(S)$ and therefore has an mgu. Notice also, that the skeleton S_i for $i \geq 1$ is obtained from S_{i-1} by combining it with the clause skeleton $Csk(c_i)$ at node i. Now the sequence:

$$\langle Csk(g), \{\}\rangle, \langle S_1, mgu(Eq(S_1)))\rangle, \dots \langle S, mgu(Eq(S)))\rangle$$

is an SLDT-computation.
□

As an immediate corollary of Proposition 2.2 and Proposition 2.3 we have

Theorem 2.2

The SLDT-resolution is a full RS.

□

Proof. If an SLDT-computation terminates successfully then, by definition, the skeleton component S of the final state is complete. Then, by Proposition 2.2 the computed substitution is an mgu of $Eq(S)$. On the other hand, Proposition 2.3 shows that every most general derivation tree can be constructed.

□

We now modify SLDT-resolution for the case when one is not interested in derivation trees but only in the computed substitutions. The resulting scheme will be called SLD-resolution. To find computed substitutions one has to construct equations associated with the skeletons, but the skeletons need not be constructed.

Notice that at each step of an SLDT-computation an incomplete node of the state skeleton is selected. Thus, the complete nodes of the skeleton do not participate in the computation and can be removed. This idea gives a new notion of state. The state is a pair $\langle g, \sigma \rangle$ where g is a sequence of atoms, called the *actual goal*, and σ is a substitution. Intuitively, the atoms of g represent the incomplete nodes of a skeleton and σ is the mgu of the set of equations associated with the skeleton. At each step of the computation a new equation e of the form $a\sigma = h\theta_g$ is created, where a is a selected atom of g, h is the head of a clause c of the program and θ_g is a renaming substitution on the variables of c such that the image of the variables of c is disjoint with all the variables appearing in previous selected renamed clauses. Denoting by g' the sequence of atoms obtained by replacing a in g by the body of $c\theta_g$ and putting $\sigma' = \sigma mgu(e)$ one defines $\langle g', \sigma' \rangle$ to be the new state of SLD-computation.

The idea presented above is now described as the scheme of SLD-resolution presented in Table 2.6. In this scheme the notation $g[a/b]$, where g and b are sequences of atoms and a is an atom in g will be used to denote the sequence of atoms obtained by replacing a selected occurrence of a in g by the sequence b. An SLD-computation for a given definite program P starts with an initial sequence of atoms g_0 which is

Table 2.6
SLD-resolution

begin

   $g := g_0$
   $\sigma := \{\}$;
   while g is not the empty sequence
     do
         choose an occurrence of an atom a in g;
         choose a clause c of head h and body B in P
          such that $a\sigma$ unifies with $h\theta_g$
         if no such c exists **then fail**;
         $\sigma := \sigma mgu(a\sigma, h\theta_g)$
         $g := g[a/B\theta_g]$
     od

end

a representation of a definite goal clause.

It is easy to see that there is a one-one correspondence between SLDT-computations and SLD-computations. Consider an SLDT-computation $\langle S_0, \sigma_0 \rangle \ldots \langle S_k, \sigma_k \rangle$. Then the sequence $\langle g_0, \sigma_0 \rangle \ldots \langle g_k, \sigma_k \rangle$, where g_i for $i = 1, \ldots, k$ is a sequence including all atoms $atom(n)$ such that n is an incomplete node of S_i is an SLD-computation.

On the other hand, let $\langle g_0, \sigma_0 \rangle \ldots \langle g_k, \sigma_k \rangle$ be an SLD-computation. Let a_i for $i = 1, \ldots, k$ be the atom selected in g_i and let c_i be the clause used to construct the equation at the step i. Then there exists an SLDT-derivation $\langle Csk(\leftarrow g_0), \sigma_0 \rangle \ldots \langle S_k, \sigma_k \rangle$. This derivation can be constructed as follows. Its initial state is fully determined and includes an incomplete node n such that $atom(n) = a_0$. The next state is obtained by choosing this node and the clause c_1 for construction of the skeleton S_1. The mgu of the resulting equation is σ_1 and includes an incomplete node n_1 such that $atom(n_1) = a_1$. The construction continues with $c_2, \ldots, c_k$ and gives as a result an SLDT-computation which at every step computes the same substitution as the original SLD-computation.

Example 2.8

The SLDT-computation of Example 2.7 p. 57 corresponds to the following SLD-computation:

$$\langle[rev(X,Y)],\{\}\rangle,$$
$$\langle[rev(Y^1,V^1),app(V^1,l(X^1,nil),Z^1],\{X/l(X^1,Y^1),Y/Z^1\}\rangle,$$
$$\langle[rev(Y^2,V^2),app(V^2,l(X^2,nil),Z^2),app(V^1,l(X^1,nil),Z^1)],$$
$$\{X/l(X^1,l(X^2,Y^2)),Y/Z^1,Y^1/l(X^2,Y^2),V^1/Z^2\}\rangle$$
$$\langle[rev(Y^2,V^2),app(V^2,l(X^2,nil),Z^2,app(Y^3,U^3,W^3)],$$
$$\{X/l(X^1,l(X^2,Y^2)),Y/l(X^3,W^3),Y^1/l(X^2,Y^2),V^1/l(X^3,Y^3),$$
$$Z^2/l(X^3,Y^3),U^3/l(X^1,nil),Z^1/l(X^3,W^3)\}\rangle$$

□

As an immediate consequence of the correspondence between SLD-computations and SLDT-computations we have by Theorem 2.2 p. 61:

Theorem 2.3

The SLD-resolution is a full RS.

□

Another example of a resolution scheme concerns the GLD-Resolution defined in [WML84]. It is an extension of the SLD-resolution. The difference is that in the GLD-resolution more than one atom of the goal may be selected in one step. For each of them a fitting clause is chosen. This results in a number of equations, which are solved immediately.

The GLD-resolution may be presented by the scheme in Table 2.7, which applies to arbitrary definite program P with goal g_0.

Example 2.9

We illustrate the notion of GLD-resolution by an example of a GLD-computation for the definite program of Example 2.1 p. 26 and for the initial goal $g = \leftarrow rev(l(1(2,nil)),X)$.

At each step of the computation all atoms of the goal are selected and the sequence of the clauses applied is indicated. For each clause c in the sequence a natural number m_c is specified. The standardizing substitution applied to c renames each variable X of c into a new variable X^{m_c}.

$$\langle[rev(l(1(2,nil)),X)],\{\}\rangle$$

$c_2(1)$

Table 2.7
GLD-resolution

begin

      $g := g_0$
      $\sigma := \{\};$
      while g is not the empty sequence
            do
               if there exists
                      a sequence of atoms a_i, $(1 \leq i \leq n)$ in g;
                      and a sequence of clauses c_i, $(1 \leq i \leq n)$ in P
                      of heads h_i and bodies B_i
                  such that $\{a_i\sigma = h_i\theta_{g,i} | 1 \leq i \leq n\}$
                      has a mgu
               then
                  $\sigma := \sigma mgu(\{a_i\sigma = h_i\theta_{g,i} | 1 \leq i \leq n\})$
                  $g := g[a_i/B_i\theta_{g,i}, 1 \leq i \leq n]$
               else fail
            od

end

$$\langle [rev(Y^1, V^1), app(V^1, l(X^1, nil), Z^1)], \{X/Z^1, X^1/1, Y^1/l(2, nil)\}\rangle$$

$c_2(2), c_4(3)$

$$\langle [rev(nil, V^2), app(V^2, l(2, nil), l(X^3, Y^3)), app(Y^3, l(1, nil), W^3)],$$
$$\{X/l(X^3, W^3), X^1/1, Y^1/l(2, nil), Z^1/l(X^3, W^3), V^1/l(X^3, Y^3),$$
$$X^2/2, Y^2/nil, Z^2/l(X^3, Y^3), U^3/l(1, nil)\}$$

$c_1(4), c_3(5), c_3(6)$

$$\langle [], \{X/l(2, l(1, nil)), X^1/1, Y^1/l(2, nil), Z^1/l(2(l(1, nil)),$$
$$V^1/l(2, nil), X^2/2, Y^2/nil, V^2/nil, Z^2/l(2, nil),$$
$$U^3/l(1, nil), X^3/nil, Y^3/nil, W^3/l(1, nil), X^5/l(2, nil), X^6/l(1, nil)\}$$

□

2.2 Semantics of definite programs

This section outlines six kinds of semantics of definite programs and discusses relations between them. These are: *the model-theoretic semantics, the proof-theoretic semantics, the unification semantics, the fixpoint semantics, the operational semantics,* and *the completion semantics.*

The model-theoretic semantics is based on the notion of interpretation, as defined in the preliminaries. It corresponds to the logical reading of the program which is a set of definite clauses. One is interested in the logical consequences of these axioms, i.e. in the formulae which are valid in every model of the program. The semantics of the program is characterized by the set of all atomic logical consequences of the program. This set will be called the *denotation* of a definite program. It turns out that this set can be also seen as a model of the program. The domain of this model is a set of not necessarily ground terms. Thus, the presentation differs from the usual approach where the ground term models are considered. Since the latter are special cases of the models discussed in this chapter, the results presented here apply directly also to the ground term models. The advantage of using the generalization of the usual approach is simplification of some proofs. The model-theoretic semantics based on nonground terms seems also to have closer connection to the operational semantics where, as in Prolog, the answers to queries may include variables.

The proof-theoretic semantics is based on the syntactic notion of proof tree introduced in Section 2.1.2. The semantics of a program is defined to be the set of the head atoms (Definition 2.5 p. 34) of all proof trees of the program. The main result shows that in the case of definite programs the proof-theoretic semantics is equivalent to the model-theoretic semantics.

The unification semantics is defined in terms of equations associated with skeletons. It consists of the heads of the most general proof trees which can be obtained from all complete proper skeletons. Thus it is a subset of the proof-theoretic semantics. On the other hand, every element of the proof theoretic-semantics is an instance of the unification semantics.

The fixpoint semantics is related to the computational aspects and to the proof-theoretic semantics. It allows also to give a theoretical foundation to the "procedural view" of logic programming. It is a way to look at definite programs as a set of recursive procedures for which a fixpoint semantics can be defined and the classical results of the fixpoint theory can be applied. To define this semantics one looks at a definite program as an operator called "immediate consequence operator" operating on sets of not necessarily ground terms. Some aspects of the theory will be developed here for such terms. Obviously most of the results will apply also to ground terms. The fixpoint semantics will be used here more as a technical tool for obtaining some results rather than a new semantics of its own right.

An operational semantics can be given by a (not necessarily deterministic) algorithm which constructs proof trees or elements of the denotation. The common approach is to use an algorithm derived from the general resolution scheme of Section 2.1.4, usually based on SLD-resolution. The general resolution scheme shows a whole spectrum of other possible approaches. The main problem here is soundness and completeness of the operational semantics. That is, one has to be sure that the procedure applied constructs only and all proof trees of a given program. We develop a general technique for proving soundness and completeness of the resolution schemes derived from the GRS. We illustrate its use for some schemes of Section 2.1.4, including the special case of the SLD-resolution. Thus we demonstrate a general framework for developing correct operational semantics. Its application to the SLD-resolution allows to obtain the classical results with relatively simple proofs.

In its pure logical reading a definite clause program provides no negative information. Formally speaking it has no negative atomic logical consequences. However, definite clauses may be sometimes read as "if and only if" statements. In this case a negative information can be logically inferred. This idea is formalized by the notion of completion semantics. The last subsection discusses this concept and outlines some related results.

2.2.1 Model-theoretic semantics

A definite program is a set of logical formulae. Therefore we first discuss a logical reading of a program. This can be made precise by referring to the notion of interpretation, model, and logical consequence, as defined in Chapter 1.

As already pointed out, the idea of logic programming is to describe structures of interest by sets of logic formulae and to infer the information about the described structure from its description. A formal counterpart of this informal idea is to say that the structure described is a model of the program. It is sometimes called the *intended model* or *intended semantics*. The inference is guided by queries to the program and the answers obtained are to be valid in the intended model of the program. However, this model has no other documentation as the program itself. Thus, the only answers which are guaranteed to be valid in it are those which are valid in all models of the program. By the definition these are logical consequences of the program. The queries have the form of goal clauses, whose components are atomic formulae. The answers to a query are instances of its body and can be presented in form of substitutions. The answers are supposed to be logical consequences of the program. Since they are conjunctions of atomic formulae, the component atoms must also be logical consequences of the program. Therefore, the semantics of a program may be defined as the set of all atomic logical consequences of the program; these are building blocks of any answer. This section shows that the set of all atomic logical consequences of a given program can also be seen as a term model of the program.

The domain of such an interpretation is a set of (not necessarily ground) terms. The functors of the language are to be interpreted as term constructors. Thus the domain must be closed under term construction. The valuations on the term domain map variables to terms. They are thus substitutions. Hence the domain must be closed under the substitutions ranging over the domain. This motivates the following definition.

Definition 2.14

Let F and V be, respectively, a set of functors and a set of variables. A *term domain* over F and V is the set $T(F, V')$ of all terms over F and some, possibly empty, subset V' of V.
□

A substitution ranging over a term domain H will be called an H-*substitution*.

Definition 2.15

For a set P of predicate symbols a *term base* $B(H)$ on a term domain H is the set of all atoms $p(t_1, ..., t_n)$ such that p is in P and $t_1, \ldots, t_n$ are in H. Elements of $B(H)$ will be called H-*based atoms*.
□

A *term base for a logical language* L is any term base for the set of predicate symbols of P and for some term domain for L.

Note that if the set of variables V is empty, then the only term domain is the set $T(F)$ of all ground terms over F, and the corresponding term base is the set of all ground atoms. These will be called respectively the *Herbrand universe* (HU) over F and the *Herbrand base* (HB) over P and F. This terminology will be used exclusively for term domains and term bases without variables. If V is not an empty set then the greatest term domain is the set $T(F, V)$ of all terms over F and V. For fixed F and fixed infinite denumerable set of variables V the domain $T(F, V)$ will be denoted $TERM$. Note also that for any term domain H the following relation holds:

$$\text{HU} = T(F, \{\}) \subseteq H \subseteq T(F, V) = TERM$$

where $\{\}$ denotes the empty set.

Thus, every term domain contains all ground terms. In practice, the restrictions we obtained for the term domains reduce the notion of the term domain to only two interesting cases: the Herbrand universe and the domain $TERM$ of all terms.

We now give a formal definition of the notion of term interpretation for a language over a set F of function symbols, a set P of predicate symbols and a denumerable set V of variables. It is an interpretation as defined in the preliminaries and such that its domain is a term domain.

Definition 2.16 Term interpretation, term preinterpretation

A *term interpretation* $\mathcal{I}$ for a language $\mathcal{L}$ over a set F of function symbols, a set P of predicate symbols and a denumerable set V of variables is defined by specifying:

- a nonempty term domain H over F and V,

- for each n-ary function symbol f in F the function $f_{\mathcal{I}}$ such that for any $t_1, ..., t_n$ in H $f_{\mathcal{I}}(t_1, ..., t_n) = f(t_1, ..., t_n)$,

- a subset $B_{\mathcal{I}}$ of $B(H)$ which furthermore is closed under H–substitution.

The two first items define a term preinterpretation.

We will use the notation $\mathcal{I} \models a$ for $a \in B_{\mathcal{I}}$, and therefore write also $B_{\mathcal{I}} \models P$ instead of $\mathcal{I} \models P$, identifying the term interpretation with the relevant subset of the term base defining the truth of the predicates.
□

This definition has to be related to the definition of interpretation in Section 1.7.3. In particular one has to say which atomic formulae are true in a given term interpretation. The valuations of $\mathcal{I}$ range over terms of H and can be represented as substitutions. Now an atomic formula $p(t_1, \ldots, t_n)$ is true in $\mathcal{I}$ for a given valuation ν iff $p(t_1, \ldots, t_n)\nu \in B_{\mathcal{I}}$. Thus an atomic formula a is true in $\mathcal{I}$ if and only if a belongs to $\mathcal{I}$. This is equivalent to saying that all H-instances of a are in $\mathcal{I}$ or that $\mathcal{I} \models \forall(a)$.

Definition 2.17

A *term model* of a set of formulae S is a term interpretation which satisfies all the formulae of S. A term model of S on a term domain H will be called H-*based* term model (or H-*model*) of S.
□

As mentioned at the beginning of this section there are good reasons to define semantics of logic programs through term models. Usually it is done by referring to Herbrand models. Our objective is to obtain general results concerning term models which are parametrized by the term domain. It turns out that most of the results concerning Herbrand interpretations extends also for interpretations on term domains with variables. Nonground term models provide more information about programs than Herbrand models; they allow for identification of the nonground atoms which are logical consequences of the program. Such atoms are assumed to be universally quantified.

We now summarize some results related to term models of definite programs, possibly with definite goals, i.e. to term models of Horn clauses. The clauses have the logical reading:

- A definite clause of the form $h \leftarrow a_1, \ldots, a_m$ for $m \geq 0$ is defined to be a shorthand for the formula $\forall(h \vee \neg a_1 \vee \ldots \vee \neg a_m)$.
- A definite goal clause of the form $\leftarrow a_1, \ldots, a_m$ for $m > 0$ is defined to be a shorthand of the formula $\forall(\neg a_1 \vee \ldots \vee \neg a_m)$. The empty goal clause $(m = 0)$ is considered as a constant $false$.

The following theorem shows the importance of term models for definite programs with definite goal clauses.

Theorem 2.4

Let S be a set of Horn clauses. If S has a model then it has a model on any term domain.
□

Proof. Let I be a model of S. Consider the following term interpretation on an arbitrary term domain H: $I' = \{p(t_1, \ldots, t_n) \in B(H) | I \models \forall(p(t_1, \ldots, t_n))\}$. We show that I' is a model of S. Let c be a clause in S. It is either a definite clause
(c_1): $\forall(a \leftarrow b_1 \wedge \ldots b_m)$ or a definite goal clause
(c_2): $\forall(\neg d_1 \vee \ldots \neg d_m)$.
Assume the contrary, i.e. that I' is not a model of S. Then there is a clause in S for which I' is not a model. We consider separately two cases when this clause is of the form c_1 or of the form c_2.

Case c_1. In this case there exists a substitution σ such that $b_1\sigma, \ldots,$ $b_m\sigma$ are in I' but $h'\sigma$ is not in I'. Denote the atoms $b_i\sigma$ for $i = 1, \ldots, m$ by b_i' and the atom $h\sigma$ by h'. Then $I \models \forall b_i'$ and $I \models \forall h'$. Consequently $I \models \forall (b_1' \wedge \ldots \wedge b_m')$. Thus for every valuation ν in I $(I, \nu) \models b_1' \wedge \ldots \wedge b_m'$. On the other hand, as I is a model of S we have also $(I, \nu) \models b_1' \wedge \ldots \wedge b_m' \to h'$. Thus for every valuation ν $(I, \nu) \models h'$, hence $I \models \forall h'$. Thus, by the definition of I' we obtain the contradiction $h' \in I'$, which ends the proof of case c_1.

Case c_2. In this case there exists a substitution σ such that $d_i\sigma$ are in I' for $i = 1, \ldots, m$. Then, by the definition of I', $I \models \forall d_i\sigma$ for $i = 1, \ldots, m$, hence $I \models \forall (d_1\sigma \wedge \ldots \wedge d_m\sigma)$, or equivalently $I \models \neg\forall(\neg d_1\sigma \vee \ldots \vee \neg d_m\sigma)$. Hence I is not a model of c_2, which contradicts the assumption that I is a model of S. Therefore I' is a model of c_2. □

Corollary 2.1

A set S of Horn clauses is unsatisfiable iff it does not have any term model. □

Proof. If S has no term model, then by Theorem 2.4 it has no model. On the other hand an unsatisfiable set of formulae has no model at all, in particular no term model. □

As already discussed we are particularly interested in atomic logical consequences of logic programs. The notion of logical consequence is closely related to the notion of unsatisfiability. The unsatisfiability result for sets of clauses allows us to restrict the attention to term models. To state the result we introduce a new notation.

Let P be a definite program and let H be a term domain for the language of P. Note that the terms of H may also include function symbols that do not occur in P. We will use the notation $P \models_H a$ to denote that a is a formula which is true in every H-based term model of P.

Theorem 2.5

For any definite program P and atom a in $B(H)$, $P \models \forall a$ iff $P \models_H a$.

$\square$

Proof. Assume $P \models_H a$ and assume that $\forall a$ is not a logical consequence of P. Then there exists a model M of P such that $\forall a$ is not true in M. Consider the term interpretation $M' = \{p(t_1, \ldots, t_n) \in B(H) | M \models \forall p(t_1, \ldots, t_n)\}$. The proof of Theorem 2.4 shows that M' is a model of P and by the definition of M' we know that $a \notin M'$. This contradicts the hypothesis. It follows by this contradiction that if $P \models_H a$ then $P \models \forall a$. The reverse implication follows directly by the definition of logical consequence.
$\square$

Notice that for a ground atom a it is not necessary to refer to the nonground part of the model M'. One can take instead the ground part of M' which is a Herbrand model. This gives the following result.

Corollary 2.2

Given a definite program P and a ground atom a in HU, $P \models a$ iff $P \models_{HU} a$.
$\square$

Term models of a definite program are sets of atoms. They have the following property.

Lemma 2.1 Intersection property of the term models

If $\mathcal{S}_H(P)$ is a (possibly infinite) set of term models of a definite program P on a term domain H then the intersection $\cap \mathcal{S}$ of all elements of $\mathcal{S}_H(P)$ is also a term model of P on H.
$\square$

Proof. Clearly $I = \cap \mathcal{S}_H(P)$ is a term interpretation of P on H. We show that it is also a model of P. Assume the contrary. Then for some clause instance $a \leftarrow b_1, \ldots, b_n$ under a substitution over H the atoms $b_1, \ldots, b_n$ are in I but a is not in I. But in this case at least one of the elements of $\mathcal{S}_H(P)$ is not a model of the clause. This contradicts the assumption. Since all elements are subsets of the term base on H then

also I is a subset of this term base.
□

It is worth noticing that every definite program has a term model. Let H be a term domain for a language L and let P be a definite program in this language. Then the term base $B(H)$ is a model of P. This leads to the following result.

Lemma 2.2 Minimal models
For every definite program P every term domain H there exists the least (in the sense of set inclusion) term model $LTM_H(P)$ which is the intersection of all H-based models of P.
□

Proof. The set of H-based term models of P is not empty. Hence by lemma 2.1 the intersection of all H-based models of P is an H-based model of P. It is also the least H-based model in the sense of set inclusion.
□

Notice that the least models of a program depend on the chosen term base.

Example 2.10
Consider the definite program $P = \{p(X_1) \leftarrow\}$ in a logical language over the alphabets $P = \{p\}$, $F = \{zero, s\}$ and $V = \{X_1, X_2, \ldots\}$. Choosing as the term domain the Herbrand universe we obtain the following least term model:
$$M_g = \{p(zero), p(s(zero)), \ldots\}.$$
On the other hand, the least term model for the term domain $TERM$ is:
$$M_v = \{p(X_1), p(X_2) \ldots p(s(X_1)) \ldots\} \cup M_g$$
where $X_1, X_2, \ldots$ are all variables of the term base.
□

For a fixed term base the least term model of a program can be considered a candidate for its meaning. We now study the relation between such a meaning and the semantics of definite programs based on the concept of logical consequence.

Definition 2.18

The *model-theoretic* semantics of a definite program P with respect to a term domain H is the set of all atomic logical consequences of P in $B(H)$. This set will be called the *denotation* of P with respect to H and is to be denoted $DEN_H(P)$, i.e.:

$$DEN_H(P) = \{a|a \in B(H), P \models a\}$$

□

As mentioned above the denotation depends on the term domain considered. The denotation associated with the Herbrand base gives the set of all ground atomic logical consequences of the program. Using $TERM$ as the domain, one gets the set of all not-necessarily ground atomic logical consequences, including as a subset all ground atomic logical consequences. Obviously a denotation is closed on the substitutions ranging on H.

As an immediate result we get.

Theorem 2.6

For any definite program P and for any term domain H of the language of P $DEN_H(P) = LTM_H(P)$.

□

Proof. Let a be an atom in $DEN_H(P)$. Then a is in $B(H)$ and a is true in every model of P. Hence, in particular in $LTM_H(P)$. Hence $DEN_H(P) \subseteq LTM_H(P)$.

It remains to prove $LTM_H(P) \subseteq DEN_H(P)$. Assume the contrary. Then there exists an atom a in $LTM_H(P)$ and a (non-term) model M of P in which a is false. Then a is also false in the term interpretation $M' = \{p(t_1, \ldots, t_n) \in B(H)|M \models p(t_1, \ldots, t_n)\}$ which is also a model of P as shown in the proof of Theorem 2.4 p. 70. This contradicts the assumption that a is in $LTM_H(P)$. Hence $LTM_H(P) \subseteq DEN_H(P)$.

□

It follows that $DEN_H(P)$ is a model of P, but this is also a consequence of the definition of the denotation, leading to an alternative proof of the inclusion $LTM_H(P) \subseteq DEN_H(P)$.

The equivalence of the ground denotation and the least Herbrand model of a definite program is a classical result. Here it is generalized for other term domains. In particular nonground term models on the domain $TERM$ are also covered.

2.2.2   Proof-theoretic semantics

In Section 2.1.2 a notion of proof tree of a program was introduced. We first define another semantics of programs based on this notion. It will be called proof-theoretic semantics. Then we relate this semantics to denotations.

The proof trees are combinations of not necessarily ground instances of program clauses. Creation of the instances requires substitutions ranging over some term domain. The domain may include an infinite set of variables to cope with the standardization necessary for the equational characterization of the proof trees (Section 2.1.3). One can also consider the restricted class of ground proof trees. In this case the term domain is the Herbrand universe.

This observation gives a motivation for introducing the domain of interpretation as a parameter of the notion of derivation tree. We will even consider a generalization of this notion, using non-term preinterpretations. The idea is as follows. In the usual derivation tree every complete node is labeled by a pair $\langle c, \sigma \rangle$, where c is a clause and σ is a substitution. As indicated in Section 2.2.1, a substitution may be considered a valuation in a term interpretation. We now allow to use not only substitutions but also valuations in non-term preinterpretations. The application $t\nu$ of valuation ν to term t denotes the value determined by the preinterpretation.

Example 2.11

Consider usual arithmetic expressions preinterpreted on the domain of integers. The application $(x + y)\nu$, where ν is a valuation such that $\nu(x) = 2$ and $\nu(y) = 3$ denotes the integer 5.
□

Application of a valuation ν to an atom $p(t_1, \ldots, t_n)$, where p is an n-ary predicate gives an object of the form $p(v_1, \ldots, v_n)$ and $v_1, \ldots, v_n$ are elements of the domain of the preinterpretation. For a given preinterpretation J such objects will be called J-*based atoms* or, in short,

J-atoms. A J-atom $p(v_1, ..., v_n)$ is called a J-based instance (in short *J-instance*) of an atomic formula $p(t_1, ..., t_n)$ iff there exists a valuation ν in the domain of J such that the value of each term t_i under ν and J is v_i. The concept of J-instance extends for every quantifier-free formula: the atoms of the formula are to be replaced by their J-instances under some fixed valuation.

Definition 2.19 J-based interpretation, preinterpretation

A *J-based interpretation* $\mathcal{I}$ for a language $\mathcal{L}$ over a set F of function symbols, a set P of predicate symbols and a denumerable set V of variables is defined by specifying:

- a nonempty domain I,
- for each n-ary function symbol f in F a total function $f_{\mathcal{I}}$: $I^n \rightarrow I$,
- a set $B_{\mathcal{I}}$ of J-based atoms.

The two first items define the preinterpretation J.
□

A J-based interpretation is thus defined by a preinterpretation J and by a set of J-based atoms built with predicates of P. Sometimes the notation $B_{\mathcal{I}} \models \phi$ will be used instead of $\mathcal{I} \models \phi$ if the preinterpretation is clear by the context. For example one may write $DEN_H(P) \models P$ or $DEN_H(P)$ is a model of P, to express that the interpretation I defined by the term preinterpretation whose term domain is H and by the subset $DEN_H(P)$ of $B(H)$ is a model of P.

Using this notions one can now introduce a concept of a proof tree parameterized by preinterpretation. The concept of instance name is extended to include any valuation.

Definition 2.20 Preinterpretation based derivation tree

For a definite program P and a preinterpretation J of the language a *J-based derivation tree* is any labeled ordered tree T such that

1. every leaf node of T is labeled by the "empty label" $\perp$ or by a pair $\langle c, \nu \rangle$, where c is a unit clause of P and ν is a valuation in J.

2. Every non-leaf node of T is labeled by by a pair $\langle c, \nu \rangle$, where c is a non-unit clause of P and ν is a valuation in J.

3. Let n be a node labeled by an instance name $\langle c, \nu \rangle$, where c is the clause $h \leftarrow a_1, \ldots, a_m$ and $m \geq 0$. Then n has m children and for $i = 1, \ldots, m$ the i-th child of n is labeled either

- $\langle c', \nu' \rangle$, where c' is a clause with the head h' such that $a_i \nu = h' \nu'$, or
- $\perp$.

□

Notice that a term preinterpretation is determined by its domain. Thus in the case of a term preinterpretation based on a domain H the trees will be called H-based derivation trees. It is easy to see that a derivation tree, as defined in Section 2.1.2 is a $TERM$-based derivation tree for the term preinterpretation on the domain $TERM$. On the other hand, HU-based derivation trees are ground derivation trees. The terminology concerning derivation trees will be extended for the case of J-based derivation trees.

Definition 2.21

Let T be a J-based derivation tree with the root labeled by $\langle h \leftarrow a_1, \ldots, a_m, \theta \rangle$. Then the J-atom $h\theta$ will be called the *head* of T.
□

A node with the empty label will be called an *incomplete* node of the tree. The other nodes will be called the *complete* nodes.

Definition 2.22

A J-based derivation tree without incomplete nodes is called a *J-based proof tree*. A J-based derivation tree which is not a proof tree is said to be *incomplete*. A J-based derivation tree complete or not is also said *partial*. The set of all J-based proof trees of a program P will be denoted $\mathcal{T}_J(P)$.
□

Example 2.12

Figure 2.17 shows examples of J-based derivation trees of the following program for two different preinterpretations J. The first of them is $TERM$-based, the other, denoted $\mathcal{N}$, interprets $+$ and $\times$ as arithmetic operations on natural numbers.

$c_1 : fac(0, 1) \leftarrow$

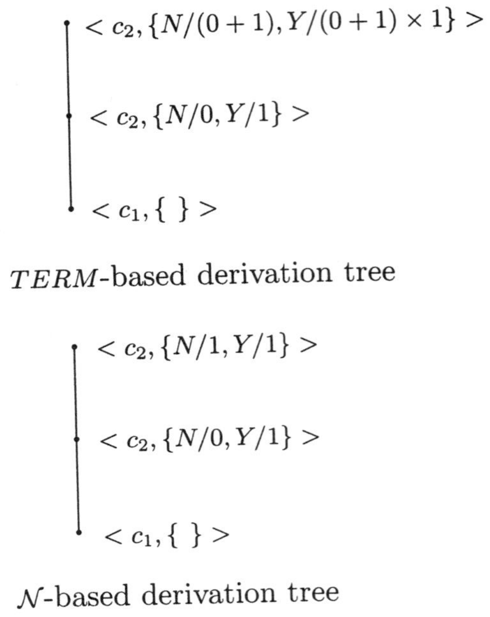

$$< c_2, \{N/(0+1), Y/(0+1) \times 1\} >$$

$$< c_2, \{N/0, Y/1\} >$$

$$< c_1, \{ \ \} >$$

$TERM$-based derivation tree

$$< c_2, \{N/1, Y/1\} >$$

$$< c_2, \{N/0, Y/1\} >$$

$$< c_1, \{ \ \} >$$

$\mathcal{N}$-based derivation tree

Figure 2.17
Example J-based derivation trees (Example 2.12)

$$c_2 : fac(N+1, (N+1) \times Y) \leftarrow fac(N, Y)$$

□

The derivation tree construction methods of Section 2.1.4 can be adapted to construct J-based derivation trees. The difference is that the set of equations generated for a given skeleton should now be solved in a given preinterpretation J. Clearly, solving equations in the term preinterpretation $TERM$ can be done by computing the mgu.

We now use the generalized notion of derivation tree to define semantics of programs.

Definition 2.23 Proof tree semantics
Let P be a definite program and let J be a preinterpretation of the language of P. The *proof tree semantics* of a definite program P with respect to J is the set of all J-based proof trees of P, i.e. $\mathcal{T}_J(P)$.

□

This definition applies in particular to a term preinterpretation determined by a term domain for the language of P. To relate this meaning to the denotation we define yet another semantics, which is also related to the notion of proof tree.

Definition 2.24 Proof-theoretic semantics

Let P be a definite program and let J be a preinterpretation of the language of P. The *proof-theoretic semantics* of P with respect to J is the set of the heads of all J-based proof trees of P, denoted $PT_J(P)$.
□

This definition applies in particular to term preinterpretations determined by term domains for the language of P. Two particularly interesting special cases are the $TERM$-based proof trees and the ground proof trees.

We now relate the proof-theoretic semantics defined on a term domain to the model-theoretic semantics on this domain.

The following theorem follows by the definition of J-based proof trees.

Theorem 2.7

For any definite program P and any preinterpretation J, $PT_J(P)$ is a model of P.
□

Proof. It follows directly from the definitions 2.24 of the proof tree semantics and of models.

More precisely assume the contrary. Then there exists a clause c in P of the form $h(\overline{t_0}) \leftarrow b_1(\overline{t_1}), ...b_m(\overline{t_m})$, where $\overline{t_1}, ..., \overline{t_m}$ are vectors of the argument terms, and a valuation ν in J, such that the J-atoms $b_1([\overline{t_1}]_{J,\nu})$ $..., b_m([\overline{t_m}]_{J,\nu})$ are in $PT_J(P)$ but the atom $h([\overline{t_0}]_{J,\nu})$ is not in $PT_J(P)$. By the definition of $PT_J(P)$ it follows that there exist J-based proof trees $T_1, ..., T_m$ with the heads $b_1([\overline{t_1}]_{J,\nu})$ $..., b_m([\overline{t_m}]_{J,\nu})$. Then there exists a J- based proof tree with the root label $\langle c, \nu \rangle$ and such that the children of the root are the roots of the trees $T_1, ..., T_m$. But the head of this tree is $h([\overline{t_0}]_{J,\nu})$, hence the contradiction with the assumption. Thus, the theorem holds.
□

In particular for a term domain H, the set $PT_H(P)$ of all H-based proof tree roots, defines a model of P and $DEN_H(P) \subseteq PT_H(P)$ by Theorem 2.6 p. 74. The opposite inclusion is a consequence of the following result.

Theorem 2.8 Definite logical consequences of a definite program

Let P be a definite program and let H be a term domain for P. $P \models \forall(B \to a)$ where B is a conjunction of H-based atoms and a an H-based atom, if and only if there exists an H-based derivation tree with head a and such that all the node atoms of its incomplete leaves (cf. Definition 2.6 p. 34) are in B.
□

In particular, given a definite program, all its logical consequences which have the form of a universally quantified clause are such that the conclusion is the head of a $TERM$-based proof tree built with the clauses of P and the atoms of B (note that if many occurrences of the same atoms are used they are all identical).

Proof. ($\Leftarrow$) follows by the definition of J-based proof trees. Any model M of P is an interpretation that uses the preinterpretation J. An induction on the J-based proof tree of the hypothesis shows that for any valuation ν in M if $B\nu \in M$ then $a\nu \in M$.

($\Rightarrow$) $P \models \forall(B \to a)$ implies $P \models_H \forall(B \to a)$ implies $P \models_H B\sigma \to a\sigma$ for any ground substitution σ. Choose H and σ such that all the free variables of $B \to a$ are replaced by new constants not in P nor in $B \to a$. This implies $P \cup B\sigma \models_H a\sigma$ if B is viewed as a set of atoms. This implies also that $PT_H(P \cup B\sigma) \models a\sigma$, hence $a\sigma \in PT_H(P \cup B\sigma)$ and $a\sigma$ is the head of an H-based proof tree for $P \cup B\sigma$. By replacing the new constants by the original variables everywhere they occur in this proof tree one gets the result.
□

Corollary 2.3 Equivalence of the proof-theoretic and model-theoretic semantics

Let P be a definite program and let H be a term domain for P. Then $PT_H(P) = DEN_H(P)$.
□

Remark 1 All the results are parametrized by a term domain H. It may be useful to observe that any element of an H-based model is also an instance of an element of a $TERM$-based model. In particular:

$$PT_H(P) = \{b\sigma | b \in PT_{TERM}(P), \sigma \text{ is an } H\text{-substitution } \}$$

This happens because every H-based proof tree is an H-based instance of a proof tree of the $TERM$-based proof-theoretic semantics. This holds only for term domains and term preinterpretations.

We studied definite programs as a formalism for specifying classes of proof trees. The proof-theoretic semantics has been derived from this purely syntactic view of definite programs. Corollary 2.3 relates this view to the classical model-theoretic semantics of logic programs.

2.2.3   Unification semantics

As described in Section 2.1.4, derivation trees of a program can be constructed by solving equations associated with skeletons. This allows to give yet another semantics of definite programs. Let P be a definite program. With every skeleton S of P we associate the set of equations $Eq(S)$. If $Eq(S)$ has an mgu the construction of Section 2.1.3 defines a unique (up to renaming) derivation tree denoted $D(S)$.

Definition 2.25
   The *unification semantics* of a definite program P is the set of the equivalence classes, by the variant relation, of the heads of the most general derivation trees $D(S)$ constructed for all complete proper skeletons S of P. The unification semantics will be represented by a set $US(P)$ of atoms in which each equivalence class is represented by one atom. This representation is unique up to renaming[2].
□
   Observe that there may be less atoms in $US(P)$ than there are derivation trees $D(S)$. An atom is said to *belong to $US(P)$* iff it is a variant of some element in $US(P)$.

---

[2]$US(P)$ will also be called *unification semantics* if there is no ambiguity, confusing the unification semantics and one of its representations.

Example 2.13 Consider the following program P:

$c_1 : p(X) \leftarrow$
$c_2 : p(X) \leftarrow$
$c_3 : p(a(X)) \leftarrow$

$US(P)$ is $\{p(X), p(a(X))\}$

□

Notice, that the derivation trees considered are $TERM$-based proof trees. Thus a natural question concerns the relation between the unification semantics of P and the proof-theoretic semantics $PT_{TERM}(P)$. The answer is given by Theorem 2.1 p. 41 and Remark 1 p. 80. If T is an H-based proof tree of P and S is its skeleton then $Eq(S)$ has an mgu and T is an instance of the tree $D(S)$.

Theorem 2.9

The H-based proof theoretic semantics of a definite program P is the set of all H-based instances of the atoms of $US(P)$, i.e. :

$$PT_H(P) = \{b\sigma | b \in US(P), \sigma \text{ is an } H\text{-substitution }\}$$

□

In particular:

Corollary 2.4

The $TERM$-based proof-theoretic semantics of a definite program P is the set of all instances of the atoms of $US(P)$.

In particular the least Herbrand model of a definite program P is the set of all ground instances of $US(P)$.

□

It should be noted that the unification semantics gives more information about programs than the $TERM$-based proof-theoretic semantics. For example, consider the following programs with two constants a and b in the function alphabet of $TERM$: $P_1 = \{p(X) \leftarrow , p(a) \leftarrow\}$ and $P_2 = \{p(X) \leftarrow , p(b) \leftarrow\}$. Both of them have the same $TERM$-based proof-theoretic semantics but different unification semantics.

An mgu of a set of equations associated with a skeleton S is a solution of this set in the term algebra on the domain $TERM$. Such a solution makes it possible to construct the tree $D(S)$. Finding a solution of this set in a preinterpretation J would allow to construct a J-based proof tree based on S. This observation allows one to define a general concept of J-based *equational semantics*. Such a semantics would include the heads of all J-based proof trees obtained by taking solutions in J of the sets of equations associated with all complete skeletons of the program[3]. Such a set of equations may have more than one solution and thus it may contribute with more than one element to the equational semantics. In the case of $TERM$-based semantics any solution of a set of equations is an instance of the solution defined by an mgu. This makes possible to use instead the unification semantics.

Finally, $US(P)$ is in general a proper subset of $PT_{TERM}(P)$ and thus is not a model of P. A short example may help to illustrate this point. Consider the definite program P:

$$p(X) \leftarrow q(Y)$$
$$q(a) \leftarrow$$

$US(P)$ is $\{p(X), q(a)\}$. Assume H is $T(\{a\}, V)$. The H-instance of the first clause $p(a) \leftarrow q(a)$ is such that its body is included in $US(P)$ but its head does not belong to $US(P)$.

The unification semantics appears to be a kind of minimal complete representation of the proof-theoretic semantics of a definite program. This semantics reflects the operational behaviour of a definite program taking into account the use of the unification. In this sense it is "more operational" than the proof theoretic semantics. In Section 5.3.2 a method to describe this semantics will be given in order to prove operational or run-time properties of definite programs. Presently, the main interest of this semantics can be stated by the following proposition.

Proposition 2.4 Relating $US(P)$ and answer substitutions
Let P be a definite program, g an atomic goal and $\mathcal{R}$ a full RS. Any $\mathcal{R}$-computed answer substitution for P and g is a most general unifier of g and some renamed element of $US(P)$ which does not share any variable with g, restricted to the variables of g.
□

---

[3]The case of the root which may contain unassigned variables should be considered for a rigorous treatment of this approach.

2.2.4   Operational semantics

We related the unification semantics to the proof-theoretic semantics, which in turn is equivalent to the model-theoretic semantics. None of these semantics gives an explicit algorithm for computing the semantic objects. However, the results presented relate construction of the semantic objects to construction of proof trees. Such algorithms may be developed as discussed in Section 2.1.4 where the general resolution scheme was introduced as a framework for construction of derivation trees. Instances of the scheme describe computations, which for a given definite program P and goal g produce substitutions, called the computed substitutions. A computed substitution restricted to the variables of g is called a computed answer substitution, or briefly an answer substitution. This section discusses the use of resolution schemes for computing logical consequences of programs. Since a resolution scheme relates programs with computations it can be seen as an operational semantics of programs. We are interested in resolution schemes with the following properties.

Definition 2.26

A resolution scheme $\mathcal{R}$ is called *sound* iff for every definite program P and definite goal clause $\leftarrow g$, any $\mathcal{R}$-computed answer substitution σ for P and g is such that $P \models g\sigma$. A resolution scheme $\mathcal{R}$ is called *complete* iff for every finite program P, definite goal clause g and for every substitution γ such that $Dom(\gamma) \subseteq Var(g)$ and $P \models g\gamma$ there exists a computed answer substitution σ for P and $\leftarrow g$ such that $\gamma = \sigma|_{Var(g)}\delta$ for some substitution δ
□

A sound and complete resolution scheme $\mathcal{R}$ allows for computation of elements of the $TERM$-based denotation of a program P. Construct all complete $\mathcal{R}$-computations for any goal clause $\leftarrow p(x_1, \ldots, x_n)$ such that $x_1, \ldots, x_n$ are distinct variables. It follows by soundness that for any computed answer substitution σ, $P \models p(x_1, \ldots, x_n)\sigma$. On the other hand, every atom $q(t_1, ..., t_k)$ in $DEN_{TERM}(P)$ is an instance of $q(x_1, \ldots, x_k)$ under the substitution $\gamma = \{x_1/t_1, \ldots, x_k/t_k\}$. Hence, by completeness, for the goal clause $\leftarrow q(x_1, \ldots, x_k)$ there exists a computed substitution σ which is more general than γ. Thus the denotation can be constructed by taking all instances of the atoms $p(x_1, \ldots, x_n)\sigma$, where σ is any computed substitution for P and $\{\leftarrow p(x_1, \ldots, x_n)\}$.

The semantic properties of soundness and completeness of a resolution scheme can be given a syntactic sufficient condition.

Theorem 2.10

Every full resolution scheme is sound and complete.

$\square$

Proof. Let $\mathcal{R}$ be a full resolution scheme, let P be a definite program and let g be a definite goal. Thus g is of the form $\leftarrow a_1, \ldots a_n$ for some $n \geq 1$.

We first prove soundness of $\mathcal{R}$. By the definition of full RS we know that for every $\mathcal{R}$-computed substitution σ for P and g there exists a skeleton S with the root labeled by g such that $\sigma = mgu(Eq(S))$. Consider the derivation tree $D(S)$. Its root is labeled by the pair $\langle \leftarrow a_1 \ldots a_n, \sigma \rangle$. Hence the immediate subtrees of $D(S)$ are proof trees with the heads $a_1\sigma, \ldots a_n\sigma$. Consequently, by Corollary 2.3 p. 80, $P \models a_i\sigma$ for $i = 1, \ldots, n$, hence $\mathcal{R}$ is sound.

We now prove completeness of $\mathcal{R}$. Let γ be a substitution such that $Dom(\gamma) \subseteq Var(g)$ and $P \models (a_1, \ldots, a_n)\gamma$. Equivalently by Corollary 2.3 p. 80 and by the definition of derivation tree, there exists a proof tree T with the head $(\leftarrow a_1, \ldots, a_n)\gamma$. By Theorem 2.1 p. 41 the proof tree $D(Sk(T))$ obtained by finding the mgu of the set of equations associated with the skeleton of T is more general than T. The head of this tree is $(\leftarrow a_1, \ldots, a_n)\sigma$, where $\sigma = mgu(Eq(Sk(T)))$. By the definition of σ and γ it follows by Theorem 2.1 that there exists a substitution δ such that $\gamma = \sigma|_{Var(g)}\delta$. On the other hand, as $\mathcal{R}$ is a full resolution scheme, there exists a computation for P and g with the computed answer substitution σ since the skeleton of T is a complete skeleton with the root labeled by g.

$\square$

The theorem shows a general approach to developing sound and complete resolution schemes: it suffices to guarantee that the scheme is full. By Theorem 2.2 p. 61 we obtain at once:

Corollary 2.5

The SLDT-resolution is sound and complete.

$\square$

Similarly, by Theorem 2.3 p. 63

Corollary 2.6
The SLD-resolution is sound and complete.
□

Controlling SLD-computations
The objective of this section is to show how a deterministic operational semantics can be derived from the nondeterministic scheme of SLD-resolution presented in Section 2.1.4. There are two sources of nondeterminism of the scheme. One of them is selection of the atom a from the actual goal g. The other is the choice of the clause whose head unifies with a. The first kind of nondeterminism can be eliminated specifying a selection function that applies in every state to the actual goal and selects one of its atoms. A more sophisticated way of selection may consider the history of computation. The selection mechanism will be called *computation rule*. The choice of a fixed computation rule is a modification of SLD-resolution. The new scheme will be called *R-controlled* SLD-resolution. The scheme is still nondeterministic since the selected atom may unify with the heads of many clauses. However, for a given initial goal g the set of possible computations is determined only by the number of clauses whose heads unify with the atom selected in every state.

A fixed computation rule R makes the choice of an atom in the goal deterministic. Clearly, this restricts the class of SLD-computations constructed. We now show that for any computation rule R the R-controlled SLD-resolution is still a full resolution scheme. As pointed out in Section 2.1.4, there is a one-one correspondence between SLD-computations and SLDT-computations. Selection of a goal atom in a state of SLD-computation corresponds to selection of an incomplete node in the skeleton of the corresponding state of the corresponding SLDT-computation. We will use this observation to prove the following theorem.

Theorem 2.11
For any computation rule R the R-controlled SLD-resolution is a full resolution scheme.
□

Proof. Let P be a definite program and let g be a definite goal. Every R-controlled SLD-computation is an SLD-computation. Hence if σ is a computed substitution for P and g obtained by an R-controlled SLD-computation then it is also an SLD-computed substitution. As SLD-resolution is full, there exists a complete skeleton with the root labeled by g such that $\sigma = mgu(Eq(S))$.

To complete the proof it suffices to show that for every complete and proper skeleton S of P with the root labeled by g there exists a terminated R-controlled SLD-computation that computes mgu of $Eq(S)$. We first use the computation rule to construct S in a top-down way starting from the skeleton of the goal clause. Notice that it is a topmost part of S: its root corresponds to the root of S and its incomplete nodes correspond to the roots of the direct subtrees of S. The construction is done in such a way that at each step the actual skeleton is a top-most part of S. The computation rule R selects an incomplete node n of the actual skeleton which corresponds to a complete node n' of S. The label of n' identifies the clause whose skeleton should be composed with the actual one at the node n. Since S is a finite tree the process will reconstruct it in a finite number of steps. Let $S_0 = Csk(g), S_1, \ldots, S_k = S$ be the sequence of the skeletons constructed. As S is proper, also S_i for $i = 0, \ldots, k$ are proper. Hence the sequence $\langle S_0, \{\}\rangle, \langle S_1, mgu(Eq(S_1))\rangle, \ldots, \langle S, mgu(Eq(S))\rangle$ is an SLDT-computation. The corresponding SLD-computation is an R-controlled terminated SLD-computation which computes $Eq(S)$.
□

By Theorem 2.10 p. 85 we obtain at once:

Corollary 2.7

For any computation rule R the R-controlled SLD-resolution is sound and complete.
□

We now consider the question whether the answer substitutions computed for a given program P and goal g by the SLD-resolution depend on the choice of the computation rule. Let σ be such an answer substitution computed with some computation rule. Thus σ is obtained by solving equations associated with the state skeleton of the final state of the computation. The same skeleton will be constructed by any computation rule and will result in the same set of equations, even if the computations leading to its construction are different. Hence we obtain:

Proposition 2.5 Independence of the computation rule

Let P be a definite program and g a definite goal. If σ is an SLD-computed answer substitution for P and g, then for any computation rule R there exists an R-controlled SLD-computation for P and g that computes σ (up to a renaming).
□

As a matter of fact the change of the computation rule may change the order in which the equations are created and solved. This may result in renaming of variables in the range of the computed substitutions.

Since R-controlled SLD-resolution is nondeterministic, we still do not have a deterministic procedure to construct answer substitutions for given program and goal. When searching for such a procedure it may be helpful to investigate the space of all R-controlled SLD-computations for a given computation rule R. We first introduce some auxiliary notion.

For any state of an R-controlled SLD-computation the next state is determined by the choice of a clause, whose head unifies with the selected atom. To show the choices made during an R-controlled SLD-computation a notion of SLD-derivation is introduced.

Definition 2.27 SLD-derivation, SLD-refutation

Let R be a computation rule. An R-controlled SLD-derivation for a program P and a goal clause g_0 is a finite or infinite sequence of the form $s_0, c_0, s_1, c_1 \ldots, c_{n-1}, s_n \ldots$ such that:

- Each s_i for $i = 0, 1, \ldots$ is a state of SLD-computation, i.e. it is a pair $\langle g_i, \sigma_i \rangle$ for some goal g_i and some substitution σ_i; $s_0 = \langle g_0, \{\} \rangle$.

- The sequence $s_0, \ldots, s_n \ldots$ is an SLD-computation and c_i for $i = 0, 1, \ldots$ is the program clause chosen in the state s_i which for the atom selected by the computation rule R causes the transition from the state s_i to the state s_{i+1}.

An R-controlled SLD-refutation for P and g is a finite SLD-derivation $s_0, c_0, s_1, c_1, \ldots, c_{n-1}, s_n$ such that $s_0, \ldots, s_n$ is a terminated SLD-computation (g_n is the empty sequence).
□

The set of all SLD-derivations with a given computation rule for given program and goal clause can be represented by a possibly infinite tree defined as follows:

Definition 2.28 SLD-tree, search trees

For a given computation rule R an *SLD-tree* (or *search tree*) of a definite program P and a definite goal clause g_0 is a tree with labeled nodes and arcs defined as follows:

- The label of each node is a state of an R-controlled SLD-computation of P and g_0,
- The label of each arc is a clause of P,
- The root node is labeled by the initial state $\langle g_0, \{\} \rangle$,
- A node n labeled by the state s is connected by an arc labeled c with a node n' labeled s' iff s, c, s' is an R-controlled SLD-derivation.

□

Clearly, every path in the search tree represents an SLD-derivation. The paths of maximal length will be called *branches*. A finite branch (or the corresponding SLD-derivation) is said to be *successful* if the goal of at least one of its leaves is empty and *failed* otherwise. A successful branch corresponds to a refutation; the answer substitution computed by this refutation will be called the answer substitution of the branch. Clearly a branch is failed iff the atom selected by the computation rule in the goal of its leaf is not unifiable with the head of any clause. An SLD-tree is said to be *finitely failed* iff all its branches are failed.

Example 2.14

Consider the following program:

$$c_1 : path(X, X) \leftarrow$$
$$c_2 : path(X, Y) \leftarrow arc(X, Z), path(Z, Y)$$
$$c_3 : arc(a, b) \leftarrow$$

For the initial goal $\leftarrow path(X, a)$ consider the following computation rules: L that selects the leftmost atom of the goal and R that selects the rightmost atom of the goal, give different SLD-trees. The SLD-tree for L is finite. It is outlined in Figure 2.18 without showing its node labels.

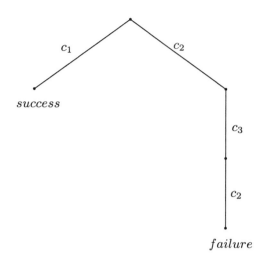

Figure 2.18
Example SLD-tree for standard computation rule in Example 2.14

For the same goal the rule R results in an infinite SLD-tree outlined in Figure 2.19.
□

Definition 2.29 Finite failure set

Given a term domain H, the *finite failure set* for P is the subset of $B(H)$ consisting of all atoms b such that for some computation rule the SLD-tree for P and $\leftarrow b$ is finitely failed. This set is denoted $FF_H(P)$.
□

Theorem 2.12

The finite failure set is closed under substitutions.
□

Proof. Let b be an atom in the finite failure set of a program P. Thus some SLD-tree S of P and $\leftarrow b$ is finitely failed. Every branch of the tree corresponds to an incomplete skeleton such that for none of its extensions the set of equations has an mgu. Consider a substitution σ that maps variables of b into terms in H. Such a substitution can be

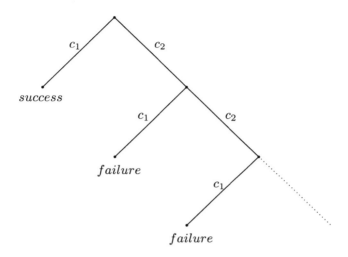

Figure 2.19
Example SLD-tree for rightmost-selection computation rule in Example 2.14

seen as a finite set of additional equations on the variables of b. Assume that $b\sigma$ is not in $FF_H(P)$. Two cases are possible.

1. $\leftarrow b\sigma$ has a successful SLD-derivation under some computation rule. Then there exists a computed answer θ for P and $\leftarrow b\sigma$. This means that there exists a proof tree T with the head $b\sigma\theta$. Hence there exists an mgu of $Eq(Sk(T))$. But the skeleton $Sk(T)$ must be an extension of the skeleton corresponding to a branch of S, since with any computation rule SLD-resolution is a full resolution scheme. This contradicts the assumption about b.

2. $\leftarrow b\sigma$ has an infinite SLD-derivation under any computation rule. This is possible only if $\leftarrow b$ has an infinite SLD-derivation under any computation rule since any finite prefix of a derivation of $\leftarrow b\sigma$ can be obtained from an incomplete skeleton Q for b by finding the mgu of $Eq(Q) \cup \sigma$. But the solution of $Eq(Q)$ gives an incomplete derivation tree for b. Thus b has derivation trees of arbitrary depth and cannot be in $FF_H(P)$.

□

Let T be an SLD-tree for a definite program P and a definite goal g. Every successful branch of T represents a refutation, and consequently a proof tree of P which has a unique proper and complete skeleton with root label g. As the SLD-resolution is complete, every complete and proper skeleton of P with root label g must be represented by a successful branch of T. Thus, there exists a one-one correspondence between the successful branches of any two different SLD-trees for P and g obtained by different computation rules. The corresponding branches are those, which represent the same skeleton. Clearly, they must have the same length. For the infinite branches there is no such direct correspondence. For discussing this issue some auxiliary notions are needed.

An incomplete proper skeleton S is said to be *fallible* iff it has an incomplete leaf l such that either no clause skeleton fits S at l or for every fitting clause skeleton c the set of equations of the l-composition of S and c has no unifier. The concept of fallible skeleton shows the problem with infinite derivations. If the computation rule selects the atom corresponding to l the derivation will immediately fail. However, another computation rule may select another incomplete leaf and it may succeed in extending the fallible skeleton. The extension itself will correspond to a new fallible skeleton. In some cases this process may not terminate. To avoid this one can put some restriction on the computation rule that allows to discover in a finite number of steps that the skeleton is fallible.

Definition 2.30 Fair computation rule

A non failed SLD-derivation is *fair* iff for every state each atom of its goal is selected after a finite number of steps. An SLD-tree is *fair* iff all its infinite branches are fair.

A computation rule is *fair* iff all SLD-trees built with this rule are fair (i.e iff all infinite branches are fair in all SLD-trees).
□

It is worth noticing that if a computation rule is a selection function, i.e. if the choice of the goal atom depends only on the goal, then it is not fair. Generally, to guarantee fairness of an SLD-derivation, information about the "age" of the atoms of the actual goal is needed. This information is not present in the goal itself.

Theorem 2.13

For a given definite program P and definite goal g, if a fair SLD-tree has an infinite branch then all SLD-trees for P and g have an infinite branch. Equivalently, if there exists a finitely failed SLD-tree then all fair SLD-trees are finitely failed.

$\square$

Proof. If a fair SLD-tree has an infinite branch, then every prefix of this infinite derivation corresponds to an unfallible skeleton. Since the derivation is fair any of the leaves will be selected in a finite number of steps and since the derivation is infinite it can be extended. Thus for any natural number k the program has an unfallible skeleton of depth greater than k. Now assume that another SLD-tree is finite. This means that all its branches are successful or failed. The skeletons corresponding to the successful branches are complete and cannot be extended. On the other hand any extension of the skeleton corresponding to a failed branch is fallible. Let n be the maximal depth of a skeleton corresponding to a branch of the SLD-tree. Thus the program has no unfallible skeletons with head g of the length greater than n. The contradiction shows that every SLD-tree for P and g has an infinite branch.

$\square$

Now we can conclude that there is a correspondence between infinite branches of all fair SLD-trees. Each of the infinite branches corresponds to a unique infinite skeleton, such that any of its subskeletons is unfallible. Note that fairness is necessary, as a non fair SLD-tree may have an infinite branch with a fallible skeleton.

Computation rules and computation strategies

The SLD-resolution scheme is nondeterministic. To derive from it a deterministic algorithm that constructs answer substitutions one has to define a computation rule and to replace the nondeterministic choice of the clause by some deterministic computation *strategy*. For a given computation rule the strategy will describe a systematic traversal of the SLD-trees induced by the rule. We now outline some possible computation rules and computation strategies.

- The *standard computation rule* selects the leftmost atom of the actual goal. Since the initial goal is given and the selected atom at each step of the derivation is replaced by the body of a clause, the standard computation rule follows the textual ordering of the atoms in the bodies of the clauses. It selects the leftmost "youngest" (most recently) introduced atom of the actual goal. This computation rule is used in Prolog.

- A *one-sweep computation rule* is defined by associating with each program clause and goal clause a total ordering on its body atoms. The ordering induces a total ordering on every goal: during a computation step the selected atom of the goal is replaced by a body with totally ordered atoms. The selection follows the ordering on the actual goal. Note that the standard computation rule is a special case of a one-sweep rule where the ordering of the body atoms of each clause is their textual ordering.

- A *data-driven computation rule* makes as a selection criterion the degree of instantiation of the atoms of the goal or of some positions of these atoms. For example ground atoms of the goal may be selected with the highest priority.

- The *"leftmost eldest" computation rule* uses the information about the history of the computation. Each atom of the actual goal has been introduced at some previous step of the computation, or is an atom of the initial goal. The age of an atom is the number of computation steps performed after the step introducing this atom. The rule selects the leftmost of the eldest atoms of the goal. It is a fair computation rule. It is a modification of the standard computation rule in which the bodies of the used clause are placed at the end of the sequence representing the actual goal. It is a simple but inefficient rule.

In the SLD-resolution the choice of the clause is nondeterministic. The nondeterminism makes it possible to find any of the existing computed answer substitutions. Thus, for a fixed computation rule the nondeterminism allows for construction of any of the branches of the corresponding SLD-tree. Now we want to find a deterministic algorithm that also has this property. This requires a systematic method for SLD-tree traversal, to be called *computation strategy*. We now assume that the clauses of the program are totally ordered, e.g. by the textual ordering, or in any other way. This introduces total ordering on all arcs outgoing from any node of the SLD-tree (and also on the branches of the tree), since the arcs are labeled by clauses. Consequently the children of every node are also ordered. We will call this ordering a left-to-right ordering since this is the way of graphical representation of the ordered SLD-trees. We now outline two common computation strategies.

- The *standard strategy* consists in the top-down, left to right visit of the ordered SLD-tree. In other words, for every visited node the next node to be visited is its least child. After visiting all children of a node the search proceeds to its next brother in the ordering.

- The *horizontal* strategy consists in visiting of a search tree level by level. Level 1 consists of the root of the tree. Level $n+1$ consists of all children of the nodes at level n. The nodes of every level are visited in the left-to-right order.

  With the horizontal strategy all nodes of any finite branch will be visited in a finite number of steps. Thus, any computed answer substitution will be found in a finite time. However, the computation process can be seen as interleaved construction of many different derivations. On the other hand, the standard strategy will never find a refutation preceded in the SLD-tree by an infinite branch. Thus, the completeness of the SLD-resolution is lost with the standard strategy. On the other hand, the standard strategy constructs derivations one by one and is therefore easier to implement.

Remark 2 The notion of SLD-tree and the unification semantics, both operational, can be related.

Call a *most general goal* a clause of the form $\leftarrow p(X_1, \ldots, X_n)$ where p is an n-ary predicate for some $n \geq 0$ and the X_i's are pairwise distinct variables. Then the unification semantics of a program P can be characterized as the set of all atoms $b\sigma$ such that b is a most general goal and σ is the computed answer of a successful branch in an SLD-tree for P and $\leftarrow b$.

2.2.5 Fixpoint semantics

The model-theoretic semantics of definite programs resulted in the notion of the least term model parameterized by the term domain used. This section gives another characterization of such models. We obtain it as a special case of a result which holds for arbitrary models of definite programs. The intuition behind the formal concepts discussed below concerns the nature of definite clauses. Assume that a domain of interpretation is defined together with interpretation of the function symbols of a given definite program P. In the terminology of Section 2.2.1 this means that a preinterpretation J of P is given. The preinterpretation can be extended to an interpretation by specifying the meaning of the predicates. Any such an extension is called *J-based* interpretation of P. Following the example of term interpretations we will consider any J-based interpretation to be a set of J-atoms, as discussed in Section 2.2.1. For an atomic formula a of the form $p(t_1, \ldots, t_n)$ and for a valuation ν in J the J-atom $p(t_{1J,\nu}, \ldots t_{nJ,\nu})$ will be denoted $a_{J,\nu}$. The set of all J-based interpretations together with the set-theoretic operations of union and intersection is a complete lattice.

Let $\mathcal{I}$ be a J-based interpretation for some preinterpretation J. A clause $h \leftarrow a_1, \ldots, a_m$, where $m \geq 0$ is true in $\mathcal{I}$ iff for every valuation ν such that $a_{1J,\nu}, \ldots, a_{mJ,\nu}$ are in $B_{\mathcal{I}}$ the J-atom $h_{J,\nu}$ is also in $B_{\mathcal{I}}$. This can be used to define a transformation on J-based interpretation which attempts to extend a given interpretation in such a way that the clauses of the program become true.

Definition 2.31 Immediate consequence operator

Let J be a preinterpretation for a definite program P. The *immediate consequence operator* for J and P is the function $T_{P,J}$ on J-based interpretations defined as follows: $a \in T_{P,J}(I)^4$ iff for some clause $h \leftarrow a_1, \ldots, a_m$ of P there exists a valuation ν such that $a_{iJ,\nu} \in I$ for $i = 1, \ldots, m$ and $h_{J,\nu} = a$.
□

For a fixed preinterpretation the index J will be omitted. For example, if J is a fixed term preinterpretation then I is a term interpretation and valuations are substitutions. In this case the definition of T_P becomes:

$a \in T_P(I)$ iff for some clause $h \leftarrow a_1, \ldots, a_n$ of P there exists a substitution σ such that $a_i\sigma \in I$ for $i = 1, \ldots, n$ and $h\sigma = a$.

The operator $T_{P,J}$ is a function on the complete lattice of J-based

---

[4]In this section I is used to denote sets of J-based atoms. Hence I is also a shorthand to denote the corresponding J-based interpretation.

interpretations of P. It allows to give the following characterization of the J-based models of P.

Proposition 2.6 Characterization of models of a DCP
  For a definite program P, $T_{P,J}(I) \subseteq I$ iff I is a model of P.
□

Proof. Assume $T_{P,J}(I) \subseteq I$. I is a model of P iff it is a model of every clause. Consider a clause c. We show that it is true in I for every valuation ν. Two cases are possible:

1. Some body atom b of c is false in I for ν. Then the body of c is also false in I for ν and the clause is true in I for ν.
2. All body atoms are true in I for ν. Then by the assumption also the head of c is true in I for ν. Hence the clause is true in I for ν.

Thus I is a model of P.
  If I is a model of P then $T_{P,J}(I) \subseteq I$ by the definition of $T_{P,J}$.
□

Our intention now is to use this characterization for "construction" of some models of P. It follows directly from the considered condition that a J-based interpretation I such that $T_{P,J}(I) = I$ is a model of P. For a function f, a value x such that $f(x) = x$ is called a *fixpoint*. The models we want to consider are fixpoints of T_P. We now quote some definitions and results concerning fixpoints which will allow us to construct models of definite programs.
  A function f on a partially ordered set is called *monotonic* iff $f(x) \geq f(y)$ for every $x \geq y$. A subset S of a partially ordered set is called *directed* iff for every finite subset X of S includes an upper bound of X. This terminology applies in particular to functions on complete lattices.

Definition 2.32
  A function f on a complete lattice L is called *continuous* iff $f(lub(X)) = lub\{f(x)|x \in X\}$ for every directed subset X of L.
□

Every continuous function is also monotonic. Let f be a continuous function and let $x \geq y$. Clearly the set $\{x, y\}$ is directed and its least

upper bound is x. Hence $lub\{f(x), f(y)\} = f(x) \geq f(y)$. We now
show that every continuous function has the least fixpoint[5]. Let f be a
continuous function on a complete lattice L. To formulate the fixpoint
theorem the following notation will be used:

- $\bot$ for $glb(L)$,

- $f \uparrow 0$ for $\bot$,

- $f \uparrow i$, where $i = 1, 2, \ldots$ for $f^i(\bot)$, i.e. for i times composed function f
  applied to $\bot$

- $f \uparrow \omega$ for the least upper bound of the set $\{f \uparrow i \mid i = 0, 1, 2 \ldots\}$

Theorem 2.14
  Every continuous function f on a complete lattice L has a least fixpoint $lfp(f)$ and $lfp(f) = f \uparrow \omega$.
□

Proof. We show first that $f \uparrow \omega$ is a fixpoint of f. Since $\bot$ is the
least element of L, $f \uparrow 1 \geq f \uparrow 0$. The function is continuous, hence
monotonic. Consequently $f \uparrow (i + 1) \geq f \uparrow i$ for $i = 0, 1, \ldots$ and the
set $\{f \uparrow i \mid i = 0, 1, \ldots\}$ is a directed subset of L. By continuity of f,
$lub(\{f \uparrow i \mid i = 0, 1, \ldots\}) = lub(\{f \uparrow i \mid i = 1, \ldots\})$. Hence $f(f \uparrow \omega) =$
$f(lub(\{f \uparrow i \mid i = 0, 1, \ldots\}) = f(lub(\{f \uparrow i \mid i = 1, ..\})) = lub(\{f \uparrow i \mid i =$
$0, 1, ..\}) = f \uparrow \omega\}$.
  The remaining question is whether $f \uparrow \omega$ is the least fixpoint. Let y be
any fixpoint of f. Thus $f(y) = y$. Clearly $y \geq \bot$. Since f is monotonic,
$y = f^i(y) \geq f^i(\bot)$ for i=1,2.... Hence $y \geq f \uparrow \omega$.
□

  The theorem characterizes the least fixpoint of a function f as the limit
of the approximations $f \uparrow i$. The elements of the lattices we consider
are sets of J-based atoms and the ordering relation is the set inclusion.
Hence $\bot$ is the empty set and the lub is the set of all the J-based atoms.

  In some cases it may be possible to compute the approximations. We
now show that $T_{P,J}$ is continuous, so that the theorem can be applied for

---

[5]This result holds for any monotonic function but for our purposes the restriction
to continuous case is sufficient.

construction of approximations of the least J-based model. In particular, it may be applied to construct the least term models.

Theorem 2.15

The function $T_{P,J}$ on the complete lattice L of all J-based interpretations of a definite program P is continuous.
□

Proof. We show that $T_{P,J}(lub(X)) = lub\{T_{P,J}(x)|\ x \in X\}$ for each directed subset X of L.

Let X be a directed subset of L. The elements of X are J-based interpretations, i.e. sets of J-interpreted atoms, that is sets of the objects of the form $p(v_1, \ldots, v_n)$ where p is a predicate of P and $v_1, \ldots, v_n$ are values in the domain of J. The ordering on L is the set inclusion. Assume that J-interpreted atoms $a_1, \ldots, a_m$ are in $lub(X)$. Then each a_i must be in some interpretation I_i in X. Since X is directed it must include an upper bound of the set $\{I_1, \ldots, I_m\}$. It is an interpretation I including $a_1, \ldots$ and a_m. On other other hand, if $a_1, \ldots a_m$ are elements of some interpretation I in X they are also in $lub(X)$.

Let a be an atom in $T_{P,J}(lub(X))$. By the definition of $T_{P,J}$ there exists a clause $a_0 \leftarrow a_1, \ldots, a_m$ and a valuation ν in J such that $a_{1J,\nu}, \ldots a_{mJ,\nu}$ are in $lub(X)$ and $a = a_{0J,\nu}$. Hence $a_{1J,\nu}, \ldots a_{mJ,\nu}$ are in some interpretation I in X.

Thus a is in $T_{P,J}(I)$, and consequently in $lub(\{T_{P,J}(x)|\ x \in X\}$. Now, if a is in $T_{P,J}(I)$ then there exist a clause $a_0 \leftarrow a_1 \ldots a_m$ and a valuation ν such that $a_{1J,\nu}, \ldots a_{mJ,\nu}$ are in I and $a_{0J,\nu} = a$. Hence $a_{1J,\nu}, \ldots a_{mJ,\nu}$ are in $lub(X)$ and a is in $T_{P,J}(lub(X))$. This concludes the proof.
□

The meaning of a definite program P can now be defined as the least fixpoint of $T_{P,J}$ for some chosen preinterpretation J. We now want to show the relation between such a definition and the other kinds of semantics.

Theorem 2.16

$T_{P,J} \uparrow \omega = PT_J(P)$
□

Proof. It follows directly by the definitions that for $i = 1, \ldots$ the set $T_{P,J} \uparrow i$ consists of the heads of all J-based proof trees of P of depth less than i. Thus, $T_{P,J} \uparrow \omega$ is the set of the heads of all J-based proof trees of P.

□

For a term preinterpretation on a term domain H from Corollary 2.3 p. 80 we obtain by Theorem 2.16 :

Corollary 2.8 Fixpoint characterization of the denotation

Let H be a term preinterpretation. Then $DEN_H(P)$ is the least fixpoint of $T_{P,H}$ and $DEN_H(P) = T_{P,H} \uparrow \omega$.

□

We now use the operator $T_{P,H}$ to characterize the finite failure set $FF_H(P)$ of the program P. For this the following notation will be used:

- $T_{P,H} \downarrow 0$ for $B(H)$,

- $T_{P,H} \downarrow i$, where $i = 1, 2, ..$ for $f^i(B(H))$, i.e. for i times composed operator $T_{P,H}$ applied to $B(H)$,

- $T_{P,H} \downarrow \omega$ for the greatest lower bound of the set $\{T_{P,H} \downarrow i \mid i = 0, 1, 2...\}$.

The intuition of the set $T_{P,H} \downarrow i$ is as follows. Let D be a derivation tree of P such that for each incomplete node n of D the path from the root to n is of length i. Call any such D a *full* tree of depth i.

The set $T_{P,H} \downarrow i$ consists of the heads of all full derivation trees of depth i. If an atom a is in $T_{P,H} \downarrow i$ but not in $T_{P,H} \downarrow i + 1$ then it has some full derivation trees of depth i with the head a but each of them is fallible. There may also exist some full and fallible derivation trees with the head a of depth less than i, but there is no such tree of depth greater than i. This gives the following conclusion.

Proposition 2.7

Let P be a definite program and let H be a term domain. An atom a is in the finite failure set $FF_H(P)$ iff it is not in $T_{P,H} \downarrow i$ for some $i \geq 1$, i.e. $FF_H(P) = B(H) - T_{P,H} \downarrow \omega$.

□

Relations between various kinds of semantics are schematically illustrated in Figure 2.20.

2.2.6   Completion semantics

A definite program has no logical consequences in the form of negative literals. This follows from the fact that a term base is a term model of the program, as discussed in Section 2.2.1. Any negated atom is false in this model and thus cannot be a logical consequence of the program. In this section we present the notion of completion that allows to deal with negation in the case of definite programs and in the case of more general programs called *normal programs*, which are not discussed in this book. The idea is to consider a logic program as a shorthand for another set of formulae called the *completion* of the program. Intuitively, a logic program defines some predicates using *if* sentences. Now the idea is that the definitions should be read as *if-and-only-if* sentences. The completion of a program is obtained by a transformation that reflects this idea. Since *if-and-only-if* reading entails the *if* reading, the logical consequences of a program become also the logical consequences of the completion. Additionally the completion has the consequences originating from the *only-if* part of the *if-and-only-if* sentences. Even in the case of definite programs the set of logical consequences of the completion may include negative literals. For a given term domain H the negation of an atom $a \in B(H)$ is a logical consequence of the completion of a definite program P iff a has a finitely failed SLD-tree for P. This result allows to use finite failure of SLD-computation for an atomic goal a for concluding $\neg a$. Such an inference rule is called *negation as failure*.

The remaining part of this section gives a formal presentation of the notion of completion and summarizes some classical results related to this notion in the case of definite programs.

We now describe construction of the completion of a given definite program P. For a given predicate p that appears in P consider all clauses of P such that p is the predicate of the head. Intuitively, this set "defines" p and will be denoted $def(p)$. Notice that $def(p)$ is empty if p appears only in the body of some clause. For the purpose of our construction we would like to combine the clauses of $def(p)$ into one *if* sentence. To this effect we add to the alphabet the equality predicate $=$. The intention is to transform the head of every clause in $def(p)$ into the same form. The original arguments of the heads are then to be moved into the bodies using $=$, which intuitively should represent the identity of terms. Let c be a clause in $def(p)$. Thus c is of the form $p(t_1, \ldots, t_n) \leftarrow$

$a_1, \ldots a_m$, where $m \geq 0$ and $a_1, \ldots a_m$ are body atoms. Denote by $E(c)$ the formula: $\exists y_1, \ldots, y_l (x_1 = t_1 \wedge \ldots x_n = t_n \wedge a_1 \wedge \ldots \wedge a_m)$, where $y_1, \ldots, y_l$ are all variables of c and $x_1, \ldots, x_n$ are "new" variables not appearing in P.

Let $def(p) = \{c_1, \ldots, c_k\}$ for some $k \geq 0$. The formula $IF(p, P)$ is defined as follows:

- $p(x_1, \ldots, x_n) \leftarrow E(c_1) \vee \ldots \vee E(c_k)$ if $k > 0$,
- $p(x_1, \ldots, x_n) \leftarrow false$ if $k = 0$.

In this way a definition of a predicate p is contracted into one *if* sentence. Notice that if p has no defining clauses in P then the resulting formula in the definition is equivalent to stating that $p(x_1, \ldots, x_n)$ is universally false. Now $IF(P)$ is defined to be the set of formulae $IF(p, P)$ for all predicates p that appear in P.

The transformation defined above uses a new predicate $=$. As mentioned above $=$ should represent identity on terms. This intention is formalized by the following axioms, called *Clark's equality theory (CET)*.

1. $\forall (x = x)$.
2. $\forall (f(x_1, \ldots, x_n) = f(y_1, \ldots, y_n) \leftrightarrow (x_1 = y_1 \wedge \ldots x_n = y_n))$ for every function symbol f.
3. $\forall ((p(y_1, \ldots, y_n) \leftarrow p(x_1, \ldots, x_n)) \leftarrow (x_1 = y_1 \wedge \ldots x_n = y_n))$ for all predicates, including "$=$".
4. $\forall (f(x_1, \ldots, x_n) \neq g(y_1, \ldots, y_m))$ for all pairs of distinct function symbols f and g.
5. $\forall (t[x] \neq x)$ for all terms $t[x]$ containing the variable x and different from x.

We now give a formal definition of the completion of a definite program. Denote by $IFF(P)$ the set of formulae obtained by replacing every occurrence of the connective $\leftarrow$ in any formula of $IF(P)$ by the connective $\leftrightarrow$.

Definition 2.33 Completion of a definite program
Let P be a definite program. The set of formulae $IFF(P) \cup CET$ is called the *completion* of P. It will be denoted $COMP(P)$.
□

The motivation for introducing completion was to give a logical re-construction of the intuitive concept of reading clauses of a program as "iff"-statements. Thus, the completion should only augment the usual "if" reading of the clauses by the "only-if" reading. This can be precisely formulated as follows.

Theorem 2.17

Let P be a definite program and let H be a term domain. The set of all atoms in $B(H)$ which are logical consequences of $COMP(P)$ is the H-based denotation of P, i.e: For any atom $a \in B(H)$, $a \in DEN_H(P)$ iff $COMP(P) \models \forall(a)$.

□

The theorem follows from the definition of completion. As the deno-tation is the set of the atomic logical consequences of the program, the theorem shows that the atomic logical consequences are the same for a program and its completion. This is a formal counterpart of the intuition that the if-reading of the clauses is not affected by the completion. This also allows to use operational semantics of definite programs to construct atomic logical consequences of the completion of a program. The "only-if" reading of the clauses allows to draw negative conclusions: negative literals may be logical consequences of the completion of a program.

Example 2.15 Negative logical consequences

The IFF version of the program of Example 2.14 p. 89 is:

$\forall U, V(path(U, V) \leftrightarrow \exists X(U = X \wedge V = X) \vee \exists X, Y, Z(U = X \wedge V = Y \wedge arc(X, Z) \wedge path(Z, Y)))$

$\forall U, V(arc(U, V) \leftrightarrow U = a \wedge V = b)$

The negative literal $\neg path(b, a)$ is a logical consequence of the com-pletion. To show this notice that the formula

$\neg path(b, a) \leftrightarrow$

$\neg(\exists X(b = X \wedge a = X)) \wedge \neg(\exists Z arc(b, Z) \wedge path(Z, a)))$

is a logical consequence of the completion of the program. The formula $\neg(\exists X b = X \wedge a = X)$ is true in every model of the completion of P. The same holds for $\neg(\exists Z arc(b, Z) \wedge path(Z, a))$, since $arc(b, Z)$ is false in every model of CET. Hence $\neg path(b, a)$ is a logical consequence of the completion.

□

Existence of negative logical consequences of a program leads us to
the question of their construction. The answer is given by the following
theorem which relates the problem to the concept of finite failure.

Theorem 2.18
   Let P be a definite program and let H be a term domain. For any
atom $a \in B(H)$, $a \in FF_H(P)$ iff $COMP(P) \models \forall(\neg a)$.
□

The theorem is a classical result and its proof for the term domain
$TERM$ can be found in many sources. For example it is a direct corollary of Theorem 15.4 and Theorem 16.1 of [Llo87]. It allows to check
whether the formula $\forall(\neg a)$ is a logical consequence of the completion of
the program. For this it suffices to construct a fair SLD-tree for a. If the
tree is finitely failed than the answer is "yes". If the tree has a success
branch, the answer is *no*. The remaining case is an infinite tree with
no success branches. Such a tree cannot be constructed in a finite time.
This way of deriving negative conclusions from finitely failed SLD-trees
is called *negation as failure*. Theorem 2.18 is sometimes called soundness and completeness theorem for negation as failure.

2.3   Summary and bibliographical comments

In this chapter we defined and related different kinds of semantics. Most
of them are defined relative to preinterpretations. The logical view of
logic programming gives the concepts of denotation and of the least
term model, both parameterized by term domains. On every term domain both notions coincide. The notion of proof tree leads to the proof-
theoretic semantics for every preinterpretation. For every term domain
proof-theoretic semantics is equivalent to the least model semantics and
associates with each program its denotation on the term domain. We
gave an equational characterization of proof trees which allows us to
define an equational semantics depending on the preinterpretation used.
We restricted our considerations to solving equations on the domain
$TERM$ of all terms, where the solutions are represented by the most
general unifiers. In this way we associated with every program a se-

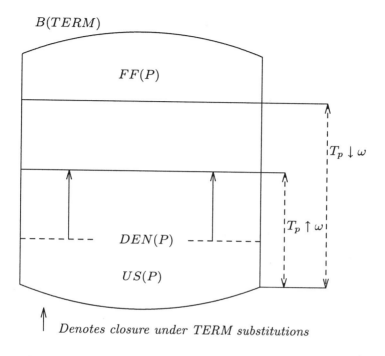

$\uparrow$ Denotes closure under TERM substitutions

Figure 2.20
Splitting of the term base $B(TERM)$

mantics, called the unification semantics, characterized by a set of not
necessarily ground atoms, denoted $US(P)$. All instances of this set under substitutions ranging over some term domain give the denotation of
the program on this term domain. We used our equational characterization of the proof trees also for defining a framework for deriving operational semantics, called the general resolution scheme. We introduced
the SLD-resolution as an instance of the scheme. We outlined a general
technique for proving soundness and completeness of any operational
semantics derived from the general resolution scheme. We presented a
fixpoint semantics of definite programs and we proved that it is equivalent to the other kinds of semantics. We introduced the notion of finite
failure set for a given term domain and we gave its characterization in
terms of the immediate consequence operator.

The summary of some results presented in this chapter is shown in Figure 2.20, where the nonground term base for the domain $TERM$ of all terms is divided into three parts:

- the denotation of a given program,

- the finite failure set,

- the subset consisting of the atoms such that some but not all instances of every atom are in the denotation, or those for which every fair SLD-tree includes only infinite and failed branches.

The denotation includes the set $US(P)$, characterizing the unification semantics of the program. It is the closure of this subset under all substitutions.

Most of the notions and results presented in this chapter appeared previously in the literature. Ground term models and their relation to SLD-resolution have been discussed in many sources; standard references are the book by Lloyd [Llo87] and the article by Apt [Apt90]. Extensions of some results to nonground term bases have been proposed simultaneously by several authors. The concept of proof tree with variables has been already introduced by Clark [Cla79]. Ferrand [Fer87] used the notion of nonground term base for presentation of a theory of algorithmic debugging. Deransart and Ferrand [DF86] presented foundations of logic programming (including normal programs) in the framework of nonground term domains. The organization of this chapter is strongly influenced by that presentation. Falaschi, Levi, Martelli and Palamidessi published a collection of papers on the "observational semantics" (e.g.[FLMP88, FLMP89]), called *S-semantics*, which coincides with the unification semantics presented in this chapter. However, the S-semantics was defined as a declarative semantics, while the unification semantics has been derived from our notion of resolution process and has therefore an operational flavour. Also Gaifman and Shapiro introduced the unification semantics, but with slightly different motivation, as a "fully abstract" semantics [GS89] providing a minimal representation. Yet another presentation of the unification semantics was done by Fages in [Fag89], where proof trees are discussed in the framework of the type theory. In this paper the elements of $US(P)$ are called *most general theorems* and the result stated by Proposition 2.4 p. 83 is presented as an instance of the theorem of Hindley, Milner and Huet on the most

general type [Hue88]. The use of nonground term bases is also proposed
by Deville [Dev90a].

The original contribution of this chapter is the attempt to give a
uniform presentation of various results. Two aspects of the presentation
may be stressed:

Parametrization. The classical results on foundations of logic programming are presented using two kinds of parameters: the term domains and the resolution schemes. The parametrization by the term
domains makes it possible to show that certain results hold for nonground term bases as well as for ground ones. The use of variables does
not strengthen the results but contributes to a more uniform treatment
of the declarative and the operational semantics. The parametrization
by the resolution schemes which are as general as possible helps to distinguish the results which are independent from the strategies from the
results which depend on them. It also facilitates formalization of the concept of strategy, and other related concepts important for formulation of
problems related to validation, to occur-check or to non-classical strategies, like strategies using delays or parallelism. The increased complexity
introduced by this parametrization is compensated by simplification of
proofs which are mostly based on the notion of proof tree.

Systematic use of the notion of proof tree. Most of the existing pre-
sentations of foundations of logic programming put more emphasis on
the model-theoretic semantics, on the operational semantics and on the
fixpoint semantics. The notion of proof tree and the proof theoretic semantics have attracted relatively little attention. This presentation uses
proof-tree as the main fundamental concept. Many results, even those
concerning the operational semantics, become easier to formulate and
to understand when presented in this framework. In the same time the
concept of proof tree is essential for viewing definite programs as grammars and for exploring their relations to other grammatical formalisms.
It is also a fruitful concept as concerns validation methods.

The notion of proof tree seems to be of little use for presentation of
completion. This is not surprising since the completion of a program
may appear as an ad hoc solution for formalization of finite failure. A
characterization of negation in terms of denotation proposed by Deransart and Ferrand in [DF86] relates negation to proof trees. Consider
$DEN_H(P)$ for some program P and term domain H. It is also the
least model of P. Hence $DEN_H(P) \models \forall \neg a$ iff no instance of a is in

$DEN_H(P)$. Denote by $NEG_H(P)$ the set of all atoms such that no H-instance of an atom in this set is in $DEN_H(P)$. The following properties follow directly by this definition:

- $a \in NEG_H(P) \Leftrightarrow DEN_H(P) \models \forall \neg a$.
- $a \in DEN_H(P) \Leftrightarrow DEN_H(P) \models \forall a$.
- $FF_H(P) \subseteq NEG_H(P)$.

However, there may be no recursively enumerable set of axioms describing $NEG_H(P)$. A more recent paper by the same authors [Fer92] uses proof trees for characterization of the well-founded semantics [GRJ91] of normal logic programs.

3 Grammatical Extensions of Logic Programs

Proof trees of definite programs are constructed by pasting together instances of clauses. This resembles construction of parse trees of context-free grammars. One difference is that production rules of a context-free grammar do not include variables. The only instances of a production rule are thus its copies and parse trees of a grammar are constructed by pasting together copies of its production rules. In this chapter we present and compare two classes of grammars that extend both the notion of context-free grammar and the notion of definite program. The semantics of both formalisms will be given in terms of parse trees.

The first formalism to be presented is that known as *Van Wijngaarden grammars (W-grammars)* or *two-level grammars*. It was introduced as a generalization of BNF to be used for defining non-context-free syntax of programming languages. The notion of W-grammar has been one of the sources of inspiration for development of Prolog (see [Coh88, CC79]), although the formal relation between W-grammars and Prolog was originally not investigated. Variants of W-grammars, like *affix grammars*, and *extended affix grammars* have been used for compiler construction. The reader interested in these variants is referred to the literature indicated in Section 3.3.

The second formalism to be discussed in this chapter known as *definite clause grammars (DCG's)* is used in many Prolog systems. The notion was developed to facilitate logic programming of linguistic problems. It originates from the *metamorphosis grammars* of Colmerauer. Some other kinds of grammars have been defined with the same objective, e.g. the *extraposition grammars*, the *definite clause translation grammars*, the *discontinuous grammars*, to mention only a few. These kinds of grammars specialized towards natural language processing will not be discussed here. The interested reader is referred to the book [DA89].

3.1 W-grammars

3.1.1 The notion of W-grammar

The notion of W-grammar will be first informally presented as a generalization of Backus-Naur notation (BNF).

Example 3.1

Consider the following set of the context-free production rules specified in BNF:

$\langle arithm\ expr \rangle$ ::= $\langle simple\ arithm\ expr \rangle | \langle if\ clause \rangle$
                                    $\langle simple\ arithm\ expr \rangle else \langle arithm\ expr \rangle$
$\langle boolean\ expr \rangle$ ::= $\langle simple\ boolean\ expr \rangle | \langle if\ clause \rangle$
                                    $\langle simple\ boolean\ expr \rangle else \langle boolean\ expr \rangle$
$\langle design\ expr \rangle$ ::= $\langle simple\ design\ expr \rangle | \langle if\ clause \rangle$
                                    $\langle simple\ design\ expr \rangle else \langle design\ expr \rangle$

One can abbreviate this specification by introducing a variable X ranging over the finite language $L_X = \{arithm, boolean, design\}$:

$\langle X\ expr \rangle$ ::= $\langle simple\ X\ expr \rangle | \langle if\ clause \rangle \langle simple\ X\ expr \rangle$
                              $else \langle X\ expr \rangle$

Each of the original production rules can be obtained from the scheme by a substitution $\{X/s\}$ where $s \in L_X$.
□

The notion of W-grammar generalizes the above example in that that the languages associated with the variables of BNF rule schemes are possibly infinite context-free languages. A W-grammar consists thus of a finite set of BNF production rule schemes with variables and of a finite set of context-free production rules that specify the domains of the variables. Each variable is associated with a nonterminal of the context-free production rules. The domain of the variable is the context-free language consisting of the strings derivable from the nonterminal associated with the variable by the context-free production rules. If the context-free languages associated with the variables are infinite then the W-grammar is a finite specification of an infinite set of context-free production rules (in Backus-Naur notation). It also specifies a possibly infinite set of nonterminals, but the terminal alphabet is finite. Thus the basic notions of the formalism, like derivation, parse tree, the language associated with a nonterminal, etc. carry over without change from the formalism of context-free grammars.

Context-free grammars can be seen as the subclass of W-grammars, where no variables appear in the rule schemes. Introduction of variables allows one to define non-context-free languages.

Example 3.2

Consider the following context-free grammar:

$$
\begin{aligned}
\langle s\rangle &::= \langle a\rangle\langle b\rangle\langle c\rangle \\
\langle a\rangle &::= a \\
\langle a\rangle &::= a\langle a\rangle \\
\langle b\rangle &::= b \\
\langle b\rangle &::= b\langle b\rangle \\
\langle c\rangle &::= c \\
\langle c\rangle &::= c\langle c\rangle
\end{aligned}
$$

Clearly, $L(G, \langle s\rangle) = \{a^k b^m c^n | k, m, n > 0\}$. We now transform the rules of the grammar into the rule schemes in such a way that for the resulting W-grammar W the language $L(W, \langle s\rangle)$ becomes the non-context-free language $\{a^n b^n c^n : n = 1, 2, ...\}$. The idea is that each nonterminal $\langle a\rangle, \langle b\rangle$ or $\langle c\rangle$ gives rise to the nonterminal scheme $\langle a\ to\ N\rangle$, $\langle b\ to\ N\rangle$ and $\langle c\ to\ N\rangle$, respectively, where the variable N ranges over some representation of natural numbers. We choose to represent natural numbers by sequences of the symbol i, where the length of the sequence is the natural number represented, e.g. ii represents 2. Now the rule schemes are developed in such a way that a nonterminal of the form $\langle x\ to\ n\rangle$ can derive only one terminal string: x^n. The information about the length of the string derived can be passed to the context by multiple occurrences of the variable N.

This idea is implemented by the following W-grammar:

$$
\begin{aligned}
\langle s\rangle &::= \langle a\ to\ N\rangle\langle b\ to\ N\rangle\langle c\ to\ N\rangle \\
\langle a\ to\ Ni\rangle &::= a\langle a\ to\ N\rangle \\
\langle b\ to\ Ni\rangle &::= b\langle b\ to\ N\rangle \\
\langle c\ to\ Ni\rangle &::= c\langle c\ to\ N\rangle \\
\langle a\ to\ i\rangle &::= a
\end{aligned}
$$

$$\langle b \, to \, i\rangle \quad ::= \quad b$$
$$\langle c \, to \, i\rangle \quad ::= \quad c$$

The variable N is associated with the nonterminal N of the following context-free grammar:

$N ::= i | Ni.$

To derive a terminal string from the nonterminal $\langle s \rangle$ one has to construct an appropriate production rule. To this effect the variable N in the first scheme has to be replaced by a string i^n for some $n = 1, 2, \ldots$. Consider for example the case $n=2$. Now $\langle s \rangle$ derives $\langle atoii\rangle\langle btoii\rangle\langle ctoii\rangle$. For $\langle a \, to \, ii\rangle$ the only matching production rule that can be constructed is $\langle a \, to \, ii\rangle ::= a\langle a \, to \, i\rangle$. It is obtained by instantiating N to i in the corresponding scheme. Now $\langle a \, to \, i\rangle$ derives a. A similar construction for $\langle btoii\rangle$ and for $\langle ctoii\rangle$ would allow to derive bb and cc respectively. Thus the terminal string $aabbcc$ will finally be derived. Generally, replacing N by i^n in the first scheme makes it possible to derive the string $a^n b^n c^n$, and only this string.

□

For formal definition of W-grammar the following terminology originating mostly from the literature on W-grammars will be used:

- The nonterminals of the context-free grammar specifying the domains are called *metanotions*.

- The terminals of the context-free grammar specifying the domains are called *metaterminals*.

- The production rules of the context-free grammar are called *metarules*. No special assumptions are made about the metarules. In particular, the right-hand side of a metarule may be the empty string and the grammar may be ambiguous.

- The nonterminals with variables are called *hypernotions*. Notice that the hypernotions are strings without any structure.

- The production rule schemes with variables are called *hyperrules*.

The informal presentation of W-grammars may be summarized by the following definition:

Definition 3.1

A W-grammar W is a 7-tuple $\langle X, M, Q, V, T, H, R\rangle$ where

- X is a finite auxiliary alphabet.
- M is a finite set of metanotions.
- Q is a finite set of metarules: it is a subset of $M \times (M \cup X)^*$ [1].
- V is a denumerable set of variables: each variable v has an associated metanotion $M(v)$ which determines its domain $L_{M(v)}$. The metanotion is called the *sort* of v.
- T is a finite set of terminal symbols.
- H is a finite set of basic hypernotions ; it is a subset of the set $\{\langle h \rangle : h \in (V \cup X)^+\}$.
- R is a finite set of basic hyperrules: it is a subset of $H \times (H \cup T)^*$.

□

It is sometimes assumed that the variables of a sort v have the form vi, where $i = 0, 1, \ldots$. This notational convention simplifies definition of W-grammars, since the sorts of variables need not be defined separately. Another notational convention allows to omit index i of the variable vi if it is the only variable of sort v used in a given context. A W-grammar specifies a (generally infinite) family of languages. For more precise explanation some further auxiliary concepts are needed. Let $W = \langle X, M, Q, V, T, H, R \rangle$ be a W-grammar. The context-free grammar $G = \langle M, X, Q \rangle$ is called its *metagrammar*. It is used to construct production rules from the hyperrules. Let m be in M. A string s in $(V \cup X)^*$ is called *grammatical term* of sort m iff m derives s', where s' is obtained from s by replacing each variable by its sort. For example, the string $N1ii$ is a grammatical term of sort N for the W-grammar of Example 3.2 since N derives Nii in the metagrammar. Note that $N1$ is a grammatical variable of sort N. The justification for this terminology is the algebraic view of context-free grammars discussed in Section 1.5. In this view a context-free grammar is a many-sorted algebra whose operations are the production rules. Terms in the signature of this algebra correspond to parse trees of the grammar. The grammatical terms defined above give rise to parse trees, thus to the terms of the many-sorted algebra corresponding to the grammar. However, in the case of ambiguous grammars a grammatical term may give rise to many parse trees.

---

[1] Thus, the auxiliary alphabet includes the metaterminals of the grammar.

It is now possible to extend the notion of substitution to the case of
grammatical terms: a *grammatical substitution* is a many-sorted map-
ping σ from V into grammatical terms such that the set $\{v|\sigma(v) \neq v\}$ is
finite.

A *hypernotion* is the image of any basic hypernotion under a grammatical substitution. Similarly, a *hyperrule* is the image of any basic
hyperrule under a grammatical substitution.

Any variable-free hyperrule of a W-grammar is a context-free production rule with nonterminals being variable-free hypernotions. This
allows one to extend for W-grammars the notion of derivation introduced
for context-free grammars. An example of such a derivation was given
above. However, since generally there are infinitely many variable-free
hyperrules it may be difficult to use them in practice. To overcome this
difficulty one may try to construct derivations with the basic hyperrules,
or with their instances created "by need". This gives rise to a concept
of *hyperderivation* defined below as a generalization of the concept of
derivation. The idea is to work with hypernotions and hyperrules instead of nonterminals and production rules. Let h, g be strings over
hypernotions and terminal symbols, i.e. $h, g \in (H \cup T)^*$. The string g
is said to be *directly hyperderivable from* h iff there exist strings h_1, h_2, b
and a hypernotion x such that $h = h_1 x h_2$, $g = h_1 b h_2$ and the pair $\langle x, b \rangle$
is a hyperrule. The relation of *hyperderivability* is a transitive and reflexive closure of the relation of direct hyperderivability. A *hyperderivation*
is a sequence $h_1, \ldots, h_n$ of strings over $(H \cup T)^*$ such that for every $i > 0$
the string $h_i + 1$ is directly hyperderivable from h_i.

Example 3.3
For the W-grammar of Example 3.2 one can construct the following
hyperderivation:

$\langle s \rangle$,
$\langle a \, to \, Kii \rangle \langle b \, to \, Kii \rangle \langle c \, to \, Kii \rangle$,
$a \langle a \, to \, Ki \rangle \langle b \, to \, Kii \rangle \langle c \, to \, Kii \rangle$,
$aa \langle a \, to \, K \rangle \langle b \, to \, Kii \rangle \langle c \, to \, Kii \rangle$,
$aa \langle a \, to \, K \rangle b \langle b \, to \, Ki \rangle \langle c \, to \, Kii \rangle$,
$aa \langle a \, to \, K \rangle bb \langle b \, to \, K \rangle \langle c \, to \, Kii \rangle$,
$aa \langle a \, to \, K \rangle bb \langle b \, to \, K \rangle c \langle c \, to \, Ki \rangle$,

$aa\langle a \text{ to } K\rangle bb\langle b \text{ to } K\rangle cc\langle c \text{ to } K\rangle$

where K is a grammatical variable of sort N. This hyperderivation cannot be extended: none of the hypernotions in the last string is identical with the left-hand side of a hyperrule of the grammar.
□

The fundamental concept of the language specified by a W-grammar is defined in terms of hyperderivations.

Definition 3.2
For a given W-grammar the *language $L(W, h)$ derived from a hypernotion h* is the set of all terminal strings hyperderivable from h.
□

Example 3.4
Putting $K = i$ in Example 3.3 one can extend the hyperderivation so that the last element obtained is the terminal string *aaabbbccc*. This is thus one of the elements of the language $L(W, \langle s \rangle)$.
□

The notion of hyperderivation can also be used for associating relations with hypernotions of a W-grammar.

Definition 3.3
Let $h = \langle \alpha_0 v_1 \alpha_1 \ldots v_n \alpha_n \rangle$, be a hypernotion of a W-grammar where $\alpha_0, \ldots, \alpha_n$ are strings over the auxiliary alphabet and $v_1, \ldots, v_n$ are distinct variables. The *relation $R(W, h)$ associated with h* consists of all n-tuples $\langle \gamma_1, \ldots, \gamma_n \rangle$ such that:

- $\gamma_i \in L_{M(v_i)}$ for $i = 1, \ldots, n$,
- There exists a terminal string hyperderivable from the nonterminal $\langle \alpha_0 \gamma_1 \alpha_1 \ldots \gamma_n \alpha_n \rangle$.

□

Example 3.5
Consider the W-grammar W defined by the following basic hyperrules:
$\langle N1i \; succ \; N2i \rangle ::= \langle N1 \; succ \; N2 \rangle$
$\langle ii \; succ \; i \rangle ::= \varepsilon$

The metarules are:

$N ::= i|Ni$

The relation $R(W, \langle N1\ succ\ N2\rangle)$ consists of all pairs $\langle i^{n+1}, i^n\rangle$, for $n = 1, 2, ...$

□

3.1.2 Definite programs are W-grammars

By analogy to the context-free grammars one can introduce a concept of parse tree of a W-grammar. However, since the hyperrules may include variables, the parse trees are constructed from instances of the basic hyperrules and not from their copies. Therefore the definition resembles the notion of derivation tree of definite program (Definition 2.3 p. 27).

A pair $\langle h, \sigma\rangle$ where h is a basic hyperrule of a W-grammar W and σ is a grammatical substitution will be called an *instance name* of the hyperrule h. Clearly every instance name $\langle h, \sigma\rangle$ determines the unique hyperrule $c\sigma$ of W. Now the concept of parse tree of W is defined in terms of instance names.

Definition 3.4

For a W-grammar W a *parse tree* is any labeled ordered tree T such that

1. Every leaf node is labeled by the "empty label" $\perp$ or by an instance name of a basic hyperrule of W,

2. Every non-leaf node of T is labeled by an instance name of a basic hyperrule of W,

3. Let n be a node labeled by an instance name $\langle h, \sigma\rangle$, where h is the hyperrule $x ::= t_0 x_1 t_1 \ldots t_m x_m t_{m+1}$ with hypernotions $x, x_1, \ldots x_m$, with possibly empty terminal strings $t_0, \ldots, t_{m+1}$ and such that $m \geq 0$. Then n has m children and for $i = 1, \ldots, m$ the i-th child of n is labeled either

   - $\langle h', \sigma'\rangle$, where h' is a hyperrule with the left-hand side x' such that $x_i\sigma = x'\sigma'$, or

   - $\perp$.

□

The intuition behind this definition is that a parse tree is obtained by combining appropriate instances of basic hyperrules. The precise meaning of "appropriate instances" is expressed by condition 3 of Definition 3.4 . The empty label $\perp$ indicates nodes where the parse tree may be extended, if there exists an appropriate instance of a basic hyperrule. A node with the empty label will therefore be called an *incomplete node* of the tree. The other nodes will be called the *complete nodes.*

Notice that the parse trees of W-grammar hide the information about the string derived but make explicit the basic hyperrules used during the derivation[2].

The notion of parse tree is illustrated by the example in Figure 3.1.

The notion of parse trees will now be used to show that definite programs can be considered as a special class of W-grammars.

Theorem 3.1

For every definite program P there exists a W-grammar W_P and a bijection between proof trees of P and parse trees of W_P such that the corresponding trees are isomorphic.

□

Proof. We construct the grammar W_P and we show that it has the required property. Proof trees of P are constructed by combining instances of the clauses. Thus the clauses play a similar role in construction of a proof tree as the basic hyperrules of a W-grammar in construction of a parse tree. The variables of a clause are instantiated to terms. Therefore it may be assumed that each variable is of the same sort and the domain associated with this sort is the Herbrand universe of the program. Thus a definite program P can be seen as a W-grammar with the empty terminal alphabet. The idea is formalized by the following construction of a W-grammar W_P for a given program P:

- The auxiliary alphabet of W_P consists of the predicate symbols of P, function symbols of P and auxiliary symbols "(", ")" and ",".
- The alphabet of the metanotions is the singleton $\{H\}$.
- The variables of W_P are those of the language of P, every variable of W_P is of the sort H, where H is the only metanotion of the metagrammar.
- The metarules describe the Herbrand universe of P; to this effect the following metarules are constructed: for each constant c the metarule of

---

[2]The conventions of graphical representation of parse trees discussed in Section 1.5 may be extended for parse trees of W-grammars to show the strings derived.

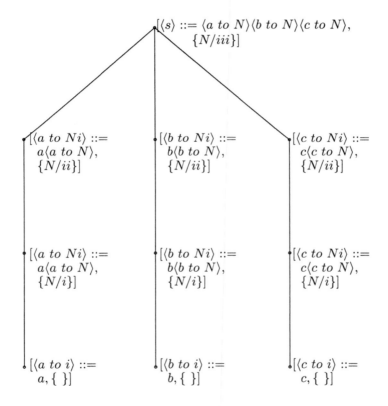

Figure 3.1
A parse tree of the string *aaabbbccc* of the W-grammar of Example 3.2 p. 111

the form $H ::= c$ is created and for each n-ary function symbol f the metarule of the form $H ::= f(H, .., H)$ is created, where the number of occurrences of H in the parentheses is n.

- The terminal alphabet of W_P is empty.

- The set of basic hypernotions consists of all strings $\langle a \rangle$ such that a is an atomic formula appearing in a clause of P.

- For each clause $h \leftarrow b_1, \ldots, b_k$ of P the grammar W_P includes the basic hyperrule $\langle h \rangle ::= \langle b_1 \rangle \ldots \langle b_k \rangle$. These are the only basic hyperrules of W_P.

Clearly, the grammatical substitutions of the grammar W_P are substitutions of the program P. Each clause c of P is transformed by the construction to a basic hyperrule r_c with the same variables. By the construction the correspondence between the clauses and the hyperrules is a bijection. The clause corresponding to a basic hyperrule r will be denoted c_r. A proof tree of P has its nodes labeled by pairs $\langle c, \sigma \rangle$, where c is a clause and σ is a substitution, or by $\bot$. Replacing each label $\langle c, \sigma \rangle$ by the label $[r_c, \sigma]$ one obtains a parse tree of W_P. Conversely, by the definition of parse tree, replacing each label $[r, \sigma]$ of a parse tree by the label $\langle c_r, \sigma \rangle$ one obtains a proof tree of P.
$\square$

The concept of the relation associated with a hypernotion of a W-grammar when applied to the grammar W_P allows one to characterize the least Herbrand model of P. This model is the set of all atoms $p(t_1, ..., t_n)$ such that p is an n-ary predicate in P for some $n = 1, 2, ...$ and $\langle t_1, ..., t_n \rangle \in R(W_P, \langle p(x_1, ..., x_n) \rangle)$, where $x_1, ..., x_n$ are distinct variables.

The construction of the grammar W_P shows in what sense the notion of W-grammar extends the concept of definite program:

- The variables of a W-grammar are many-sorted. The sorts are non-terminals of the metagrammar. The variables range over grammatical terms which, in the unambiguous case are string representations of many-sorted terms. The many-sorted term corresponding to a grammatical term can be reconstructed by parsing of the latter in the meta-grammar. However, in case of ambiguous metagrammar this term may not be unique.

- Every atom of a definite programs has a unique tree structure. In contrast to that a hypernotion of a W-grammars may be an unstructured string.

- The terminal alphabet of a W-grammar need not be empty, while a definite program can be seen as a W-grammar with the empty terminal alphabet.

Thus, definite programs constitute a proper subclass of W-grammars, with tree-structured hypernotions.

3.1.3   Transparent W-grammars

Proof trees of a definite program can be constructed by resolution. In case of W-grammars resolution is not directly applicable since the hypernotions are unstructured strings. A resolution step is based on finding a most general unifier of two atomic formulae. In case of W-grammar one should find instead a grammatical substitution that makes two given hypernotions into the same string. The domains of the variables are specific context-free languages defined by the metagrammar. Consider the simplest case when the hypernotions are of the form $\langle X \rangle$ and $\langle Y \rangle$, where X and Y are variables of different sorts R and S. Thus one has to find a grammatical term t such that all variable-free instances of t are in the intersection of the context-free languages $L(G, R)$ and $L(G, S)$, where G is the metagrammar of the considered W-grammar. It is known, that in general the non-emptiness of intersection of context-free languages is undecidable (see e.g. [HU79]). This means that there is no algorithm which terminates on every input and finds the required grammatical substitution or indicates non-existence of such a substitution. The problem can be solved for a special class of W-grammar where each hypernotion has a unique tree structure. This class is defined as follows.

Definition 3.5 A W-grammar W is said to be *transparent* iff it includes a metanotion Φ such that

- each string derivable from Φ in the metagrammar of W has a unique parse tree,

- for each hypernotion $\langle h \rangle$ of W the string h is a grammatical term of sort Φ.

□

Example 3.6

The W-grammar of Example 3.2 p. 111 is not transparent. However, it is rather straightforward to transform it into a transparent one by specifying the structure of hypernotions. For this purpose the following metagrammar may be used:

$(m_0)\ \Phi \rightarrow s$
$(m_1)\ \Phi \rightarrow a\ to\ N$
$(m_2)\ \Phi \rightarrow b\ to\ N$
$(m_3)\ \Phi \rightarrow c\ to\ N$
$(m_4)\ N \rightarrow i$
$(m_5)\ N \rightarrow Ni$

□

For a transparent grammar each hypernotion is a grammatical term. It can be seen as a representation of a term in the term algebra corresponding to the metagrammar. For example the hypernotion $\langle a\ to\ Xii \rangle$ of the considered W-grammar represents the term $m_1(m_5(m_5(X)))$.

Consequently, the hyperrules of the grammar may be given a term representation by transforming their hypernotions into corresponding terms. Similarly, the hypernotions of a hyperderivation can be represented by the corresponding terms. This allows for application of the resolution technique for construction of hyperderivations.

Let $h_1, \ldots h_n$ be a hyperderivation and let $\langle g \rangle$ be a hypernotion in h_n. We want to extend the hyperderivation: the string h_{n+1} is to be constructed by replacing the hypernotion $\langle g \rangle$ in h_n by the right-hand side of the appropriate hyperrule. That is h_n is of the form $d_1 \ldots d_{m-1} \langle g \rangle d_{m+1} \ldots d_q$, where $d_1 \ldots d_q$ are hypernotions or terminal symbols. The problem reduces to finding a grammatical substitution θ such that $\langle g \rangle \theta = \langle a \rangle \theta$ where $\langle a \rangle \leftarrow b_1, \ldots b_k$ is a (renamed) basic hyperrule with b_i's being hypernotions or terminal symbols. But g and a have unique term representations $t(g)$ and $t(a)$. By construction of the term representation it follows that θ can be obtained from an mgu of $t(g)$ and $t(a)$. The mgu can be found by existing term unification algorithms. Now the original hyperderivation gives rise to the extended hyperderivation $(h_1, \ldots, h_n, h_n + 1)\theta$, where $h_n + 1$ is of the form $d_1 \ldots d_{m-1} b_1 \ldots b_k d_{m+1} \ldots d_q$. Notice that the new hyperderivation not only extends the old one but also specializes it.

Example 3.7

Using the metarules of Example 3.6 one can give the following term representation to the basic hyperrules of the grammar of Example 3.2 p. 111.

(1) $\langle m_0 \rangle \rightarrow \langle m_1(N) \rangle \langle m_2(N) \rangle \langle m_3(N) \rangle$

(2) $\langle m_1(m_5(N)) \rangle \rightarrow a \langle m_1(N) \rangle$

(3) $\langle m_2(m_5(N)) \rangle \rightarrow b \langle m_2(N) \rangle$

(4) $\langle m_3(m_5(N)) \rangle \rightarrow c \langle m_3(N) \rangle$

(5) $\langle m_1(m_4) \rangle \rightarrow a$

(6) $\langle m_2(m_4) \rangle \rightarrow b$

(7) $\langle m_3(m_4) \rangle \rightarrow c$

We now construct a hyperderivation starting with the hypernotion $\langle s \rangle$. At every step the term representation of the actual form is indicated and the grammatical rule used to obtain the extension.

1. $\langle s \rangle$
   $\langle m_0 \rangle$
   use (1)

2. $\langle a\,to\,X \rangle \langle b\,to\,X \rangle \langle c\,to\,X \rangle$
   $\langle m_1(X) \rangle \langle m_2(X) \rangle \langle m_3(X) \rangle$
   use (2): the mgu is $\{X/m_5(X_1)\}$

3. $a \langle a\,to\,X_1 \rangle \langle b\,to\,X_1 i \rangle \langle c\,to\,X_1 i \rangle$
   $a \langle m_1(X_1) \rangle \langle m_2(m_5(X_1)) \rangle \langle m_3(m_5(X_1)) \rangle$
   use (5): the mgu is $\{X_1/m_4\}$

4. $aa \langle b\,to\,ii \rangle \langle c\,to\,ii \rangle$
   $aa \langle m_2(m_5(m_4)) \rangle \langle m_3(m_5(m_4)) \rangle$
   use (3): the mgu is $\{N_4/m_4\}$

5. $aab \langle b\,to\,i \rangle \langle c\,to\,ii \rangle$
   $aab \langle m_2(m_4) \rangle \langle m_3(m_5(m_4)) \rangle$
   use (6): the mgu is $\{\}$

6. $aabb \langle c\,to\,ii \rangle$
   $aabb \langle m_3(m_5(m_4)) \rangle$
   use (4): the mgu is $\{N_6/m_4\}$

7. $aabbc \langle c\,to\,i \rangle$
   $aabbc \langle m_3(m_4) \rangle$
   use (7): the mgu is $\{\}$

8. *aabbcc*
   aabbcc
   no other hyperrule can be applied.

   The hyperderivation constructed is the following derivation

   $\langle s \rangle$,
   $\langle a \text{ to } ii \rangle \langle b \text{ to } ii \rangle \langle c \text{ to } ii \rangle$,
   $a \langle a \text{ to } i \rangle \langle b \text{ to } ii \rangle \langle c \text{ to } ii \rangle$,
   $aa \langle b \text{ to } ii \rangle \langle c \text{ to } ii \rangle$,
   $aab \langle b \text{ to } i \rangle \langle c \text{ to } ii \rangle$,
   $aabb \langle c \text{ to } ii \rangle$,
   $aabbc \langle c \text{ to } i \rangle$,
   aabbcc.
   □

3.1.4 Conclusions

The conclusion of this section is that the notion of W-grammar is an extension of the notion of definite program. Thus, definite programs can be seen as a special kind of W-grammars, but generally a W-grammar is not a definite program. The main features of this extension are the following:

- The notion of atom, used in definite programs, is replaced by the concept of hypernotion. An atom is constructed from a predicate and from functors of the language and always has unambiguous structure, which can be represented by a tree. A hypernotion is constructed by concatenation of strings and grammatical terms. A grammatical term may have unambiguous tree structure. Hence, in a special case also a hypernotion may have a tree structure, but not in a general case.

- The terms of a definite program are one sorted while the grammatical terms of a W-grammar are many-sorted. The many-sorted discipline is imposed implicitly by the concept of metagrammar.

- A W-grammar has a well-defined notion of a language derived from a hypernotion. In the special case of a definite program the language derived from an atom is either empty or a singleton consisting of the empty string.

Table 3.1
Example Turbo Prolog program

domains
    title, author = symbol
    pages   = integer
    publication = book(title,pages)
predicates
    written_by(author,publication)
    long_novel(title)
clauses
    written_by(fleming,book("DR NO",210)).
    written_by(melville,book("MOBY DICK",600)).
    long_novel(Title):-written_by(_,book(Title,Length)),Length>300.

We have shown that in the full generality the formalism of W-grammars is of little practical interest because of the undecidability of the unification problem for hypernotions. The notion of transparent W-grammars allows to structure the hypernotions implicitly by means of the metagrammar, while still preserving their textual form. A subclass of the transparent W-grammars can be obtained by the following restrictions:

- The terminal alphabet is empty.

- The hypernotions are constructed with predicates, as atoms in definite programs.

- The arguments of each predicate are grammatical terms, whose syntax is defined by a metagrammar.

The W-programs in this class can be seen as many-sorted definite programs. The idea of using a metagrammar in a definite program has been explored in Turbo Prolog [Bor86] for improving efficiency of the compiled programs. For illustration we quote in Table 3.1 an example Turbo Prolog program from the manual. The metarules of a program are called domain declarations. In the example the metarules are non-recursive. The notation *title,author = symbol* is a shorthand for two rules:

    title → symbol
    author → symbol

The example metarules include the metanotions: *title author symbol integer publication*, the metaterminals: *book ()*, and refer to the standard domains of *integers* and *symbols* for which no metarules are given in the program.

The predicate declarations specify the types of the arguments by using metanotions. The terms of the clauses have to observe these declarations: if the type of an argument is specified by a metanotion *s* then the argument is to be a grammatical term of sort *s*. The variables are implicitly typed by parsing of the grammatical terms according to the predicate declarations: the variable *Title* is of type *title*, hence *symbol*, the variable *Length* is of type *pages*, hence *integer*.

Another subclass of transparent W-grammars can be defined by introducing only the third extension, that is by allowing terminal symbols without changing the syntax of atoms or introducing a metagrammar. This gives rise to an abstract concept of *definite clause grammar* (DCG) to be discussed in the next section.

3.2 Definite clause grammars

Definite clause grammars can be defined in two ways: either as an independent grammatical formalism or as a "syntactic sugar" i.e. as a notational shorthand for a class of Prolog programs. In this section we follow the first way, and we explain then how a DCG can be transformed into a definite program, which is equivalent to it in some rigorously defined sense.

3.2.1 Metamorphosis grammars and DCG's

Historically, the notion of DCG originates from Colmerauer's notion of *metamorphosis grammar* (MG), a formalism for tree rewriting. Both the nonterminals and the terminals of a MG are trees. More precisely, they are ground terms over some given alphabet of function symbols. A metamorphosis grammar defines a rewriting relation over sequences of such terms. The rewriting may be "context-sensitive": one step of rewriting consists in replacing a selected subsequence of a given sequence of terms. The subsequence may consist of more than one term.

We now quote the original definition of MG [Col78] in order to derive from it a formal definition of DCG.

Definition 3.6 Metamorphosis grammar

A *metamorphosis grammar* G is a quintuple $\langle F, T, N, S, \rightarrow \rangle$ where

1. F is a set of function symbols.

2. T is a subset of HU, the Herbrand universe over F, to be called the *terminal vocabulary*.

3. N is a subset of HU, to be called the *nonterminal vocabulary*; it is assumed that T and N are disjoint, their union is denoted V.

4. $S \subset N$ is called the set of *start nonterminals*.

5. $\rightarrow$ is a rewriting relation on V^* such that if $x \rightarrow y$ then x is not ε.

□

The notion of MG has been introduced to define languages in terms of the rewriting relation. For this the relation $\rightarrow$ on V^* is extended as follows:

- $x \rightarrow^0 y$ iff $x = y$,
- $x \rightarrow^{i+1} y$ iff there exist $u, v, r, s \in V^*$ such that $x = urv$ and $r \rightarrow s$ and $usv \rightarrow^i y$,
- $x \rightarrow^* y$ iff there exists $i \geq 0$ such that $x \rightarrow^i y$.

The language $L(G, s)$ generated by the grammar G for a start nonterminal s is defined as follows:

$$L(G, s) = \{t \in T^* : s \rightarrow^* t\}.$$

The language $L(G)$ of G is the union of all languages $L(G, s)$ for s in S.

Notice that the vocabularies of a MG need not be finite. The relation $\rightarrow$ may also be infinite. In this case the formalism gives no effective way for describing it. The example from [Col78] following the original definition shows this situation and seems to suggest an extension to the definition which would solve this problem.

Example 3.8

Here is the example of MG originating from Colmerauer.

- $F = \{a,\ b,\ zero,\ suc,\ bs,\ suite\}$ where a b and $zero$ are constants and the remaining function symbols are unary.
- $T = \{a,\ b\}$.
- $N = S \cup \{bs(x) : x \in HU\}$.
- $S = \{suite(x) : x \in HU\}$.
- The pairs of strings satisfying the relation $\rightarrow$ are the following:

  - $suite(x) \rightarrow a\ suite(suc(x))$ for all $x \in HU$,
  - $suite(x) \rightarrow bs(x)$ for all $x \in HU$,
  - $bs(suc(x)) \rightarrow b\ bs(x)$ for all $x \in HU$,
  - $bs(zero) \rightarrow \varepsilon$ for all $x \in HU$.

  For this grammar $suite(suc(suc(zero))) \rightarrow^* abbb$, and generally, for a natural number n represented by the term $suc^n(zero)$ we have $suite(suc^n(zero)) \rightarrow^* a^i b^j$, where $j - i = n$.
  $\square$

  In the above example the infinite relation $\rightarrow$ has been specified in an "ad hoc" way. A more systematic approach to defining the relation $\rightarrow$ would be to provide a finite set of rule schemes of the form $\alpha \rightarrow \beta$ where both α and β are sequences of (not necessarily ground) terms and α is a non-empty sequence including at least one term which can be instantiated to a nonterminal. The relation $\rightarrow$ is then defined by the set of all ground instances of the schemes. By the instance of a rule scheme $\langle s_1, ..., s_n, t_1, ..., t_m \rangle$ under a substitution σ we mean the pair $\langle s_1\sigma, ..., s_n\sigma, t_1\sigma, ..., t_m\sigma \rangle$ This formalizes the approach of the Example 3.8 , which includes only four schemes.

  We now consider the class of MGs defined by such schemes with the following additional restrictions:

- The set F of function symbols has a distinguished subset P.
- The nonterminals of a grammar are all terms of the form $p(t_1, \ldots, t_{n_p})$, where p is a symbol in P, n_p is its arity and each t_i is a ground term over F.
- The left hand side of each rule scheme is a not necessarily ground term such that its ground instances are nonterminals.

Such grammars will be called *definite clause grammars*. Notice that construction of nonterminals and terminals of a DCG resembles construction of atomic formulae and terms of a logic language. We summarize the discussion by introducing a formal definition:

Definition 3.7 Definite clause grammar
A DCG is a metamorphosis grammar $\langle A, T, N, S, \rightarrow, \rangle$, such that:

- A is the union of disjoint finite alphabets P of predicates and F of functors.
- T is a subset of the Herbrand universe over F.
- N is a subset of the Herbrand base over P and F.
- $S \subseteq N$ [3].
- $\rightarrow$ is the rewrite relation defined by a finite set $R \subset B(T(F, V)) \times (B(T(F, V)) \cup T(F, V))^*$, where V is a denumerable set of variables [4]:

  $x \rightarrow y$, iff $\langle x, y \rangle$ is a ground instance of a scheme in R.
- $T(F, V)$ is the set of all (not necessarily ground) terms over F.

□

The elements of R will be called *rule schemes*. A rule scheme will be represented in the form $a \rightarrow b_1, \ldots, b_n$. where a is atom, called the *head* of the scheme, and the sequence $b_1, \ldots, b_n$, whose elements are either atoms or terms, is called the *body* of the scheme.

The right arrow separates the head atom from the body and the components of the body are separated by commas. The empty string of terms will be denoted ε. Any ground instance of a rule scheme will be called a *production rule* of the DCG. Thus, a DCG usually has an infinite number of production rules. Its nonterminals are ground atomic formulae over P and F. Unless otherwise specified we will assume that the sets N and T of a DCG consists of all nonterminals and terminals that appear in the production rules. Notice that T may be infinite. The production rules define the rewrite relation of the DCG, and consequently the language for each of the nonterminals of the DCG. Introduction of rule schemes and atoms with variables makes it possible to introduce the

---

[3]If S is not explicitly specified we will assume $S = N$.
[4]Recall that $T(F, V)$ is the set of all terms over F and V and $B(T(F, V))$ is the term base over this term domain.

notion of language generated by a given DCG and given atom. Let G be a DCG and let a be a not necessarily ground atom over the predicates and the functors of G. By the language $L(G, a)$ we mean the set of all sequences of terms derivable in G from all ground instances of a.

Example 3.9

The metamorphosis grammar G of Example 3.8 is not a DCG since no formal splitting of the alphabet is defined. The language of the MG can, however, be defined by the DCG G' where:

- $P = \{suite\ bs\}$
- $F = \{zero\ suc\ a\ b\}$
- $R =$
  $\{suite(x) \rightarrow a\ suite(suc(x))$
  $suite(x) \rightarrow bs(x)$
  $bs(suc(x)) \rightarrow b\ bs(x)$
  $bs(zero) \rightarrow \varepsilon\ \}$

and S is defined as in G. The rewrite relation of G' is defined by the production rules obtained from the rule schemes. It is a proper subset of the rewrite relation of the original MG: the predicate symbols *suite* and *bs* are no more used for construction of the terms that instantiate the variables of the schemes. However, the restriction does not influence the languages generated: for every start nonterminal s of G we have: $L(G, s) = L(G', s)$.
□

3.2.2 Definite clause grammars as an extension of definite programs

The syntax of rule schemes of DCG's resembles very much the syntax of clauses of definite programs. An important difference is that the rule schemes may include terms which play the role of terminal symbols. On the other hand the rule schemes can be used to derive the elements of the language in a way similar to the use of clauses for construction of the proof trees.

We now introduce a syntactic concept of parse tree of a DCG which allows us to relate DCG's and definite programs. Let c be a rule scheme of a DCG. A pair $\langle c, \sigma \rangle$ where c is a rule scheme and σ is a substitution will be called an instance name of c. Clearly every instance name $\langle c, \sigma \rangle$ determines the unique instance $c\sigma$ of the scheme c. Now the concept of parse tree is defined in terms of instance names.

Definition 3.8

For a definite clause grammar G a *parse tree* is any labeled ordered tree T such that

1. Every non-leaf node of T is labeled by an instance name of a rule scheme of G,

2. Let n be a node labeled by an instance name $\langle (h \rightarrow t_0, a_1, t_1 \ldots a_k, t_k), \sigma \rangle$, where $k \geq 0$, $a_1, ..., a_k$ are atoms and $t_0, ..., t_k$ are possibly empty sequences of terms. Then n has k children. and for $i = 1, \ldots, k$ the i-th child of n is labeled either

  - $\langle c', \sigma' \rangle$, where c' is a rule scheme with the head h' such that $a_i\sigma = h'\sigma'$, or

  - $\perp$.

□

The intuition behind this definition is that a parse tree is obtained by combining appropriate instances of rule schemes. The precise meaning of "appropriate instances" is expressed by condition (2). The empty labels $\perp$ indicate nodes where the parse tree may be extended, if there exists an appropriate instance of a rule scheme. A parse tree is said to be *complete* if none if its nodes has the empty label, otherwise it is *incomplete*. It is also *partial* if it is either complete or incomplete. A complete parse tree represents a sequence of terms:

  - A one-node complete parse tree τ has its root labeled by an instance name $\langle c, \sigma \rangle$ of a rule scheme c such that the right-hand side of c includes no atomic formulae. Thus c is of the form $a \rightarrow t_1 \ldots t_n$ for some $n \geq 0$ where $t_1 \ldots t_n$ are terms. The sequence $s(\tau)$ of terms associated with the tree τ is defined to be $t_1\sigma \ldots t_n\sigma$.

  - A many-node complete parse tree τ has its root labeled by an instance name $\langle c, \sigma \rangle$ of a rule scheme c such that the right-hand side of c includes at least one atomic formula. Thus c is of the form $a \rightarrow t_0 a_1 \ldots t_{k-1} a_k t_k$ where $k \geq 1$, t_i for $i = 0 \ldots k$ are sequences of terms and a_j for $j = 1 \ldots k$ are atomic formulae. Clearly the root has k children, which are the roots of the proof trees $\tau_1 \ldots \tau_k$. These are direct components of τ. The sequence $s(\tau)$ is now defined to be $(t_0\, s(\tau_1)\, t_1 \ldots t_{k-1}\, s(\tau_k)\, t_n)\sigma$ where $s(\tau_i)$ for $i = 1 \ldots k$ are the sequences associated with the component proof trees, and by application of the substitution σ to the sequence of terms we mean its application to every term in the sequence.

Notice that the sequence of terms associated with a complete parse tree may include variables. Considering DCG's as a subclass of MG's, we see that the *language* defined by a DCG G is the set of all ground instances of sequences associated with all complete parse trees of G. A natural extension of this definition would be to consider as the language of a DCG all (not necessarily ground) sequences associated with all complete parse trees. An example of a parse tree of the DCG of Example 3.9 and its associated sequence is shown in Figure 3.2.

The notion of parse tree shows the relation between DCG's and definite programs: a definite program can be seen as a special case of a DCG where the right-hand side of each production rule is either empty or is a sequence of atomic formulae. This observation gives also an alternative perspective of the semantics of DCG's. The language of a DCG has been related to the concept of parse tree: it is the set of all terminal sequences associated with the complete parse trees of the grammar. But, since the parse trees are proof tree-like objects, they also define a family of relations indexed by the predicate symbols of the grammar. For a given parse tree τ with the root labeled $\langle c, \sigma \rangle$ denote by $r(\tau)$ the atomic formula $h\sigma$, where h is the head of the rule scheme c. The semantics of a given DCG G can now be considered as the set of pairs $\langle r(\tau), s(\tau) \rangle$ for all parse trees τ of G. In the case of a definite program P considered as a DCG this reduces to the set $\langle r(\tau), \varepsilon \rangle$. Forgetting the second (constant) component of each pair we obtain in this case $DEN_{TERM}(P)$. This kind of semantics shows that the extension of the concept of definite program to DCG is obtained by associating with each parse tree the derived sequence of terminals. Consequently, an atomic formula $a = p(t_1, \ldots t_n)$ may or may not have a tree τ such that $r(\tau) = a$. The predicate p can now be associated with $(n + 1)$-ary relation r_p defined as follows: $\langle t_1, \ldots, t_n, s \rangle \in r_p$ iff there exists a parse tree τ such that $p(t_1, \ldots, t_n) = r(\tau)$ and $s = s(\tau)$. The last element of each tuple is a sequence of terms. However, a sequence of terms can itself be considered as a term created by means of an infix right-associative operator "." and a constant

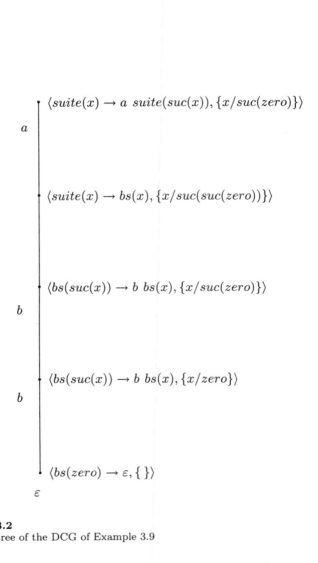

Figure 3.2
A parse tree of the DCG of Example 3.9

nil representing the empty sequence. Thus, a sequence $t_1 \ldots t_n$ can be represented by the term $(t_1.(\ldots(t_n.nil)\ldots))$.

The outlined semantics of DCG's associates with every n-ary predicate of a DCG an $(n+1)$-ary relation. The question arises, whether it is possible to transform a given DCG into a definite program defining the same family of relations. This would amount to "compiling" a DCG into a definite program. The answer for this question is positive. We now present and prove correct a construction used in Prolog implementations of DCG's. A standard reference explaining the idea is [PW80], where the notion of DCG is defined as a syntactic sugar for the program obtained by this construction. In contrast to that, our presentation stresses the grammatical nature of the DCG's with precisely defined semantics. The correctness of the construction will be proved with respect to this semantics.

The construction associates with each n-ary predicate of a given DCG a $n+2$-ary predicate of the resulting definite program. Both additional arguments of an n-ary predicate p represent sequences of terms as lists. By a *list* we mean here a term which is either a constant *nil* or a compound term of the form $t_1.t_2$, where "." is a binary functor used in the (right-associative) infix notation and t_2 is a list. A sequence $t_1,\ldots,t_n$ of terms will be represented by the list $t_1.(\ldots(t_n.nil))$. The list representation of a sequence s will be denoted $[s]$.

We now explain the idea of the construction. An atom $p(t_1,\ldots,t_n,[s_1],[s_2])$ is in the denotation of the resulting definite program iff the following conditions are satisfied:

1. s_2 is a suffix of s_1, i.e. $s_1 = ss_2$ for some sequence s.

2. For some parse tree τ of the DCG $r(\tau) = p(t_1,\ldots t_n)$ and $s(\tau) = s$.

Thus, the idea is to represent a sequence s by a pair of lists $\langle[ss_1],[s_1]\rangle$, for some sequence s_1. In particular s_1 may be the empty sequence, represented by the empty list *nil*. Such a representation allows one to use the resulting definite program as a relatively efficient Prolog parser for a given DCG.

Let G be a DCG with an alphabet P of predicates, an alphabet F of functors and with a set R of the rule schemes. We construct a definite program P_G defined as follows:

- For each n-ary predicate p in P there is a $n+2$-ary predicate p' in P_G.

- The alphabet of the function symbols of P_G is F.

- Let r be a rule scheme in R. Then r is of the form
$$p_0(t_{01}, \ldots, t_{0n_0}) \rightarrow s_0 p_1(t_{11}, \ldots, t_{1n_1}) s_1 \ldots s_{m-1} p_m(t_{m1}, \ldots t_{mn_m}), s_m,$$
where $m \geq 0$, s_i for $i = 0 \ldots m$ is a sequence of terms, and $p_j(t_{j1}, \ldots, t_{jn_j})$ is an atomic formula. For each r the program P_G includes the clause of the form

$$p_0'(t_{01}, \ldots t_{0n_0}, [s_0 S_1], C) \leftarrow p_1'(t_{11}, \ldots, t_{1n_1}, S_1, [s_1 S_2]), \ldots,$$
$$p_m'(t_{m1}, \ldots, t_{mn_m}, S_m, [s_m C])$$

if $m > 0$, or

$$p_0'(t_{01}, \ldots t_{0n_0}, (s_0 C)', C) \leftarrow$$

if $m = 0$.

The construction is illustrated by the following example.

Example 3.10
Let
$$p(Y) \rightarrow a \, q(Y) \, b \, r(Y) \, c$$
be a rule scheme of a DCG. The terminal symbols involved in this rule scheme are constants a, b and c. The construction transforms the scheme into the following clause:
$$p'(Y, a.S_1, C) \leftarrow q'(Y, S_1, b.S_2), r'(Y, S_2, c.C)$$
Figure 3.3 shows how the sequences: α derived from $q(Y)$, β derived from $r(Y)$ and $a\alpha b\beta c$ derived from $p(Y)$ can be expressed in terms of the sequences represented by the lists S_1, S_2 and C[5].
□

We now prove that the construction is correct, i.e. that the semantics of a given DCG G is properly simulated by the semantics of P_G.

Theorem 3.2
Let τ be a complete parse tree of a DCG G and let $r(\tau) = p(t_1, \ldots, t_n)$. Then for any sequence c of terms there exists a proof tree of P_G with the head $p'(t_1, \ldots, t_n, [s(\tau)c], [c])$.
□

---

[5]In Figure 3.3 the difference list notation is used.

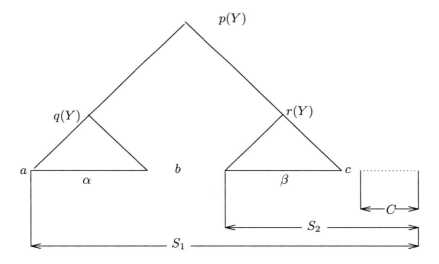

$$a\alpha b\beta c = aS_1 - C$$

$$\alpha \;=\; S_1 - bS_2$$

$$\beta \;=\; S_2 - cC$$

Figure 3.3
The principle of compilation of DCG's into definite programs (Example 3.10)

Proof. The theorem is proved by induction on the depth d of the tree τ.

For $d = 1$ the label of the root is $\langle r, \sigma \rangle$, where r is a rule scheme $p(t'_1, \ldots, t'_n) \rightarrow s$ such that $t'_i \sigma = t_i$ for $i = 1, \ldots, n$, and $s(\tau) = s\sigma$. By the construction r is transformed into the unit clause r' of the form $p'(t'_1, \ldots, t'_n, [sC], C) \leftarrow$, which gives rise to the proof tree of depth 1 with the root labeled $\langle r', \sigma\{C/[c]\} \rangle$.

Assume that the theorem holds for every parse tree of depth less than m. Consider a parse tree of depth m. Its root label is $\langle r, \sigma \rangle$, where r is a rule scheme

$$p(t_{01}, \ldots t_{0n_0}) \rightarrow s_0 p_1(t_{11}, \ldots t_{1n_1}) s_1 \ldots s_{k-1} p_k(t_{k1}, \ldots t_{kn_k}) s_k$$

such that $k > 0$. The tree has k immediate subtrees $\tau_1, \ldots \tau_k$, such that $r(\tau_i) = p_i(t_{i1}, \ldots, t_{in_i})\sigma$, for $i = 1, \ldots, k$. The depth of each subtree does not exceed m. The trees are such that $s(\tau) = s_0 \sigma s(\tau_1) s_1 \sigma \ldots s(\tau_k) s_k \sigma$.

By the induction hypothesis for each τ_i and for any sequence c there exists a proof tree $\pi_i(c)$ in P_G with the head $p'_i(t_{i_1}\sigma, \ldots t_{i_n}\sigma, [s(\tau_i)c], [c])$.

Consider the clause r' associated with r by the construction. It is of the form

$$p'(t_{01}, \ldots t_{0n_0}, [s_0 S_1], C) \leftarrow p'_1(t_{1_1}, \ldots t_{1n_1}, S_1, [s_1 S_2]), \ldots,$$
$$p'_k(t_{k1}, \ldots t_{kn_k}, S_k, [s_k C])$$

Let c be an arbitrary sequence of terms. Denote by c_i the sequence $s(\tau_i) s_i \sigma \ldots s(\tau_k) s_k \sigma c$ and by d_i the sequence: $s_i \sigma \ldots s(\tau_k) s_k \sigma c$. Notice: $s_0 c_1 = s(\tau)c$.

Consider the substitution $\gamma = \{S_1/[c_1], \ldots, S_k/[c_k], C/[c]\}$.

The proof tree with the root labeled $\langle r', \gamma \rangle$ and with the immediate components $\pi_i(d_i)$ for $i = 1, \ldots k$ has the required property.
□

We proved that every element of the denotation of the original DCG is coded by an element of the denotation of the constructed definite program. To prove correctness of the construction it is necessary to show also that the DCP, if "properly used", can only produce such codes. This is formalized by the following proposition.

Proposition 3.1
Let G be a DCG and let π be a proof tree of the definite program

P_G with the head of the form $p'(t_1, \ldots, t_n, [sc], [c])$. Then there exists a complete parse tree τ of G such that

$$r(\tau) = p(t_1, \ldots, t_n) \text{ and } s(\tau) = s.$$

□

The proposition can be proved by induction on the depth of the proof tree.

It should be noticed that the terminal alphabet of a DCG G is a set of ground terms and the language $L(G)$ is a set of sequences of terms. However, every ground term t can be represented as a sequence $r(t)$ of symbols from a finite alphabet. Thus one can also associate with G a representation language $R(G)$ in which every sequence $t_1, \ldots, t_n$ of $L(G)$ is represented by the concatenation of the strings $r(t_1) \ldots r(t_n)$.

3.2.3 DCG's and W-grammars

Both DCG's and W-grammars are extensions of the notion of definite program. As discussed above, both extensions introduce terminal objects to the bodies of the clauses. However, a W-grammar has only a finite terminal alphabet, while the terminal alphabet of a DCG is a possibly infinite set of ground terms. The following example shows a DCG with infinitely many terminals.

Example 3.11

Consider a DCG G where

- $P = \{even\}$
- $F = \{0, s\}$
- $R =$
  $\{even(0) \rightarrow 0$
  $even(s(s(X))) \rightarrow s(s(X))\, even(X)\}$

The language $L(G)$ consists of all finite sequences of terms of the form $s^{2n}(0)\, s^{2(n-1)}(0) \ldots s(s(0))\, 0$ for $n = 0, 1, \ldots$.

□

The essential feature of the example is that the terminal component of the body of the second rule scheme is a nonground term. Its variable X may be instantiated by infinitely many ground terms of the universe, thus allowing the language to include infinitely many terminal symbols.

A DCG whose terminals do not include variables can be seen as a W-grammar. This class of DCG's will be called *ground* DCG's. Let G be a ground DCG and let P, F and R be the predicate alphabet, the functor alphabet and the set of the rule schemes of G. Denote by $\Sigma(G)$ the set of terminal terms that appear in the rule schemes. Now G can be seen as the W-grammar $W_G = (X, M, Q, V, T, H, R')$ where:

- $X = F \bigcup P$.

- M is the singleton set $\{Term\}^6$.

- Q is defined as follows. The metarules describe the Herbrand universe over F; to this effect the following metarules are constructed: For each constant c the metarule of the form $Term ::= c$ is created and for each n-ary function symbol f the metarule of the form $Term ::= f(Term, .., Term)$ is created, where the number of occurrences of the metanotion $Term$ in the parentheses is n.

- V is a denumerable set of variables. All variables are of sort $Term$.

- $T = \Sigma(G)$.

- $H = \{\langle h \rangle : h$ is an atomic formula that appears in a rule scheme of $R\}$.

- R' is obtained from R by replacing each occurrence of an atomic formula h in R by the corresponding basic hypernotion $\langle h \rangle$.

This transformation of a ground DCG into a W-grammar is rather straightforward, as illustrated by the following example.

Example 3.12 Consider the DCG with the following rule schemes, which derives strings of even length over a singleton alphabet.
  $string(0) \rightarrow \varepsilon$
  $string(s(N)) \rightarrow ii\ string(N)$
A parse tree of this DCG brings in the root label the information about the length of the underlying string.
  The metagrammar of the corresponding W-grammar is
  $Term ::= 0 | s(Term)$
  Its terminal alphabet is $\{i\}$ and its basic hyperrules are almost identical with the rule schemes of the DCG.
  $\langle string(0) \rangle ::= \varepsilon$

---

[6]That is $Term$ is the only metanotion.

$$\langle string(s(N)) \rangle ::= ii \ \langle string(N) \rangle$$
□

It is easy to see that the parse trees of G and W_G are isomorphic. Thus the class of ground DCG's can be seen as a subclass of W-grammars.

It is left as an exercise to construct a W-grammar that generates the representation language for a given nonground DCG.

3.3 Bibliographical comments

The notion of W-grammar, called also *two-level grammar* has been introduced in [Wij65]. It has been applied to define non-context-free syntax of Algol 68 [WMP$^+$75]. The presentation of W-grammars in this chapter differs from the original one in the concrete syntax used to represent W-grammars. The original presentation introduces many notational conventions which must be mastered to understand the idea of the formalism. Our presentation following [Mał84] refers to well-known BNF notation. This should allow the reader to grasp the idea of the formalism without being faced to new notational conventions. The notion of hyperderivation does not appear in the original definition. It has been introduced in [Mał84], together with the concept of transparent W-grammar. The idea of transparency was already suggested in [Wat74]. A comprehensive introduction to W-grammars in the original notation is [CU77]. Examples of the use of W-grammars for specification of programming languages can be found in [Pag81]. Formal properties of W-grammars have been studied, among others, in [Sin67] and in [Sim81]. The result of [Sin67] is that every recursively enumerable set can be specified by a W- grammar. In view of the fact that definite programs can be seen as W- grammars this result can also be obtained as a corollary of the computability result in [Tär77]. The thesis [Sim81] studies relations between W-grammars and first-order logic. It contains also a bibliographic review of the work on W-grammars until 1981. The thesis [Bou92a] has updated it taking into account most of the work done in the field during the last decade.

The relations between W-grammars and definite programs are discussed in [MN82]. The paper [Nil83] presents a technique for compilation of many-sorted definite programs into an efficient code. An example of a many-sorted logic programming language is Turbo Prolog [Bor86].

An analysis-oriented version of W-grammar, called *affix grammar* was introduced in [Kos71] and modified in [Wat74]. Several variants of affix grammars gained acceptance as tools for compiler writing. More recent papers on this topic are e.g. [Mei90, Kos91, KB91, SB92].

The metamorphosis grammars have been introduced in [Col78]. Our presentation follows that article and quotes the example given there.

The standard reference to definite clause grammars is [PW80], where the notion of DCG is introduced as a "syntactic sugar" for a Prolog program. In contrast to that we present the notion of DCG as a special case of a metamorphosis grammar. The grammatical nature of the DCG's is made clear through precisely defined notions of derivation, and parse tree. This makes it possible to view the notion of DCG as an extension of the notion of definite program and to compare it to the notion of W-grammar. The transformation of DCG's into definite programs presented in [PW80] as a semantics of DCG's, which is often used as a basis for implementation of DCG's in Prolog, can now be proved correct with respect to the grammatical semantics of DCG's. Other implementations of DCG's or similar grammatical formalisms in Prolog are e.g. [MTH+83, Nil86]. The thesis [Saï92] defines a Prolog extension which can be used for debugging of W-grammars. It surveys some important issues in the design of the so-called grammatical unification algorithm [Mał84]. A discussion on using Prolog for parsing and compiling can be found in [CH87]. The notion of DCG has been defined with the motivation of natural language processing. Other kinds of grammars defined for that purpose are surveyed in [DA89]. Also the collection [SDS90] is devoted to logic grammars. The topic of natural language processing in Prolog is discussed in [GM89].

This chapter contains some of the material previously presented in [DM89, DM90].

4 Attribute Grammars

This chapter presents some notions related to the formalism of attribute grammars. The original motivation for introducing attribute grammars has been to facilitate compiler specification and construction. Subsequently other applications appeared and it became clear that the formalism is very general and can be used as a high-level programming language. The purpose of the presentation of attribute grammars in this book is to relate them to logic programming. Therefore the material of this chapter is in principle restricted to the notions relevant for this purpose. The chapter includes an informal introduction, a survey of some formal notions and results about attribute grammars, and a presentation of proof methods for attribute grammars. The objective is to give a background on attribute grammars for the material presented in the subsequent chapters. For a more comprehensive introduction to the field the reader is referred to [DJL88].

4.1 Informal introduction

The notion of attribute grammar is an extension of the notion of context-free grammar. This section presents the concept in a traditional way, following the original paper by Knuth [Knu68a, Knu68b]. The idea is to decorate parse trees of a context-free grammar by additional labels which provide a "semantics" for the grammar. Every node of a parse tree labeled by a nonterminal is to be additionally decorated by a tuple of semantic values, to be called *attribute values*. (This terminology conforms to the labelling convention for parse trees discussed in Section 1.5.) The number of attribute values is fixed for any nonterminal symbol of the grammar. Their names are called *attributes* of the nonterminal. We illustrate this idea by a variant of the well-known example originating from Knuth [Knu68a].

Example 4.1

Consider the following CFG defining the language of binary numerals:

$Z \to N.N$
$N \to NB$

$N \rightarrow \varepsilon$

$B \rightarrow 0$

$B \rightarrow 1$

It has three nonterminals:

- Z derives binary numerals,
- N derives binary representations of natural numbers,
- B derives bits 0 and 1.

Our intention is to decorate any parse tree of the grammar in the following way. Any occurrence of nonterminal

- Z should be decorated by the decimal representation v of the value of the string derived from it.
- N should be decorated by:

  – the decimal representation v of the string derived,

  – the length l of this string,

  – the rank r, which is the natural number such that 2^r is the decimal value associated with the rightmost bit position of the string.

- B should be decorated by:

  – the decimal representation v of the bit derived,

  – the rank r of the bit.

An example of a decorated tree is given in Figure 4.1.

□

To describe the decoration of all parse trees the decoration mechanism is specified on the level of production rules of the grammar. For each production rule some attribute values of its nonterminals are defined as functions of some other attribute values. These functional dependencies are required to hold for every occurrence of the production rule in any parse tree. In this way attribute values in any given parse tree are being globally related through local dependencies defined for production rules of the grammar. The local dependencies are defined in form of equations, called *semantic rules*. For providing unique and well-defined decoration a restriction on the form of the semantic rules is imposed as described below.

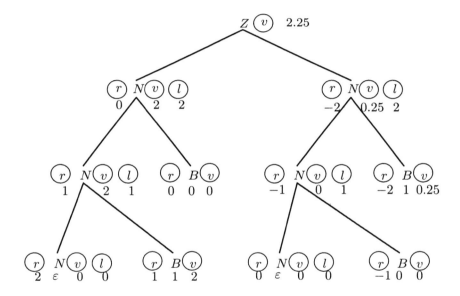

Figure 4.1
A decorated parse tree of the decorated CFG of Example 4.1

With each nonterminal symbol X of a context-free grammar we associate disjoint finite sets $Inh(X)$ and $Syn(X)$ of symbols, called *inherited* and *synthesized* attributes of X. The set of all attributes of X is denoted $Attr(X)$.

Some definitions of attribute grammars allow for associating attributes also with terminal symbols. This extension may be useful in some applications but it is not essential from the conceptual point of view. Therefore it is not discussed in this book.

We now introduce the notation for defining semantic rules. Let p be a production rule of the profile $\langle X_1...X_{n_p}, X_0 \rangle$ (i.e. p must be of the form $X_0 {\to} \alpha_0 X_1...X_{n_p} \alpha_{n_p}$, where every X_i is a nonterminal symbol and α_i is a terminal string, for $i = 0, \ldots, n_p$). An attribute a associated with X_i in p is called an *attribute occurrence* of a in p and it is denoted $a(i)$. Notice that any X_i is an occurrence of a nonterminal symbol Y and Y may have many occurrences in p. To facilitate reading, the redundant notation $a(Y_i)^1$ is used in some examples instead of $a(i)$. Generally, a semantic rule is an equation defining the value of an attribute occurrence in a production rule as a function of the values of some other attribute occurrences. We will additionally require that the semantic rules of p have the form of equations:

$$a(i) = f_{p,a,i}(a_1(i_1)...a_k(i_k))$$

where either $i = 0$ and a is a synthesized attribute of X_0 or $i > 0$ and a is an inherited attribute of X_i. An attribute grammar satisfying these conditions is said to be in *normal form*. The restriction simplifies handling of attribute grammars and does not cause any loss of the expressive power.

Example 4.2

We now illustrate the concept of attribute grammar by defining appropriate semantic rules for the grammar of Example 4.1 . The grammar has three nonterminals: Z, N and B. According to discussion in Example 4.1 the following attributes are associated with the nonterminal symbols:

$$Attr(Z) = \{v\}, Attr(N) = \{r, l, v\}, Attr(B) = \{r, v\}.$$

---

[1] With this notation the indice of Y_i may often be omitted or replaced by quotation.

The attribute r is inherited, l and v are synthesized. The following semantic rules associated with the production rules express the fact that the decimal value of a bit string is the sum of powers of 2 corresponding to the rank of non-null bits.

$$
\begin{aligned}
Z \to N.N \quad & v(Z) = v(N_1) + v(N_2) \\
& r(N_1) = 0 && r(N_2) = -l(N_2) \\
N \to NB \quad & v(N_0) = v(N_1) + v(B) && l(N_0) = l(N_1) + 1 \\
& r(B) = r(N_0) && r(N_1) = r(N_0) + 1 \\
N \to \varepsilon \quad & v(N) = 0 && l(N) = 0 \\
B \to 1 \quad & v(B) = 2^{r(B)} \\
B \to 0 \quad & v(B) = 0
\end{aligned}
$$

□

Denote by $Attr(p)$ the set of all attribute occurrences in a production rule p:

$$Attr(p) = \{a(i) | a \in Attr(X_i), 0 \le i \le n_p\}$$

The semantic rules induce an ordering on $Attr(p)$ called *local dependency relation* and denoted $D(p)$. It is defined as follows: for any $a(i), b(j) in Attr(p)$ $\langle b(j), a(i) \rangle \in D(p)$ iff $b(j)$ occurss in the right-hand side of the semantic rule, whose left-hand side is $a(i)$.

Any production rule may be represented as an elementary parse tree with attribute occurrences marked as additional node labels. In this case the relation $D(p)$ may be visualized as a directed graph with nodes being attribute occurrences such that for every $\langle b(j), a(i) \rangle \in D(p)$ there is an arc from $b(j)$ to $a(i)$. Such a graph will be called *local dependency graph*. When no confusion arises the notation $D(p)$ will be also used for local dependency graphs. The local dependency graphs for the grammar of Example 4.2 are given in Figure 4.2.

For defining the local dependencies we use a graphical convention. Each production rule is represented by a box. The upper edge of the box corresponds to the left-hand side of the production rule. It includes the head nonterminal and its attributes. The inherited attributes appear to the left of the nonterminal and the synthesized attributes to the right of the nonterminal. The lower edge of the box represents the body of the production rule and the attributes of the body nonterminals using the same convention. The local dependency relations are represented as arrows connecting the attributes.

Given a parse tree T we construct the *global dependency graph* for

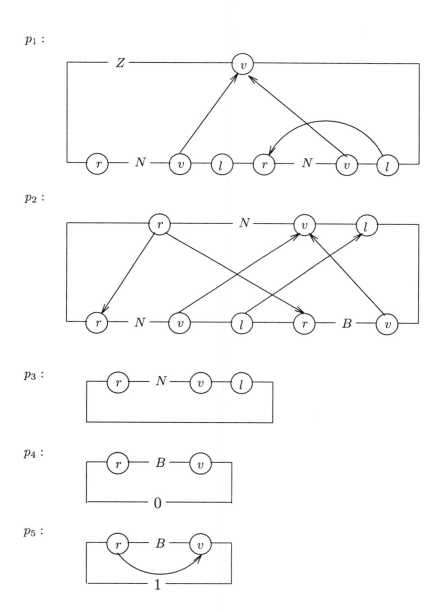

Figure 4.2
Local dependency graphs of the attribute grammar of Example 4.2

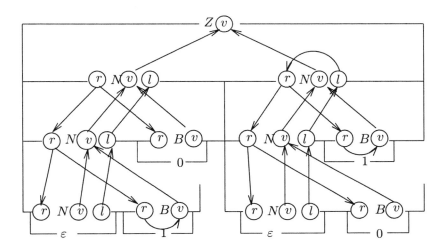

Figure 4.3
A global dependency graph in a parse tree of the attribute grammar of Example 4.2

T by composing the graphs $D(p)$ corresponding to all occurrences of the production rules in T. If the resulting graph is non-circular then it defines a partial ordering on all attribute occurrences of T. Now any attribute value in T can be computed as a function of the minimal elements in this ordering. The global dependency graph for the string 10.01 generated by the grammar of Example 4.2 is shown in Figure 4.3.

Notice that using this graph and the semantic rules one can easily compute the decorated tree of Figure 4.1.

4.2 Definitions of attribute grammars

4.2.1 Relational attribute grammars

An attribute grammar as defined in Section 4.1 associates a dependency graph with each parse tree of the underlying context-free grammar. The graph can be used for controlling computation of all attribute values of the nodes of the tree. The notion of dependency may be seen as an auxiliary one, while the main concept is that of decorated tree, which emerges as the result of computation. For example, for the parse tree of Figure 4.3 the result of the computation is the decorated tree in Figure 4.1. This observation allows us to give a more abstract definition of the concept of attribute grammar, which brings only a declarative concept of decorated tree while abstracting of the "operational" notion of dependency relation. Notice that each semantic rule of an attribute grammar can be seen as a definition of the relation between local attribute values of the neighboring nodes of the parse tree. This relation is defined for a production rule and should hold for every occurrence of this production rule in any parse tree. The definition of the relation has the form of the equation and the decoration of any given parse tree can be described as a solution of a finite set of equations. The discipline of writing of the semantic equations enforced by the original definition of the attribute grammar guarantees uniqueness of the solution regardless of the attribute domains provided that the semantic operations used are total. Taking this declarative view it is possible to generalize even more and allow the semantic rules to be arbitrary formulae, not necessarily equalities. To be more precise we extend the notation of Section 4.1.

Definition 4.1
Let T be a parse tree of a context-free grammar, and let n be a node of T labeled by a nonterminal X. Let a be an attribute of X. Then the pair $\langle a, n \rangle$, denoted $a(n)$, will be called an *attribute occurrence* (of a) in T. The set of all attribute occurrences in T will be denoted $Attr(T)$.
□

In many publications the notion *attribute occurrence* is used only for the attribute occurrences in the production rules, while attribute occurrences in parse trees are called *attribute instances*. Since we view production rules as parse trees (cf. Section 1.5) we do not make this distinction. The definition covers the case of attribute occurrences in a production rule, since a production rule of the profile $\langle X_1 \ldots X_n, X_0 \rangle$ can be considered a parse tree with the nodes labeled $\{X_0, \ldots X_n\}$.

Now we generalize the notion of attribute grammar. It is assumed that for some set of sorts S an S-sorted algebraic structure A is given and an S-sorted alphabet of function symbols and predicates.

Definition 4.2 Relational attribute grammar

A *relational attribute grammar* (RAG) is a 7-tuple $\langle N, P, S, Attr, \mathcal{L}, \Phi, \mathcal{I} \rangle$ where :

- N is a finite set of nonterminal symbols.
- P is an N-sorted signature.
- S is a set of sorts.
- *Attr* is a finite set of attributes; each nonterminal X in N has associated a set of attributes $Attr(X)$. Each attribute a has a sort $s(a)$ in S. The *attribute occurrences* in the terms of P are defined as in Definition 4.1 . Every attribute occurrence of a has also the sort $s(a)$.
- $\mathcal{L}$ is an S-sorted logical language [2] whose variables include all attribute occurrences of attributes of *Attr*.
- Φ is an assignment of a logic formula Φ_p of $\mathcal{L}$ to each production rule p in P. The only free variables of Φ_p are attribute occurrences of p. The formula Φ_p will be called the *semantic condition* of p or *attribute definitions*. Notice that for every interpretation of $\mathcal{L}$ the formula Φ_p defines some relation between the values of the attribute occurrences of p.
- $\mathcal{I}$ is an interpretation of $\mathcal{L}$ in some S-sorted algebraic structure $\mathcal{A}$: it associates the function symbols of $\mathcal{L}$ with functions of $\mathcal{A}$ and the predicates of $\mathcal{L}$ with relations of $\mathcal{A}$.

□

Notice, that a context-free grammar $\langle N, \Sigma, R \rangle$ can be seen as the N-sorted signature $\mathcal{R}'$, where $\mathcal{R}'$ associates with the name of every production rule of R its profile, with the interpretation on the N-sorted domain of context-free languages over the terminal alphabet Σ (cf. Section 1.5). Hence the definition of the relational attribute grammar applies in particular to the case when the signature P is given by a context-free grammar. On the other hand, an N-sorted signature P can be seen as a context-free grammar with empty terminal alphabet and, possibly, with some production rules appearing more than once, so that the set of the production rules becomes a multiset. Having this in mind, and to preserve a uniform terminology we use the notion *parse tree* also for

---

[2]Usually $\mathcal{L}$ is a first order language, but the definition does not impose this restriction.

referring to terms in the signature P of a relational attribute grammar. The pair $\langle N, P \rangle$ will be called the *underlying context-free grammar* of the relational attribute grammar.

We now define a semantics of relational attribute grammars. The parse trees of a relational attribute grammar are to be decorated by values in the domains of the algebraic structure $\mathcal{A}$ in such a way that certain restrictions defined by the semantic conditions are observed. This means that for every node n every attribute occurrence $a(n)$ is to be given a value in the appropriate domain. If n is labeled by the nonterminal X (i.e. by the sort $X \in N$) then the number of attribute occurrences of n equals the number of elements in $Attr(X)$. This holds for every occurrence of the label X in any parse tree. Thus the assignment of the values to attribute occurrences in every node of the tree can be represented by a tuple of values of the length determined by the nonterminal labelling the node. This assignment can be represented by an additional labelling of the nodes of the tree by the tuples of values.

We now specify a condition that is to be satisfied by the labelling. Let m be a node of a parse tree labeled by a production rule p_m of the profile $\langle X_1 \ldots X_k, X_0 \rangle$. (Thus, cf. Section 1.5, m is additionally labeled by X_0 and it has k children labeled by the nonterminals $X_1, \ldots, X_k$.) Consider the semantic condition Φ_m of p_m. Its free variables are in $Attr(p_m)$. According to the definition each of the elements of $Attr(p_m)$ is of the form $a(i)$ where $0 \leq i \leq k$ and $a \in Attr(X_i)$. Let σ_m be a renaming substitution $\{a(i)/a(m_i) | i = 0, 1, \ldots, k\}$. In this way we associate with each node m of a parse tree T the formula $\Phi_m \sigma_m$.

Definition 4.3

Let G be a relational attribute grammar and let T be a parse tree of the underlying context-free grammar. The conjunction of all formulae $\Phi_m \sigma_m$ where m is a node of T is called the *associated formula* of T and it is denoted $\phi(T)$. A valuation ν of $Attr(T)$ is called a *T-assignment*. It is said to be *valid* iff $\phi(T)$ is satisfied in the interpretation $\mathcal{I}$ under ν.

□

The T-assignments will be generally called *tree assignments*.

A T-assignment can be thought of as an additional labelling of T: a node of T labeled by a nonterminal X is additionally labeled by a valuation of $Attr(X)$ represented by a tuple of values. A parse tree with

such an additional decoration will be called a *decorated tree*. For a valid
T-assignment, whenever an occurrence of a production rule appears in T
then the attribute values of the corresponding nodes satisfy the semantic
condition associated with the production rule. A parse tree with an
additional decoration satisfying this condition will be called a *valid tree*.

Example 4.3

The following RAG specifies $i!$, factorial of a natural number i. The
underlying context-free grammar is highly ambiguous. The depth of the
skeleton tree depends on the number i whose factorial is to be found.
The grammar has only one nonterminal symbol: fac with 2 attributes:
a to denote the value of the argument and v to denote the value of the
function. The formal definition is as follows:

- N is $\{fac\}$.
- P is $\{fac \rightarrow \varepsilon, \ fac \rightarrow fac\}$.
- S is the singleton $\{Int\}$.
- *Attr* is $\{a, v\}$, the sort of each attribute is Int.
- $\mathcal{L}$ is a one-sorted logical language with the alphabet including the predicate $=$ and the binary function symbols $-$ and $*$; it employs the usual
  infix notation.
- Φ is :

  - $\Phi_{fac \rightarrow \varepsilon}$: $(a(fac) = 0) \wedge (v(fac) = 1)$,
  - $\Phi_{fac \rightarrow fac}$: $(a(fac_1) = a(fac_0) - 1) \wedge (v(fac_0) = v(fac_1) * a(fac_0))$.

- $\mathcal{I}$ associates with the sort Int the domain of integers, $=$ is interpreted as
  equality on integers, $-$ and $*$ are interpreted as the arithmetic operations
  of subtraction and multiplication.

A valid decorated tree for the given RAG is shown in Figure 4.4.
□

Now the semantics of relational attribute grammars can be defined to
be a function that associates with a relational attribute grammar the set
of all valid trees. Another possible semantics is to consider only the root
labels of all valid trees. More precisely, this semantics is a function that
associates with any RAG a family $\{R_X | X \in N\}$ of relations indexed by
the nonterminals of the grammar. These relations are defined as follows.

$$\begin{array}{cc}
\text{tree} & \text{satisfied relation} \\
<fac>3\ 6 & \\
\mid & 2 = 3 - 1 \wedge 6 = 2 * 3 \\
<fac>2\ 2 & \\
\mid & 1 = 2 - 1 \wedge 2 = 1 * 2 \\
<fac>1\ 1 & \\
\mid & 0 = 1 - 1 \wedge 1 = 1 * 1 \\
<fac>0\ 1 & \\
\mid & 0 = 0 \wedge 1 = 1 \\
\varepsilon &
\end{array}$$

Figure 4.4
A valid decorated tree of Example 4.3

For every nonterminal X consider the set of all parse trees with the roots labeled by X. Let T be such a tree and let σ be a valid T-assignment. Then σ determines a label of the root of T. It is an n-tuple of values where n is the number of attributes of X. The relation R_X consists of all such tuples. The relation associated with the nonterminal fac of Example 4.3 is the set of pairs $\langle i, i! \rangle$ for $i \geq 0$.

4.2.2   Functional attribute grammars

Relational attribute grammars define decorated trees but their semantics is purely declarative. No information is provided about the way to compute valid assignments for given parse trees. We now re-introduce the restrictions of Section 4.1 to define a subclass of RAG's called *functional attribute grammars* (FAG's). The functional attribute grammars are essentially the attribute grammars of Section 4.1. The difference is that we still abstract of the dependency relation. Thus the functional attribute grammars still have only the declarative semantics, though one can find algorithms that would compute valid assignments, at least in some cases. Another difference is that we abstract from the terminal symbols in the underlying CFG's.

   The idea of the syntactic restrictions is to guarantee that in any parse tree the value of each attribute occurrence of each tree node is defined as a function of some attribute occurrences of neighboring nodes. A tool for achieving this goal is a discipline of writing functional definitions based on splitting of the attributes into two disjoint categories: synthesized attributes and inherited attributes.

Definition 4.4

A *functional attribute grammar* is a relational attribute grammar $\langle N, P, S, Attr, \mathcal{L}, \Phi, \mathcal{I} \rangle$ such that:

- *Attr* is the union of two disjoint sets: *Inh* (inherited attributes) and *Syn* (synthesized attributes). For a nonterminal X the set of inherited attributes in $Attr(X)$ is denoted $Inh(X)$. Similarly, the set of synthesized attributes of X is denoted $Syn(X)$. For each $p \in P$ of the profile $\langle X_1 \ldots X_n, X_0 \rangle$ the set $Attr(p)$ of the attribute occurrences is now partitioned into the set $In(p)$ of *input attribute occurrences* and the set $Out(p)$ of *output attribute occurrences*:
  $In(p) = \{a(i) | a \in Inh(X_0) \text{ and } i = 0 \text{ or } a \in Syn(X_i) \text{ and } 1 \leq i \leq n\}$
  $Out(p) = \{a(i) | a \in Syn(X_0) \text{ and } i = 0 \text{ or } a \in Inh(X_i) \text{ and } 1 \leq i \leq n\}$.
- The formula Φ_p for the production rule p is a conjunction of the form

$$\bigwedge_{w \in Out(p)} w = t_w$$

where t_w are terms of $\mathcal{L}$ whose only variables are elements of $Attr(p)$. The conjuncts are called the *semantic rules* of p or *attribute definitions*. If the term t_w of an attribute definition is an attribute occurrence, the definition is called a *copy rule*. If all variables of the terms t_w are in $In(p)$ then the FAG is said to be in *normal form*.

$\square$

Example 4.4

To illustrate the notion of functional attribute grammar we reformulate in our notation an example originating from [KH81]. The intuition of this example is that the only attribute of the root of a linear tree represents the height of the tree multiplied by four. The example was used to illustrate some proof techniques (cf. Example 7.14 p. 353).

$$
\begin{aligned}
N : & \quad \{X, Y\} \\
P : & \quad \{p_1 : X \to Y, p_2 : Y \to Y, p_3 : Y \to \varepsilon\} \\
S : & \quad \{Nat\} \\
Attr : & \quad Attr(X) \cup Attr(Y)
\end{aligned}
$$

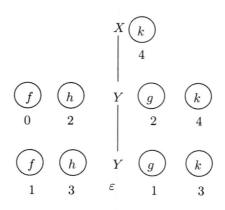

Figure 4.5
A decorated tree of a functional attribute grammar (Example 4.4)

$$
\begin{aligned}
Attr(X) : & \quad \{k\} \\
Attr(Y) : & \quad \{f, h, g, k\} \\
Inh : & \quad \{f, h\} \\
Syn : & \quad \{g, k\}
\end{aligned}
$$

The following formulae are associated with the production rules:

$$
\begin{aligned}
\Phi_{p_1} : \quad & k(X) = k(Y) \wedge \\
& f(Y) = 0 \wedge \\
& h(Y) = g(Y) \\
\Phi_{p_2} : \quad & g(Y_0) = g(Y_1) + 1 \wedge \\
& k(Y_0) = k(Y_1) + 1 \wedge \\
& f(Y_1) = f(Y_0) + 1 \wedge h(Y_1) = h(Y_0) + 1 \\
\Phi_{p_3} : \quad & g(Y) = f(Y) \wedge \\
& k(Y) = h(Y)
\end{aligned}
$$

The formulae are interpreted on the natural numbers.

An example of a decorated tree of this grammar is given in Figure 4.5

□

4.2.3 Conditional attribute grammars

A functional attribute grammar defines the values of the output attribute occurrences of a production rule as a (total) function of the input attribute occurrences. Due to this definition, a functional attribute grammar allows for decoration of every parse tree: for every occurrence of the production rule in the tree the value of every output attribute occurrence can be computed knowing the values of the input attribute occurrences[3].

The concept of functional attribute grammar can be generalized to allow for a natural restriction of the class of parse trees which have a valid decoration. Such a restriction turns out to be useful in many applications. For instance, programming languages are often defined by context-free grammars with additional context conditions. A requirement that every variable used in a program has a declaration in this program is a typical example of such a condition. It may be convenient to describe context conditions within an attribute grammar based on the context-free grammar of the language in such a way that only the parse trees of the programs satisfying the context conditions have a valid decoration. The idea of the generalization is to add to the semantic rules of a production rule a condition on the values of its input attribute occurrences.

This does not cause difficulties in decorating parse trees. Intuitively, the decoration of a parse tree can be constructed by computing the values of output attribute occurrences from the values of input attribute occurrences for every occurrence of a production rule in a given parse tree. Thus a natural extension is to impose restrictions on the input values. Before computing the output values of such an occurrence the condition on the input values is checked. If it is not satisfied the tree has no decoration.

This is formalized by the notion of *conditional attribute grammar*.

The only difference between FAG's and conditional attribute grammars is in the allowed form of the formulae Φ_p. In the case of a conditional attributes grammars each of them is of the form:

$$< B_p, E_p >$$

[3]An algorithm decorating parse trees based on this idea will be discussed in Section 4.3.6.

where B_p is a (possibly empty) conjunction of literals whose only variables are attribute occurrences of $In(p)$ and

$$E_p = \bigwedge_{w \in Out(p)} w = t_w.$$

Notice that every functional attribute grammar is a (special case of) conditional attribute grammar. Notice also that conditional attribute grammar with total interpretation is a (special case of) relational attribute grammar where the definitions have the form

$$\Phi_p : B_p \wedge \bigwedge_{w \in Out(p)} w = t_w$$

The purpose of the conditional attribute grammars is to allow the use of partial functions in the definitions of the attributes. To this effect it is required that the conditions are total. On the other hand the functions referred to by the terms t_w need not be total but have to be defined for all argument values satisfying the condition.

A *valid* tree for a conditional attribute grammar is a parse tree T together with a T-assignment ν such that $\Phi(T)$ is true in the interpretation $\mathcal{I}$ under ν. Notice that for some trees and assignments such that in some rule B_p is false, some formulae of the form $w = t_w$ may be undefined. These trees and assignments are not considered.

Now the semantics of conditional attribute grammars can be defined to be a function that associates with a conditional attribute grammar the set of all valid trees or the root labels of all valid trees.

4.3   Attribute dependency schemes

4.3.1   Introduction and definition

The concept of dependency relation discussed in Section 4.1 applies to FAG's and CAG's. For such grammars each production rule p has an associated dependency relation $D(p)$ on $Attr(p)$: an attribute occurrence a depends on a' iff p has a semantic rule of the form $a = t$, where a' occurs in t (or in the conditional part in the case of a conditional attribute grammar). The relations $D(p)$ determine the relation $D(T)$ for every parse tree T of the grammar, as explained in Section 4.1.

An operational semantics of attribute grammars should provide an algorithm for computing valid decoration of any given parse tree. Any parse tree T such that $D(T)$ is an ordering relation can be effectively decorated. In this case the value of any element in $Attr(T)$ can be expressed as a function of the minimal elements of $D(T)$. Thus any instantiation of these elements determines a valid decoration of the tree. Also in the case of conditional attribute grammar $D(T)$ gives a basis for computing a decoration, though in some cases the computation may fail. The dependency ordering characterizes all restrictions on the control of computations. The actual sequence of function calls must preserve this ordering. The nature of the semantic functions involved does not influence the sequencing. For studying sequencing problems we now introduce the notion of *attribute dependency scheme*. It can be seen as a "control component" of a functional attribute grammar, since it only describes an abstract dependency relation on the attribute occurrences within every parse tree.

Definition 4.5

An *attribute dependency scheme* (ADS) is a 4-tuple $\langle N, P, Attr, D \rangle$ such that:

- N is a finite set of nonterminal symbols.

- P is an N-sorted signature (thus defining a context-free grammar with empty set of terminal symbols and a set of parse trees).

- $Attr$ is a finite set of attributes. Each nonterminal X has associated a subset $Attr(X)$ of attributes.

- D is a mapping associating with every p in P a binary relation

$$D(p) \subset Attr(p) \times Attr(p)$$

$D(p)$ may be also considered as a graph with the set of vertices $Attr(p)$. This graph is called the *local dependency graph* of p.

□

For a given parse tree T the *global dependency graph* $D(T)$ is constructed by combining the local dependency graphs at all nodes of T. An ADS can be used as an abstraction of a FAG (or CAG).

Definition 4.6

Let G $\langle N, P, S, Attr, \mathcal{L}, \Phi, \mathcal{I} \rangle$ be a FAG and let $D(p)$ be the dependency relation associated in G with a production rule p. Then the ADS $\langle N, P, Attr, \{D(p)|p \in P\}\rangle$ is called the *associated* ADS of G.
□

An ADS can be also used for describing the control of a tree decoration process. In this case the underlying context-free grammar of the ADS is the same as for the FAG whose parse trees are to be decorated. However, the ADS ordering for each tree may be different from the dependency relation defined by the FAG: the dependencies should be observed but some independent attribute occurrences may be ordered by the ADS. Thus, in this case, the original dependency ordering of $Attr(T)$ for any parse tree T is a subset of the ADS-defined ordering.

We now introduce a classification of ADS's. It applies also to FAG's[4] : a FAG is said to be in a class C iff its associated ADS is in C. The classification gives a basis for the construction of algorithms for decoration of parse trees.

4.3.2   Dependency indicators

The dependency relations of ADS are associated with parse trees (including production rules as a special case of parse trees). As an auxiliary concept we will consider dependency relations on attributes of nonterminals. A natural idea is to project the transitive closure of the dependency relation of a tree on attribute positions of its root. Thus for a given parse tree T with the root $X \in N$ denote by $D_T(X)$ the transitive closure $D(T)^+$ restricted to $Attr(X)$ [5]. Since $Attr(X)$ is a finite set, the family of all such relations is finite. It will be denoted $D_0(X)$. We now introduce an auxiliary concept of dependency indicator.

Definition 4.7

Let G be an ADS. A *dependency indicator* R of G is any family of finite sets of relations $\{R(X)|X \in N\}$ such that each element of $R(X)$

---

[4]It applies also to CAG's, in which the condition is considered to be part of each attribute definition.
[5]The same relation will be sometimes denoted $D_0(T)^+$ in order to avoid explicit indication of the root nonterminal.

is a binary relation on $Attr(X)$.

□

An example of dependency indicator is the family $D_0 = \{D_0(X)|X \in N\}$.

Let R be a dependency indicator and let X' for some X in N be an occurrence of X in a parse tree T. Then $R(X')$ will denote an isomorphic copy of the graph $R(X)$. Such graphs can be combined by the usual operations to characterize relations on $Attr(X)$. We shall compare two dependency indicators R and R' by letting $R \preceq R'$ iff for every nonterminal X and relation r in $R(X)$ there exists r' in $R'(X)$ such that $r \subseteq r'$.

We are interested in dependency indicators that approximate the indicator D_0 in the sense that for every X they "cover" $D_0(X)$ according to the relation $\preceq$. Additionally it may be required that the local dependencies within a production rule combined with relations of the indicator and projected on the left-hand side of the rule do not add any dependencies. This requirement gives rise to the following definition:

Definition 4.8

Let R be a dependency indicator. R is said to be *closed* iff for any production rule p of the form $X_0 \rightarrow X_1 \ldots X_n$ and for any relations r_i in $R(X_i)$ there exists a relation r_0 in $R(X_0)$ such that

$$((D(p) \cup \bigcup_{i=1}^{n} r_i))^+|_{Attr(X_0)} \subseteq r_0$$

□

Thus It follows directly from the definition that D_0 is a closed dependency indicator. It also turns out that any closed dependency indicator is also an approximation of the indicator D_0.

Lemma 4.1

If R is a closed dependency indicator then for every X in N $D_0(X) \preceq R(X)$.

□

The lemma can be proved by structural induction on parse trees. One has to show that for any proof tree T with the root label X there exists a relation r in $R(X)$ such that the relation $D(T)^+$ restricted to the

attribute positions of the root of T is a subset of r. The base case
concerns the parse trees which are production rules with terminal bodies.
For such trees the conclusion follows directly from the definition of closed
dependency indicator. The induction step takes into consideration the
subtrees combined into a new parse tree by a production rule. The proof
is left as an exercise.

4.3.3   Non-circular ADS's

As already discussed, it is desirable that the dependency relation on
each parse tree of a FAG is a partial order. This guarantees existence of
a valid decoration. We now formulate this requirement as a property of
attribute dependency scheme.

Definition 4.9

An ADS is said to be *non-circular* iff, for every parse tree T, the graph
$D(T)$ has no cycle.
□

The same terminology applies to the functional attribute grammars
and to the conditional attribute grammars. Non-circular FAG's are
sometimes called *well-formed*. The question arises whether it is possible to test a given ADS for non-circularity.   The problem is decidable
but it has intrinsically exponential complexity [Jaz81]. Sometimes the
question may be answered by some sufficient conditions. Such conditions
may be given in terms of dependency indicators.

Definition 4.10

Let R be a dependency indicator. R is said to be *non-circular* iff for
any production rule p of the form $X_0 \rightarrow X_1 \ldots X_n$ and for any relations
r_i in $R(X_i)$ the graph

$$D(p) \cup \bigcup_{i=1}^{n} r_i$$

has no cycle.
□

Since closed dependency indicators approximate D_0 we obtain the
following result.

Lemma 4.2

An ADS $\langle N, P, Attr, D \rangle$ is non-circular iff D_0 is non-circular iff it has a closed and non-circular dependency indicator.
□

Proof. Notice first that an ADS is circular iff there exist a production rule p, and parse trees $T_l, ..., T_n$ such that the graph

$$D(p) \cup \bigcup_{i=1}^{n} D_0(T_i)$$

has cycles. Hence the ADS is non-circular iff D_0 is non-circular. But D_0 is non-circular iff the ADS has some non-circular and closed dependency indicator. If R is such an indicator then by Lemma 4.1 $D_0 \preceq R$. Thus D_0 is non-circular. On the other hand D_0 is closed, so if it is non-circular it is a dependency indicator with the required properties.
□

This lemma gives a basis for standard non-circularity tests described in the literature. The idea is that construction of some closed dependency indicators is relatively inexpensive. Clearly, if the constructed indicator is circular the grammar may still be non-circular. However, some indicators cover large classes of non-circular grammars. Many such classes have been defined in the literature. We now present some of them. The selection is restricted to classes used in some compiler construction systems.

4.3.4 Strongly non-circular ADS

The concept of dependency indicator has been introduced with the motivation to approximate D_0. Generally, in distinct parse trees the attributes of a given nonterminal X depend on each other in a different way. Therefore the elements $D_0(X)$ of the family D_0 are generally sets of relations. One can attempt to approximate $D_0(X)$'s by a single relation that includes all possible dependencies, thus to construct a closed dependency indicator with elements of the family being singleton sets. For some ADS's any such dependency indicator would be circular. But there is a large class of ADS's for which it is not the case. This leads to the following concept.

Definition 4.11

An attribute dependency scheme $A = \langle N, P, Attr, D \rangle$ is *strongly non-circular* iff there exists a closed and non-circular dependency indicator R of A such that $R(X)$ is a singleton for any X in N.
□

This definition originates from [CFZ82]. It is equivalent to another definition given in [KW76]. Testing for strong non-circularity can be done in polynomial time [CFZ82].

The class of strongly non-circular FAG's is interesting as it allows for construction of a conceptually simple algorithm for decoration of parse trees.

Let G be a strongly non-circular FAG and let R be its dependency indicator satisfying the conditions of Definition 4.11 . For a given synthesized attribute a of a nonterminal X denote by $Use(X, a)$ the set of inherited attributes of X on which a depends in the only relation $r(X)$ of $R(X)$. Thus $Use(X, a) = \{b | b \in Inh(X), (b, a) \in r(X)\}$. The set $Use(X, a)$ is sometimes called *argument selector* [CFZ82].

By the definition of R in every parse tree T with root X the actual dependency relation $D_T(X)$ on the attributes of the root is covered by $R(X)$. It follows that the value of any synthesized attribute a in the root of T is determined by T and by the values of the inherited attributes in $Use(X, a)$. The argument selectors $Use(X, a)$ are determined by R. The problem of decoration of any parse tree T can thus be described by a set of functions recursively defined over the structure of T, as shown by Courcelle and Franchi-Zannettacci [CFZ82]. Kennedy and Warren [KW76] gave an iterative version of an evaluator based on this idea. For decorating a tree T one has to keep only the tree, the synthesized attributes of its root and a stack containing in each element the values of the inherited attributes in $Use(X, a)$ for every synthesized a. The maximal height of the stack equals the height of T.

4.3.5   l-ordered ADS

An important class of ADS's is obtained by imposing a further restriction on strongly non-circular ADS's. In a strongly non-circular ADS each family $R(X)$ is a singleton $\{r(X)\}$ which defines a partial order on the attributes of X. The class of l-ordered ADS results from the additional requirement that the order is total. The intuition behind this condition is as follows. If $a \ r(X) \ b$ then a does not depend on b (i.e. there is no such parse tree T that $bD_T(X)a$). This means that for every node labeled X the value of a can be computed before the value of b. On the other hand, if c and d are incomparable in the ordering $r(X)$ it may happen that in some node labeled X, c depends on d and in some other node in the same or another parse tree d depends on c, so that it is not possible to have one fixed ordering of evaluation of these attributes (see Example 4.5). Such an ordering exists for l-ordered FAG's and allows to construct a deterministic algorithm that decorates the tree.

Definition 4.12

An attribute dependency scheme $G = \langle N, P, Attr, D \rangle$ is *l-ordered* iff there exists a closed and non-circular dependency indicator R of G such that $R(X)$ is a singleton and for all X in N the only relation $r(X)$ in $R(X)$ is a total order on $Attr(X)$.
□

It follows directly from the definition that every l-ordered ADS is also strongly non-circular. However, a strongly non-circular ADS need not be l-ordered.

Example 4.5

We give an example of a strongly non-circular ADS which is not l-ordered. The example ADS is defined in Figure 4.6.

The dependency indicator $R(Z) = \{\lambda\}, R(X) = \{r(X)\}$, where λ is the empty relation and $r(X) = \{(a, c), (b, d)\}$ has the properties required by the strong non-circularity. Notice that $R=D_0$. Thus, if the ADS is l-ordered then the relations of the corresponding indicator must preserve the partial orders defined by R. However, any total ordering on $Attr(X)$ preserving $r(X)$ causes a circularity.
□

4.3.6 Attribute evaluation by tree walk

We now present a general nondeterministic algorithm that decorates a given parse tree. The algorithm is applicable to any non-circular FAG. We then specialize it in various ways and we get as a result various sub-categories of l-ordered AGs. Up to now these classes have given rise to the largest number of implementations. In addition to that, some sub-categories seem to play an interesting role from a theoretical point of view.

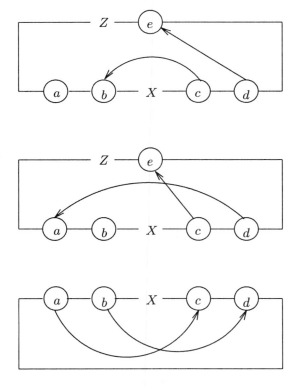

Figure 4.6
A strongly non-circular ADS which is not l-ordered (Example 4.5)

The general algorithm is called *pure-visit* algorithm as it is based
on the idea of visiting nodes of a parse tree to evaluate their attribute
occurrences. The algorithm is presented as introduced by Filé [Fil83].
The notation used refers to the notion of abstract parse tree where the
nodes are labeled by the production rules.

Algorithm

1. **procedure** visit-and-evaluate(u)
   { u is the current node of tree T, labeled $X \rightarrow X_1 \ldots X_n$ }

2. **begin** $C(u) := C(u) + 1$
   { C is a counter associated to each node u, initialized to 0 }

3. compute some inherited attributes of X_u

4. choose a sequence $v = \langle v_1, v_2, ..., v_m \rangle$ such that $m \geq 0$
   and $v_j \in [1..n]$ for $1 \leq j \leq m$

5. **for** $j := 1$ **to** m **do** visit-and-evaluate(v_j-th child of u)

6. compute some synthesized attributes of X_u
   end visit-and-evaluate

7. **procedure** evaluate(T)
   { T is the tree to decorate}

8. **begin** initialize all the counters to 0

9. guess k_0 { $k_0 \geq 1$ }

10. **while** $C(root(T)) \leq k_0$ **do** visit-and-evaluate($root(T)$)
    end evaluate

It is important to note in which sense the procedure *evaluate* is nondeterministic. It describes a way of visiting a tree T and recursively
calls the procedure *visit-and-evaluate* at nodes of the tree. Each time a
node is visited, the counter associated to this node is incremented (line
2) and some inherited attributes (maybe none) are chosen and evaluated
(line 3). The choice is not defined here and this is one of the reasons
for the nondeterministic nature of the algorithm. Then a finite sequence
(possibly with repetitions) of children of node u is chosen (line 4). It is
called a visit-sequence. Procedure *visit-and-evaluate* is then recursively

invoked for each node in the visit-sequence following the order specified by the sequence (line 5). Upon return some synthesized attributes
(maybe none) of node u are chosen and evaluated (line 6). The main
procedure *evaluate* is easy to understand. After successful termination
of *evaluate*(T), the visit-counter $C(u)$ of every node u of T contains the
number of calls to *visit-and-evaluate (u)* that have been executed during
the computation. Each such call is in fact the beginning of a visit of the
subtree issued from u. Therefore, we say that the call to *evaluate*(T) is
k-visit ($k \geq 1$) if, after the computation, the visit-counter of each node
is at most k (with $k_0 \leq k$).

A computation of *evaluate*(T) may fail before evaluating all attribute
occurrences if one chooses to evaluate some attribute that depends on
not yet evaluated attributes. If this does not happen and the computation stops after evaluating all attributes of the tree T, it is said to be
complete.

Now we present a classification of attribute grammars based on the
way of restricting the nondeterminism inside the algorithm. As pointed
out in [Fil83], there are basically two kinds of nondeterminism:

- Nondeterminism of *type a*: at each visit to a node u, attributes to be
evaluated are chosen arbitrarily (lines 3 and 6).

- Nondeterminism of *type b*: at each node labeled p, the visit-sequence is
chosen arbitrarily (line 4).

Now we introduce the following classification of possible algorithms
derived from the presented scheme:

- *Pure* algorithms with unrestricted nondeterminism of type a,

- *Simple* algorithms which are deterministic.

We consider first the pure algorithms. Several ways of removing the
nondeterminism of type b have been suggested:

- visiting once all children in the order of their occurrence in the production rule; the algorithms using this strategy are called $L - pass$ algorithms.

- visiting once all children in the order reverse to their occurrence in the
production rule; the algorithms using this strategy are called $R - pass$
algorithms.

- visiting once all children in the order of their occurrence in the production rule or in the reverse order, depending on the count of the visit; the algorithms using this strategy are called *alternating-pass* (or *alt*) algorithms.

- visiting once all children in an order which is a permutation of their occurrence in the production rule; the algorithms using this strategy are called *sweep* algorithms.

The algorithms with unrestricted nondeterminism of type b are called *visit* algorithms.

The class of simple algorithms removes also the nondeterminism of type a. This is done by introducing a partition on attributes of each nonterminal. For a nonterminal X a partition is a family $A_l(X)$ for $l = 1, \ldots, k$ of disjoint sets of attributes such that the union of all sets is $Attr(X)$. The partition defines which attributes should be evaluated during the consecutive visits of a node u labeled by a production rule with head X. In concrete terms this means that lines 3 and 6 of the algorithm are replaced by:

compute the inherited attributes of $A_{C(u)}(X)$
compute the synthesized attributes of $A_{C(u)}(X)$.

For the simple $L - pass$ and $R - pass$ algorithms no further changes are introduced. For the other kinds of visiting strategies one has to be specific about the way of alternating or selecting the permutation. Generally, we may assume that a function v is given that for every production rule p of the grammar and for every natural number determines the visit sequence for the nodes of p. The line 4 of the algorithm is then to be replaced by:

take the visit-sequence $v(p, C(u))$.

We outlined a number of suggestions for specializing the given algorithm. To summarize, we will call the outlined specializations X-k-Y algorithms, where:

- $X \in \{simple, \ pure\}$.

- $k = 1, 2, \ldots$ denotes the maximal allowed number of visits in a node. Unrestricted k is denoted as *multi*.

- $Y \in \{visit, \ sweep, \ alt, \ L\text{-}pass, \ R\text{-}pass\}$.

This allows for classification of attribute grammars.

Definition 4.13

An attribute grammar is $X - k - Y$ iff for any tree T, the computation of $evaluate(T)$ with strategy $X - k - Y$ is complete.

An attribute grammar is $X - \text{multi} - Y$ iff there exists some k such that it is $X - k - Y$.

$\square$

It is clear that any well-formed FAG is pure-multi-visit, since by an appropriate choice of the attributes to evaluate and of the order of the visits to the nodes there exists an integer k (equal to the maximum number of attributes associated to a nonterminal symbol) such that the pure-k-visit strategy is complete.

It may be proved that the class of simple-multi-visit FAG's is exactly the class of l-ordered FAG's.

In order to illustrate how the classification should be used, for modifying the basic algorithm we give the algorithms for simple-k-sweep and pure-k-alt grammars.

Simple-k-sweep evaluation

Each node is visited at most k times. A partition over the attributes $A_i(X) \subset Attr(X)$ for $1 \leq i \leq k$ is given. In each production $p \in P$, k permutations on the right hand side non-terminal symbols are defined for each visit; let v_i^p be the i-th permutation for $1 \leq i \leq k$.

procedure Simple-sweep-evaluate(u)
{ u is the current node of tree T, labeled by $p : X \rightarrow X_1 \ldots X_n$ }
{ i is a global variable }
begin
compute the inherited attributes in $A_i(X)$
for $j := 1$ **to** n **do** Simple-sweep-evaluate($v_i^p(j)$-th child of u)
compute the synthesized attributes in $A_i(X)$
end Simple-sweep-evaluate

procedure evaluate(T)
{ T is the tree to decorate }
begin
for $i := 1$ **to** k **do** Simple-sweep-evaluate($root(T)$)
end evaluate;

This algorithm performs k walks over the tree in an order depending on the production and the visit number.

In the case of a Simple-k-L-pass strategy, there are k top-down left-to-right walks.

Pure-k-alt evaluation

The only restriction is the following one: v_i^p tells whether the right hand side nonterminals of production p are processed in a left-to-right order (L) or a right-to-left one (R).

procedure Pure-alt-evaluate(u)
{ u is the current node of tree T, labeled by $p : X \rightarrow X_1 \dots X_n$ }
{ i is a global variable }
begin
compute some inherited attributes of X_u
for $j := 1$ **to** n **do** Pure-alt-evaluate($v_i^p(j)$-th child of u)
compute some synthesized attributes of X_u
end Pure-alt-evaluate

procedure evaluate(T)
{ T is the tree to decorate }
begin
for $i := 1$ **to** k **do** Pure-alt-evaluate($root(T)$)
end evaluate;

4.3.7   One-sweep ADS's and simple-one-sweep evaluation

The class of simple-one-sweep FAG's seems to be particularly important. As shown in [CD88] it has the ability to model program schemes. In the sequel we also discuss its relevance for logic programming. The attribute dependency scheme of a simple-one-sweep FAG is called *one-sweep* ADS. Indeed the notion "simple" in the context of ADS is meaningless since no attribute evaluation takes place for ADS. It would be desirable to give a characterization of one-sweep ADS's in terms of the dependency relation. This can be done in a very simple way. Let A be an ADS in the normal form and let D_1 be the dependency indicator such that $D_1(X) = Inh(X) \times Syn(X)$. Notice that D_1 is necessarily closed by the normal form hypothesis:

Lemma 4.3

An attribute dependency scheme ADS in normal form is one-sweep (equivalently one-visit) iff its dependency indicator D_1 is non-circular.
□

The proof can be found in [Cou84].

A subclass of one-sweep ADS's that deserves special attention is the class of L-ADS's. The corresponding class of attribute grammars is called L-*attribute grammars*, or in our terminology, L-*functional attribute grammars*. According to the terminology of the previous section these are the ADS's of the simple-1-L-pass FAG's. They can be also characterized in the following way. Let A be an ADS and let p be its production rule of the profile $\langle X_1 \ldots X_n, X_0 \rangle$. Consider the relation $D(p)$ on $Attr(p)$. The ADS is an L-ADS iff for every p and for any $a \in X_i$ and $a' \in X_j$ such that $aD(p)a'$ either $i < j$ or $a' \in Syn(X_j)$ and $j = 0$. Thus an L-ADS is an ADS such that dependencies between attributes of different nodes of a production rule go always "from left to right" with possible exception of the synthesized attributes of the head, which may depend on some attributes of the body.

A special attention must be paid to the evaluators of L-FAG's. For obvious efficiency reasons (the number of visits is known and equal to 1), numerous systems have been and still are built for this category: MUG1 [WRC+76], HLP84 [KNPS86], RIE [SISN85] among others. They have a practical and theoretical interest as, in this case, attributes evaluation can be done during parse tree construction. Although the existing systems are essentially devoted to compiler construction, in view of the relations between attribute grammars and logic programs discussed in Chapter 5 the attribute evaluation algorithm for L-FAG's can be adopted for implementation of logic programs.

4.3.8   Classification of the attribute dependency schemes

The two following figures extracted from [DJL88] may help to understand the relationships between the different categories of attribute dependency schemes. In the Figure 4.7 a classification of ADS's (holding for FAG's and CAG's) based on the tree walk evaluation algorithms is shown [6]. The arrows indicate strict inclusion of the classes.

Figure 4.8 shows a simplified classification of ADS's (holding also for FAG's and CAG's) discussed in this chapter. Every class is represented by a node of the graph. The additional label of every node shows the worst case complexity of the decision procedure testing whether a given ADS belongs to the class.

---

[6]The classification, borrowed from [DJL88], is made for functional attribute grammars. But the categories are defined by the local dependencies only, hence the classification is the same for attribute dependency schemes.

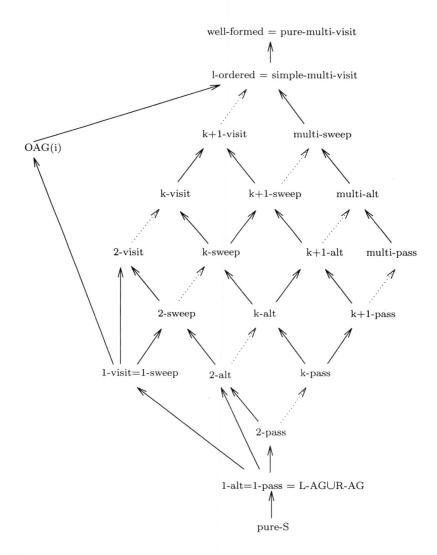

Figure 4.7
Classification of ADS's based on tree walks

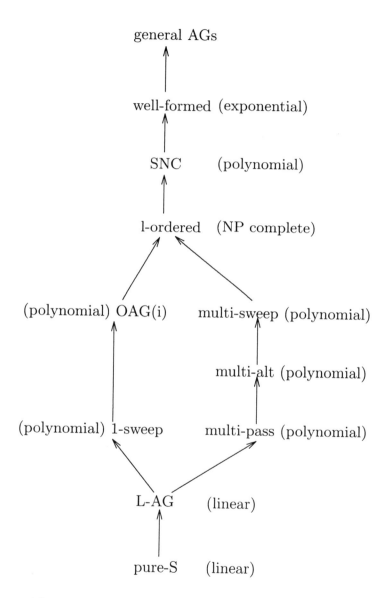

Figure 4.8
General classification of ADS's, and test complexity

4.4   Proof methods for partial correctness

This section introduces a notion of specification of attribute grammar and defines a concept of correctness of an attribute grammar with respect to a specification. A proof method allowing to establish the correctness of an attribute grammar w.r.t. a specification is presented and proved sound. The method is also complete in an abstract sense. The completeness result presented is analogous to the theorem of De Bakker and Meertens [BM75] stating the completeness of the inductive assertion method for flowcharts. However, if the specification language is a first-order language then the incompleteness result of Wand [Wan78] extends to our proof method. The method is thus extended to prove properties holding inside some particular decorated parse trees.

4.4.1   Specifications

We now give formal definitions of the notions related to specifications of relational attribute grammars.

A relational attribute grammar uses a logical language and an interpretation. The semantics associates with each nonterminal X of the grammar the relation R_X over the domain(s) of the interpretation, defined at the end Section 4.2.1. The semantics of a grammar may or may not coincide with the intentions of its designer. We now introduce a notion of specification of attribute grammar. A specification allows for independent definition of the relations which are to be associated with the nonterminals by the semantics of the attribute grammar. A specification is a family S of logical formulae indexed by nonterminals of the grammar. The free variables of each formula S_X are attributes of nonterminal X. The logical language of the specification includes the language used in the specified attribute grammar. It has an interpretation which is an extension of its interpretation.

Consider a valuation of the free variables of the specification formula S_X associated with a nonterminal X. Assuming some ordering of attributes such a valuation can be represented as a tuple of values. The set of all valuations satisfying S_X is a relation Q_X on the domain(s) of the interpretation.

Definition 4.14

A *specification* for a relational attribute grammar with language $\mathcal{L}$

and interpretation $\mathcal{I}$ is a family $S = \{S_X\}_{X \in N}$ of formulae in a logical language $\mathcal{L}'$ [7] with interpretation $\mathcal{I}'$ such that for each non terminal X the free variables of S_X are in the set $Attr(X)$.

We will assume that $\mathcal{L}'$ includes $\mathcal{L}$ and that $\mathcal{I}'$ is an extension of $\mathcal{I}$. Therefore, if no confusion arises, we will only refer to one language and one interpretation, denoted usually $\mathcal{L}$ and $\mathcal{I}$.

□

The notation $S_X(a_1, ..., a_m)$ will be used to indicate that a nonterminal X has the attributes $\{a_1, ..., a_m\}$. We will also need renamed variants of specification formulae: for u being a node of a parse tree of G labeled by a nonterminal X we denote by $S_X(u)$ the formula obtained from S_X by replacing each attribute a_i by the attribute occurrence $a_i(u)$. Notice that the attribute occurrences play the role of variables, while the tree assignments of Definition 4.3 p. 150 are valuations. As mentioned above S_X defines the relation Q_X consisting of all tuples $\langle d_1, ..., d_m \rangle$ such that $\mathcal{I} \models S_X(d_1, ..., d_m)$.

A specification describes a required property of the attribute grammar. The grammar may or may not have this property. In the first case the grammar will be called (partially) correct with respect to the specification. The notion can be formalized by the following definition.

Definition 4.15

A relational attribute grammar G is *correct* with respect to a specification S iff for every nonterminal X the relation R_X defined by G is a subset of the relation Q_X defined by S.

□

A specification S of G such that G is correct with respect to S will be called a *valid* specification of G. Note that the relations specified by S may include tuples which are not present in the actual semantics of the attribute grammar. Thus, the notion introduced is essentially *partial correctness* and says nothing about non-emptiness of the relations R_X.

The concept of correctness can be equivalently reformulated by referring to the interpretation $\mathcal{I}$ of the specification language. As mentioned above this interpretation is an extension of the interpretation defined by the attribute grammar.

An attribute grammar G is *correct* w.r.t. the specification $\langle S, \mathcal{I} \rangle$ iff

---

[7] not necessarily first order.

for every parse tree T of G and for every valid T-assignment ν,

$$(\mathcal{I}, \nu) \models S_X(r)$$

where r is the root of T and X is the nonterminal labelling the root.

The equivalence of both formulations follows by the definitions of the relations R_X and Q_X.

The notion of correctness refers to the roots of all valid trees of the attribute grammar. However, every internal node of a valid tree is the root of a subtree which itself must be a valid tree. Hence

Proposition 4.1

If $\langle S, \mathcal{I} \rangle$ is a specification valid for an attribute grammar G then, for every parse tree T of G, for every valid T-assignment ν and for every node u of T

$$(\mathcal{I}, \nu) \models S_X(u)$$

where X is the nonterminal of the node u.
□

As mentioned above, a specification describes some required properties of the attribute grammar. The properties described by different specifications can be formally compared.

Definition 4.16

Let $\langle S, \mathcal{I} \rangle$ and $\langle S', \mathcal{I} \rangle$ be specifications for a relational attribute grammar G. S is said to be *weaker* than S' iff for all nonterminals X of G,

$$\mathcal{I} \models (S'_X \to S_X)$$

This will be denoted by $S' \to S$ in $\mathcal{I}$.

If S is weaker than S' then S' is said to be *stronger* than S.
□

Note that if S is valid for G and $S \to S'$ then S' is valid for G. The specification $TRUE$ with every formula identical to *true* is always valid for G in a trivial way. It is the weakest valid specification for G. If the specification language is sufficiently expressible, there may exist a specification S_G that describes exactly the relations determined by G, i.e. such that $R_X = Q_X$ for every nonterminal X of G. Clearly, S_G is then a strongest valid specification for G.

4.4.2   Structural induction on decorated trees

We now formulate a method for proving correctness of an attribute grammar with respect to a given specification. We restrict our discussion to relational attribute grammars since other kinds of attribute grammars can be considered subclasses of this general category. The relations associated with a relational attribute grammar are defined in terms of valid trees. For a grammar to be correct the root label of each valid tree must be in the corresponding relation defined by the specification. Call such a tree a correct valid tree. The production rules of the underlying grammar can be considered operations on valid trees. To prove correctness of a relational attribute grammar with respect to a given specification it suffices to show that every production rule applied to correct valid trees can only produce a correct valid tree. To formalize this intuition we introduce a notion of *inductive* specification.

Definition 4.17 Inductive specification

Let G be a relational attribute grammar. A specification $\langle S, \mathcal{I} \rangle$ for G is said to be *inductive* with respect to G if, for any production rule p

$$\mathcal{I} \models \Phi_p \wedge S_{X_1}(1) \wedge \ldots \wedge S_{X_n}(n) \rightarrow S_{X_0}(0)$$

where $\langle X_1 \ldots X_n, X_0 \rangle$ is the profile of p.
□

Intuitively, a specification is inductive with respect to G iff any production rule of G applied to valid trees correct with respect to the specification can only construct a valid tree which is also correct. The definition captures this intuition by referring to the semantic rule Φ_p: if the attribute values of p satisfy the semantic rule and the attributes of the right-hand side nonterminals of p (i.e. the root attributes of the valid trees to be combined) satisfy the specification formulae S_{X_i} then the attributes of the left-hand side (i.e. the attributes of the root of the resulting tree) should satisfy the specification formula S_{X_0}. The following proposition shows that the notion of inductive specification may be used in correctness proofs.

Proposition 4.2

If a specification S is inductive with respect to a relational attribute

grammar G then S is valid for G.
□

Validity of the specification can be proved by structural induction on the structure of the decorated trees, considering simultaneously trees with roots labeled by different nonterminals.

A specification may be valid without being inductive as shown by the following example.

Example 4.6
The attribute grammar is defined as follows:
$N = \{X, Y\}$
$P = \{p:\ X \rightarrow Y,\ q:\ Y \rightarrow \varepsilon\}$
$Attr(X) = \{a\}$
$Attr(Y) = \{b\}$
$\Phi_p:\ a(0) = b(1)$
$\Phi_q:\ b(0) = 0$
$\mathcal{I}$ is the interpretation $\mathcal{N}$ on the domain of natural numbers.
Let S be the specification defined as follows:
$S_X:\ a = 0$
$S_Y:\ true$
The specification S is valid but it is not inductive since the following does not hold in $\mathcal{N}$ (rule p):

$$\forall a(0), b(1)[a(0) = b(1) \land true \rightarrow a(0) = 0]$$

□

Proposition 4.3
If S is a strongest valid specification for G then S is inductive.
□

Proof. Let p be a production rule of G with the profile $\langle X_1 ... X_n, X_0 \rangle$ and let ν be any attribute assignment of p. We have to show that

$$(\mathcal{I}, \nu) \models \Phi_p \land S_{X_1}(1) \land ... \land S_{X_n}(n) \rightarrow S_{X_0}(0)$$

Assume that the premise of the implication holds. Since S is a strongest specification, for each $i = 1, ..., n$ the assumption that $S_{X_i}(i)$

holds implies that there exists a tree T_i and a valid T_i-assignment ν_i such that $\nu_i(a(r_i)) = \nu(a(i))$ for all a in $Attr(X_i)$, where r_i is the root of T_i. We now use the production rule p to combine the trees T_i into a new tree T. Thus, every node u_i of the tree T_i for $i = 1, \ldots, n$ becomes now a node u'_i of T. The root r of T will be labeled X_0. Let ν' be the T-assignment such that $\nu'(a(r)) = \nu(a(r))$ for a in $Attr(X_0)$ and $\nu'(a(u'_i)) = \nu_i(a(u_i))$ for all attribute occurrences $a(u_i)$ in the tree T_i. Since ν satisfies Φ_p, ν' satisfies Φ_T. Thus, since S is a strongest valid specification of G, ν' (and ν) satisfy $S_{X_0}(r)$. Hence S is inductive.
□

By the results presented above we obtain immediately the following theorem.

Theorem 4.1
Let G be a relational attribute grammar. A specification S for G is valid iff it is weaker than some inductive specification S'.
□

The "if" part of the theorem follows from Proposition 4.2 and Definition 4.16 . The theorem allows us to prove correctness of a grammar G with respect to a specification S in the following way:

1. define a specification S',

2. prove that S' is inductive,

3. prove that S is weaker than S'.

The "if" part of the theorem gives soundness of this method.

The "only if" part of the theorem follows from Proposition 4.3 . It can be seen as a completeness theorem for the proof method in the case of the specification language expressible enough to give a strongest specification for any attribute grammar in the considered class.

We now illustrate the use of the method.

Example 4.7
It is not difficult to prove the correctness of Katayama-Hoshino's attribute grammar of Example 4.4 p. 153 with respect to the specification (on $\mathcal{N}$):
$S_X : \exists n \; k = 4 \times n$
$S_Y : \exists n (g = f + 2 \times n \wedge k = h + 2 \times n)$

In this case the method reduces to showing that the specification is inductive. This amounts to checking some conditions for every production rule of the grammar.

For example, for $p1 : X \rightarrow Y$ one has to check that
$\exists n\ k(X) = 4 \times n$
using the assumption
$\exists n(g(Y) = f(Y) + 2 \times n \wedge k(Y) = h(Y) + 2 \times n)$
and the semantic rule
$k(X) = k(Y) \wedge f(Y) = 0 \wedge h(Y) = g(Y)$.
By applying the semantic rule to the assumption we obtain at once:
$\exists n(g(Y) = 0 + 2 \times n \wedge k(X) = g(Y) + 2 \times n)$
hence
$\exists n\ k(X) = 2 \times n + 2 \times n$
thus
$\exists n\ k(X) = 4 \times n$.
Similarly one can check the conditions for $p2$ and $p3$.
□

We complete this section with one more example.

Example 4.8 Factorial

We prove that the "factorial" grammar of Example 4.3   p. 151 is correct with respect to the specification:

S_{fac}: $a \geq 0 \wedge v = a!$

Φ is defined as follows:

- in $r_1 : fac \rightarrow \varepsilon$, Φ_{r_1}: $a(0) = 0 \wedge v(0) = 1$.
- in $r_2 : fac \rightarrow fac$, Φ_{r_2}: $a(1) = a(0) - 1 \wedge v(0) = v(1) * a(0)$.

We show that S_{fac} is inductive, hence valid. We check the conditions for every rule.

The condition for r_1 is:
$a(0) = 0 \wedge v(0) = 1 \rightarrow a(0) \geq 0 \wedge v(0) = a(0)!$
It holds in $\mathcal{N}$ since $0 \geq 0$ and $1 = 0!$ as ! is interpreted as the factorial.

The condition for r_2 is as follows:

$((a(1) \geq 0 \wedge v(1) = a(1)! \wedge a(1) = a(0) - 1 \wedge v(0) = v(1) * a(0)) \rightarrow$
$a(0) \geq 0 \wedge v(0) = a(0)!$

Elimination of attribute occurrences and simplification gives the following condition, which is true in $\mathcal{N}$:

$a(0) > 0 \rightarrow (a(0) \geq 0 \wedge (a(0) - 1)! * a(0) = a(0)!)$

Notice that the specification:

$a \geq 0 \rightarrow v > 0$ is also (trivially) valid, because the conclusion is a consequence of the valid specification S_{fac}. However, this specification is not inductive, since the corresponding verification condition for rule r_2 does not hold.

□

4.4.3   The annotation method

The practical usability of the proof method of Theorem 4.1 suffers from its theoretical simplicity. The inductive specification S' to be found to prove the validity of some given specification S will usually consist of complex formulae, since there will be only one formula S_X for each nonterminal X. In this section we discuss a technique for structuring specifications. For a nonterminal X of the grammar we want to represent the specification S_X as a formula $\bigwedge A \rightarrow \bigwedge B$ where A and B are finite sets of formulae, to be called *assertions*. The formulae in A will be considered as inherited attributes of X and those in B as synthesized ones within a certain attribute dependency scheme. The underlying grammar of the scheme originates from the relational attribute grammar whose specification is provided by the assertions. For a decorated tree of this grammar the attribute values provide valuation for the occurrences of the assertions.

A formula $\bigwedge A \rightarrow \bigwedge B$ of the specification reflects the fact that the synthesized attributes of a node depend on the inherited ones (via the subtree issued from the node). For each production rule we will have a local dependency scheme. The dependency is to be interpreted as implication.

The idea of the annotation proof method is as follows. For each assertion of a production rule show that its truth follows from the truth of all assertions on which it locally depends. Since the number of production rules and attributes is finite, the number of such proofs is also finite. If the attribute dependency scheme is non-circular, existence of all these local proofs guarantees validity of the specification.

The idea presented seems to be particularly well suited for functional attribute grammars. For such grammars structuring of specifications is facilitated by the functional nature of the semantic rules.

We now give a formal presentation of the method. We first introduce an auxiliary concept which will be used to define structured specifications of attribute grammars.

Definition 4.18 Annotation

Let $G = \langle N, P, S, Attr, \mathcal{L}, \Phi, \mathcal{I} \rangle$ be a relational attribute grammar. An *annotation* of G is a mapping Δ assigning to every X in N two finite sets $\Delta_I(X)$ and $\Delta_S(X)$ of formulae in a language $\mathcal{L}'$ with interpretation $\mathcal{I}'$ and such that any free variable of a formula in one of these sets is an attribute of X.

It is assumed that $\mathcal{L}'$ includes $\mathcal{L}$ and that $\mathcal{I}'$ is an extension of $\mathcal{I}$. Therefore, if no confusion arises we will only refer to one language and one interpretation, denoted usually $\mathcal{L}$ and $\mathcal{I}$.
□

The elements of $\Delta_I(X)$ will be called *inherited assertions* of X. The elements of $\Delta_S(X)$ will be called *synthesized assertions* of X. An *assertion* of Δ is an inherited assertion or a synthesized assertion of some nonterminal of G. The set of all assertions of Δ will be denoted A_Δ. An annotation is introduced to determine a specification.

Definition 4.19

For a given annotation Δ the formula
$$\bigwedge \Delta_I(X) \to \bigwedge \Delta_S(X)$$
is called the *specification associated* with Δ and is denoted S_Δ.
□

Every specification $\langle S, \mathcal{I} \rangle$ can be seen as the specification associated with the purely synthesized annotation $\langle \Delta, \mathcal{I} \rangle$ such that for every nonterminal X, $\Delta_I(X) = \vee$ and $\Delta_S(X) = \{S_X\}$.

We shall now give sufficient conditions ensuring the validity of an annotation. The intuition behind these conditions is to formalize the proof technique outlined above.

We first introduce a notion of logical dependency scheme for a given annotation Δ. Let ϕ be an assertion associated by Δ with a nonterminal X. For an occurrence of X in a node n of a parse tree T we denote by

$\phi(n)$ the instance of ϕ obtained by replacing each free variable x of ϕ by a new variable $x(n)$. The set of all such instances will be denoted $\Delta(T)$. For a production rule p of the profile $\langle X_1 \ldots X_m, X_0 \rangle$ denote by $\Delta(p)$ the set of all instances of the assertions of X_i, $i = 0, \ldots, n$. The instances of the inherited assertions of X_0 and the instances of the synthesized assertions of each X_i for $i > 0$ are called the *input* assertions of $\Delta(p)$. The remaining assertion instances are called the *output* assertions of $\Delta(p)$. $\Delta(n)$ denotes the set of asertions $\phi(n)$ at node n^8.

Definition 4.20 Logical dependency scheme

Let Δ be an annotation for a relational attribute grammar G with nonterminals N and production rules P. Let D be a mapping associating with each production rule p a binary relation D_p on $\Delta(p)$ such that if $\langle \phi, \gamma \rangle$ is in D_p then ϕ is an input assertion of $\Delta(p)$ and γ is an output assertion of $\Delta(p)$. The quadruple $\langle N, P, \Delta, D \rangle$, is called a *logical dependency scheme* (LDS) for G and Δ.
□

Clearly, a logical dependency scheme can be seen as an attribute dependency scheme. The intention is to find a logical dependency scheme that gives a structure of a validity proof of the specification associated with a given annotation Δ. This is stated formally by the following definition.

Definition 4.21 Soundness of an annotation for a LDS

Let Δ be an annotation of a relational attribute grammar $G = \langle N, P, S, Attr, \mathcal{L}, \Phi, \mathcal{I} \rangle$ and let $L = \langle N, P, \Delta, D \rangle$ be a logical dependency scheme for G and Δ. The annotation Δ is said to be *sound* for L iff for every $p \in P$ and for every output assertion ψ of p

$$\mathcal{I} \models (\bigwedge_{\delta \in D_p^{-1}(\psi)} \delta \wedge \Phi_p) \rightarrow \psi$$

□

Thus an annotation is sound iff every output assertion follows from the assertions on which it depends by the semantic rules of the attribute grammar. To check soundness of a given annotation for a given dependency scheme one has to prove a finite number of implications: one

---

[8] $\Delta(n) = \Delta_X(n)$ where X is the label of the node n.

implication for each output assertion of every production rule. The following theorem shows that soundness of the annotation together with non-circularity of the logical dependency scheme is sufficient for validity of the specification associated with the annotation.

Proposition 4.4 Validity condition of an annotation

Let Δ be an annotation of a relational attribute grammar $G = \langle N, P, S, Attr, \mathcal{L}, \Phi, \mathcal{I} \rangle$ and let $L = \langle N, P, \Delta, D \rangle$ be a logical dependency scheme for G and Δ. If Δ is sound for L and L is non-circular, then S_Δ is valid.
□

Proof. Let T be an arbitrary parse tree of G and let ν be a valid T-assignment. To show that the specification S_Δ is valid it is sufficient to prove that for every assertion $\phi \in \Delta(T)$, $(\mathcal{I}, \nu) \models \phi$.

As L is a non-circular dependency scheme, $D(T)$ is an ordering relation on $\Delta(T)$. For a given assertion ϕ in $\Delta(T)$ let rank r of ϕ be the largest number such that there exists a path of length r connecting ϕ with a minimal element of $\Delta(T)$ in this ordering. Now we prove that $(\mathcal{I}, \nu) \models \phi$ by induction on the rank. An assertion ϕ of rank 0 either occurs in an output position of a rule or in the input positions of the root of the parse tree. In the former case it does not depend on any other assertion; in the later it is one of the assertion in the hypotheses of S_Δ. Thus, in the tree T there is exactly one occurrence of a production rule where ϕ is an output assertion. Hence by soundness of the dependency scheme $(\mathcal{I}, \nu) \models \phi$.

Now assume that for every assertion ϕ in $\Delta(T)$ such that rank of ϕ does not exceed n, $(\mathcal{I}, \nu) \models \phi$. Consider an assertion ψ of rank $n+1$. Let $\psi_1, \ldots, \psi_k$ be all assertions on which ψ directly depends in T. Clearly, each of them is of the rank not exceeding n. On the other hand both ψ and $\psi_1, \ldots, \psi_k$ are assertions of neighboring nodes of T. Thus, there exists a production rule p of G such that ψ and $\psi_1, \ldots, \psi_k$ are assertions of an occurrence of p in T. Hence, by soundness of Δ and by induction hypothesis $(\mathcal{I}, \nu) \models \phi$.
□

The theorem justifies the following method for specifying relational attribute grammars and proving validity of the specifications:

- Give specification S of a grammar G in the form of annotation Δ, thus $S_X = \bigwedge \Delta_I(X) \rightarrow \bigwedge \Delta_S(X)$.
- For each production rule p of G define a logical dependency relation D on $\Delta(p)$; in this way an attribute dependency scheme L is defined on the context-free grammar of G.
- Prove soundness of Δ; in other words for each production rule prove a finite number of implications which are constructed from the assertions of the denotation according to the dependency relation D.
- Prove non-circularity of the logical dependency scheme.

The inductive specification method is a special case of the annotation method, where the annotation is reduced to a single synthesized assertion associated with each nonterminal and the logical dependency scheme is purely synthesized. Using the strongest specification with a purely synthesized LDS, one gets the completeness of the method.

Theorem 4.2

Let G be a relational attribute grammar. A specification S for G is valid if and only if there exists an annotation Δ and a non-circular LDS L for Δ such that :

- Δ is sound for L,
- S_Δ is weaker than S.

□

We now illustrate the use of annotation method.

Example 4.9

We reconsider the Katayama-Hoshino's example (Example 4.4 p. 153) using the annotation method.

The intention is to prove that in every complete parse tree of the grammar the decoration of the root is a multiple of 4, i.e. we want to prove validity of the specification of Example 4.7 p. 179 $S_X : \exists n \ k = 4 \times n$.

We do that using the following annotation interpreted on $\mathcal{N}$:

$$\Delta = \{\alpha, \beta, \gamma, \delta\}$$
$$\Delta_I(X) = \{\}, \Delta_S(X) = \{\delta\}$$

$\Delta_I(Y) = \{\beta\}, \Delta_S(Y) = \{\alpha, \gamma\}$
$\alpha : \exists n \ g = f + 2 \times n$
$\beta : h = 2 \times f + g$
$\gamma : k = f + 2 \times g$
$\delta : \exists n \ k = 4 \times n$

and the logical dependency relation D is given by the diagrams in Figure 7.5 p. 356 with X as $fourmultiple$ and Y as p.

The specification determined by the annotation is:

$S_{\Delta X} : \exists n \ k = 4 \times n$
$S_{\Delta Y} : h = 2 \times f + g \rightarrow (\exists n \ g = f + 2 \times n \wedge k = f + 2 \times g)$

While the specification for X is as required, the specification for Y is quite complicated and gives no intuition about the nature of the grammar.

We illustrate the proof of soundness of Δ by proving the implication $(\Phi_{X \rightarrow Y} \wedge \gamma \wedge \alpha) \rightarrow \delta$. By the semantic rule (see Example 4.4 p. 153) $\Phi_{X \rightarrow Y}$ we have: $f(Y) = 0$ and $k(X) = k(Y)$. Hence, using γ and α we obtain: $k(Y) = f(Y) + 2 \times g(Y) = 2 \times g(Y)$. Consequently, $\exists n \ g(Y) = f(Y) + 2 \times n$ hence $\exists n \ g(Y) = 2 \times n$. Thus $\exists n \ k(Y) = 2 \times 2 \times n$, hence $\exists n \ k(X) = 4 \times n$. Since the last formula is δ at X, we proved the implication. The rest of the proof of soundness of Δ is left as an exercise. Since the dependency scheme is obviously non-circular the specification S_Δ is valid for the example grammar.
□

The annotation proof method will be adapted to the case of definite programs and illustrated by more examples in Chapters 6 and 7.

4.5   Proof methods for decorated parse trees

In the previous section annotations were introduced as a tool for structuring correctness proofs. Such proofs concern the properties of the roots of valid trees. However, since the nodes inside a parse tree are roots of subtrees, the annotation method can also be applied for proving properties of the internal nodes of valid trees. Properties of the roots of valid trees are properties of unconstrained trees. If one constrains some attribute values of the root of valid trees, this must have some repercussion on the values of the attributes of all the nodes.

This leads to the idea of *valid annotation*.

4.5.1   Valid annotation

An annotation is said to be *valid* for a RAG G iff every valid decorated tree of G satisfying the inherited assertions of its root satisfies all assertions of its every node. More, precisely:

Definition 4.22

Let Δ be an annotation of a relational attribute grammar $G = \langle N, P, S, Attr, \mathcal{L}, \Phi, \mathcal{I} \rangle$. Δ is valid for G iff for every parse tree T of G and every valid T-assignment ν such that $(\mathcal{I}, \nu) \models \bigwedge_{\phi \in \Delta_I(r)} \phi$, where r is the root of T, it follows that $(\mathcal{I}, \nu) \models \psi$ for every $\psi \in \Delta(u)$, for every node u of T.
□

We now give a sound and complete method for proving validity of an annotation. Denote by $\iota_\Delta(X)$ the conjunction of all assertions in $\Delta_I(X)$ and by $\sigma_\Delta(X)$ the conjunction of all assertions in $\Delta_S(X)$.

Theorem 4.3

An annotation Δ for an attribute grammar G is valid if and only if there exists an annotation Δ' for G and a non-circular logical dependency scheme L' for G and Δ' such that :

- (i) Δ' is sound for L',
- (ii) for every nonterminal X and for every valuation ν of $Attr(X)$ in $\mathcal{I}$

  $(\mathcal{I}, \nu) \models \iota_\Delta(X) \leftrightarrow \iota_{\Delta'}(X)$ and

  $(\mathcal{I}, \nu) \models \sigma_{\Delta'}(X) \rightarrow \sigma_\Delta(X)$.

□

Proof. The if part of the theorem follows from the validity of Δ' by (ii).

The only if part will be proved by construction of an annotation Δ' with required properties.

Let Δ be an annotation valid for G and let S_G be the strongest specification for G[9]. Thus S_Δ is valid and $S_G \rightarrow S_\Delta$. Hence at every node u of a valid tree the formula $\iota_\Delta(u) \wedge S_G(u) \rightarrow \sigma_\Delta(u)$ is true in $\mathcal{I}$. But also for every valid decorated occurrence of a production rule $p : X_0 \rightarrow X_1...X_n$ the formula $\Phi_p \wedge S_G(1) \wedge \ldots \wedge S_G(n) \rightarrow S_G(0)$ is true in $\mathcal{I}$.

We now define an annotation Δ'. For every nonterminal X: $\Delta_I'(X) = \{\iota_\Delta(X)\}$ and $\Delta_S'(X) = \{\sigma_\Delta(X), S_G(X)\}$. It verifies trivially condition (ii). To fulfill condition (i) we have to define a logical dependency scheme L' for G and Δ'. Let $p : X_0 \rightarrow X_1...X_n$ be a production rule of G for some $n \geq 0$. The output assertions in a rule p are $\sigma_\Delta(0)$, $S_G(0)$ and $\iota_\Delta(k)$ for $k = 1, ..., n$. The local dependencies specifying L' will be defined as follows: $\sigma_\Delta(0)$ depends on $\iota_\Delta(0)$ and on all $S_G(k)$ for $k = 1, ..., n$; $S_G(0)$ depends on all $S_G(k)$ for $k = 1, .., n$; every attribute occurrence $\iota_\Delta(k)$ for $k = 1, ..., n$ depends on all $S_G(k)$ for $k = 1, ..., n$.

L' is non-circular. It can be checked that it is an l-ordered logical dependency scheme with the assertions of S_G in the first class and all assertions of Δ' in the second class.

Δ' is sound for L'. For the assertions $\sigma_\Delta(0)$ and $S_G(0)$ the verification conditions for soundness follow directly from the properties of S_G and Δ discussed at the beginning of this proof. Consider the remaining output assertions: $\iota_\Delta(k)$ (for $k = 1, ..., n$). Each of them depends on $S_G(k)$ for $k = 1, ..., n$. Assume that these input assertions are satisfied for some valuation ν. As S_G is the strongest specification of G then the occurrence of p decorated with ν is the root rule of a valid tree. Hence, as Δ is a valid annotation then $\iota_\Delta(0)$ must also be satisfied, as well as $\iota_{\Delta'}(0)$. By validity of Δ it follows also that $(\mathcal{I}, \nu) \models \iota_\Delta(k)$, for $k = 1, ..., n$. Hence, by (ii) $(\mathcal{I}, \nu) \models \iota_{\Delta'}(k)$, for $k = 1, ..., n$. This concludes the proof of soundness of Δ' for L'.
$\square$

4.5.2   Proving properties of incomplete parse trees

The proof methods presented in this chapter apply to complete decorated parse trees. In practice, the construction of a parse tree is sometimes combined with attribute evaluation. The properties of the incomplete decorated trees constructed in such a way might be interesting for op-

---

[9]Existence of such a specification depends on the expressive power of the specification language. Assumption about the existence of S_G means that we are discussing relative completeness of the method rather than its completeness.

timization of the computation process. The annotation method can be used for this purpose provided that the assertions include only those attributes whose values are known in every incomplete tree built by the process. For example, in the following typical situations the values of all attributes are known:

- The parse tree is built in a bottom up manner and all the attributes and assertions are synthesized.

- The parse tree is built in a top down manner and all the attributes and assertions are inherited.

- The parse tree is built in a top down left to right manner, the grammar is an L-RAG and all assertions are ordered by an L-logical dependency scheme.

This topic will be discussed in more detail in Chapter 6.

4.6   Proof methods for completeness

In the previous section we discussed the notion of a specification valid for a relational attribute grammar. If S is a valid specification of G, and T is a valid decorated tree of G with root labeled X then the tuple of attribute values decorating T satisfies S_X. However, for a tuple of attribute values satisfying S_X there may be no valid tree such that this tuple is a decoration of its root. This observation motivates the following definition.

Definition 4.23 Completeness of a grammar w.r.t. a specification

An attribute grammar G is *complete* with respect to a specification S iff for every nonterminal X the relation Q_X defined by S is a subset of the relation R_X defined by G.
□

This section presents two methods for proving completeness of grammars with respect to specifications.

4.6.1 Co-inductive specifications

We now present the first method for proving completeness of grammars. A grammar G is complete with respect to a specification S iff for a given tuple $\bar{v}$ in the relation Q_X there exists a valid tree of G with the root decorated by $\bar{v}$. A necessary condition for this is the existence of a production rule of the profile $\langle X_1...X_n, X \rangle$ which can be decorated by the attributes in such a way that $\bar{v}$ is the decoration of X. Having achieved this one has to complete the partial decorated tree. Let $n > 0$ and let $\bar{v}_i$ be the tuple decorating X_i for $i = 1, ..., n$. Now for each i one has to find a production rule with the left-hand side X_i, which can be decorated in such a way that the decoration of its left-hand side is $\bar{v}_i$. One has to continue until this process terminates; i.e. until a complete valid tree is constructed. There are two ways in which the process may not achieve this goal: the failure, when no production rule satisfying the above requirement can be found, and nontermination when the constructed tree grows forever. The condition for completeness we are going to formulate consists of two independent subconditions, preventing failure and nontermination.

For formulating the second subcondition we need some auxiliary notions.

Let p be a production rule of the profile $\langle X_1...X_n, X \rangle$ be a production rule of a grammar G. The nonterminal X_i is called a *mutually recursive* nonterminal with X in p iff $X_i \Rightarrow_G^* \alpha X \beta$ for some strings α and β.

For every nonterminal X of G let f_X be a function on the Cartesian product of the domains of attributes of X into a well-founded domain. The ordering on the domain will be denoted $\succ$. Such a function will be called an *ordering* function.

A familly f of ordering functions is said to be *decreasing* on p with root X and an attribute valuation ν of p iff $f_X(\nu(Attr(0))) \succ f_{X_i}(\nu(Attr(i)))$ for every nonterminal X_i mutually recursive with X in p.

We now introduce the main notion of this section.

Definition 4.24 Co-inductive specification

Let S be a specification of a RAG $G = \langle N, P, S, Attr, \mathcal{L}, \Phi, \mathcal{I} \rangle$ and let Q_X be the relation specified by S for the nonterminal X.

S is said to be *co-inductive* iff for some familly f of ordering functions and for every tuple $\bar{v}$ in Q_X there exists a production rule $p : X \rightarrow$

$X_1 \dots X_n$ and a valuation ν such that:

- $(\mathcal{I}, \nu) \models \Phi_p$ and $\bar{v} = \nu(Attr(0))$,
- $\nu(Attr(i))$ is in the relation Q_{X_i} for $i = 1, \dots, n$,
- f is decreasing on p and ν.

□

It is not difficult to see that for any tuple in the relation defined by a co-inductive specification it is possible to build finite valid tree with the root decorated by this tuple. In fact the first two conditions of the definition say that any leave of an incomplete parse tree satisfies the specification and can always be extended by some grammatical rule so that this property is preserved. This excludes the "failure" cases in a "top-down" construction of a valid tree with given root decoration. The last condition guarantees that the construction process will terminate (necessarily successfully by the previous conditions). This observation leads to the following theorem (originating from [Der84]) which states soundness and completeness of a method for proving completeness of grammars.

Theorem 4.4 Proof method for completeness
A relational attribute grammar G is complete with respect to a specification S iff S is stronger than some co-inductive specification S'.
□

Proof. (Soundness.) If a specification S' is co-inductive then G is complete w.r.t. S'. As discussed above, this follows directly by the definition of co-inductive specification, which excludes failure and nontermination in the process of top-down construction of parse tree with the root labeled by any tuple defined by the specification.

(Completeness.) Assume that the specification language allows for expression of the strongest specification S_G and that the attribute grammar G is complete w.r.t. a specification S. Obviously $\mathcal{I} \models S \rightarrow S_G$. It remains to show that S_G is co-inductive. Note that for every nonterminal X the relation Q_{GX} defined by S_{GX} is exactly the relation R_X. Thus, by definition of R_X, for every tuple $\bar{v} \in S_{GX}$ there exists a valid tree with the root decorated by $\bar{v}$. Define the family f of ordering functions by putting $f_X(\bar{v})$ equal to the minimum of the depths of all valid trees with the roots labeled by $\bar{v}$. Now, for a given tuple $\bar{v} \in Q_{GX}$ take the production rule p used in construction of a tree with the minimal depths. Clearly, it is satisfying the conditions of the definition of co-inductive specification for the valuation ν used in this tree:

- ν satisfies the semantic rule Φ_p;
- Under this valuation the decoration of every right-hand side nonterminal X_i is in the relation R_{X_i}, hence in the relation Q_{GX_i};
- f is decreasing on p and ν.

□

Notice that the completeness of the method stated in Theorem 4.4 is relative to the existence of a formula corresponding to the strongest specification. As the result assumes the existence of such a formula, the method is as complete as the correctness proof method, i.e. it is not complete if one restricts the specification language to be first order.

Example 4.10 Factorial revisited

Let us consider again the example of factorial with one more unnecessary rule. The additional rule is introduced to give better understanding of the concept of decreasing functions.

- N is $\{fac\}$.
- R is $\{ r_1 : fac \rightarrow \varepsilon, r_2 : fac \rightarrow fac, r_3 : fac \rightarrow fac \}$.
- $Attr$ is $\{a, v\}$, the sort of each attribute is Int.
- $\mathcal{L}$ is a one sorted logical language with the alphabet including the predicate name $=$, the unary postfix function $!$ and the binary function names $-$ and $*$ with the usual infix notation.
- Φ is:

  - $\Phi_{r_1} : a(0) = 0 \wedge v(0) = 1.$
  - $\Phi_{r_2} : a(1) = a(0) - 1 \wedge v(0) = v(1) * a(0).$
  - $\Phi_{r_3} : a(1) = a(0) \wedge v(0) = v(1).$

- $\mathcal{I}$ associates with the sort Int the domain of integers, $=$ is interpreted as equality on integers, $-$ and $*$ are interpreted as the arithmetic operations of subtraction and multiplication, $n!$ is factorial of n.

We show that the specification: S_{fac}: $a \geq 0 \wedge v = a!$ is co-inductive. Consider the ordering function defined as follows: $f_{fac}(\langle x_1, x_2 \rangle) = x_1$. Let $\langle x_1, x_2 \rangle$ be a pair in Q_{fac}. Two cases should be considered:

- $x_1 = 0$: in this case the only "applicable" production rule in top-down construction of a valid tree is r_1 and the conditions of the definition of co-inductive specification are trivially satisfied.

- $x_1 > 0$: in this case the production rule r_2 with the valuation $a(0) = x_1, a(1) = x_1 - 1, v(0) = x_2 = x_1!, v(1) = x_2/x_1 = (x_1 - 1)!$ satisfies the conditions of the definition of co-inductive specification.

Hence S_{fac} is co-inductive. Notice that for no valuation the production rule r_3 satisfies the decreasing condition. Notice also that the same proof of completeness would also hold for the grammar obtained by removing the rule r_3. This is a general observation: if an attribute grammar is complete with a subset of rules, it is also complete with the whole set of rules.

□

At first glance proofs of completeness are relatively more complex than proof of correctness because of the termination condition. However they are very natural. The main difficulty is to find appropriate family of ordering functions. This "termination condition" can be replaced by other equivalent formulations or by some sufficient conditions which are easier to check.

4.6.2 Existential completeness

In many attribute grammars, especially in the functional ones, some attributes of a tuple decorating the root of the tree depend functionally on some other ones. This can be sometimes used for proving completeness of the grammar. The motivation is to structure completeness proofs; a completeness proof is to be obtained by composition of a simplified completeness proof with a correctness proof. We now present a proof method based on this idea.

The approach is first presented by an example. Consider again the specification S_{fac}: $a \geq 0 \wedge v = a!$ of Example 4.10 . Notice that in every node of a valid tree the value of v is a function of a. Thus a top-down construction of a valid tree may be performed by constructing first a skeleton partially decorated by appropriate values of the first attribute of every node. The decoration of every such a tree can be augmented to a complete valid tree using the semantic rules. The question of completeness reduces in this case to the question about existence of the partially decorated tree with a given root value a. This amounts to asking about completeness of the grammar with respect to the specification $S'_{fac} : a \geq 0$. Notice that this specification refers to a subset of the attributes of the nonterminal fac. The completeness of the grammar with respect to the original specification will follow then by the functional dependency of v on a. We now introduce general concepts motivated by this example.

Let G be an attribute grammar and let A be a proper subset of its attributes. By $R_{X|_A}$ we denote the restriction of the relation defined by G for a nonterminal X to the positions corresponding to the attributes of A. Similarly, for a tuple $\bar{v}$ of attribute values we denote by $\bar{v}_{|_A}$ the tuple obtained from $\bar{v}$ by removing the elements which do not correspond to the attributes of A.

Definition 4.25 Existential completeness

Let G be a relational attribute grammar and let S be a specification of G involving a subset A of its attributes. G is said to be *existentially complete* with respect to S iff for every nonterminal X the relation Q_X defined by S is a subset of $R_{X|_A}$.
$\square$

In other words, if a grammar is existentially complete with respect to S then for every tuple in Q_X there exists its extension to a root label of a valid tree. This observation justifies the terminology used. Note that completeness is a special case of existential completeness, where A is the set of all attributes of G.

Existential completeness of a grammar can sometimes be used for proving completeness of the grammar with respect to a stronger specification. This idea is formalized by the following theorem.

Theorem 4.5 Proof method for completeness, using existential completeness

Let G be a relational attribute grammar with attributes in disjoint sets A and B. G is complete with respect to a specification S iff there exist specifications S_1, using the attributes of A, and S_2 such that:

1. $S \rightarrow S_1 \wedge S_2$,

2. G is existentially complete with respect to S_1,

3. G is partially correct with respect to $S_1 \rightarrow S_2$,

4. The relation defined by S_2 is a function on the tuples satisfying S_1; that is, for every nonterminal X if $\bar{v}, \bar{v}' \in Q_2$ and $\bar{v}_{|A} = \bar{v}'_{|A} \in Q_1$ then $\bar{v} = \bar{v}'$. S_2 will be said *functional w.r.t.* S_1.

☐

Proof. It follows by (2) and (3) that for any tuple $\bar{v}$ satisfying S_1 there exists a valid tree such that its root label $\bar{v}'$ satisfies S_2 and $\bar{v} = \bar{v}'_{|A}$. By (4) (i.e. by the functionality of S_2 w.r.t. S_1) G is complete with respect to $S_1 \wedge S_2$. Hence the result by (1).

The only if condition is obtained by taking S_1 as the strongest specification S_G and S_2 equivalent to *true*. All conditions are then trivially fulfilled.

☐

The introductory example of this section can now be presented in the framework of the method.

Example 4.11

It can be checked that the attribute grammar G for factorial (Example 4.10 p. 192) is existentially complete w.r.t. the specification $S1_{fac} : a \geq 0$. This specification involves only a proper subset of the attributes of the grammar. An approach to proving existential completeness will be discussed separately.

The specification S for this grammar discussed above is
$S_{fac}: a \geq 0 \wedge v = a!$

Hence S is in the form $S1 \wedge S2$, where $S2_{fac} : v = a!$ Hence the condition (1) of the theorem is trivially satisfied. As mentioned, above (2) also holds. The condition (3) of the theorem requires correctness of G with respect to the specification $S1 \rightarrow S2$. It is satisfied, as G is correct with respect to S (see Example 4.8 p. 180). To complete the proof of completeness of G with respect to S it suffices to check the functionality condition (4):
$(x_1 > 0 \wedge y_1 > 0 \wedge x_2 = x_1! \wedge y_2 = y_1!) \rightarrow x_2 = y_2$

☐

We presented a structured method for proving completeness of a grammar. The essential component of a completeness proof is the proof of existential completeness. We now present a method for proving existential completeness for certain class of relational attribute grammars.

Let G be a relational attribute grammar and let S be a specification involving a subset A of attributes of G. We want to prove existential completeness of G with respect to S. We make the additional assumption about the form of the attribute definitions of G: for every production rule r the formula Φ_r is a conjunction of a formula Φ_r^A whose only free variables are occurrences of attributes of A and a formula Φ_r'. No restrictions are imposed on the form of Φ_r'. The attributes in A will be called the *decisive attributes*. We will call G an *A-conjunctive attribute grammar*. Notice that the splitting of Φ_r into Φ_r^A and Φ_r' may be ambiguous.

For an A-conjunctive attribute grammar G we denote by $G_{|A}$ the grammar obtained from G by replacing each definition Φ_r by Φ_r^A.
Clearly the set of valid trees of $G_{|A}$ includes the trees obtained from valid trees of G by restricting the elements of the labels to the attribute values of A.

Let G be an A-conjunctive attribute grammar and let S be a specification involving only the attributes of A. We want to find a sufficient condition for existential completeness of G with respect to S. Denote by R_X' the relation defined for a nonterminal X by the grammar $G_{|A}$. As stated above, $R_{X|A} \subseteq R_X'$. Existential completeness means $Q_X \subseteq R_{X|A}$, hence we obtain the necessary condition $Q_X \subseteq R_X'$, or in other words $G_{|A}$ should be complete with respect to S. For existential completeness it suffices to guarantee that $R_{X|A} = R_X'$. This means that satisfaction of the restricted attribute definitions of $G_{|A}$ by a decoration of a tree of G such that S is satisfied should enforce satisfaction of definitions of G. Thus, we put a requirement on G which can be expressed as a specification involving attributes of G. This discussion gives a background for the following method of proving existential completeness.

Theorem 4.6 Proof method for existential completeness
Let G be an A-conjunctive attribute grammar and let S be a specification involving only the attributes of A. G is existentially complete with respect to S if there exists a specification U such that S and U specify all the attributes and:

1. $G_{|A}$ is complete with respect to S,

2. G is partially correct with respect to $S \to U$,

3. For every production rule $r : X \to X_1...X_n$ with $n \geq 0$:

   $\bigwedge_{i \geq 0} S_{X_i}(i) \wedge \bigwedge_{i > 0} U_{X_i}(i) \wedge \Phi_r^A \to \exists \Phi_r'$

   where $\exists$ denotes existential closure on those variables which do not appear in the predecessor of the implication.

   $\square$

   The theorem can be proved by structural induction on decorated trees.

Example 4.12

Consider again the attribute grammar for factorial Example 4.10 p. 192. The grammar is A-conjunctive with $A = \{a\}$ and the restricted attribute definitions are as follows:

$\Phi_{r_1}^A : a(0) = 0$
$\Phi_{r_2}^A : a(1) = a(0) - 1$
$\Phi_{r_3}^A : a(1) = a(0)$

The complementary definitions are thus:

$\Phi_{r_1}' : v(0) = 1$
$\Phi_{r_2}' : v(0) = v(1) * a(0)$
$\Phi_{r_3}' : v(0) = v(1)$

We want to prove existential completeness of G with respect to the specification S: $a \geq 0$, involving only the attribute a. We use Theorem 4.6 with the auxiliary specification U: $v > 0$.

(1) To prove completeness of $G_{|A}$ with respect to S we show that S is co-inductive. The rules satisfying the conditions are r_1 for $a = 0$ and r_2 for $a > 0$. As the ordering function we take the identity function.

(2) It has been proved in Example 4.8 p. 180 (final remark) that the specification $S \to U$ is valid for G.

(3) The last condition is to be checked for every rule of G:

For r_1: $\exists v(0)$ $v(0) = 1$ holds trivially.

For r_2: $a(0) > 0 \wedge a(1) = a(0) - 1 \wedge v(1) \geq 0 \wedge a(1) \geq 0$ implies $\exists$ $v(0)v(0) = a(0) \times v(1)$

For r_3 the condition holds trivially.

This example shows that the auxiliary specification U needed to prove existential completeness may be rather weak.

$\square$

Notice that Theorem 4.6 suggests a "bottom-up" method for proving existential completeness, but there may be many other ways to do it. It is sufficient to replace the conditions 2 and 3 by a proof that any valid decorated tree of $G_{|A}$ may be extended into a complete valid decorated tree. In Chapter 6 an other method will be used to obtain the same kind of results in the framework of logic programs.

4.6.3 Organizing the proof of completeness

In the definition of a co-inductive specification one uses the following condition:

For every tuple of values $\bar{v}$ in Q_X there exists a production rule p and a valuation ν such that $(\mathcal{I}, \nu) \models \Phi_p$ and $\bar{v} = \nu(Attr(0))$.

The above condition is implied by the following one:

There exists a family of relations Q_X^r, defined on the attributes of the left hand side X of r, for a subset of rules r such that:

- Q_X is included into the union of the Q_X^r's,
- and for each of these rules r the following holds:

For every tuple of values $\bar{v}$ in Q_X^r there exists a valuation ν such that $(\mathcal{I}, \nu) \models \Phi_r$ and $\bar{v} = \nu(Attr(0))$ and the other conditions of Definition 4.24 p. 190 are verified.

This leads to a reformulation of the proof method closer to practice: find a family of auxiliary assertions $\{S^r\}$, indexed by a subset of the rules, whose free variables are in $Attr(X)$ (X being the sort of the root of r), and a family f of ordering functions such that:

1. For every nonterminal X the disjunction of all the formulae S^r such that the root of r is of sort X is implied by S_X in the interpretation $\mathcal{I}$.

2. For every rule r, for every assignment ν of the attribute occurrences of the root such that $(\mathcal{I}, \nu) \models S^r$, there exists some assignment ν' of the remaining attributes occurrences in $Attr(r)$ such that all the assertions $S_{X_i}, i > 0$, and the relation Φ_r are true together in $(\mathcal{I}, \nu \cup \nu')$, and such that f is decreasing for r and ν.

Example 4.13 Factorial revisited

Let us consider again the Example 4.10 p. 192 of factorial.

- N is $\{fac\}$.
- R is $\{\ r_1 : fac \to \varepsilon,\ r_2 : fac \to fac,\ r_3 : fac \to fac\ \}$.
- *Attr* is $\{a, v\}$, the sort of each attribute is *Int*.
- $\mathcal{L}$ is a one sorted logical language with the alphabet including the predicate name $=$ and the binary function names $-$ and $*$; it employs the usual infix notation.
- Φ is:

  - r_1: $a(0) = 0 \wedge v(0) = 1$,
  - r_2: $a(1) = a(0) - 1 \wedge v(0) = v(1) * a(0)$,
  - r_3: $a(1) = a(0) \wedge v(0) = v(1)$.

- $\mathcal{I}$ associates with the sort *Int* the domain of integers, $=$ is interpreted as equality on integers, $-$ and $*$ are interpreted as the arithmetic operations of subtraction and multiplication, $n!$ is factorial of n.

We show that the specification: S_{fac}: $a \geq 0 \wedge v = a!$ is co-inductive, i.e. that there exists a valid decorated tree with attribute root values satisfying S_{fac}.

Let us consider the subset of rules: $\{\ r_1, r_2\ \}$.

The first condition is:

$S_{fac} \Rightarrow S_{fac}^{r_1} \vee S_{fac}^{r_2}$

with $S_{fac}^{r_1}$: $a = 0 \wedge v = a!$ $S_{fac}^{r_2}$: $a > 0 \wedge v = a!$

Then the second condition is satisfied with the decreasing function:

$$f_{fac}(a, v) = a.$$ Indeed:

In r_1: $S_{fac}^{r_1}(0)$: $a(0) = 0 \wedge v(0) = a(0)!$ implies: $\Phi_1 : a(0) = 0 \wedge v(0) = 1$ for all $a(0)$ and $v(0)$ trivially.

In r_2: for all $a(0)$ and $v(0)$, $S_{fac}^{r_2}$: $a(0) > 0 \wedge v(0) = a(0)!$ implies that there exists $a(1)$ and $v(1)$ such that Φ_2 and $S_{fac}(1)$ hold, i.e.:

Φ_2: $a(0) > 0 \wedge a(1) = a(0) - 1 \wedge v(0) = v(1) * a(0)$ and $S_{fac}(1)$: $a(1) \geq 0 \wedge v(1) = a(1)!$

and f_{fac} is decreasing on r_2 and any valuation such that $a(0) > 0$:

$f_{fac}(a(0), v(0)) \succ f_{fac}(a(1), v(1))$

which is easy to verify.

□

4.7 Some remarks

4.7.1 The power of the annotation method and its complexity

Let $\langle \Delta, \mathcal{I} \rangle$ be a valid annotation of a relational attribute grammar. It
has been shown in [CD88] that there exists an annotation $\langle \Delta', \mathcal{I} \rangle$ such
that :

- for every nonterminal X $\Delta'_I(X)$ is empty and the elements of $\Delta'_S(X)$ are
  constructed from the assertions of Δ. The validity of Δ' implies validity
  of Δ.

- there exists a LDS for which Δ' is sound, which by the definition must
  be purely synthesized, hence non-circular.

Thus, the specification associated with Δ' is inductive. This shows that
the annotation method does not permit to prove more valid specifications than the induction method, hence the methods have the same
theoretical power. However it is shown in [CD88] that the size of the
inductive specification induced by Δ' may be exponential with respect
to the size of the annotation Δ. This shows that the complexity of the
proof may be reduced by using annotations. From the practical point
of view, as demonstrated by the examples, it may be much more convenient to check separately a number of more simple verification conditions
induced by the assertion method, than one complex verification condition of the induction method. Even a relatively simple formula of the
form $S1 \rightarrow S2$ can be naturally split into the inherited assertion $S1$
and the synthesized assertion $S2$. Then for a simple recursive clause
the verification conditions of the annotation method include two simple
implications of the form $S1(0) \rightarrow S1(1)$ and $S2(1) \rightarrow S2(0)$. In the
case of induction method there will be only one, but relatively complex
verification condition of the form $(S1(1) \rightarrow S2(1)) \rightarrow (S1(0) \rightarrow S2(0))$
The use of the inductive method becomes totally unnatural if properties
to be proved depend on particular upper context inside the tree.

4.7.2   Relative completeness of the proof methods

All the results of this chapter concerning the completeness of the proof method have been obtained under the assumption that the specification language can express the strongest specification.

In [CD88] it is shown that Wand's incompleteness result established for Hoare's like deductive systems [Wan78] holds also for inductive proofs in attribute grammars. This result says that a first order assertion language may not be rich enough to express the (inductive) properties needed to achieve the proof of some specification. The proof from [CD88] is reformulated in Section 7.2.3 in the context of logic programming.

4.8   Bibliographical comments

The notion of attribute grammar was introduced in [Knu68a, Knu68b]. It has been the subject of active research and the number of publications on attribute grammars is very large. A comprehensive survey of the field with a structured bibliography is [DJL88]. The collection [AM91] includes also a number of introductory articles.

The notion of relational attribute grammar has been introduced in [DM85b] as a common denominator for attribute grammars and definite programs. The original concept of attribute grammar is a special case of a relational attribute grammar, called in this book a functional attribute grammar.

The general algorithm for attribute evaluation which gives a basis for classification of functional attribute grammars originates from [Fil83].

The attribute grammars give a general scheme for computations. A formal treatment of this issue can be found in [CFZ82, CD88] where attribute grammars are compared with recursive program schemes. The notion of dependency indicator has been introduced in [CD88].

Many systems for attribute based compiler construction or editors and attribute evaluation have been developed (see [DJL88] for a comprehensive review of some of them). Earlier affix grammar based compiler compiler as CDL [Kos71] or LET [Bou92a] can be considered as evaluators of L-FAG's.

The problem of partial correctness of attribute grammars has been studied by several authors, in, among others, [PAN76, KH81, Cou84]. The proof methods for attribute grammars (partial correctness and completeness) presented in this chapter originate from [Der83, Der84]. A comprehensive presentation of the methods for partial correctness and annotations can be found in [CD88], where it is also shown that the methods apply to recursive procedures and to logic programs.

5 Attribute Grammars and Logic Programming

This chapter discusses relationships between definite programs and various kinds of attribute grammars. The declarative semantics of these formalisms has been developed using similar concepts of trees: proof trees in the case of definite programs and decorated trees in the case of attribute grammars. However, the formalisms are not equivalent. This chapter introduces a number of formal constructions which allow to identify equivalent subclasses of attribute grammars and logic programs. The constructions explain the nature of some similarities between the formalisms. On the other hand they make possible application of techniques known for one of them to the other, at least for the restricted subclasses defined by the constructions. The study of the differences can be used as a source of inspiration for possible extensions of both formalisms.

Both definite programs and attribute grammars have declarative semantics and operational semantics. Definite programs are interpreted on term domains and proof tree construction is based on term unification. Traditionally the operational semantics of definite programs is based on SLD-resolution, but the general resolution scheme of Section 2.1.4 shows a whole spectrum of unification based proof tree construction algorithms. Attribute grammars are interpreted on arbitrary domains and valid tree construction algorithms are usually restricted to non-circular functional attribute grammars. Thus, the notion of dependency relation plays important role in operational semantics of attribute grammars. It is abstracted in the notion of attribute dependency scheme and leads to the important classification of functional attribute grammars discussed in Chapter 4. This shows that definite programs and attribute grammars can be compared with respect to the declarative semantics and with respect to various kinds of operational semantics. In this chapter the following questions are discussed:

- What is the relation between declarative semantics of definite programs and declarative semantics of attribute grammars.

- What is the counterpart of attribute dependency scheme for a definite program.

- How to model some operational semantics of definite programs by functional attribute grammars.

- Which attribute grammars can be transformed into definite programs with equivalent declarative semantics.

  We now give some motivation for raising these questions.

- *From definite programs to attribute grammars with the model-theoretic view.* We show that for every definite program there exists a relational attribute grammar with the same declarative semantics. Thus relational attribute grammars can be seen as a uniform general framework incorporating both definite programs and attribute grammars. On the other hand this allows to identify a subclass of the relational attribute grammars that can be given a correct operational semantics by compilation into definite programs.

- *Dependency relations for logic programs.* Functional attribute grammars constitute a proper subclass of the relational attribute grammars. A natural question is then when a definite program can be transformed into a functional attribute grammar with equivalent declarative semantics. The study of this problem leads to the notion of dependency relation for logic programs. This is an abstraction related to information flow through the parameters of the predicates of a logic program. It gives an insight into some logic programming techniques and allows to identify some interesting classes of logic programs.

- *Modelling operational semantics of logic programs by functional attribute grammars.* The notion of a full resolution scheme of Definition 2.13 p. 55 gives a foundation for development of correct and complete interpreters of definite programs. We discuss a possibility of using functional attribute grammars for that purpose. For a given definite program a functional attribute grammar is constructed depending on the resolution scheme considered. The attributes of this grammar represent the arguments of the equations constructed for skeletons and solutions of such equations. The declarative semantics of this attribute grammar describes only some declarative aspects of the computations of the resolution scheme for the program considered, but allows to prove correctness and completeness of the computed substitutions. To construct these substitutions some operational semantics of the attribute grammar is to be used.

- *From functional attribute grammars to definite programs.* An interesting question is whether a functional attribute grammar can be transformed into a definite program with the same declarative semantics. Potentially this would allow for using of attribute grammar techniques for logic programs. Generally the answer for this question is negative since the function symbols of an attribute grammar have explicit interpretation as "semantic functions" on given domains. In contrast to that, the model-theoretic semantics of definite programs is given by considering logical consequences of the program. As shown in Section 2.2.1 this can be reduced to considering the least term models where the function symbols are interpreted as term constructors. Thus, to compare functional attribute grammars and definite programs one has either to restrict domains of the attribute grammars considered to the term domains or to consider definite programs with a priori given interpretations. We discuss both cases. We show that a functional attribute grammar with a term interpretation can be seen as a special kind of a definite program. On the other hand, the notion of preinterpretation based derivation tree of Definition 2.20 p. 76 allows us to handle definite programs with a priori given interpretation of function symbols. This can be seen as a special kind of constraint logic programming (cf. [JL87]). For such programs a general operational semantics would require equation solving over a given domain instead of unification. Generally there may be no algorithm for solving the equations produced. We show that a functional attribute grammar with any interpretation of functors can be considered to be a definite program with the same interpretation. For such a program the set of equations associated with a complete skeleton of the program can always be solved, regardless of the interpretation of function symbols. The reason for this is that the syntactic restrictions on the programs of this class originating from the attribute grammar guarantee existence of a strategy under which every equation can be solved by evaluation of ground terms and elimination of variables. The interpretation is only used for evaluation of ground terms. In practice, the interpretation can be given by associating with each function symbol a functional procedure in some programming language. This results in an approach to integration of logic programs with procedures written in other languages. Several Prolog systems allow for the use of foreign procedures in Prolog programs. The notion of functional attribute grammar gives a conceptual foundation for studying such integration.

In this chapter, for sake of simplification, definitions and constructions are presented for definite programs. However, all these definitions and contructions extend in a simple way to goal clauses and thus to Horn programs. Many examples are given with definite programs augmented by goal clauses.

5.1 From definite programs to attribute grammars with the declarative semantics

We now show that definite programs can be viewed as a special kind of attribute grammars. We present a construction that transforms a given definite program into a relational attribute grammar with the same declarative semantics. We also discuss the cases when the program can be transformed into a functional attribute grammar.

5.1.1 Modelling declarative semantics of a definite program P by a relational attribute grammar $\mathcal{R}(P)$

The first objective is to construct a relational attribute grammar whose valid trees are isomorphic to the proof trees of a given definite program.

Let P be a definite program over an alphabet $Pred$ of predicates and an alphabet F of function symbols. A preinterpretation J of P is assumed to be given. We now define a relational attribute grammar $\mathcal{R}(P)$ which has the required property. A general idea of the construction is to take the clause skeletons of P as the underlying context-free grammar. Thus, the nonterminals of the grammar are the predicates of the program. The attributes of every nonterminal represent the arguments of the predicate and range over the domains of J: a nonterminal with its attribute values is a J-atom. The semantic rules guarantee that every valid tree of the grammar is built of the J-instances of the clauses of the program. This idea is formalized by the following construction.

Definition 5.1

For a given definite program P with a preinterpretation J the relational attribute grammar $\mathcal{R}(P)$ is defined to be the 7-tuple

$\langle N, R, S, Attr, \mathcal{L}, \Phi, \mathcal{I} \rangle$

where

- N is *Pred*.

- R is the *Pred*-sorted signature:
  $r_c : \langle p_1 \ldots p_m, p_0 \rangle$ is in R iff
  $c : p_0(t_{01}, \ldots, t_{0n_0}) \leftarrow p_1(t_{11}, \ldots, t_{1n_1}), \ldots, p_m(t_{m1}, \ldots, t_{mn_m})$
  is a clause of P. Thus, the elements of the signature correspond to
  clause skeletons of P. The signature can also be seen as a context-free
  grammar with the empty terminal alphabet.

- S is a singleton, i.e. the logical language used for specification of the
  semantic rules is one-sorted.

- *Attr* is a set of attributes denoting the arguments of the predicates. The
  j-th argument of the predicate p corresponds to the attribute denoted
  p_j.

- $\mathcal{L}$ is a first-order language with the alphabet of functors F and such
  that its alphabet of variables includes all attribute occurrences of the
  attributes in *Attr*. The only predicate of this language is the binary
  equality predicate "=".

- Φ is defined as follows. Let c be a clause of the form: $p_0(t_{01}, \ldots, t_{0n_0}) \leftarrow$
  $p_1(t_{11}, \ldots, t_{1n_1}), \ldots, p_m(t_{m1}, \ldots, t_{mn_m})$
  Then Φ associates with r_c the following formula ϕ_c

$$\exists V(c) \bigwedge_{k=0}^{m} \bigwedge_{j=1}^{n_k} p_j(k) = t_{kj}$$

where

- $\exists V(c)$ denotes existential quantification over all variables of the clause
  c,

- $p_j(k)$ is the occurrence of the attribute p_j of the nonterminal p_k in r_c.
  (This notation has been defined in Section 4.1),

- $\bigwedge$ denotes conjunction and n_k is the arity of the predicate p_k,

- t_{kj} is the j-th argument of the k-th atom of c.

- $\mathcal{I}$ is a J-based interpretation of $\mathcal{L}$ (the functors of $\mathcal{L}$ are interpreted in $\mathcal{I}$
  as in the preinterpretation J of the program P) and the only predicate $=$

is interpreted as the identity on the domain of $\mathcal{I}$. $\mathcal{I}$ is assumed without loss of generality to be one sorted; its domain is denoted I.

□

The existential quantifier over all free variables of the clause expresses the fact that proof trees are built from J-instances of the renamed clauses. The only free variables of ϕ_c are the attribute occurrences $p_j(k)$. The formula ϕ_c is true for a given valuation ν (assigning values to the attribute occurrences) iff there exists a valuation μ (assigning values to the variables of the clause c) such that $[p_j(k)]_{\mathcal{I},\nu} = [t_{kj}]_{\mathcal{I},\mu}$ for every $k = 0, \ldots, m$ and for every $j = 1, \ldots, n_k$.

In case I is a term domain the formulae ϕ_c have the form $\exists V(c) \bigwedge_{j,k} \nu(p_j(k)) = t_{kj}$, which means that each term $\nu(p_j(k))$ must be an instance of the term t_{kj} (one must assume that the codomain of ν contains no variable of c, because the variables of c are locally quantified).

Example 5.1 Program *plus*

Consider the following program P.

1. $plus(zero, X, X) \leftarrow$
2. $plus(s(X), Y, s(Z)) \leftarrow plus(X, Y, Z)$

Its underlying set of production rules is:

1. $plus \rightarrow \varepsilon$
2. $plus \rightarrow plus$

The domain of interpretation is $TERM$. The corresponding semantic rules of $\mathcal{R}(P)$ are

1. ϕ_1

   $\exists X \; plus_1(0) = zero \wedge plus_2(0) = X \wedge plus_3(0) = X$

2. ϕ_2

   $\exists X, Y, Z \; plus_1(0) = s(X) \wedge plus_2(0) = Y \wedge plus_3(0) = s(Z) \wedge plus_1(1) = X \wedge plus_2(1) = Y \wedge plus_3(1) = Z$

   □

We now discuss the relation between J-based proof trees of P and valid trees of $\mathcal{R}(P)$. Let S be a parse tree of $\mathcal{R}(P)$ (that is S an *Pred*-sorted term in the signature R). By the construction of $\mathcal{R}(P)$ each production rule of the underlying context-free grammar corresponds to a clause of P. Thus, the label of each node u of S corresponds to a clause c_u of P. Therefore S can also be seen as a skeleton of P. The formula ϕ_u associated with u is existentially quantified. It is of the form $\exists V(c_u)\gamma_u$ where $V(c_u)$ is the sequence consisting of all variables of c_u and γ_u is a conjunction of equations. For each formula ϕ_u it is possible to rename the bound variables in such a way that they become unique for u. The formula ϕ'_u obtained in this way is of the form $\exists V'(c_u)\gamma'_u$, where $V'(c_u)$ is the sequence of all new variables renaming those of $V(c_u)$ and γ'_u is the image of γ_u under the renaming. Clearly, ϕ'_u is logically equivalent to ϕ_u. Now the formula

$$\phi(S) = \bigwedge_{u \in S} \phi_u$$

is logically equivalent to the formula

$$\phi'(S) = \exists V'(S) \bigwedge_{u \in S} \gamma'_u$$

where $V'(S)$ is the concatenation of all sequences $V'(c_u)$ for $u \in S$. (Notice that these sequences have no common variables).

Let u be a non-root node of S and let p be the head of the clause c_u. For every attribute p_i of p the formula $\phi'(S)$ includes exactly two equations of the form $p_i(u) = t_1$ and $p_i(u) = t_2$ where $p_i(u)$ is a free variable, while t_1 and t_2 have no common variables and all their variables are existentially quantified in $\phi'(S)$. One of the equations originates from the formula ϕ_{c_u} and the other from the formula $\phi_{c_{u'}}$, where u' is the parent of the node u.

For any attribute occurrence $p_i(u)$ of the root node u, $\phi'(S)$ includes only one equation of the form $p_i(u) = t_1$. Thus for any valuation ν on $Attr(S)$ that satisfies $\phi'(S)$ there exists a valuation μ of all the clause variables V' such that $[p_i(u)]_{\mathcal{I},\nu} = [t_1]_{\mathcal{I},\mu} = [t_2]_{\mathcal{I},\mu}$.

Hence any valid tree of $\mathcal{R}(P)$ corresponds to an J-based proof tree of P built on the same skeleton with the same valuation μ, and vice versa. Hence the theorem:

Theorem 5.1 Correctness of $\mathcal{R}(P)$

Every J-based proof tree of a definite program P is isomorphic to a

valid tree of $\mathcal{R}(P)$ with J-based interpretation and vice versa.
$\square$

Theorem 5.1 shows that definite programs can be considered as a special subclass of relational attribute grammars with term interpretations. This result is mostly of theoretical interest: it allows to put logic programs and functional attribute grammars in the same framework of relational attribute grammars for studying their similarities and differences.

5.1.2   Modelling declarative semantics of definite programs by conditional attribute grammars

The next question to be discussed is whether the relational attribute grammar $\mathcal{R}(P)$ can be transformed into a functional attribute grammar with the same declarative semantics. The problem reduces to the question whether it is possible to find such a splitting of the attributes that allows to express each output attribute occurrence of every production rule as a function of its input attribute occurrences. The question will be discussed for the case of term interpretation.

We first show attribute splittings that allow to transform $\mathcal{R}(P)$ into an equivalent conditional attribute grammar. Additional restrictions on the splittings will lead to empty conditions in the constructed conditional attribute grammars, which thus becomes a functional attribute grammar.

The attributes of $\mathcal{R}(P)$ correspond to the argument positions of the predicates of P. We now split them into inherited attributes and synthesized attributes. Each production rule of $\mathcal{R}(P)$ corresponds to a clause of P and the terms which are arguments of the predicates in the clause correspond to attribute occurrences of the rule. The introduced splitting divides the latter into input attribute occurrences and output attribute occurrences, as defined in Section 4.2.2. Consequently, the corresponding argument terms of the clause will be called its *input* terms and *output* terms. We now define an important class of attribute splittings.

Definition 5.2 Simple splitting
Let P be a definite program. A splitting of attributes of $\mathcal{R}(P)$ is *simple* iff in every clause of P each variable of an output term occurs in at least one input term.
$\square$

Example 5.2

Let P be the following program:

1. $append(nil, L, L) \leftarrow$

2. $append(cons(E, L_1), L_2, cons(E, L_3)) \leftarrow append(L_1, L_2, L_3)$

The relational attribute grammar $\mathcal{R}(P)$ has the following semantic rules:

1. ϕ_1

$\exists L \; append_1(0) = nil \wedge append_2(0) = L \wedge append_3(0) = L$

2. ϕ_2

$\exists E, L_1, L_2, L_3 \; append_1(0) = cons(E, L_1) \wedge append_2(0) = L_2 \wedge$
$append_3(0) = cons(E, L_3) \wedge append_1(1) = L_1 \wedge append_2(1) = L_2 \wedge$
$append_3(1) = L_3$

Consider the following splitting of the attributes of $\mathcal{R}(P)$:

- Inherited attributes: $\{append_1, append_2\}$

- Synthesized attributes: $\{append_3\}$

According to the definition the input terms of the first clause are nil and L. The output term of this clause is L. In the second clause the input terms are $cons(E, L_1)$, L_2 and L_3 and the output terms are $cons(E, L_3)$, L_1 and L_2. Hence the splitting is simple.
□

We now show that a simple splitting allows for construction of a conditional attribute grammar with the same set of valid trees as $\mathcal{R}(P)$. For the construction we will use the following notion of selector.

Definition 5.3

Let f be an n-ary functor, $n > 0$, in the alphabet F and let $i \leq n$. By s_i^f we denote a partial *selection* operation on terms over F such that $s_i^f(t) \rightarrow_{def} d_i$ if t is a term of the form $f(d_1, \ldots, d_i, \ldots, d_n)$, and it is undefined otherwise. The unary function symbol s_i^f is called a *basic selector*.
□

The composition of the selection operations denoted by basic selectors will be represented by the sequence of these selectors, to be called *composed* selector. The composed selector $s\pi$, where s is a basic selector and π is a selector, applied to a term t, is π applied to $s(t)$.

Introduction of basic selectors to the language makes it necessary to extend the term interpretation $\mathcal{I}$ by the new (partial) interpretation $\mathcal{I}'$, where the selectors are interpreted as the selection operations and the only predicate $=$ is interpreted as identity on terms without selector.

The following examples illustrate the concept of selector. Let f be a binary function symbol, let g be a unary function symbols and let a, b be constants. Their respective selectors are s_1^f, s_2^f, and s_1^g. In the extended interpretation the formula $s_1^g s_2^f(g(f(a, b))) = s_1^g(g(b))$ is true but $s_2^f(f(s_1^g(g(a)), b)) = s_2^f(f(a, b))$ and $s_1^g(a) = s_1^g(b)$ are undefined.

In the following constructions the semantic rules of the constructed attribute grammars may apply selectors to the terms over the alphabet of functors of the definite program.

The formula ϕ_c associated with the production rule r_c corresponding to a clause c is an existentially quantified conjunction of all equations of the form $x = t$ where x is an attribute occurrence of r_c and t is the corresponding argument term of c (cf. Example 5.3). The intuition behind the splitting of the attributes is to express the values of the output attribute occurrences of every clause in terms of its input attribute occurrences. The equation of $\mathcal{R}(P)$ involving an input attribute occurrence restricts the form of the terms which may appear as its value. For example, the value of the first input attribute of the rule *append* $\to \varepsilon$ is required to be *nil*, while the value of the first input attribute of the rule *append* $\to$ *append* is required to be a term of the form $cons(t_1, t_2)$, where t_1 and t_2 are some terms. For any term t satisfying this requirement we can use selectors to extract its components: t_1 can be represented as $s_1^{cons}(t)$ and t_2 as $s_2^{cons}(t)$. Such a use of selectors is safe since for the arguments satisfying the conditions the selection functions can be eliminated.

For a simple attribute splitting every variable of an output term appears in at least one input term. Thus, the value of any output attribute occurrence can be expressed as a term, possibly including selectors, whose only free variables are some input attribute occurrences. This observation allows for transformation of the relational attribute grammar $\mathcal{R}(P)$ into a conditional attribute grammar. For each production rule r of $\mathcal{R}(P)$ we transform the formula ϕ_r into an equivalent conditional semantic rule of the form $\langle B_r, E_r \rangle$, where B_r is a condition and E_r is the conjunction of definitions of all output attribute occurrences of r. Each definition is of the form $a = t$, where a is an output attribute occurrence of r and t is a term, possibly including selectors, whose only variables are input attribute occurrences of r.

We first construct the condition B_r: it is the existentially quantified conjunction of all equations of ϕ_r including input attribute occurrences; the quantification concerns all variables of the input terms of r.

Let $\alpha = (a_1 = t_1 \wedge, \ldots, \wedge a_n = t_n)$ be the conjunction of all remaining equations. Then each a_i for $i = 1, \ldots, n$ is an output attribute occurrence of r. Since the splitting is simple, each variable x that appears in some t_i occurs also in the condition B_r, in the right-hand side of an equation $b = w$ where b is an input attribute occurrence. Let π_x be a selector such that $\pi_x(w) = x$. We now define E_r to be the formula obtained from α by replacing all occurrences of every variable x by the term $\pi_x(b)$.

Recall that we work with term domains. It follows by the construction that a valuation ν over a term domain satisfies ϕ_r iff ν satisfies $\langle B_r, E_r \rangle$ in the interpretation $\mathcal{I}'$ which extends $\mathcal{I}$ with the interpretation of the selectors. Hence we have the following proposition.

Proposition 5.1

Let P be a definite program. For every simple splitting of attributes of $\mathcal{R}(P)$ with term based interpretation there exists a conditional attribute grammar G with extended term based interpretation, such that every proof tree of P is isomorphic to a valid tree of G and vice versa.
$\square$

Notice that the construction described is nondeterministic: a variable that appears more than once in the condition B_r may be represented by different selectors when constructing E_r.

The construction is applicable to a restricted class of programs, since for a given program a simple splitting of the attributes of $\mathcal{R}(P)$ may not exist.

Example 5.3

For the program and attribute splitting of Example 5.2 the construction gives the following conditional attribute grammar.

1. *append* → ε

   Condition part B_1: $\exists L\ append_1(0) = nil \wedge append_2(0) = L$

   Definition part E_1: $append_3(0) = append_2(0)$

2. *append* → *append*

   Condition part B_2:

   $\exists E, L_1, L_2, L_3\ append_1(0) = cons(E, L_1) \wedge append_2(0) = L_2 \wedge$
   $append_3(1) = L_3$

   Definition part E_2:

   $append_1(1) = cdr(append_1(0)) \wedge append_2(1) = append_2(0) \wedge$
   $append_3(0) = cons(car(append_1(0)), append_3(1))$

   In this example the selectors s_1^{cons} and s_2^{cons} are denoted *car* and *cdr*. For the splitting considered no alternative choice of selectors is possible. Notice also that a condition of the form $\exists x(y = x)$, where x has a unique occurrence is satisfied by any valuation of y. Thus, the conditions of our example can be simplified to the following equivalent forms:

- $B_1' : append_1(0) = nil$

- $B_2' : \exists E, L_1\ append_1(0) = cons(E, L_1)$

   ☐

   As illustrated by the above example, if an input term is a variable, which does not appear in other input terms then the corresponding condition is satisfied by any valuation and can be removed. Splittings that allow to remove all conditions of the constructed conditional attribute grammars can be characterized by the following definition.

Definition 5.4 Nice splitting

   Let P be a definite program. A splitting of attributes of $\mathcal{R}(P)$ is *nice* iff in every clause of P the input terms are pairwise distinct variables.
   ☐

   For a nice and simple splitting the construction described above produces attribute definitions with empty conditions and without selectors.

Thus, in any such case, a unique functional attribute grammar is obtained, whose valid trees are isomorphic to the proof trees of the original definite program.

Example 5.4

For the program *plus* of Example 5.1 p. 208 the splitting: $Inh = \{plus_2\}$ and $Syn = \{plus_1, plus_3\}$ is nice and simple. For this splitting our construction gives the following functional attribute grammar.

1. $plus \to \varepsilon$

   $plus_1(0) = zero \land plus_3(0) = plus_2(0)$

2. $plus \to plus$

   $plus_2(1) = plus_2(0) \land plus_1(0) = s(plus_1(1)) \land plus_3(0) = s(plus_3(1))$

Each parse tree of this grammar has a valid assignment. The inherited attribute of the root may be assigned to any term t. If the depth of the tree is n then the values of the attribute occurrences at its root are $s^n(zero)$, t, and $s^n(t)$.

□

For a splitting which is nice but not simple the construction does not work. What is then the intuition of nice splittings? This question will be discussed in the next section.

The conditional attribute grammar constructed for a given program has the valid trees isomorphic to the proof trees of the program. An interesting question is whether an attribute evaluator applied to the grammar can be used for construction of the proof trees of the program. Generally this is not possible, even if the grammar is non-circular. Even if the attribute evaluator is able to interleave parsing with attribute evaluation, which is not always the case, it needs values of the inherited attributes of the root to construct a decorated tree. Generally, these values are not known in the case of definite program. Some special cases will be discussed in the subsequent sections.

5.2   Attribute dependency schemes for definite programs

As discussed in the previous section a definite program can be seen as
a relational attribute grammar. The dependency relation introduced by
attribute splitting of this grammar allows to investigate its properties,
and, indirectly, properties of the original definite program. We want to
use it for analysis of information flow in proof trees.

5.2.1   Direction assignment, the attribute dependency scheme $\mathcal{A}_\alpha(P)$

We now attempt to define a notion of dependency relation for definite
programs without referring to the attribute grammars of the previous
section. The dependency relation will be formally introduced by associating with a definite program an attribute dependency scheme whose
attributes are argument positions of the predicates. The underlying
context-free rules are clause skeletons. The local dependency relation
relates the argument positions of the clause which have common variables. We first modify the notion of attribute splitting for the case of
definite programs.

Definition 5.5 Direction assignment

Let P be a definite program. A *direction assignment* (in short *d-
assignment*) for P is a partial mapping from arguments of the predicate
symbols into the two-element set $\{inherited, synthesized\}$.
□

A direction assignment is *total* if the mapping is defined for all arguments of the predicate symbols. Such a partial mapping will be some-
times denoted by a n-tuple of elements in $\{\downarrow, \uparrow, -\}$ associated to every
predicate symbols. The d-assignments discussed in this section will be
assumed to be total unless explicitly stated. A program P with a total
(partial) d-assignment α will be denoted P_α and will be called a *directed*
program (*partially directed* program). Notice that a directed program is
a special case of a partially directed program. For a given d-assignment
the inherited arguments of the head of a clause and the synthesized arguments of its body atoms are called the *input* terms of the clause. The
synthesized arguments of the head and the inherited arguments of the
body atoms are called the *output* terms of the clause. This terminology
originates from attribute grammars. The motivation for its introduction

was discussed in Section 4.2.2. The definitions extend for the terms of goal clauses (the goal is thus regarded as a body).

We now use d-assignments to define dependency relations on proof trees of definite programs.

Definition 5.6 ADS induced by a d-assignment

Let P be a definite program with the alphabet of predicates $Pred$ and let α be a d-assignment for P. We denote by $\mathcal{A}_\alpha(P)$ the attribute dependency scheme $\langle Pred, R, Attr, D \rangle$,where

- R is the following $Pred$-sorted signature: $r_c : \langle p_1 \ldots p_m, p_0 \rangle$ is in R iff $c : p_0(t_{01}, \ldots, t_{0n_0}) \leftarrow p_1(t_{11}, \ldots, t_{1n_1}), \ldots, p_m(t_{m1}, \ldots, t_{mn_m})$ is a clause of P. Thus, the elements of the signature correspond to clause skeletons of P. The signature can also be seen as a context-free grammar with the empty terminal alphabet.

- $Attr = \{p_i | p \in Pred, i = 1, \ldots, arity(p)\}$; The splitting of the attributes is defined by α, i.e. $Inh = \{a \in Attr | \alpha(a) = inherited\}$ and $Syn = \{a \in Attr | \alpha(a) = synthesized\}$

- D is the family of local dependency relations defined as follows: Let c be a clause of P of the form
$p_0(t_{01}, \ldots, t_{0n_0}) \leftarrow p_1(t_{11}, \ldots, t_{1n_1}), \ldots, p_m(t_{m1}, \ldots, t_{mn_m})$. Every attribute occurrence $a \in Attr(r_c)$ corresponds to exactly one term t_{ij} for some $0 \leq i \leq m$ and $1 \leq j \leq n_i$. Let a be an input attribute occurrence and let b be an output attribute occurrence in $Attr(r_c)$. $aD(c)b$ iff the terms of c corresponding to a and b share a variable.

□

The attribute dependency scheme $\mathcal{A}_\alpha(P)$ defines a dependency relation on the attibute occurrences of every parse tree. Since the parse trees are skeletons of P, it defines also a dependency relation on argument positions of every proof tree. The local dependencies indicate possible direction of information flow between variable sharing positions. Thus, the dependency relation on a skeleton shows a possible data flow in the process of construction of a proof tree based on this skeleton.

We now develop a terminology to be used for directed programs.

Definition 5.7

A d-assignment α for a definite program P is said to have a property X (or to be an X d-assignment) if the attribute dependency scheme $\mathcal{A}_\alpha(P)$

has this property. A definite program P with a total d-assignment α, denoted P_α, is said to have a property X (or to be an X directed program) if α has this property.
□

This definition allows us to extend the classification of attribute dependency schemes discussed in Section 4.3 for d-assignments and for partially directed programs. For example, the concept of non-circular d-assignment is covered by this generic definition.

We now use the notion of d-assignment to identify some classes of logic programs with interesting properties. Some of them have been already mentioned in the previous section.

5.2.2 Nice directed programs

For a given definite program P the scheme $\mathcal{A}_\alpha(P)$ and the relational attribute grammar $\mathcal{R}(P)$ of Section 5.1.1 have the same set of attributes. A total d-assignment for a program P determines a splitting of this set. In the previous chapter we defined two kinds of interesting splittings: a nice splitting and a simple splitting. We pointed out that a nice and simple splitting makes it possible to transform a definite program into an equivalent functional attribute grammar. We now extend the terminology concerning splitting for d-assignments.

Definition 5.8 Nice d-assignment
A d-assignment for a definite program P is said to be *nice* iff in every clause of P any input term is a variable different from the other input terms. A definite program is said to be *nice* if there exists a nice total d-assignment for this program.
□

This definition applies without change also to Horn programs.

Since for a given program there exists only a finite number of d-assignments, it is decidable whether a definite program is nice. As non-circularity of an attribute dependency scheme is decidable it is thus decidable whether a given program has a nice and non-circular d-assignment.

We now give an example of a nice d-assignment.

Example 5.5 Nice append

1. $append(nil, L, L) \leftarrow$
2. $append(E.L1, L2, E.L3) \leftarrow append(L1, L2, L3)$

   $Inh = \{append_2\}$
   $Syn = \{append_1, append_3\}$

1. input terms: $\{append_{02} = L\}$
2. input terms: $\{append_{02} = L2, append_{11} = L1, append_{13} = L3\}$

   (The variable E appears in the output arguments only).

The d-assignment of this example is a kind of artificial construction obtained by the attempt to fulfill the conditions of the definition. Intuitively, the first two arguments of the predicate *append* represent the lists to be appended and the third argument the result of this operation. This would be reflected by the following d-assignment:
   $Inh = \{append_1, append_2\}$
   $Syn = \{append_3\}$
   This d-assignment is not nice.
□

For a functional attribute grammar every parse tree has a valid attribute assignment that transforms it into a valid tree. For a complete skeleton of a definite program there may be no decoration that makes it into a proof tree. The notion of nice d-assignment allows to identify a class of definite programs such that for every skeleton there exists a decoration that makes it into a proof tree.

Proposition 5.2 Basic property of a nice program
   If there exists a nice and non-circular total d-assignment for a definite program P, then for every skeleton S of P the set of equations $Eq(S)$ has a solution.
□

Proof. Let $t = r$ be an equation of $Eq(S)$. Since a d-assignment for P is defined then one of the terms t and r is an input term of a clause variant, while the other is an output term of another clause variant.

Consider the set of equations E obtained from $Eq(S)$ by reordering the
equations in such a way that the left-hand side of every equation is the
input term. Clearly, E has the same set of solutions as $Eq(S)$. By the
definition of nice d-assignment the left-hand side of every equation of E
is a variable different from the left-hand side of any other equation. By
the definition of $Eq(S)$ this variable does not appear in the right-hand
side of the equation.

Thus, the most general unifier of a single equation $x = t$ is the substitution $\{x/t\}$. The most general unifier of $Eq(S)$ is a composition of
this substitution and the mgu of the set of equations $E - \{x = t\})\{x/t\}$.
The left-hand sides of these equations are distinct variables since x is
the left-hand side of only one equation of E. On the other hand, the
non-circularity condition guarantees that in this set there is no equation such that the variable which is its left-hand side occurs also in its
right-hand side. Successive application of this transformation will produce decreasing sets of equations with the same property and finally will
result in an idempotent most general unifier of $Eq(S)$.
□

This result holds also for Horn programs.

Notice that the mgu produced by the variable elimination process
described above may not be ground. This happens if a variable occurs
only in output arguments of some program clause or goal clause. Assume
that such a clause is used for construction of a parse tree. Consider the
equations of E originating from its use. The right-hand sides of these
equations are variants of the output arguments. Thus, at least one of
them includes a variable which does not appear as a left-hand side of any
equation of E. This variable cannot be instantiated during the variable
elimination process.

The basic step of the variable elimination process described in the
proof of Proposition 5.2 is transformation of an equation $x = t$, where
x is a variable, into the substitution $\{x/t\}$. This resembles the elementary step of the unification algorithm of Section 1.6.3. The difference
is that the unification algorithm imposes the "occur-check" condition
that x does not occur in t. As mentioned above, non-circularity of the
d-assignment guarantees that in any equation which might be created
during the described process x cannot appear in t. It turns out that nice
and non-circular definite programs can be executed by SLD-resolution
without occur-check. This is discussed in more detail in Chapter 8 (The-

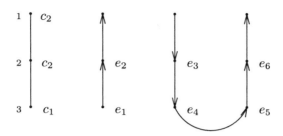

Figure 5.1
The dependency relation in a skeleton of nice append program of Example 5.5
p. 219

orem 8.3 p. 403).

Example 5.6

For the program and d-assignment of Example 5.5 consider the standardized skeleton S shown in Figure 5.1 together with the ordering relation determined by the d-assignment.

The set $Eq(S)$ consists of the following equations (following the dependencies):

$e_1 : L1^2 = nil$
$e_2 : L1^1 = E^2.L1^2$
$e_3 : L2^2 = L2^1$
$e_4 : L3 = L2^2$
$e_5 : L3^2 = L3$
$e_6 : L3^1 = E^2.L3^2$

The mgu obtained by the elimination method is the substitution:
$\{L1^2/nil, L1^1/E^2.nil, L2^2/L2^1, L3/L2^1, L3^2/L2^1, L3^1/E^2.L2^1\}$.
□

The class of nice programs is very restricted. Typical examples in the textbooks of logic programming usually do not belong to it. However, for many programs it is possible to find a partial d-assignment which is nice. For a partial d-assignment only some arguments of the clauses are assigned as input terms or output terms. The remaining arguments will be called, following [Bou92b], the *decisive* arguments of the clause. The intuition of the decisive arguments is that they determine whether a given skeleton is proper or not. We now make this statement more precise.

Let P be a definite program and let α be a nice and non-circular partial d-assignment such that in every clause of P the input terms do not share variables with decisive arguments. Let S be a skeleton of P. The equations of $Eq(S)$ originate from the arguments of the clauses of P. Let $Eq_1(S)$ be the subset of $Eq(S)$ originating from all decisive arguments of the clauses. Then it follows by Proposition 5.2 p. 219 that $Eq(S)$ has a solution iff $Eq_1(S)$ has a solution. Thus, to construct a proof tree based on S one can consider first only the equations of $Eq_1(S)$. Their mgu may or may not exist. If it exists it determines a partial decoration of the skeleton. The remaining equations correspond to the arguments with the nice d-assignment. By Proposition 5.2 they have an mgu and by the restriction on variable sharing the mgu does not affect the partial decoration determined by $Eq_1(S)$. Thus, their mgu composed with the mgu of $Eq_1(S)$ determines the missing part of the decoration of S. If $Eq_1(S)$ has no unifier the remaining equations need not be considered. This is summarized by the following corollary.

Corollary 5.1 Basic property of a Horn program with partial nice d-assignment

Let P be a definite program and let α be a nice and non-circular partial d-assignment such that in every clause of P the input terms do not share variables with decisive arguments. Every skeleton of P which is proper with the decisive arguments only is proper with all arguments.

□

Example 5.7 Program with a nice partial d-assignment

Consider the following definite program:

1. $rev(nil, L, L) \leftarrow$
2. $rev(A.L, Q, R) \leftarrow rev(L, Q, A.R)$

Assume that it will be always called with a goal g of the form $\leftarrow rev(t, X, nil)$, where t is a ground term. It is easy to check that there is no nice total d-assignment for this program augmented with such a goal. Indeed, any direction assigned to the first position of the predicate violates the niceness condition. However, the partial d-assignment: $Inh = \{rev_3\}$, $Syn = \{rev_2\}$ is nice, since the input terms in clause 1: $\{rev_{03} = L\}$, the input terms in rule 2: $\{rev_{03} = R, rev_{12} = Q\}$, and the input terms in the goal: $\{rev_{12} = X\}$ satisfy the niceness condition.

It is also easy to see that the d-assignment is non-circular. The only variable shared between non-decisive and decisive arguments of a clause is A in the second clause. It appears only in an output argument of this clause.

To check whether a given (standardized) skeleton can be decorated it suffices to solve the equations associated with decisive argument positions. For example, for the skeleton of Figure 5.2, where r_g denotes the skeleton of the goal clause $\leftarrow rev(1.(2.nil), X^0, nil)$ these equations are:

$$e_1 : A^1.L^1 = 1.(2.nil)$$
$$e_2 : A^2.L^2 = L^1$$
$$e_3 : L^2 = nil$$

and have the mgu that binds A^1 to 1 and A^2 to 2. By Proposition 5.2 the remaining equations associated with the skeleton have an mgu and since the program satisfies the restriction on variable sharing this mgu does not influence the partial decoration constructed so far. This unifier binds X^0 to the list $2.(1.nil)$.
□

To summarize, nice definite programs constitute a very restricted class of logic programs, such that any skeleton of a program gives rise to a proof tree. Any computation of a program that has a nice partial d-assignment can be done in two phases, first of which is a construction of partially decorated skeleton while the second is the computation of the remaining part of the decoration. It is not clear whether this observation has some practical importance for logic programming.

5.2.3 Simple directed programs

An interesting class of directed programs is related to the notion of simple splitting defined in Section 5.1.2.

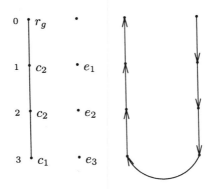

Figure 5.2
A skeleton of the reverse program in Example 5.7 p. 222 with partial dependency
graph

Definition 5.9 Simple d-assignment
   A d-assignment for a definite program P is said to be *simple* iff in
every clause of P each variable of an output term occurs in at least one
input term.
□
   This definition extends without change for Horn programs.
   Using the convention of Definition 5.7 p. 217 we obtain the class
of simple directed programs, to be called briefly *simple programs*. As
discussed in Section 5.1.2 every simple program can be transformed into
a conditional attribute grammar with the same declarative semantics.

Example 5.8
   Consider a definite program consisting of the clause
   $grandpar(X, Y) \leftarrow par(X, Z), \ grandpar(Z, Y)$
   and of a finite number of unit clauses of the form $par(c_1, c_2) \leftarrow$ where
c_1 and c_2 are constants. The d-assignment which defines all positions
of the predicates to be synthesized is simple and non-circular for this
program.
□
   The following theorem shows that simple d-assignments give a sufficient condition for achieving groundness of the constructed proof trees.

Theorem 5.2 Groundness condition for simple programs

Let P_α be a simple and non-circular directed definite program. If the inherited arguments of the head of a proof tree of P are ground then the proof tree is ground.

□

Proof. The proof trees of P can be seen as the valid trees of the relational attribute grammar $\mathcal{R}(P)$. We prove the theorem by applying to $\mathcal{R}(P)$ the annotation method of Section 4.4.3. The attributes of $\mathcal{R}(P)$ correspond to the arguments of the predicates. The splitting and the dependency relation is defined by α. To each attribute p_i we associate the assertion $ground(p_i)$ interpreted on the domain of all terms of the language. The local dependency relations on the assertions follow the dependency of the attributes defined by the d-assignment.

It is easy to check that the resulting annotation is sound (Definition 4.21 p. 183) since in every clause the variables of the output terms occur in the input terms. By non-circularity of the d-assignment we obtain the result.

□

This result holds also for Horn clauses.

The program of Example 5.8 has no inherited positions. Thus, any of its proof trees is ground.

Assume that for a simple program we construct an SLD-derivation starting with a goal clause. Theorem 5.2 gives a condition for the goal which is sufficient for groundness of any computed answer substitution: the d-assignment must be simple also on the goal clause. This means that every variable that appears in an output term of the goal must also appear in some input term of the goal.

Groundness of arguments of goal atoms is a property used for optimization of compiled code of logic programs. However, Theorem 5.2 says nothing about groundness of goals during computations: groundness of the inherited arguments of the body atoms of a clause instance does not follow from groundness of the inherited arguments of its head. Consider for example the program of Example 5.8 with the following d-assignment: $grandpar : \{\uparrow, \downarrow\}$ and $par : \{\uparrow, \downarrow\}$. This is another simple d-assignment for this program. The goal $\leftarrow grandpar(X, john)$ conforms with this d-assignment but the SLD-computation with the standard computation rule transforms this goal into the goal of the form

$\leftarrow par(X, Z), grandpar(Z, john)$ where the inherited argument of the
selected atom is not ground. The selected atomic subgoal can be seen
as the call of a procedure. Its inherited arguments are input arguments
of the call. In our example they are not ground. We now define a restriction on simple d-assignments which guarantees groundness of the
inherited arguments of each goal atom selected during the computation.

Definition 5.10 Data driven directed programs
   A directed program P_α is said to be *data driven* iff α is a one-sweep
simple[1] d-assignment.
□

Consider the relation on the body atoms of a clause which holds for
atoms a and b iff some output term of b shares a variable with some input
term of a. For a one-sweep program this relation is a partial ordering.
An important subclass of data driven programs are L-programs (cf. the
notion of L-ADS in Section 4.3.7). For an L-program if the atoms a and
b of a clause body are in this relation then a textually precedes b in the
clause.
   This gives an intuition for the following result.

Proposition 5.3
   Let P_α be a data driven definite program. Then there exists a simple
L-program P' with the same proof-theoretic semantics.
□

The proposition follows from the definitions of data driven programs
and L-programs. For each clause of P, rearrange its body atom, so that
the textual ordering follows the ordering of the body atoms determined
by α. The program P' consists of all clauses obtained in that way. For
this program α is an L-assignment, and by the construction the proof-
theoretic semantics of P and P' coincide.
The class of simple programs has been introduced in [DM85b]. The
L-programs have been experimentally studied by Drabent [Dra87] who
calls them "simple". The objective of the study was to analyze how often
an existing Prolog program can be given an L-assignment reflecting its
intended use. The experiment concerned both small programs published

---

[1]Notice that the word "simple" here concerns d-assignment (Definition 5.9) and
should not be confused with the simple one-sweep ADS in the sense of Section 4.3.7.

in the literature and some application programs. Many of them were not definite programs because of the use of extralogical Prolog features. About half of the analyzed programs turned out to have natural L-assignments. Many others could be treated as L-programs with except of their minor fragments.

Drabent's study shows some typical reasons for a program not to be an L-program:

- *Variable as data*: Some variables in the clauses are not bound to ground terms during the computation. This is essential for programming techniques using open data structures like difference lists.

- *Multidirectional use of a predicate*: For example, the append program of Example 5.2 p. 211 may be used for appending two ground lists or for decomposition of a ground list. These two different uses can be indicated by different d-assignments. A larger program may include the append program and use it in both ways.

- *Communication variables*: Definite programs are sometimes used for simulation of concurrent processes. In this case variables of a clause may play role of communication channels between processes. It is essential that such variables are never bound to ground terms, hence such programs are not L-programs.

- *Glued arguments*: A d-assignment is given for arguments of predicates. However, one can artificially reduce a number of arguments of a predicate by combining arguments into tuples. Such a transformation of L-program may lead to a non-L-program. Drabent gives examples of programs which could be made into L-programs by the opposite transformation, i.e. by decomposition of predicate arguments.

Some Prolog systems use a unification algorithm without occur-check and it is well-known that this may lead to obtaining unsound answers (see e.g. [Llo87]). When executing non-circular simple programs (and in particular data driven programs) every answer obtained by such a Prolog system is sound. This results from the fact that the complete proof tree must be ground. However, omitting occur-check may delay a failure which should be otherwise caused by the check. The delay may sometimes lead to an infinite loop. The occur-check problem is discussed in more detail in Chapter 8.

5.2.4 Multi d-assignment

As mentioned above, some programs do not have any simple or nice d-assignment because of multiple occurrences of the same predicate with different uses. This leads to the idea of "multiple d-assignment" as a generalization of the d-assignment. We first give an example of such a program.

Example 5.9 Fabulous mutants

The purpose of the program is to combine names of animals into names of fabulous mutants. It uses the database of animal names where each name is a list of components. The list constructor is represented by $|$ and the empty list is denoted ".". e.g. $e|leph|ant|$. or $ant|ilop|e|$. A new name can be created from the names x and y iff x has a nonempty postfix which is a prefix of y. The new name is the concatenation of the prefix of x with y, e.g. $e|leph|ant|ilop|e|$. or $ant|ilop|e|leph|ant|$.. The program consists of the following definite clauses:

$$c_1 : mutant(Z) \leftarrow animal(X), animal(Y),$$
$$append(V1|X1, V2|X2, X),$$
$$append(V2|X2, Y1, Y),$$
$$append(V1|X1, Y, Z)$$
$$c_2 : append(., X, X) \leftarrow$$
$$c_3 : append(V|X, Y, V|Z) \leftarrow append(X, Y, Z)$$
$$c_4 : animal(ant|ilop|e|.) \leftarrow$$
$$c_5 : animal(e|leph|ant|.) \leftarrow$$
etc.

□

We want to generate (ground) "mutants", thus the intended d-assignment should specify $mutant_1$ as a synthesized position. We now show that there is no simple d-assignment satisfying this requirement. If $mutant_1$ is synthesized, then the second occurrence of Z in c_1 must be an input term. Thus, $append_3$ must be a synthesized position. Consequently, by the structure of c_2, $append_2$ must be inherited. But in this case the variable $Y1$ does not appear in any input term of c_1, so that the conditions of simple d-assignment are violated. The reason of non-simplicity of the example program is the multi-directional use of the predicate $append$. One could avoid the problem by introducing two "copies" of the predicate *append* with different directions and provide copies of the defining clauses for each of them. We now make this idea more precise.

Definition 5.11 Multi d-assignment

A *multi d-assignment* μ for a definite program P is a mapping on the predicates of P which associates with every predicate p a nonempty set μ_p of n_p-tuples of symbols $\downarrow$, $\uparrow$ and $-$, where n_p is the arity of p.
□

Let μ be a multi d-assignment for P. Select one tuple from each set μ_p. In this way each argument of p is mapped into the corresponding symbol of the tuple. Interpreting the symbol $-$ as "undefined" we obtain a partial d-assignment. Thus, a multi d-assignment can be seen as a way for specifying a finite number of partial d-assignments for P. If all sets μ_p are singletons, then μ can be seen as a d-assignment. A multi d-assignment is *total* if all of its d-assignments are total.

The following definition formalizes the intuition of transforming a logic program with a multi d-assignment into a logic program with a single d-assignment. The transformation is such that the semantics of the original program can be reconstructed from the semantics of the resulting program.

Definition 5.12

Let P be a definite program and let μ be a multi d-assignment for P. A μ-*extension* of P is any definite program P^* defined such that:

- The predicates of P^* are all pairs $\langle p, a \rangle$, (to be denoted p_a) where p is a predicate of P and $a \in \mu_p$.

- For every predicate p of P, for every $a \in \mu_p$ and for every clause of P of the form

$$p(\bar{t}_0) \leftarrow p^1(\bar{t}_1), \ldots, p^n(\bar{t}_n)$$

where $n \geq 0$ and $\bar{t}_1, \ldots \bar{t}_n$ are the tuples of argument terms of the predicates $p^1, \ldots, p^n$, there is at least one clause in P^* of the form

$$p_a(\bar{t}_0) \leftarrow p^1_{a1}(\bar{t}_1), \ldots, p^n_{an}(\bar{t}_n)$$

where $a1 \ldots an$ are some elements of the sets $\mu_{p1}, \ldots \mu_{pn}$.

□

Notice that there may be many different μ-extensions of a program P. Notice also that every μ-extension of P is a partially directed program, whose d-assignment associates with every predicate symbol p_a the directions determined by a.

By the definition a μ-extension of a program P consists of "copies" of the clauses of P and includes at least one copy of every clause for every d-assignment of the head predicate. Thus, by the construction, every proof tree of P can be obtained from a proof tree of the extension by collapsing different copies of the same clause. Notice that the multi d-assignment μ defines a d-assignment for P^*: for every predicate p_a the directions of the argument positions are determined by a.

The notion of multi d-assignment may allow to obtain a program with required property as an extension of a given program. In particular a multi d-assignment for a program which has no simple d-assignment may allow to find its extension which has a simple d-assignment. This is illustrated by the following example.

Example 5.10 Fabulous mutant (continued)

Let us consider the following total multi d-assignment μ for the program *mutant*:

mutant: $\{1:\{\uparrow\}\}$ We impose this direction.

animal: $\{1:\{\uparrow\}\}$ It is the only possibility to get a simple d-assignment.

append: $\{1:\{\downarrow,\downarrow,\uparrow\}, 2:\{\uparrow,\uparrow,\downarrow\}\}$

We now construct a μ-extension of the program.

$c_1 : mutant_1(Z) \leftarrow animal_1(X),\ animal_1(Y),$
$\qquad\qquad\qquad\quad append_2(V1|X1, V2|X2, X),$
$\qquad\qquad\qquad\quad append_2(V2|X2, Y1, Y),$
$\qquad\qquad\qquad\quad append_1(V1|X1, Y, Z)$
$c_{21} : append_1(., X, X) \leftarrow$
$c_{31} : append_1(V|X, Y, V|Z) \leftarrow append_1(X, Y, Z)$
$c_{22} : append_2(., X, X) \leftarrow$
$c_{32} : append_2(V|X, Y, V|Z) \leftarrow append_2(X, Y, Z)$
$c_4 : animal_1(ant|ilop|e|.) \leftarrow$
$c_5 : animal_1(e|leph|ant|.) \leftarrow$

etc.
□

Let P be a definite program with a multi d-assignment μ and let P^* be a μ-extension of P. It follows by the definition of μ-extensions that by removing indices of all predicates of a clause c of P^* one obtains a clause c' of P. Similarly, any proof tree of P^* can be transformed into a proof tree of P by replacing every node label $\langle c, \sigma \rangle$ by the label $\langle c', \sigma \rangle$. Thus, the properties of proof trees of P^* carry over to proof trees of P. On the other hand, any proof tree of P is an image of a proof tree of P^* and any skeleton of P is an image of a skeleton of P^*. Notice that the transformation does not concern the argument terms of the clauses but only the predicates. Thus the equations associated with a skeleton of P^* and those associated with its image in P have the same mgu. Hence the following propositions can be obtained from the results on nice and simple programs.

Proposition 5.4
Let P be a definite program with a multi d-assignment μ. If there exists a nice and non-circular μ-extension of P then for every skeleton S of P the set of equations $Eq(S)$ has a solution.
□

Proposition 5.5
Let P be a definite program with a multi d-assignment μ. Let P_α^* be a simple and non-circular μ-extension of P. If the α-inherited arguments of the head of a proof tree of P are ground then the proof tree is ground.

□

This proposition shows that every proof tree with the head predicate *mutant* of the "fabulous mutant" program must be ground.

All the results of this section extend to Horn programs.

An interesting application of this proposition follows from the results of Section 5.2.3. If a multi d-assignment μ for a program with a goal clause has a simple and non-circular μ-extension then no computation starting with the goal requires occur-check. Existence of a multi d-assignment with this property is decidable but, following the results on the circularity test in ADS, it is intrinsically exponential in the worst case. There are indeed three factors of exponentiality: number of directions associated to each predicate, duplication of the clauses, and non circularity test. It is an open question whether there exist efficient algorithms for solving this problem for restricted but sufficiently large classes of programs. The efficient non-circularity tests discussed in Chapter 4 may provide some guidance.

5.3   Modelling the operational semantics by attribute grammars

In Section 2.1.4 we outlined a spectrum of possible operational semantics for definite programs. All of them are based on the characterization of the proof trees by equations associated with skeletons. A general framework for construction of the proof tree was presented as a general resolution scheme. This section shows that some instances of the general resolution scheme can be described by functional attribute grammars (with partial semantic functions). In that way various kinds of operational semantics of logic programs can be modelled by attribute grammars. This allows one to use verification methods of attribute grammars for proving "run-time" properties of logic programs. On the other hand, this shows a potential possibility of using attribute evaluators for execution of logic programs. This idea may be interesting also in the case of non-term preinterpretations.

The presentation is organized as follows. We first give a general nondeterministic construction which permits to associate many different attribute grammars to the same program. The parse trees of each of them are skeletons of the program and the attribute evaluation process for a given skeleton is the process of solving equations associated with that skeleton. Thus the nondeterministic choices during the construction can be seen as defining control for the resolution process. We then discuss conditions for obtaining grammars with particularly simple semantic rules. Finally we show how to model some special resolution schemes of Chapter 2.

5.3.1   General construction, the attribute grammar $\mathcal{F}(P)$

We first outline briefly the idea of the construction to be presented. The intention is to model full resolution schemes by attribute grammars.

For a given definite program the construction produces a functional attribute grammar. The underlying context-free grammar produces the skeletons and the attribute definitions describe the equation solving process. For a given skeleton S denote by $Eq(n)$ the subset of $Eq(S)$ associated with node n of S. The computation can be viewed as traversing the nodes of the skeleton. Every node is visited a fixed number of times, depending on its predicate. At every visit a fixed subset of $Eq(n)$ is selected and solved, using the information about previously solved equations given in the form of substitution.

This is reflected by the definition of the attribute grammar where:

- The number of attributes of a predicate equals to the number of scheduled visits for each corresponding node: every inherited attribute corresponds to a top-down visit, every synthesized attribute corresponds to a bottom-up visit.

- Every attribute value is a pair consisting of a sequence of terms and a substitution. The terms are halves of the equations to be solved during the visit corresponding to the attribute. They come from the context. The remaining halves originate from the clause labelling the node.

The substitution represents the solution of the equations which occur in the definitions of all attribute occurrences on which the attribute depends.

So the value of an attribute represents the instantiation of some arguments and the current substitution after some equation solving steps. The semantic rules define how an output attribute is computed using some input attributes. In other words, the definition of an output attribute describes a new equation solving step in which "external" halves of equations are given together with the solution of the previously solved subset of equations.

Notice that we do not impose any restriction on the previously solved equations. This means that the current substitution associated with different input attribute occurrences may represent solutions of subsets of equations with nonempty intersection and may share variables. The resolution of the equations is done by computing a most general unifier. As there is no restriction on the subset of equations solved in a current substitution, combination of sequential and parallel equation solving may be needed. In that case it would be necessary to use the equational representation $eq(\sigma)$ (see Section 1.6.2) of the current substitution σ. Therefore it is required that the mgu's computed are idempotent.

In our construction the terms in the first component of an attribute value are instances of some arguments under the substitution component. An alternative construction is possible where the substitution is not applied to the arguments.

The ideas outlined above are incorporated in the following construction of the attribute grammar $\mathcal{F}(P)$. The construction is nondeterministic. The parse trees of the grammar are the skeletons of P and the attribute evaluation process of Section 4.3.6 applied to a given skeleton defines control for solving the set of equations associated with this skeleton.

Definition 5.13 Construction of the grammar $\mathcal{F}(P)$

For a Horn program P we construct a functional attribute grammar $\mathcal{F}(P)$ such that

- Its underlying context-free grammar defines the skeletons of P (as in Definition 5.1 p. 206).

- Its set of attributes $Attr$ is defined as follows : Every predicate p of P has associated two subsets of attributes $Inh(p)$ and $Syn(p)$. There is a mapping τ_p of attributes of p into subsequences of the argument positions of p. Given an attribute occurrence a_i at nonterminal p in the rule r, we denote $t(a_i)$ the sequence of terms in the positions $\tau_p(a_i)$ of the clause c_r. The root of a goal clause skeleton (which has no head) may also have one synthesized attribute.

- Let a be an attribute of p. Then its value domain is the set of pairs $\langle \bar{t}, \sigma \rangle$ such that $\bar{t}$ is a sequence of n terms, where n is the number of elements of the sequence $\tau_p(a)$, possibly empty if $n = 0$, and σ is an idempotent substitution. The value of the synthesized attribute of the root of a goal clause has an empty sequence of terms.

- The semantic rules are defined as follows. Let r_c be the skeleton of a clause c .

Then for every output attribute occurrence a of r_c we construct a semantic rule of the form:

$a = \langle a^{term}, a^{subst} \rangle$ where

$a^{term} = t(a) a^{subst}$

and

$a^{subst} = mgu(\bigcup_{i=1}^{k}(eq(a_i^{subst}) \cup eq(t(a_i) a_i^{subst}, a_i^{term})))$

for some set $\{a_1, \ldots, a_k\}$ of the input attribute occurrences of r_c, where $eq(\langle t_1, \ldots, t_n \rangle, \langle s_1, \ldots, s_n \rangle)$ denotes the set of equations $t_1 = s_1, \ldots, t_n = s_n$. It is assumed that the mgu of the empty set of equations is the identity substitutions and that the computed mgu's are idempotent.

□

Notice that the constructed equations may, or may not have unifiers. Thus the grammar constructed can be seen as a conditional attribute grammar since the semantic functions are partial.

For a partial skeleton S denote by $Eq(S, a)$ the set of all the equations of $Eq(S)$ occurring in the definitions of the attribute occurrences in S on which a depends according to the global dependency relation $D(S)$.

Proposition 5.6

Let P be a definite program and let S be a partial skeleton for P. For any non-circular attribute grammar $\mathcal{F}(P)$, any attribute occurrence $a = \langle a^{term}, a^{subst} \rangle$ in S and any valid S-assignment ν, $\nu(a^{subst})$ is a most general unifier of $Eq(S, a)$.
□

This can be shown by induction following the partial order defined by the dependency relation and the form of the attribute definitions.

Thus the construction of Definition 5.13 can be used to model full resolution scheme as stated by the following theorem.

Theorem 5.3

Let P be a definite program, g a goal clauses and $\mathcal{F}(P)$ be an attribute grammar obtained by the construction of Definition 5.13 .

If

- $\mathcal{F}(P)$ is non-circular and

- g has a unique synthesized attribute occurrence $a = \langle \varepsilon, a^{subst} \rangle$ and

- in all complete skeletons S with the root labeled by g $Eq(S, a^{subst}(0)) = Eq(S)$, then every procedure which computes all the valid decorated trees of root labeled by g is a full resolution scheme.

□

As a consequence the substitution $a^{subst}(0)$ is a most general unifier of all the equations. Thus if applied to all arguments of the nodes of the skeleton S, one gets a proof tree $D(S)$.

The conditions of Theorem 5.3 may seem difficult to satisfy. However, they are decidable and can thus be automatically checked.

A better solution would be to restrict the construction in such a way that the constructed attribute grammars satisfy the conditions. For example, the following restrictions are sufficient:

- Every argument position is used in some term component of the corresponding rule of the grammar.

- Every input attribute is used in some output attribute.

- The grammar is l-ordered and the root of every rule has an occurrence of a synthesised attribute which is maximal according to the l-ordering.

In the sequel we will present a number of constructions satisfying these restrictions. We first illustrate the general construction by an example.

Example 5.11

We apply our construction to the following definite program, where parenthesis-free notation is used for terms to facilitate reading; e.g. the term f(Z) is represented as fZ.

1. $q(Y) \leftarrow p(fZ, fX, Y, Z)$
2. $p(X, Y, fX, Z) \leftarrow$
3. $p(X, Y, Z, fY) \leftarrow$

The underlying grammar has the following production rules:

1. $q \rightarrow p$
2. $p \rightarrow \varepsilon$
3. $p \rightarrow \varepsilon$

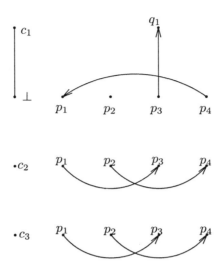

Figure 5.3
Local dependency relations in the rules of $\mathcal{F}(\mathcal{P})$ of Example 5.11 p. 236

We now choose the attributes of the predicates and associate them with the argument positions. In this example every attribute will be associated with a single argument position. An attribute of a predicate r associated with the i-th position of r, for $i \geq 1$ will be denoted r_i.

We choose the following attributes.

$Inh(q) = \{\ \}, Syn(q) = \{\ q_1\ \}$
$Inh(p) = \{\ p_1, p_2\ \}, Syn(p) = \{\ p_3, p_4\ \}$

The next decision is to impose local dependency relations. The intuition behind our construction is that the equations of the form $U = t$, where U is a variable should be solved before the equations of the form $f(U) = s$. This is reflected by the local dependency relations shown in Figure 5.3.

Using this notation we obtain the following semantic rules[2]:

1. ϕ_1

$q_1(0) = \langle Y^u \gamma_3, \gamma_3 \rangle$

---

[2]The superscript u is used to indicate standardization.

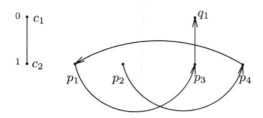

Figure 5.4
Dependency relations on a skeleton of $\mathcal{F}(\mathcal{P})$ for Example 5.11 p. 236

where $\gamma_3 = mgu(\{Y^u p_3^{subst}(1) = p_3^{term}(1)\} \cup eq(p_3^{subst}(1)))$

$p_1(1) = \langle fZ^u \gamma_4, \gamma_4 \rangle$

where $\gamma_4 = mgu(\{Z^u p_4^{subst}(1) = p_4^{term}(1)\} \cup eq(p_4^{subst}(1)))$

$p_2(1) = \langle fX^u, \epsilon \rangle$

2. ϕ_2

$p_3(0) = \langle fX^u \gamma_1, \gamma_1 \rangle$

where $\gamma_1 = mgu(\{X^u p_1^{subst}(0) = p_1^{term}(0)\} \cup eq(p_1^{subst}(0)))$

$p_4(0) = \langle Z^u \gamma_2, \gamma_2 \rangle$

where $\gamma_2 = mgu(\{Y^u p_2^{subst}(0) = p_2^{term}(0)\} \cup eq(p_2^{subst}(0)))$

3. ϕ_3

$p_4(0) = \langle fY^u \gamma_2, \gamma_2 \rangle$

where $\gamma_2 = mgu(\{Y^u p_2^{subst}(0) = p_2^{term}(0)\} \cup eq(p_2^{subst}(0)))$

$p_3(0) = \langle Z^u \gamma_1, \gamma_1 \rangle$

where $\gamma_1 = mgu(\{X^u p_1^{subst}(0) = p_1^{term}(0)\} \cup eq(p_1^{subst}(0)))$

The example satisfies the conditions of Theorem 5.3 and the additional restrictions stated above (the attribute grammar is l-ordered), hence it specifies a full resolution scheme.

Consider the skeleton S in Figure 5.4.

The figure shows also the dependency graph for this skeleton. The graph defines an ordering on the attribute occurrences. The computation determined by this ordering produces the following decoration:

$$p_2(1) = \langle fX^0, \epsilon \rangle$$
$$p_4(1) = \langle Z^1, \{Y^1/X^0\} \rangle$$
$$p_1(1) = \langle fZ^1, \{Y^1/X^0, Z^0/Z^1\} \rangle$$
$$p_3(1) = \langle ffZ^1, \{Y^1/fZ^1, Z^0/Z^1, X^0/fZ^1\} \rangle$$
$$q_2(0) = \langle ffZ^1, \{Y^1/fZ^1, Z^0/Z^1, X^0/fZ^1, Y^0/fZ^1\} \rangle$$

□

Notice that the construction is nondeterministic as the semantic rules of the constructed attribute grammar are determined by arbitrary choice of the assignment of attributes to the argument positions of the predicates and by the definition of the local dependency relations. These choices may be guided in order to obtain a construction with some desirable property. In fact even with the restrictions above the form of the attribute definitions remains complex. There are many practical situations in which it may be substantially simplified.

A careful reader may have discovered that the semantic rules defined by the general construction can be simplified in our example because of some special properties of the dependency relation chosen. We now identify these properties and corresponding simplification in the general construction. The simplifications rely on the information of variable sharing between the term components and the substitution components of the semantic rules constructed. If variables are not shared, the substitutions can be immediately applied. In this case additional restriction on the form of the local dependency relations may also make obsolete the substitution components of the attributes.

We first give auxiliary definitions concerning the attribute grammar obtained by our construction.

Definition 5.14

Let P be a definite program. A grammar $\mathcal{F}(P)$ obtained from P by our construction is said to be :

- *Natural* iff in every clause every variable occurs in exactly one output attribute definition of the corresponding skeleton;

- *Direct* iff for every input attribute occurrence a in a clause skeleton there is exactly one output attribute occurrence that depends on a.

□

Notice, that the properties listed above concern the local dependency relations of the constructed grammar. The choice of these relations is left open by our construction as a design decision. Thus it may be possible to choose them in such a way that the resulting grammar is natural and direct. We now show how the semantic rules simplify in this case.

Let a be an output attribute occurrence in a skeleton and let $a_1, \ldots, a_k$ be all attribute occurrences on which a depends. Then the main component of the semantic rule for a is construction of a most general unifier a^{subst} of the set of equations of the form

$$\{\bar{t}_1 = \bar{s}_1 \gamma_1, \ldots \bar{t}_k = \bar{s}_k \gamma_k\} \cup eq(\gamma_1) \cup \ldots \cup eq(\gamma_k)$$

where

- $\bar{t}_i$ is the tuple of terms which is the term component of the value of a_i,
- $\bar{s}_i$ is the tuple of the standardized clause arguments assigned to a_i,
- γ_i is the substitution component of the value of a_i,
- $eq(\gamma_i)$ is the set of equations obtained by representing every binding x/t of γ_i as the equation $x = t$.

Since $\bar{s}_1, \ldots \bar{s}_k$ are standardized, the substitution γ_i may affect $\bar{s}_i$ only if $\bar{s}_i$ shares some variables with some $\bar{s}_j$ where $j \neq i$. This is not the case if the grammar is natural and non-circular. Thus for a natural grammar the set of equations considered reduces to the form

$$\{\bar{t}_1 = \bar{s}_1, \ldots \bar{t}_k = \bar{s}_k\} \cup eq(\gamma_1) \cup \ldots \cup eq(\gamma_k).$$

This set of equations can be divided into two disjoint subsets:

$$\{\bar{t}_1 = \bar{s}_1, \ldots \bar{t}_k = \bar{s}_k\} \text{ and } eq(\gamma_1) \cup \ldots \cup eq(\gamma_k).$$

We want to solve them separately and to combine their results as in Section 2.1.4. Note that each set of equations $eq(\gamma_i)$ is already in solved form and that γ_i is its mgu. If the domains of all substitutions γ_i are disjoint then the solution of the second set of equations is the union of these substitutions. If the grammar obtained by our construction is also direct, then for every skeleton the graph of the dependency relation has at most one outgoing arc in every node. Thus the parents of any node do not depend on each other nor have a common predecessor. If such a grammar is also natural then for each attribute occurrence in any skeleton the domains of the substitutions γ_i are disjoint. In this case the computed most general unifier simplifies:

$$\left(\bigcup_{i=1}^{n} \gamma_i\right) mgu(\{\bar{t}_1 = \bar{s}_1, \ldots \bar{t}_k = \bar{s}_k\}).$$

Further simplification may be possible if the domain of $mgu(\{\bar{t}_1 = \bar{s}_1, \ldots \bar{t}_k = \bar{s}_k\})$ is disjoint with the domain of γ_i for $i = 1, \ldots, k$. In this case the composition of the substitutions may be reduced to their union (it is the case if furthermore attribute definitions use one input attribute occurrence only).

Example 5.12

The grammar of Example 5.11 p. 236 is non-circular, natural and direct. The domain of the local unifier computed for every node includes only the local renamed variables. Hence the semantic rules can be simplified as follows:

1. ϕ_1

   $q_1(0) = \langle p_3^{term}(1), \{Y^u/p_3^{term}(1)\} \cup p_3^{subst}(1)\rangle$

   $p_1(1) = \langle f(p_4^{term}(1)), \{Z^u/p_4^{term}(1)\} \cup p_4^{subst}(1)\rangle$

   $p_2(1) = \langle f(X^u), \epsilon\rangle$

2. ϕ_2

   $p_3(0) = \langle f(p_1^{term}(0)), \{X^u/p_1^{term}(0)\} \cup p_1^{subst}(0)\rangle$

   $p_4(0) = \langle Z^u, \{Y^u/p_2^{term}(0)\} \cup p_2^{subst}(0)\rangle$

3. ϕ_3

   $p_4(0) = \langle f(p_2^{term}(0)), \{Y^u/p_2^{term}(0)\} \cup p_2^{subst}(0)\rangle$

   $p_3(0) = \langle Z^u, \{X^u/p_1^{term}(0)\} \cup p_1^{subst}(0)\rangle$

□

A proof tree based on a given skeleton S determines a unifier of $Eq(S)$. On the other hand by Theorem 5.3 p. 235 a most general unifier of $Eq(S)$ is computed. Hence if the maximal root attribute has an argument component which is the sequence of all the arguments of the root predicate its value corresponds to a proof tree root, but the values of the argument components inside the skeleton do not necessarily correspond to elements of proof tree roots (it will be the case after applying the maximal root substitution). Thus, the question arises, whether this may

happen, or in which case the substitution components of the attributes could be ignored.
A sufficient condition for removing them is that the d-assignment chosen for construction of the natural and direct attribute grammar $\mathcal{F}(\mathcal{P})$ is nice. Since the d-assignment is nice, computation of the local mgu during the visit reduces to binding of the input terms to fresh variables. Since the grammar is natural and direct the bindings will never be updated in the later steps of computation. The local bindings are immediately used to compute the value of the local outputs which in this case are elements of the final decoration. The grammar $\mathcal{F}(\mathcal{P})$ in our example satisfies the conditions. The decoration of any of its skeletons can thus be obtained by using the following simplified semantic rules:

1. ϕ_1

   $q_1(0) = p_3(1)$

   $p_1(1) = f(p_4(1))$

   $p_2(1) = f(X^u)$

2. ϕ_2

   $p_3(0) = f(p_1(0))$

   $p_4(0) = Z^u$

3. ϕ_3

   $p_4(0) = f(p_2(0))$

   $p_3(0) = Z^u$

The attributes of the simplified grammar range over terms and represent decoration of the skeletons.

We now put together all the optimization conditions discussed above.

Let P be a Horn program and $\mathcal{F}(P)$ be an attribute grammar obtained by the construction of Definition 5.13 p. 234.

Assume that the d-assignment used to build $\mathcal{F}(P)$ is nice and that the attribute grammar is non-circular, natural, direct and that every argument position of the clause is used in some attribute definition. In this case all attribute definitions may be simplified by ignoring their substitution components. The valid trees of such a simplified grammar correspond to proof trees of P. As they are obtained by computing the most general unifier of the equations of the skeleton, they correspond to elements of the unification semantics (Section 2.2.3); i.e. any valid decorated skeleton S is $D(S)$.

Notice that if instead of being nice, $\mathcal{F}(P)$ is purely synthesized, the substitution component may also be ignored, but the valid decorated trees are not always proof trees. This will be illustrated in the next construction.

The class of logic programs for which there exists an attribute grammar $\mathcal{F}(P)$ with all these characteristics is rather restricted. As already discussed, the realistic programs are usually not nice, since existence of a nice and non-circular d-assiment for a given program means that every skeleton of this program is proper. Fortunately, as we have shown, substantial simplification may be possible also for programs which are not nice.

5.3.2 Modelling unification semantics, the attribute grammar $\mathcal{A}_{US}(P)$

The general construction of Definition 5.13 p. 234 may be used to model full resolution schemes. It may be performed for a particular program, but it may be used as a scheme which applies to any program. Some classical resolution schemes can be described in this way. We now give two examples of such schemes: nondeterministic computation of the elements of the unification semantics and the SLD-resolution. However, some full resolution schemes, like GLD-Resolution (cf. Section 2.1.4), cannot be described by any grammar $\mathcal{F}(P)$.

In this section we model the unification semantics of definite programs by an attribute grammar which describes a nondeterministic bottom up full resolution scheme.

For a given program P our construction produces an attribute grammar $\mathcal{G}(P)$ such that any valid tree of $\mathcal{G}(P)$ is isomorphic with (but not identical to) the proof tree $D(S)$ defined for S by the unification semantics of Section 2.2.3.

The grammar $\mathcal{G}(P)$ is defined as follows:

- Every predicate has only one synthesized attribute a associated with all argument positions of the predicate.

- The semantic rules are constructed as described in Definition 5.13 p. 234.

A unit clause of the form $p(\bar{s}) \leftarrow$ gives rise to the production rule[2] :

$p \leftarrow \varepsilon,$
with the semantic rule:
$a(0) = \langle \bar{s}^u, \epsilon \rangle.$

A non-unit clause of the form:
$p_0(\bar{s}_0) \leftarrow p_1(\bar{s}_1), \ldots, p_n(\bar{s}_n),$
gives rise to the production rule:
$p_0 \rightarrow p_1, \ldots, p_n,$
with the semantic rule:
$a(0) = \langle \bar{t}_0^u \sigma, \sigma \rangle,$
where
$\sigma = \bigcup(\sigma(1), \ldots, \sigma(n)) \; mgu(\{[a(1), \ldots, a(n)] = [\bar{s}_1^u, \ldots, \bar{s}_n^u]\}).$

Notice that the semantic rules have been simplified since the grammar is natural and direct.

This grammar is purely synthesized. It is a full resolution scheme by the Theorem 5.3 p. 235, as for any skeleton S all the equations in $Eq(S)$ are in some attribute definition from which the unique synthesized attribute of the root depends. The construction is defined for definite programs. However, the valid trees correspond also to the proof trees of the original program constructed for most general atomic goals[3]. Hence the value of the argument component of the root of a valid tree corresponds to the arguments of some element of the unification semantics $US(P)$.

This may be proved also directly by structural induction.

The grammar can be further simplified by removing the substitution components of the attributes. This would result in the semantic rules of the following form[4] :

Definition 5.15 Construction of $\mathcal{A}_{US}(P)$

- $a(0) = \bar{s}^u$ for unit clause skeletons.

- $a(0) = \bar{s}_0^u \sigma$
  where

---

[3]A most general atomic goal is a goal of the form $\leftarrow g$, where g is an atom whose arguments are distinct variables.

[4]The superscript u is used to indicate standardization.

Figure 5.5
A valid tree of the grammar $\mathcal{A}_{US}(P)$ modelling the unification semantics for the
short program, which is not a proof tree of P

$$\sigma = mgu(\{[a(1), \ldots, a(n)] = [\bar{s}_1^u, \ldots, \bar{s}_n^u]\})$$

for non-unit clause skeletons.

This simplified construction will be referred as $\mathcal{A}_{US}(P)$; σ will be
called the *local substitution*.
□

Figure 5.5 shows an example of a valid tree of the grammar $\mathcal{A}_{US}(P)$
of the following program P:

$$c_1 : p(X) \leftarrow q(f(X))$$
$$c_2 : q(X) \leftarrow$$

A valid decorated tree of this grammar is not a proof tree. To obtain
the corresponding proof tree it is sufficient to apply to the argument
component of each node u the composition of the local unifiers from the
root until the node u.

The grammar $\mathcal{A}_{US}(P)$ may be used for proving properties of nonground term models of P by means of inductive method of Section 4.4.2.

5.3.3   Modelling SLD-resolution, $\mathcal{A}_{SLD}(P)$

We now restrict the construction of Section 5.3.1 to model $\mathcal{R}$-controlled
SLD-resolution. At every step of an SLD-computation an atomic goal
$p(A)$ is selected and resolved. In this way a subcomputation is started
which, if successful, produces a computed substitution. The idea of our
construction is to associate with p an inherited attribute that characterizes the states in which such atomic goals are selected and a synthesized
attribute which characterizes the corresponding success states. This is
possible under the assumption that the computation rule gives a fixed

order of selection of the body atoms of every rule. The reason is that the order of selection of body atoms of the clauses can only be modelled by local dependency relations which must be fixed for every skeleton. Without further loss of generality we restrict our attention to the standard strategy, i.e. to the left to right order.

Definition 5.16 Construction of $\mathcal{A}_{SLD}(P)$

For a Horn program P we construct an attribute grammar $\mathcal{A}_{SLD}(P)$ $\langle N, R, S, Attr, L, \Phi, \mathcal{I} \rangle$ such that

- Its underlying context-free grammar defines the skeletons of P (as in Definition 5.1 p. 206).

- Its set of attributes *Attr* is defined as follows :

  Every predicate p of P has one inherited attribute and one synthesized attribute. The mapping τ_p associates the set of all argument positions of p with the inherited attribute. Thus the empty set of argument positions is associated with the synthesized attribute. In this case we will use a simplified notation, where the attributes, both being pairs, are replaced by the following three attributes representing the relevant components of the pairs:

  - *Arg* is the argument component of the original inherited attribute. Its value ranges over n-tuples of terms, where n is the arity of p,
  - σ is the substitution component of the original inherited attribute,
  - δ is the substitution component of the original synthesized attribute.

- The semantic rules are defined by the general construction[4] :

  - For a goal clause of the form $\leftarrow p_1(\bar{s}_1), \ldots, p_k(\bar{s}_k), \ldots, p_n(\bar{s}_n)$, where $n > 0$ and $\bar{s}_1, \ldots, \bar{s}_n$ are the argument sequences, the semantic rules are:
  $Arg(1) = \bar{s}_1^u$,
  $\sigma(1) = \epsilon$,
  $Arg(k) = \bar{s}_k^u \delta(k-1)$, $\sigma(k) = \delta(k-1)$ for $2 \le k \le n$.
  - For a unit clause of the form $p(\bar{s}_0) \leftarrow$, the only semantic rule is:
  $\delta(0) = \sigma(0) mgu(\{Arg(0) = \bar{s}_0^u\})$

– For a definite clause of the form
$p_0(\bar{s}_0) \leftarrow p_1(\bar{s}_1), \ldots, p_k(\bar{s}_k), \ldots, p_n(\bar{s}_n)$, where $n > 0$, the semantic rules
are:
$Arg(1) = \bar{s}_1^u \gamma$ where $\gamma = mgu(\{Arg(0) = \bar{s}_0^u\})$,
$\sigma(1) = \sigma(0)\gamma$,
$\delta(0) = \delta(n)$,
$Arg(k) = \bar{s}_k^u \delta(k-1)$, $\sigma(k) = \delta(k-1)$, for $2 \le k \le n$

□

Example 5.13
We apply the construction to the reverse program of Example 5.7
p. 222 augmented with the goal clause c_0:

$c_0 :\leftarrow rev(1.(2.nil), X, nil)$
$c_1 : rev(nil, L, L) \leftarrow$
$c_2 : rev(A.L, Q, R) \leftarrow rev(L, Q, A.R)$

The semantic rules associated with the clauses are:

1. Φ_0:
$Arg(1) = [1.(2.nil), X^u, nil]$
$\sigma(1) = \epsilon$

2. Φ_1:
$\delta(0) = \sigma(0)mgu(\{Arg(0) = [nil, L^u, L^u]\})$

3. Φ_2:
$Arg(1) = [L^u, Q^u, A^u.R^u]mgu(\{Arg(0) = [A^u.L^u, Q^u, R^u]\})$
$\sigma(1) = \sigma(0)mgu(\{Arg(0) = [A^u.L^u, Q^u, R^u]\})$
$\delta(0) = \delta(1)$

□

The local dependencies of the example grammar $\mathcal{A}_{SLD}(P)$ are shown
in Fig 5.6.
Notice that the maximal attribute of a valid tree with the root labeled
by a goal clause is the attribute δ of the last predicate of the skeleton of
the goal clause. The maximal attribute of a tree with the root labeled
by a definite clause is the attribute δ of the head of the skeleton of
this clause. The semantic rules has been obtained by simplification of

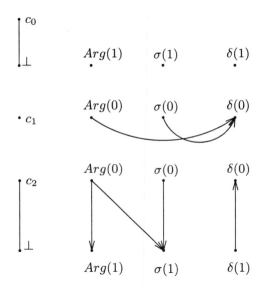

Figure 5.6
The local dependencies of the grammar $\mathcal{A}_{SLD}(P)$ of Example 5.13   p. 247

the semantic rules defined by the general construction (the attribute grammar is natural and direct).

We now show how the grammar $\mathcal{A}_{SLD}(P)$ models SLD-derivations.

Proposition 5.7

Let P be a Horn program and let T be a valid decorated tree of $\mathcal{A}_{SLD}(P)$. Let u be a node of T with the decoration $p[Arg_u, \sigma_u, \delta_u]$, where p is a predicate of P; it is assumed that at the root of T ($u = 0$) Arg_0 do not share variable with the domain of σ_0. Then: $\delta_u = \sigma_u \gamma_u$, where γ_u is the SLD-computed substitution for P with the atomic goal $p(Arg_u)$, up to a renaming.
□

The proposition shows in which sense the grammar $\mathcal{A}_{SLD}(P)$ models SLD-resolution. The proposition follows by the observation that both SLD-resolution and the process of construction of valid trees of the grammar can be seen as two different full resolution schemes working with the skeletons of the program. Thus δ_u is the result of a computation in one of the schemes. The computation starts with Arg_u and the current substitution σ_u, which do not share variables with the equations of the skeleton. As the resolution scheme is full the result must coincide up to renaming with the result σ_u obtained by the other full resolution scheme.

The relation to the SLD-resolution can be made more precise. Every node u of a valid tree with the root labeled by a skeleton of a goal clause g corresponds to a state of SLD-refutation of P and g with the standard computation rule. The substitution component of this state is σ_u. To construct its goal component define cut of u to be the empty sequence of nodes if u is the root of the tree and the sequence of all right siblings of u concatenated with the cut of the parent of u otherwise. The goal component of the state of SLD-refutation corresponding to the node u of a valid tree is then of the form

$$[p(\bar{s}^v), p_{u1}(\bar{s}^{v1}), \ldots, p_{un}(\bar{s}^{vn})]\sigma_u$$

where $u1, \ldots un$ is the *cut of* u, $p_{u1}, \ldots, p_{un}$ are predicates of the nodes of the cut and $\bar{s}^v, \bar{s}^{v1}, \ldots, \bar{s}^{vn}$ are the corresponding vector arguments in the clause of the parent node.

An example of a valid tree of the program of Example 5.13 is shown in Figure 5.7.

The grammar $\mathcal{A}_{SLD}(P)$ makes it possible to study properties of SLD-

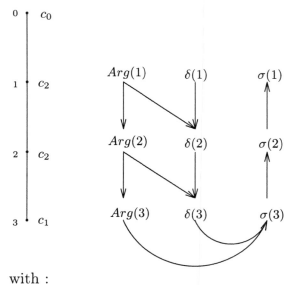

with :

$$Arg(1) = [1.2.nil, X^0, nil]$$
$$\sigma(1) = \epsilon$$
$$\delta(1) = \delta(2)$$

$$Arg(2) = [2.nil, Q^1, 1.nil]$$
$$\sigma(2) = \{A^1/1, L^1/2.nil, X^0/Q^1, R^1/nil\}$$
$$\delta(2) = \delta(3)$$

$$Arg(3) = [nil, Q^2, 2.1.nil]$$
$$\sigma(3) = \{A^1/1, L^1/2.nil, X^0/Q^2, R^1/nil,$$
$$A^2/2, L^2/nil, Q^1/Q^2, R^2/1.nil\}$$
$$\delta(3) = \{A^1/1, L^1/2.nil, X^0/2.1.nil, R^1/nil, A^2/2,$$
$$L^2/nil, Q^1/2.1.nil, R^2/1.nil, L^3/2.1.nil, Q^2/2.1.nil\}$$

Figure 5.7
A valid tree of the grammar $\mathcal{A}_{SLD}(P)$ of Example 5.13 p. 247

computations. The problem of proving such properties reduces to proving properties of this grammar by methods of Sections 4.4, 4.5 and 4.6.

5.4   From functional attribute grammars to definite programs

In this section we consider the problem of transforming an attribute grammar into a semantically equivalent definite program. We first restrict our attention to functional attribute grammars with term interpretations. Then the case of non-term interpretations will be considered.

5.4.1   From functional attribute grammars with term domains to definite programs, $\mathcal{P}_T(A)$

In this section we show that any functional attribute grammar with term interpretation can be transformed into a semantically equivalent definite program of a specific form. The attribute values of such an attribute grammar are terms. The idea of the transformation is to consider the nonterminals of the grammar to be the predicates of the corresponding program and the attributes of the nonterminals to be the argument positions of these predicates. The splitting of attributes in a given attribute grammar defines the input attribute occurrences and the output attribute occurrences in the production rules. Each production rule will now be used for construction of a clause. The skeleton of the clause is constructed by removing the terminal symbols[5]. The terms defining the output attribute occurrences of the production rule will appear on the corresponding argument positions of the skeleton. Each input attribute occurrence of the production rule will be represented by a distinct variable. This variable will appear in the corresponding argument position of the constructed clause.

Definition 5.17 Construction of $\mathcal{P}_T(A)$
For a functional attribute grammar A with term preinterpretation we construct a definite program $\mathcal{P}_T(A)$ defined as follows:

---

[5]A more elaborate version of the construction would not remove the terminal symbols and would produce a DCG instead of a definite program.

- Its predicates are the nonterminals of A: the arity of each predicate equals the number of its attributes in A; there is one-one correspondence between the attributes of p considered as a nonterminal and the arguments of p considered as a predicate.
- Its function symbols are those used in the semantic rules of A.
- Each clause is obtained from a production rule of the grammar in the following way:

  − The terminal symbols of the production rule are removed; the result of this transformation is considered to be the skeleton of the clause constructed.

  − A distinct variable is associated with each input attribute occurrence of the production rule; for each output attribute occurrence there is an "output" term which is the right-hand side of the semantic rule with the input attribute occurrences replaced by the associated variables.

  − The clause is constructed from the skeleton by adding arguments to the predicates: the arguments corresponding to the input attribute occurrences are their associated variables, the arguments corresponding to the output attribute occurrences are their output terms.

  □

We illustrate the construction by the following example.

Example 5.14

Consider the attribute grammar of Example 4.2 p. 144, which describes computation of the values of binary numerals.

$$
\begin{array}{lll}
r_1 : Z \to N.N & v(Z) = v(N_1) + v(N_2) & \\
& r(N_1) = 0 & r(N_2) = -l(N_2) \\
r_2 : N \to N.B & v(N_0) = v(N_1) + v(B) & l(N_0) = l(N_1) + 1 \\
& r(B) = r(N_0) & r(N_1) = r(N_0) + 1 \\
r_3 : N \to \varepsilon & v(N) = 0 & l(N) = 0 \\
r_4 : B \to 1 & v(B) = 2^{r(B)} & \\
r_5 : B \to 0 & v(B) = 0 &
\end{array}
$$

Consider these rules with the term interpretation. The construction described above transforms the grammar into the following definite program.

1. $z(V1 + V2) \leftarrow n(0, L1, V1), n(-L2, L2, V2)$
2. $n(R, L1 + 1, V1 + V2) \leftarrow n(R + 1, L1, V1), b(R, V2)$
3. $n(R, 0, 0) \leftarrow$
4. $b(R, 2^R) \leftarrow$
5. $b(R, 0) \leftarrow$

Figure 5.8 shows an example of a proof tree of this definite program and the corresponding decorated tree of the attribute grammar.
□

It follows directly by the construction that the definite program constructed is nice and simple with the original attribute splitting. Application of the construction of Definition 5.17 to this program allows us to construct a functional attribute grammar which is identical to the original one except of the fact that it includes no terminal symbols. The following proposition summarizes the discussion.

Proposition 5.8 From FAG to definite programs
For every functional attribute grammar A with term interpretation, there exists a nice and simple directed definite program P_α, such that the valid trees of A are isomorphic to the proof trees of P.
□

Clearly the definite program $\mathcal{P}_T(A)$ has the required property. The d-assignment α is that determined by the attribute splitting of A. Generally, for an attribute grammar with term interpretation the set of equations associated to a derivation tree has a solution iff there is no cycle or if the cycles involve attribute identities only. The solution is unique and can be obtained by attribute evaluation which in this case reduces to variable elimination. This corresponds to finding the most general unifier of the set of equations. But the derivation tree corresponds to a complete skeleton S of $\mathcal{P}_T(A)$ which has the same set of equations as the derivation tree. Thus, there exists the proof tree $D(S)$ based on S (as defined in Section 2.1.3). This tree is isomorphic to the valid tree obtained by attribute evaluation of the derivation tree.

The result establishes semantic equivalence in the sense of proof-theoretic semantics (and also in the sense of unification semantics) be-

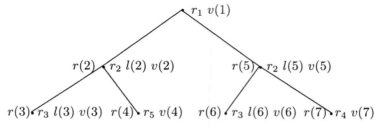

with :

$$v(1) = (0 + 0) + (0 + 2^{-(0+1)})$$
$$v(2) = 0 + 0$$
$$v(3) = 0$$
$$v(4) = 0$$
$$v(5) = 0 + 2^{-(0+1)}$$
$$v(6) = 0$$
$$v(7) = 2^{-(0+1)}$$

$$r(2) = 0 \qquad l(2) = 0 + 1$$
$$r(3) = 0 + 1 \qquad l(3) = 0$$
$$r(4) = 0 \qquad l(5) = 0 + 1$$
$$r(5) = -(0 + 1) \qquad l(6) = 0$$
$$r(6) = -(0 + 1) + 1$$
$$r(7) = -(0 + 1)$$

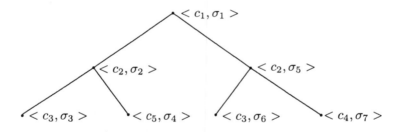

with :

$$\sigma_1 = \{V1/0 + 0, V2/0 + 2^{-(0+1)}, L1/0 + 1, L2/0 + 1\}$$
$$\sigma_2 = \{R/0, L1/0, V1/0 + 0, V2/0\}$$
$$\sigma_3 = \{R/0 + 1\}$$
$$\sigma_4 = \{R/0\}$$
$$\sigma_5 = \{R/ - (0 + 1), L1/0 + 1, V1/0, V2/2^{-(0+1)}\}$$
$$\sigma_6 = \{R/ - (0 + 1) + 1\}$$
$$\sigma_7 = \{R/ - (0 + 1)\}$$

Figure 5.8
A valid tree of attribute grammar A of Example 5.14 p. 252 and the corresponding proof tree of the program $\mathcal{P}_T(A)$

tween functional attribute grammars with term interpretations and a
subclass of definite programs.

It is worth noticing that the construction can be applied to a circular
attribute grammar. The following example shows that circularity of
a functional attribute grammar is related to existence of solutions for
the set of equations constructed by the operational semantics of the
corresponding definite program.

Example 5.15

Consider the following definite program.

1. $s \leftarrow p(X, X)$
2. $p(X, f(X))$

The program has no proof tree with the root labeled by the first clause,
since the unification of the body atom of the goal with the head of the
second clause fails by occur-check.

The following d-assignment is nice and simple for this program.
$$Inh(p) = \{ p_1 \}$$
$$Syn(p) = \{ p_2 \}$$
This program is equivalent to the following attribute grammar from
which it can be derived by the construction of Definition 5.17 p. 251.

1. $s \rightarrow p \ \{ p_1 = p_2\}$
2. $p \rightarrow \varepsilon \ \{p_2 = f(p_1)\}$

It is easy to check that this grammar is circular.
□

The relation between the circularity of functional attribute grammars
and the occur-check problem of logic programs will be discussed formally
in Chapter 8.

5.4.2   Attribute grammars with non-term interpretations and preinterpreted definite programs

Every attribute grammar has some specific interpretation which is used
for attribute evaluation. No specific interpretation is assumed for a
definite program, so that the terms involved in a computation are never
reduced. This is an essential difference between the formalisms. The

construction of Definition 5.17 p. 251 applied to an attribute grammar with non-term J-based interpretation $\mathcal{I}$ would give rise to a definite program with the function symbols interpreted in its preinterpretation J. Such programs will be called *preinterpreted definite programs*.

The declarative semantics of a preinterpreted program can be given in terms of J-based proof trees (Definition 2.22 p. 77). As noticed in Section 2.2.3, such trees could be constructed from the skeletons by solving the associated equations. This makes the operational semantics domain-dependent and requires the use of domain-specific equation solvers.

However, the attribute evaluators do not require specific equation-solvers. This is due to the syntactic restrictions on the form of the semantic rules of functional attribute grammars. These restrictions, together with non-circularity of the grammar guarantee that the set of equations associated with any skeleton can be solved by variable elimination and evaluation of ground terms. In this section we show that a similar technique can also be used for some classes of preinterpreted logic programs. These classes will be obtained by transformation of certain kinds of functional attribute grammars. The new construction is a slightly modified version of that given by Definition 5.17 p. 251. The modification is to make explicit the equations generated by the clauses constructed. Let $p \rightarrow b_1, \ldots, b_k$ be a production rule of the attribute grammar. It is first transformed into the clause $p(\bar{x}_0) \leftarrow b_1(\bar{x}_1), \ldots b_k(\bar{x}_k)$ where $\bar{x}_i$ for $i = 0, 1, \ldots, k$ is the vector of distinct variables, each of which represents an attribute value of the nonterminal p for $i = 0$ and of the nonterminal b_i for $i = 1, \ldots, k$. The vectors share no variables. Now the semantic rules of the production rule can be represented as equations of the form x *is* t, where x is a variable on an output position of the constructed clause and t is the term whose variables occur at some input positions in this clause. All these equations are inserted into the clause as body atoms; the new predicate *is* used in infix notation represents equality in the interpretation of the original attribute grammar. Note that the construction is nondeterministic since the place of insertion of the new atoms is not specified.

Example 5.16

For the attribute grammar of Example 5.14 p. 252 the modified version of the construction gives the following (preinterpreted) definite program:

$$
\begin{aligned}
z(V) \quad &\leftarrow \quad n(R1, L1, V1), n(R2, L2, V2), V \; is \; (V1 + V2), \\
& \qquad R1 \; is \; 0, R2 \; is \; (-L2) \\
n(R, L, V) \quad &\leftarrow \quad n(R1, L1, V1), b(R2, V2), V \; is \; (V1 + V2), \\
& \qquad L \; is \; (L1 + 1), R2 \; is \; R, R1 \; is \; (R + 1) \\
n(R, L, V) \quad &\leftarrow \quad V \; is \; 0, L \; is \; 0 \\
b(R, V) \quad &\leftarrow \quad V \; is \; (2^R) \\
b(R, V) \quad &\leftarrow \quad V \; is \; 0
\end{aligned}
$$

Notice, that the transformation is not specific about the place of insertion of new atoms in the body, so that we made some arbitrary decisions.

□

Clearly if the *is* predicate is interpreted as the identity on the domain of the preinterpretation, the transformation preserves the declarative semantics.

Assume that the operational semantics is like SLD-resolution with the standard computation rule. The only difference is that the *is* subgoals are to be handled as equations. The main problem now is how to solve these equations. In the program each of them has a variable as its left hand side. Thus, if the right-hand side of an "*is*"-equation is ground at the time of call, the solution of the equation can be obtained by evaluating its right-hand side. Otherwise an equation-solving procedure specific for the given interpretation may be necessary to find its solutions. We want to avoid this and therefore we require that the right-hand side of any "*is*"-equation is fully instantiated at the time of call. Clearly the left-to-right computation strategy for the program obtained by our construction may select equations with nonground right-hand sides. If the original functional attribute grammar is non-circular then the set of equations associated with any skeleton can be solved by reduction of ground terms and elimination of solved variables. Thus, if the right-hand side of the selected equation is nonground one can delay the equation and its right-hand side will eventually be instantiated. Theoretically this would solve the problem. However, in some cases it would be necessary to construct a complete skeleton before starting the resolution of some of the delayed equations. The standard strategy is much easier to apply. Therefore we would like to transform the resulting program in such a way that the standard strategy is sufficient. The remaining part of this section shows some classes of attribute grammars for which this approach can be applied.

From L-attribute grammars to preinterpreted definite programs

The modified construction does not specify the order of the new atoms in the body of the clause. Notice, that each of them corresponds to a semantic rule of the original attribute grammar. Assume now that this grammar is an L-attribute grammar. By the definition of L-attribute grammars, an inherited attribute occurrence of a nonterminal X in the right-hand side of a production rule may only depend on the attribute occurrences of the nonterminals preceding X in the rule. The synthesized attribute occurrences of the left-hand side nonterminal of the rule may depend on the inherited attribute occurrences of this nonterminal and on attribute occurrences of nonterminals of the right-hand side of the rule. The local dependency relation in this case indicates left-to-right flow of the computed attribute values during attribute evaluation. The objective is to simulate attribute evaluation by the computations of the preinterpreted definite program with the standard computation rule. A body atom of a clause in this program is either a semantic rule or a nonterminal of the grammar with the variables representing attribute values. A semantic rule defining the value of some variable representing an occurrence of an inherited attribute should precede all other occurrences of this variable. Such an ordering of atoms exists since the grammar transformed is an L-attribute grammar. Indeed, let $p \rightarrow b_1 \ldots b_k$ be a production rule of a given L-attribute grammar. Denote by $Def(p), Def(b_1), \ldots, Def(b_k)$ the sequence of is equations corresponding to the semantic rules defining the output attribute occurrences of, respectively, $p, b_1, \ldots, b_k$. The clause $p(\bar{x}_0) \leftarrow Def(b_1), b_1(\bar{x}_1), Def(b_2), \ldots, Def(b_k), b_k(\bar{x}_k), Def(p)$ where $\bar{x}_i$ for $i = 0, 1, \ldots, k$ are vectors of distinct variables, as defined in the previous construction, has the required property and its execution in given preinterpretation with the standard computation rule will simulate attribute evaluation in the original L-attribute grammar.

This construction extends naturally to conditional L-attribute grammars. The conditions of the semantic rules are translated into atoms placed in the body of the clause "as soon as" all their variables are known (i.e. as soon as possible in the L-AG order).

Example 5.17

We give an example of an L-attribute grammar with non-term domain and transform it into the equivalent logic program. Given a context-free grammar we associate with every of its nonterminals (except for the root) two attributes: the synthesized attribute l characterizes the length of the underlying terminal substring, the inherited attribute m characterizes the number of symbols preceding this substring in the string derived from the start nonterminal S. A simple concrete example is the following:

$$
\begin{array}{lll}
S \to N & l(S) = l(N) & m(N) = 0 \\
N \to BN & l(N_0) = l(B) + l(N_1) & m(N_1) = m(N_0) + l(B) \\
& m(B) = m(N_0) & \\
B \to 1 & l(B) = 1 & \\
B \to 0 & l(B) = 1 &
\end{array}
$$

The example shows a general principle for construction of the semantic rules for this problem. For the particular context-free grammar considered the rules can be simplified. For any context-free grammar we obtain an L-attribute grammar with the interpretation on integer domain. For the particular attribute grammar described above the construction yields the following logic program:

$$
\begin{array}{l}
s(L) \leftarrow n(L, 0) \\
n(L, M) \leftarrow b(L1, M), M1 \ is \ M + L1, n(L2, M1), L \ is \ L1 + L2 \\
b(1, M) \leftarrow \\
b(1, M) \leftarrow
\end{array}
$$

□

The class of L-attribute grammars is very restricted. The question arises how to transform more general attribute grammars into semantically equivalent logic programs employing "is"-predicate. We show that it is possible at the cost of increasing the complexity of the proof trees. The solution will be outlined informally referring to some known results about attribute grammars. We discuss first an auxiliary result relating recursive program schemes with preinterpreted definite programs.

From recursive program schemes to preinterpreted definite programs

Recursive program schemes play important role in the theory of programming. This section outlines briefly and informally the notion of recursive program scheme and the transformation of recursive program schemes with call by value semantics into conditional L-attribute grammars. For formal definitions and technical details the reader is referred to [CFZ82]. Combining this transformation with that defined for L-attribute grammars one can transform recursive program schemes into preinterpreted logic programs.

Syntactically a recursive program scheme is a finite set of expressions called definitions. The definitions are conditional expressions of the form $t =$ **if** c **then** t_1 **else** t_2, where t is a term of the form $f(x_1, ..., x_n)$ for some function symbol f and distinct variables $x_1, ..., x_n$, t_1, t_2 are terms, possibly including f and c is a formula, called condition. The function symbols of all terms t in the definitions of a scheme are called the defined function symbols. They may appear in the right-hand sides of the definitions of the scheme and in the conditions. The remaining function symbols play the role of functional parameters. By binding them to some specific functions one can use the scheme as a possibly mutually recursive definition of the functions denoted by the defined symbols. The value of a defined function f for the arguments $v_1, ..., v_n$ is obtained by evaluating the right-hand side of the definition. The values of the subterms are computed in the left-to-right bottom-up order which is referred-to as "call by value" semantics.

Example 5.18 Recursive program scheme
We illustrate the notion of the recursive program scheme by the following example.

$$
\begin{aligned}
reverse(x) \;\; &= \;\; \textbf{if } x == nil \textbf{ then } nil \\
&\quad\; \textbf{else } append(reverse(cdr(x)), cons(car(x), nil)) \\
append(x, y) \;\; &= \;\; \textbf{if } x == nil \textbf{ then } y \\
&\quad\; \textbf{else } cons(car(x), append(cdr(x), y))
\end{aligned}
$$

Here *reverse* and *append* are the defined functions while *cons, car, cdr* and *nil* are the functional parameters. and play a similar role as the semantic functions of attribute grammars. "$==$" denotes the term indentity as usual in Prolog. With this scheme and appropriate interpretation the term $reverse(append(cons(1, cons(2, nil)), cons(3, nil)))$ will be rewritten to $cons(3, cons(2, cons(1, nil)))$.
□

We now illustrate by an example the transformation defined by Courcelle and Deransart which translates recursive applicative program schemes with call by value semantics into semantically equivalent conditional L-attribute grammars ([CD88]). The transformation is similar to the previous one, except that the conditions are handled separately. We will assume that the same predicates are used in the logic program too.

The idea is to consider the defined function symbols as nonterminals of the attribute grammar to be constructed. An n-ary function symbol is associated with n inherited attributes, representing the arguments, and one synthesized attribute, representing the result of computation. Every definition of the original scheme corresponds to two production rules, reflecting the "then"-part and the "else"-part of the definition. The order of the nonterminals in the right-hand side of the respective production rule corresponds to the order in which the defined function symbols are encountered in the call-by-value strategy applied to the respective part of the definition transformed. The condition (if any) or its negation are included in their semantic rules. The semantic rules use the functional parameters of the scheme as the semantic functions. The resulting attribute grammar is equivalent to the program scheme in the following sense. Let f be an n-ary defined function symbol of the scheme. For any interpretation of functional parameters the call-by-value semantics of $f(v_1, ..., v_n)$ yields v iff there exists a valid tree of the attribute grammar with the head $f(v_1, ..., v_n, v)$.

Example 5.19 Recursive functional program

The transformation applied to the example recursive scheme results in the following attribute grammar.

The production rules are as follows:

1. $reverse \rightarrow \varepsilon$

2. $reverse \rightarrow reverse\ append$

3. $append \rightarrow \varepsilon$

4. $append \rightarrow append$

The attributes are:

$Inh = \{\ reverse_1,\ append_1,\ append_2\ \}$

$Syn = \{\ reverse_2,\ append_3\ \}$

The attribute definitions are:

1. Φ_1:

$reverse_1(0) == nil \wedge reverse_2(0) = nil$

2. Φ_2:

$reverse_1(0) \mathbin{\backslash}== nil \wedge reverse_1(1) = cdr(reverse_1(0)) \wedge append_1(2) = reverse_2(1) \wedge append_2(2) = cons(car(reverse_1(0)), nil) \wedge reverse_2(0) = append_3(2)$

3. Φ_3:

$append_1(0) == nil \wedge append_3(0) = append_2(0)$

4. Φ_4:

$append_1(0) \mathbin{\backslash}== nil \wedge append_1(1) = cdr(append_1(0)) \wedge append_2(1) = append_2(0) \wedge append_3(0) = cons(car(append_1(0)), append_3(1))$

Using a modified construction of the previous section the attribute grammar can be transformed into the following preinterpreted program, where the negation of the term identity is denoted $\mathbin{\backslash}==$ as usual in Prolog.

$$reverse(X, Y) \quad \leftarrow \quad X == nil,\ Y\ is\ nil$$

$$reverse(X, Y) \quad \leftarrow \quad X\mathbin{\backslash}== nil,\ X1\ is\ cdr(X),\ reverse(X1, Y1),$$
$$X2\ is\ Y1, Y2\ is\ cons(car(X), nil),$$
$$append(Y1, Y2, Y),$$
$$Y1\ is\ Y3$$

$$append(X, Y, Z) \quad \leftarrow \quad X == nil,\ Z\ is\ Y$$

$$append(X, Y, Z) \quad \leftarrow \quad X \setminus== nil, X1 \ is \ cdr(X), \ Y1 \ is \ Y,$$
$$append(X1, Y, Z1), \ Z \ is \ cons(car(X), Z1)$$

□

Notice that with the standard strategy the arguments of the conditions are ground at call.

From strongly non-circular attribute grammars to preinterpreted definite programs

As mentioned in Chapter 4 a strongly non-circular attribute grammar can be translated into a deterministic recursive program scheme taking the parse tree as an argument. The computation sequence of this scheme depends only on the parse tree argument. We illustrate this transformation by an example. The resulting scheme will then be translated to a logic program using the transformation of the previous section.

Example 5.20

Consider the attribute grammar with the following production rules:

r_1: $goal \rightarrow q$
r_2: $q \rightarrow p$
r_3: $q \rightarrow p$
r_4: $p \rightarrow \varepsilon$

The nonterminals have the following attributes:

$$Attr(goal) = Syn(goal) = \{ \ goal_1 \ \}$$
$$Inh(q) = \{ \ q_1 \ \}, \ Syn(q) = \{ \ q_2 \ \}$$
$$Inh(p) = \{ \ p_1, p_2 \ \}, \ Syn(p) = \{ \ p_3, p_4 \ \}$$

The grammar has the following semantic rules:

Φ_1:

$$goal_1(0) = q_2(1) \land q_1(1) = a$$

Φ_2:

$$q_2(0) = f(p_3(1)) \land p_1(1) = f(p_4(1)) \land p_2(1) = f(q_1(0))$$

Φ_3:

$$q_2(0) = f(p_4(1)) \land p_1(1) = f(q_1(0)) \land p_2(1) = f(p_3(1))$$

Φ_4:

$$p_3(0) = f(p_1(0)) \land p_4(0) = f(p_2(0))$$

Notice that the synthesized attributes a depend globally on the following inherited attributes, which are in the sets $Use(x, a)$:

for $x = goal$, $goal_1$ depends on no attributes,

for $x = q$, q_2 depends on q_1,

for $x = p$, p_3 depends on p_1, and

p_4 depends on p_2.

It is a strongly non-circular attribute grammar but not l-ordered (similar local dependency graphs are shown in Figure 4.5).

We now transform the grammar to a recursive program scheme. The functions defined by the scheme correspond to the synthesized attributes of the nonterminals. The number of definitions for a synthesized attribute a of a nonterminal x equals the number of production rules with the head x. The function will be denoted ϕ_a. The number of its arguments equals the number of the inherited attributes x on which a depends plus one. The additional argument is the term representation of the parse tree: the tree with the root labeled by i-th production rule is denoted by the term $r_i(X)$, where X is the vector of the term representations of the direct subtrees of the tree. This construction gives for our example the following scheme:

$$
\begin{aligned}
\phi_{goal_1}(r_1(t)) &= \phi_{q_2}(t, a) \\
\phi_{q_2}(r_2(t), q_1) &= f(\phi_{p_3}(t, f(\phi_{p_4}(t, f(q_1))))) \\
\phi_{q_2}(r_3(t), q_1) &= f(\phi_{p_4}(t, f(\phi_{p_3}(t, f(q_1))))) \\
\phi_{p_3}(r_4, p_1) &= f(p_1) \\
\phi_{p_4}(r_4, p_2) &= f(p_2)
\end{aligned}
$$

Finally, by replacing the ϕ functions of arity n by π predicates of arity $n + 1$, the last step of transformation gives the following definite program:

$$\pi_{goal_1}(r_1(T), R) \leftarrow X \text{ is } a, \pi_{q_2}(T, X, R)$$
$$\pi_{q_2}(r_2(T), Q1, R) \leftarrow R1 \text{ is } f(Q1), \pi_{p_4}(T, R1, R2), R3 \text{ is } f(R2),$$
$$\pi_{p_3}(T, R3, R4), R \text{ is } f(R4)$$
$$\pi_{q_2}(r_3(T), Q1, R) \leftarrow R1 \text{ is } f(Q1), \pi_{p_3}(T, R1, R2), R3 \text{ is } f(R2),$$
$$\pi_{p_4}(T, R3, R4), R \text{ is } f(R4)$$
$$\pi_{p_3}(r_4, P1, R) \leftarrow R \text{ is } f(P1)$$
$$\pi_{p_4}(r_4, P2, R) \leftarrow R \text{ is } f(P2)$$

Notice that in this example π_{p_3} and π_{p_4} are the same functions, hence it can be simplified as follows:

$$\pi_{goal_1}(r_1(T), R) \leftarrow X \text{ is } a, \pi_{q_2}(T, X, R)$$
$$\pi_{q_2}(r_2(T), Q1, R) \leftarrow R1 \text{ is } f(Q1), \pi_p(T, R1, R2), R3 \text{ is } f(R2),$$
$$\pi_p(T, R3, R4), R \text{ is } f(R4)$$
$$\pi_{q_2}(r_3(T), Q1, R) \leftarrow R1 \text{ is } f(Q1), \pi_p(T, R1, R2), R3 \text{ is } f(R2),$$
$$\pi_p(T, R3, R4), R \text{ is } f(R4)$$
$$\pi_p(r_4, P2, R) \leftarrow R \text{ is } f(P2)$$

Note again that both bodies of π_{q_2} are the same. They could be simplified but this would lead to a new definite program with a different proof tree semantics.

□

The preinterpreted definite programs obtained by the construction are deterministic (i.e. they can be run without backtracking) if the first argument is given. Moreover, if called with most general goals they remain operationally complete, i.e. during the computation the second argument of any call to the "*is*" predicate is ground. In this case the computation enumerates and decorates parse trees of the grammar. However, as usual, the standard strategy does not guarantee the completeness, i.e. enumeration of all parse trees of the grammar. Moreover, the construction of parse trees is "attribute driven": production rules whose attributes are not connected to synthesized attributes of the head of the tree are not used. The attribute instances not needed to compute synthesized attribute of the head are not evaluated.

From l-ordered attribute grammars to preinterpreted definite programs

The l-ordered attribute grammars are strongly non-circular and can also be handled by the transformation discussed above. However, as discussed in Section 4.3.5, l-ordered grammar is a special case of strongly non-circular grammar, where the projection of the dependency relation on the attributes of each nonterminal is a total ordering. This relation can be used to determine statically visit sequences needed for attribute evaluation of every instance of a production rule (cf. Section 4.3.6). A particular case of l-ordered grammar is an L-attribute grammar for which there is only one visit sequence in each production.

We now show a transformation of l-attribute grammars into preinterpreted logic programs that incorporates this idea.

Recall the general attribute evaluation algorithm of Section 4.3.6. For the purpose of evaluation the attributes of a nonterminal of the l-ordered grammar are partitioned into pairs of subsets. The first element of a pair is a set of inherited attributes the second element is a set of synthesized attributes. Let us denote $\{ Inh_k(p), Syn_k(p) \}$ the kth pair for $0 < k \leq m$ if there are m pairs for the nonterminal p. The intuition of this splitting is that a node corresponding to an occurrence of p will be visited m times by the evaluator. The k-th visit will be preceded by evaluation of the attributes in $Inh_k(p)$, will cause visits to all children of the node and will be completed by evaluation of the attributes in $Syn_k(p)$. Thus, for a rule c of the form $p \leftarrow p_1, ...p_n$ there are m visit sequences of the form (see Section 4.3.6):

$$visit(p, k): \ldots eval(Inh_k(p_i)), visit(p_i, k_i), \ldots, eval(Syn_k(p))$$

The idea of the construction is thus to associate with each visit sequence $visit(p, k)$ a clause defining the predicate $visit_{p,k}$ whose arguments are the parse tree and the attributes of $Inh_k(p)$ and $Syn_k(p)$. The evaluation of attributes is achieved by use of the "is" predicate. The construction is illustrated by the following example.

Example 5.21

The grammar to be transformed is that of Example 5.20 with rule 3 removed in order to obtain an l-ordered grammar. Thus we have the grammar:

r_1: $goal \rightarrow q$
r_2: $q \rightarrow p$
r_3: $p \rightarrow \varepsilon$

with the following semantic rules:

Φ_1:
$goal_1(0) = q_2(1) \wedge q_1(1) = a$
Φ_2:
$q_2(0) = f(p_3(1)) \wedge p_1(1) = f(p_4(1)) \wedge p_2(1) = f(q_1(0))$
Φ_3:
$p_3(0) = f(p_1(0)) \wedge p_4(0) = f(p_2(0))$

The attributes are partitioned as follows:

1. $Inh_1(goal) = \{\}$, $Syn_1(goal) = \{goal1\}$
2. $Inh_1(q) = \{q_1\}$, $Syn_1(q) = \{q_2\}$
3. $Inh_1(p) = \{p_2\}$, $Syn_1(q) = \{q_4\}$
   $Inh_2(p) = \{p_1\}$, $Syn_2(p) = \{p_3\}$

The generated program is thus the following:

$$\pi_{goal_1}(r_1(t), R) \leftarrow X \text{ is } a, visit_{q,1}(t, X, R)$$
$$visit_{goal,1}(r_1(t), Q2) \leftarrow Q1 \text{ is } a, visit_{q,1}(t, Q1, Q2)$$
$$visit_{q,1}(r_2(t), Q1, Q2) \leftarrow P2 \text{ is } f(Q1), visit_{p,1}(t, P2, P4),$$
$$P1 \text{ is } f(P4), visit_{p,2}(t, P1, Q2)$$
$$visit_{p,1}(r_3, P2, P4) \leftarrow P4 \text{ is } f(P2)$$
$$visit_{p,2}(r_3, P1, P3) \leftarrow P3 \text{ is } f(P1)$$

□

The logic program resulting from the transformation of an l-ordered attribute grammar has the same basic properties as the one obtained by the transformation defined for the strongly non-circular grammars:

- It terminates and it is deterministic if the first argument (the parse tree) is given.

- It is operationally complete for goals whose values of the inherited attributes are given.

- The standard strategy is generally incomplete when the program is used with most general goals.

- The generation of skeletons is "attribute driven"; this is another source of incompleteness in skeleton enumeration.

However there are some important differences:

- All attributes of a parse tree are computed in the l-ordered case, while, as mentioned above, in the case of strongly non-circular grammars the computation of attributes is "by need", so that attributes not needed for evaluation of the root attributes are not computed.

- The complexity is linear in the number of attribute occurrences. More precisely, the size of a proof tree of the produced program is proportional to the number of attribute occurrences in the corresponding parse tree. In contrast to that, the size of a proof tree of the program obtained from a strongly non-circular grammar may be exponential with respect to the original parse tree.

The construction can be extended to a restricted kind of l-ordered conditional attribute grammars, where the conditions concern attributes computed during one visit only. Such grammars can be transformed into logic programs where the conditions are introduced into the clauses describing respective visit sequences.

5.5   Bibliographical comments

The constructions relating proof trees of definite programs and decorated trees of attribute grammars originate from [DM85b]. The articles [DM88, DM90, Mał91] present also a general comparison of logic programs and attribute grammars. In [Isa85] a construction similar to the one of Section 5.1.2 is introduced with a complete treatment of the partial interpretation.

The concept of dependency relation for a definite program was introduced in [DM84]. It was used in [DM85a] for analysis of AND-parallelism and backtracking, in [DM85b, AP92b] for studying the occur-check problem, in [Dra87] for analysis of the programming techniques used in Prolog programs and in [Plü90] for termination proofs of logic programs, in

[Boy91] for analysis of operational completeness of logic programs with external procedures. It is not clear whether these examples can be used to formulate a general method for program analysis, and how they relate to the method of abstract interpretation [CC79].

The notion of decisive argument has been introduced in the thesis [Bou92b]. The thesis discusses properties of partial d-assignments and presents a polynomial algorithm for finding a nontrivial partial nice d-assignment for a given program (a program in which all the arguments are decisive is trivially partially nice), or for deciding whether there exists a total nice d-assignment.

There have been several attempts to exploit conceptual similarity of logic programs and attribute grammars. The paper [Arb86] reports on compilation of circular attribute grammars into Prolog. The idea of externally defined semantic functions of functional attribute grammars is used in [BM88, Boy91, MBB$^+$93] for declarative integration of logic programs with procedures written in other programming languages. A compiler writing system integrating logic programming and attribute grammars is presented in [Paa90, Paa91]. The TYPOL system combines attribute and logic programming techniques [AFZ88, ACG92] for working with specifications written in structured operational semantics style. The use of an attribute grammar as a logic program is discussed in [RL88].

6 Proof Methods for Definite Programs

This chapter discusses some methods for validation of logic programs. We first give a motivation for development of such methods and we discuss various aspects of validation.

6.1 Introduction

Validation of a program is usually understood as checking that the program fulfills certain requirements. In particular validation may include formal proofs of some properties of the program or testing which may show that some required properties are not satisfied. Thus, validation concerns comparison of the program at hand with some requirements, expressed often as a formal specification. The axiomatic nature of definite programs and completeness of the SLD-resolution allow for viewing such programs as executable formal specifications. This has sometimes been used as an argument for claiming that logic programs require no validation. Practical experience shows, however, that logic programs have to be validated. We now discuss some reasons for this.

6.1.1 Verification with respect to intended semantics

As mentioned above, validation is needed if there is a danger that a logic program does not fulfill certain requirements. The requirements specify some intended properties of the program.

As discussed in Chapter 2 there are many different kinds of semantics used for definite programs. The properties which are subject of validation are thus to be defined for a particular kind of semantics. For example one may be interested in properties of the denotation, properties of the unification semantics or properties of the computations performed by a specific operational semantics. In each of these cases different validation methods may be needed.

A property of the H-based denotation for some term base H can be characterized as a set of H-based atoms. The same holds for the unification semantics and for the proof-theoretic semantics based on a non-term preinterpretation. In particular one may consider a property characterizing exactly user's expectations concerning the (J-based) denotation. The corresponding set of (J-based) atoms is called the *intended semantics* of the program. We compare it to the (J-based) denotation. The considered semantics is also characterized by a set of (J-based) atoms. It will be called the *actual semantics* of the program.

Let IS be the intended semantics and let AS be the actual semantics of a program. The actual semantics has the property characterized by the intended semantics iff $AS \subseteq IS$. In this case the program is said to be *partially correct* with respect to IS, or IS is *valid* for the program. The actual semantics of a program which is not partially correct includes elements not belonging to the intended semantics. These elements can be computed using a full resolution scheme. Intuitively, this means that the program does not conform to the expectations of the user and the computed atoms are symptoms of program errors. Notice that the program with the empty actual semantics is trivially partially correct with respect to any intended semantics.

The program is *complete* with respect to IS iff $IS \subseteq AS$. Intuitively this means that the the program describes at least what is expected. If the program is not complete the intended semantics includes elements not belonging to the actual semantics. These elements cannot be computed by any full resolution scheme. Intuitively, this means that the program does not conform to the expectations of the user.

For the program which is both partially correct and complete the intended semantics coincides with the actual semantics.

In practice the actual semantics of a developed logic program is often different from the intended semantics. One of the major reasons is that the intentions of the user may not be naturally expressible in the language of definite programs in the case of realistic problems. Thus, it may not be immediately clear that a definite program of realistic size does not reflect the intentions. Therefore validation of logic programs is needed in practice.

This chapter presents some methods for proving partial correctness and completeness of programs with respect to intended semantics specified by logic formulae. Notice that the concept of actual semantics refers to different kinds of semantics. This allows for giving only one definition of partial correctness and completeness for different kinds of actual semantics considered. However, the proof methods for the denotations are different from the proof methods for the unification semantics.

Methods for proving correctness and completeness of attribute grammars have been presented in Chapter 4. The weaker concept of existential completeness has also been introduced. Constructions of Chapter 5 allow for modelling different kinds of semantics of definite programs by attribute grammars. Hence, applying the methods of Chapter 4 to grammars constructed in Chapter 5 one can prove properties of definite programs. The objective of this chapter is to elaborate on this observation in order to derive proof methods for definite programs. Different kinds of semantics give rise to different attribute grammars. Consequently, application of proof methods to these attribute grammars allows for proving properties of the original logic programs. The examples of this chapter show that the same property can often be proved in different ways by referring to the attribute grammars modelling different kinds of semantics.

6.1.2 Verification of operational properties

As we have seen there are many possible semantics which may be associated to a definite program. Given a program P its denotation $DEN_H(P)$ defines its declarative semantics (as a H-based term interpretation) and the unification semantics $US(P)$ characterizes the results of computations of any full resolution scheme. As discussed in Chapter 2 the set of atoms computed by a full resolution scheme coincides with the unification semantics, hence in some sense with the declarative semantics. But this is not the case in most operational semantics defined by implementations. Assuming that the intended semantics of a given program is identical with its declarative semantics one has still to check that all elements of this semantics can be computed by a given implementation.

The differences between the declarative semantics and the operational semantics defined by the implementation are caused by some implementation decisions aiming at efficiency of computations, simple memory management etc. We recall briefly two such decisions adopted in most Prolog implementations:

- *The use of the standard computation rule and standard strategy* (Section 2.2.4). As already discussed this leads to operational incompleteness in the sense that for some programs only a subset of $US(P)$ is computed. The objective of validation is then to establish that for a given program and for a given class of goals all answers will be computed. This question is related to the termination problem. The incompleteness is caused by a nonterminating computation, which takes place when the interpreter explores an infinite branch of the search tree before visiting some success branches.

Various concepts of termination have been extensively studied in the literature.

A widely accepted notion is that of *universal termination* [VP86]. In our framework a definite program is universally terminating w.r.t. a goal and a strategy iff the corresponding search tree is finite. If the search tree is finite then the operational completeness is preserved: all the success branches (if any) will be found. A section of this chapter outlines an approach to proving universal termination based on some attribute grammar techniques.

• *The use of "unification" without occur-check.* The occur-check (see the algorithm of Section 1.6.3) is an essential part of unification. However, for efficiency reasons many Prolog systems employ a version of unification not including the occur-check. Such algorithms may erroneously report a success of unification for non-unifiable terms. This would lead to construction of unsound answers. Consider for example the goal clause $\leftarrow plus(Y, s(X), X)$ for the definite program describing addition in the usual way (see Example 5.1 p. 208). The first clause of the program is the fact $plus(zero, X, X) \leftarrow$. The attempt to unify the atom of the goal with the fact would normally fail by occur-check but may succeed if the occur-check is not included in the implementation. Thus one may erroneously conclude that addition of *zero* and any positive integer n gives the result $n - 1$. On the other hand, for many programs and goals the positive occur-check will never occur during the computation. For such programs and goals Prolog systems without occur-check give correct answers. The programmer must detect such dangerous situations or prove that a program can be executed soundly on such interpreters. This problem will be discussed and studied in deep in Chapter 8.

The knowledge of the computational behaviour of a program in a given implementation may allow for optimization of the program. The questions of interest may concern the form of the actual subgoal selected for the resolution. This chapter also discusses the problem of proving such run-time properties. The approach proposed relies on the unification semantics. This kind of techniques may also apply to validation of Prolog programs using arithmetic and negation as failure. The arithmetic predicate *is* of Prolog requires groundness of one of its arguments at

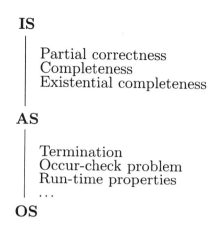

IS

Partial correctness
Completeness
Existential completeness

AS

Termination
Occur-check problem
Run-time properties
...

OS

Figure 6.1
The three semantics of a definite program and the corresponding verification
problems

call time [1]. The violation of this requirement causes so called "run-time
error". Groundness at call may also be needed in the case of negative
subgoals handled in Prolog. Nongroundess of such a goal at call time
may lead to generation of unsound answers by the Prolog system. For
detail discussion of this issue see e.g. [Llo87]. The validation of Prolog
programs is, however, outside of the scope of this book.

The above discussion is summarized in Figure 6.1. We pointed out
two different reasons for validation. The first one is to compare the
intended semantics of the program with its actual semantics. The other
is to compare the actual semantics of the program with its operational
semantics defined by a given implementation, which for some programs
produces the set of answers different from those described by the actual
semantics.

The rest of the chapter presents various proofs methods which can be
used for validation of definite programs. Most of them are being derived
from proof methods for attribute grammars by referring to the constructions of Chapter 5 relating definite programs and attribute grammars.

---

[1]In this chapter we sometimes refer to the notion of *calling a goal* which results
from the usual operational view of the SLD-resolution: "calling a goal" means to
perform SLD-resolution with this initial goal.

6.2 Verification of programs with respect to the declarative semantics

We first refer to the attribute grammar $\mathcal{R}(P)$ modelling the declarative semantics of a given definite program P, as defined in Section 5.1.1. As discussed in Chapter 5, there is a one-one correspondence between J-based proof trees of P and valid trees of $\mathcal{R}(P)$ with J-based interpretation. In particular the construction induces also a correspondence between the heads of the proof trees and the root labels of the valid trees. As discussed in Section 2.2, different kinds of declarative semantics of a program are equivalent and can be characterized by the set of the heads of all J-based proof trees of P. Therefore, the proof methods for partial correctness and completeness of attribute grammars applied to $\mathcal{R}(P)$ give proofs of properties of P.

6.2.1 Proving partial correctness

The inductive proof method of Chapter 4 can be applied to the attribute grammar modelling declarative semantics of a definite program. We show that in this case the notion of inductive specification can be simplified. As a result, one can derive proof methods for partial correctness of definite programs. This section shows only how to derive such methods. A comprehensive discussion of the methods is the topic of Chapter 7.

Let P be a definite program. Consider a specification $\langle S, \mathcal{I} \rangle$ of the attribute grammar $\mathcal{R}(P)$. Recall that S is a family of formulae indexed by the nonterminal symbols of the underlying context-free grammar. That is, according to the definition of $\mathcal{R}(P)$, the family is indexed by the predicates of P. The only free variables of a formula S_p in the family are the attributes of p, which correspond to the argument positions of p. The set of these variables will be denoted Var_p. Different occurrences of the formula S_p will be used in proofs. They will be denoted $S_p(k)$. In that case we will adopt the notational conventions used for attribute occurrences. Thus, the notation $p_i(k)$ will be used for denoting an occurrence of the variable p_i of the formula $S_p(k)$ associated with the node k of a derivation tree of a given program. In this case the predicate of the node atom of k is p and the set of all variable occurrences associated with k will be denoted $Var_p(k)$.

Intuitively, S_p characterizes a relation on the domain of interpretation.

As attributes of p in $\mathcal{R}(P)$ correspond to argument positions of p in P, the family S can be seen as a specification of P.

The language of the specification is any logical language (not necessarily first order) whose function symbols include all function symbols of the program. For simplicity we will assume that its predicate symbols do not include those of P. This case will be considered in Chapter 7. $\mathcal{I}$ is an interpretation of the language of the specification, with $=$, used in $\mathcal{R}(P)$, interpreted as identity. The interpretation of the functional symbols of P in $\mathcal{I}$ is a preinterpretation for P. It will be denoted $J_{\mathcal{I}}$ or simply J if there is no ambiguity.

For proving partial correctness of $\mathcal{R}(P)$ with respect to S^2 it suffices to show that S is inductive. We say that a specification S of a definite program P is *inductive* iff S is an inductive specification of $\mathcal{R}(P)$. Applying Definition 4.17 p. 177 of an inductive specification to $\mathcal{R}(P)$ we obtain:

Definition 6.1 Inductive specification

A specification $\langle S, \mathcal{I} \rangle$ of a definite program P is inductive iff for every clause c of the form:
$p_0(\bar{t}_0) \leftarrow p_1(\bar{t}_1), \ldots, p_k(\bar{t}_k), \ldots, p_n(\bar{t}_n)$ the following holds:

$$\mathcal{I} \models \phi_c \wedge S_{p_1}(1) \wedge \ldots \wedge S_{p_n}(n) \rightarrow S_{p_0}(0)$$

where $\bar{t}_k$ for $k = 0, \ldots, n$ denotes the argument vector $\langle t_{k1}, \ldots, t_{kn_k} \rangle$ of the predicate p_k and ϕ_c is the semantic rule associated with c in $\mathcal{R}(P)$.

□

The above definition uses the notation of Chapter 4: for u being a node of a parse tree labeled by a nonterminal X we denote by $S_X(u)$ the formula obtained from S_X by replacing each attribute a_i by the attribute occurrence $a_i(u)$.

Recall that, according to the definition of $\mathcal{R}(P)$, the semantic rule ϕ_c is of the form $\exists V(c) \bigwedge_{k \geq 0, j > 0} p_j(k) = t_{kj}$ where $V(c)$ is the set of all variables of c.

The equality predicate is defined as the identity on the domain of interpretation. Now the definition of inductive specification can be sim-

---

[2]One says also that S is *valid* for P.

plified. Let θ be the substitution $\{p_j(k)/t_{kj}|k \geq 0, j > 0\}$. Then the following definition is equivalent to the previous one:

Definition 6.2

A specification $\langle S, \mathcal{I} \rangle$ of a definite program P is inductive iff for every clause c: $p_0(\bar{t}_0) \leftarrow p_1(\bar{t}_1), \ldots, p_n(\bar{t}_n)$ of P the following holds:

$$\mathcal{I} \models \theta(S_{p_1}(1) \wedge \ldots \wedge S_{p_n}(n) \rightarrow S_{p_0}(0))$$

$\square$

Intuitively speaking, the semantic rule ϕ_c is a conjunction of equalities defining the attribute occurrences of c. The new condition defining inductive specifications is obtained by removing ϕ_c in the old condition and replacing the attribute occurrences by the defining terms of the removed semantic rule. Notice that the new definition concerns definite programs without any reference to attribute grammars. Now the induction method of Section 4.4.2 can be directly applied for proving partial correctness of definite programs without any reference to attribute grammars. In the context of attribute grammars this method has been further developed into the annotation proof method. Clearly, the same development is possible in the context of definite programs. The correctness proof methods based on the declarative semantics are discussed in more detail and illustrated by examples in Chapter 7.

6.2.2 Proving completeness

As discussed in Section 4.6 completeness of an attribute grammar with respect to a specification means that for every tuple of attribute values satisfying the specification there exists a valid tree whose root is labeled by this tuple. The method for proving completeness of attribute grammars introduced in Chapter 4 relies on the notion of co-inductive specification. This section discusses the situation when this proof method is applied to the attribute grammar modelling declarative semantics of a definite program. We show that in this case the notion of co-inductive specification is simplified. This simplified definition is then used for proving completeness of definite programs with respect to specifications.

Let P be a definite program. Consider a specification $\langle S, \mathcal{I} \rangle$ of the attribute grammar $\mathcal{R}(P)$. For proving completeness of $\mathcal{R}(P)$ with respect to S it suffices to show that S is (stronger than) a co-inductive specification. Applying Definition 4.24 p. 190 of co-inductive specification to $\mathcal{R}(P)$ we obtain:

Definition 6.3

Let P be a definite program, $Pred$ the set of its predicate symbols and let $\langle S, \mathcal{I} \rangle$ be a specification of the attribute grammar $\mathcal{R}(P)$. Denote by Q_p the relation specified by S for a predicate p in $Pred$.

The specification S is *co-inductive* iff for some family of ordering functions f: $\{f_p\}_{p \in Pred}$, for every p in $Pred$ and for every tuple $\bar{v}$ in Q_p there exists a clause c: $p_0(\bar{t}_0) \leftarrow p_1(\bar{t}_1), \ldots, p_n(\bar{t}_n)$ of P and a valuation ν such that:

- $\mathcal{I} \models \nu(\phi_c)$ and $\bar{v} = \nu(Attr(0))$,
- $\nu(Attr(i))$ is in the relation Q_{p_i} for $i = 1, \ldots, n$,
- f is decreasing on $p_0 \to p_1 \ldots p_n$ and ν.

□

The auxiliary notion of family of ordering functions decreasing on a given production rule and valuation has been defined in Section 4.6.1.

Recall that ϕ_c is of the form $\exists V(c) \bigwedge_{k \geq 0, j > 0} p_j(k) = t_{kj}$ where $V(c)$ is the set of all variables of c. This allows us to replace the attribute occurrences in the definition by tuples of argument terms in the clause. However, the concept of decreasing family of functions should be redefined so that all references to attributes can be eliminated.

Predicates p and p' are called *mutually recursive predicates* of a definite program P iff they are mutually recursive nonterminals of the underlying skeleton grammar G, i.e. iff $p \Rightarrow_G^* \alpha p' \beta \Rightarrow_G^* \alpha' p \beta'$ for some strings α, β, α' and β'.

For every predicate p of P let f_p be a function on the interpretation domain of p into a well-founded domain. The ordering on the domain will be denoted $\succ$. Such a function will be called an *ordering* function.

Let $c : p_0(\bar{t}_0) \leftarrow p_1(\bar{t}_1), \ldots, p_n(\bar{t}_n)$ be a clause of a definite program P. A given family of ordering functions $\{f_p\}_{p \in Pred}$ is said to be *decreasing* on c and on a valuation ν of variables of c iff $f_{p_0}(\nu(p_0(\bar{t}_0))) \succ f_{p_i}(\nu(p_i(\bar{t}_i)))$ for every predicate p_i in the body which is mutually recursive with p_0.

Using these notions we reformulate the definition of a co-inductive specification for the attribute grammar $\mathcal{R}(P)$ as a definition of co-inductive specification of P.

Definition 6.4

Let $\langle S, \mathcal{I} \rangle$ be a specification of a definite program P. Denote by Q_p the relation specified by S for the predicate p.

S is said to be *co-inductive* iff for some family f of ordering functions, for every predicate p and for every tuple $\bar{v}$ in Q_p there exists a clause c: $p_0(\bar{t}_0) \leftarrow p_1(\bar{t}_1), \ldots, p_n(\bar{t}_n)$ of P and a valuation ν such that:

- $\mathcal{I} \models \bar{v} = \nu(\bar{t}_0)$,

- $\nu(\bar{t}_i)$ is in the relation Q_{p_i} for $i = 1, \ldots, n$,

- f is decreasing on c and ν.

□

Notice that this definition refers only to the original definite program. Hence one can use it for proving completeness of this program with respect to a given specification. The intuition is that for any element $\bar{v}$ satisfying the specification S_p there should be a J-based proof tree with the head $p(\bar{v})$. To guarantee existence of a such a tree we require that there exists an J-instance of a clause with head $p(\bar{v})$ and such that all body atoms satisfy the specification. Consequently, each body atom can be extended with an instance of some clause. This is not sufficient for completeness since there may be no finite proof tree. Existence of the decreasing ordering functions guarantees "termination"[3], that is existence of a finite proof tree.

Clearly, the notion of co-inductive specification of a definite program allows us to use the proof method of Chapter 4 for proving completeness of definite programs with respect to specifications. Theorem 4.4 can now be reformulated in the following way:

Theorem 6.1 Proof method for completeness

A definite program P is complete w.r.t. a specification $\langle S, \mathcal{I} \rangle$ if and only if there exists a specification $\langle S', \mathcal{I} \rangle$ such that

---

[3] "termination" of the construction process. This concept refers to the existence of proof trees only and should not be confused with the operational notion of termination which depends on the operational semantics.

- $\mathcal{I} \models S \rightarrow S'$,
- S' is co-inductive for P.

□

In other words, a specification is complete iff it is stronger than a co-inductive specification. We illustrate the method by an example.

Example 6.1

Consider the following program *plus*:

$c_1 : plus(zero, X, X) \leftarrow$
$c_2 : plus(s(X), Y, s(Z)) \leftarrow plus(X, Y, Z)$

with the interpretation on the domain $TERM$ of not-necessarily ground terms. We show that it is complete w.r.t. the specification

$S_{plus} : \exists n, m \ (n, m \geq 0) \ \wedge \ plus_1 = s^n(zero) \ \wedge \ plus_2 = s^m(zero) \ \wedge \ plus_3 = s^{n+m}(zero)$.

and the ordering function:

$f_{plus}(plus_1, plus_2, plus_3) = size(plus_1)$

where $size(s^n(zero)) = n$.

To prove completeness we show that the specification is co-inductive. Let $\bar{v}$ be an element of the relation Q_{plus}. Two cases are possible and we consider them separately:

- $n = 0$, i.e. $\bar{v}$ is of the form $\langle zero, s^m(zero), s^m(zero) \rangle$.

In this case, c_1 has the properties required by the definition of co-inductive specification; the termination condition holds trivially as c_1 is a unit clause.

- $n > 0$; in this case c_2 has the required properties.

As the cases are exhaustive and cover all elements of Q_{plus} the specification is co-inductive.

□

Completeness proofs are generally complex since all arguments and variables must be taken into account. In the next section we show how in some cases the proof may be broken into several simpler proofs.

Completeness proofs using the existential completeness

In Section 4.6.2 we discussed a possibility of structuring and simplifying completeness proofs in case of functional dependencies on some attributes. In this case completeness proof can be obtained by composition of a simplified completeness proof with a correctness proof. The method, stated formally by Theorem 4.5 p. 194, applies also to logic programs.

In this case the subset A of attribute used to prove the completeness corresponds to a subset of arguments of the logic program which we also call *decisive arguments*, as in Section 5.2.2[4]. Let us denote by $P_{|_A}$ the program P restricted to the decisive arguments A.

For proving completeness of P with respect to S, according to Theorem 4.5 , it is sufficient to:

- find two specifications S_1 and S_2 such that A is the set of the free variables of S_1 and

1. $S \rightarrow S_1 \wedge S_2$, and

2. the set of the free variables of S_1 and S_2 coincides with the set of free variables of S, and

3. S_2 is functional w.r.t. S_1 (see Theorem 4.5 p. 194);

- prove completeness of $P_{|_A}$ w.r.t. S_1;
- prove existential completeness of $P_{|_A}$ w.r.t. S_1 (see Section 6.2.3);
- prove partial correctness of P w.r.t. $S_1 \rightarrow S$.

The problem of finding appropriate S_2 can sometimes be solved by putting $S_2 = S$. If the number of decisive arguments is restricted, the proof may be considerably simplified.

Example 6.2

We illustrate the method on the program *plus* and its specification S of Example 6.1 .

---

[4]The idea here is the same: the decisive arguments are those which determine the existence of a proof tree.

1. Take $A = \{plus_1, plus_2\}$ and define S_1 on $\mathcal{N}$ (natural integers) to be:

   $S_{1plus} : \exists n, m \ (n, m \geq 0 \wedge plus_1 = s^n(zero) \wedge plus_2 = s^m(zero))$

   We want to have $S \rightarrow S_1 \wedge S_2$. This can be trivially obtained by taking S_2 as S. S_2 is functional w.r.t S_1, by definition of Q_{plus} in $\mathcal{N}$:

   $S_{1plus}(plus_1, plus_2) \wedge S_{2plus}(plus_1, plus_2, b) \wedge S_{2plus}(plus_1, plus_2, c) \rightarrow b = c.$

2. $P_{|A}$ is complete with respect to S_1. Easy proof of completeness is omitted (it is the same as in Example 6.1 but with simpler formulae).

3. $P_{|A}$ is existentially complete with respect to S_1: it can be proved automatically using a partial nice d-assignment.

4. P is partially correct w.r.t. $S_1 \rightarrow S$. To check this it suffices to prove partial correctness of P with respect to S, by showing that S is an inductive specification.

   $\square$

6.2.3   Proving existential completeness

This section shows a method for proving existential completeness of a restriction of the program to a set of decisive arguments. The idea is to use the attribute grammar $\mathcal{F}(P)$ modelling an operational semantic of the program to show that computation of non-decisive arguments must succeed whenever the decisive arguments satisfy the specification. The idea is illustrated by an example. It is interesting to note that this approach leaves freedom in the choice of the computational model described by $\mathcal{F}(P)$. It is our conjecture that simple models, for example based on L-attribute grammars may often be sufficient. The method is essentially application of Theorem 5.3 p. 235. It is therefore not stated formally but only illustrated by an example.

Example 6.3

Let us consider again the program rev which uses the concatenation of difference lists.

$c_1 : rev(nil, L, L) \leftarrow$
$c_2 : rev(A.L, R1, R2) \leftarrow rev(L, Q1, Q2), cd(Q1, Q2, A.M, M, R1, R2)$
$c_3 : cd(L1, L2, L2, L3, L1, L3) \leftarrow$

Such program is not functional because there are infinitely many difference lists representing the reverse of a given list. However one is usually interested in its existential completeness only, provided that its partial correctness w.r.t. the specification "if rev_1 is a list then $rev_2 - rev_3$ is a difference list denoting the reverse of rev_1" is relatively easy to establish[5].

When programming with difference lists it is common to focus attention on concatenation since most of difficulties are usually concentrated there. The crucial property in this respect is called *compatibility*: two difference lists $L_1 - L_2$ and $L_3 - L_4$ are *compatible* if and only if L_2 and L_3 are unifiable.

Looking at the definition of cd it is relatively easy to convince oneself that with this condition a complete skeleton (which has one node only) is proper. We will use the compatibility condition for proving existential completeness of the example program with respect to the following specification interpreted on the domain $TERM$:

- S_{rev}: rev_1 is a list.
- S_{cd}: *true*.

We want to show that any partial skeleton in which all the first arguments of rev are instantiated by lists is proper.

For this, one may consider the structure of arbitrary skeleton and the associated equations. A leaf labeled c_1 creates no problems. For a node labeled c_2 the equations originating from the body atoms are solvable provided that the difference lists determined by the first four arguments of cd are compatible (i.e. provided that the second and the third argument of cd are unifiable). An experienced programmer can convince himself that it is the case. However this is a subtle point of the proof.

We show here how the construction $\mathcal{F}(P)$ of Section 5.3.1 may be used for formal proof of existential completeness. We will also show that the complex part of the proof may be fully automatized, using the notion of nice d-assignment of Section 5.2.2.

We first show that the program defining cd is existentially complete w.r.t. the specification:

---

[5]Proving completeness means proving that for every list (first argument) and every difference list (two last arguments) representing the reverse of the first argument there exists a proof tree. This is not the property of usual interest.

S_{cd}^{ec}: $cd2$ and $cd3$ are unifiable.

We now construct an attribute grammar $\mathcal{F}(P)$ describing construction of proof trees in such a way that proving of the compatibility condition is facilitated. The grammar has four attributes (sequence of terms and substitution are handled by two different attributes):

- $Arg-in$: the inherited sequence of the four first arguments, each component being referred as $cd_1, \ldots, cd_4$.

- σ: the inherited current substitution.

- $Arg-out$: the synthesized pair of the two last arguments, each component being referred as cd_5, cd_6.

- δ: the synthesized current substitution.

c_3: $cd(L1, L2, L2, L3, L1, L3) \leftarrow$

The semantic rules associated with the clause are[6]:

Φ_3:
$Arg-out(0) = [L1^u\mu, L3^u\mu]$
$\delta(0) = \sigma(0)\mu$
where $\mu = mgu([L1^u, L2^u, L2^u, L3^u]) = Arg-In(0))$.

Existential completeness is obvious (μ exists if the elements cd_2 and cd_3 of $Arg-in(0)$ are unifiable).

The proof of existential completeness of the program rev is thus as follows. The first argument of rev is to be decisive. The program restricted to the decisive arguments of rev (cd has no decisive arguments) is complete w.r.t. the specification:

- S_{rev}^1: rev_1 is a list,
- S_{cd}^1: $true$.

Thus it remains to show existence of a unifier for the non-decisive arguments, provided all the first arguments of rev are lists. Thus one extends the attribute grammar to the rules of rev as follows.

---

[6]The superscript u is used to indicate standardization.

- Arg: the synthesized pair of the two last arguments of rev, each of them being referred as rev_2 and rev_3.
- α: the synthesized current substitution of rev.

The clauses are:

c_1: $rev(nil, L, L) \leftarrow$

c_2: $rev(A.L, R1, R2) \leftarrow rev(L, Q1, Q2), cd(Q1, Q2, A.M, M, R1, R2)$

The semantic rules associated with the clauses are[6] :

Φ_1:
$$Arg(0) = [L^u, L^u]$$
$$\alpha(0) = \epsilon$$

Φ_2:
$$Arg-in(2) = [Q1^u, Q2^u, A^u\nu.M^u, M^u]\mu_1$$

where $\mu_1 = mgu(\{[Q1^u, Q2^u] = Arg(1)\})$ and $A^u\nu$ denotes the instance of A which occurs in the decisive argument.
$$\sigma(2) = \alpha(1)\mu_1$$
$$Arg(0) = [R1^u, R2^u]\mu_2$$

where $\mu_2 = mgu(\{[R1^u, R2^u] = Arg-out(2)\})$
$$\alpha(0) = \delta(2)\mu_2$$

Local dependencies for this attribute grammar are drawn in Figure 6.2. This attribute grammar describes a way to solve the equations associated to the non-decisive arguments. It fulfills conditions of Theorem 5.3 p. 235[7]. Furthermore it has a relatively simple form (it is natural and direct). To ensure existential completeness it is sufficient to show the existence of unifiers in all rule occurrences. In c_1 it is trivial. In c_2 the unifiers μ_1 and μ_2 always exist. Hence the only trouble comes from the rule c_3 (definitions Φ_3) where the existence of the unifier depends on the compatibility condition.

Indeed the only point is to verify that in $Arg-In(2)$: $Q2^u\mu_1$ and $(A^u\nu.M^u)\mu_1$ are unifiable in clause c_2. This results from the validity of the annotation associated to this grammar:

- S_{rev}: rev_3 is a variable not occurring in $rev1$. Synthesized.

---

[7]There is no goal clause, but the clause c_2 fulfills the conditions of the theorem for parse trees with root labeled by c_2.

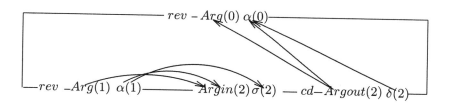

Figure 6.2
Local dependencies for the verification of the compatibility condition (Example 6.3)

- H_{cd}: cd_2 and cd_4 are distinct variables. Inherited.
- S_{cd}: cd_6 is a variable and identical to cd_4. Synthesized.

□

This proof reflects what is practically done implicitly by a programmer by trying to write such existentially complete program, using difference lists. There is however a simpler way of proving existential completeness for this program. It has a partial nice d-assignment:

$rev : \{-, \uparrow, \downarrow\}$,
$cd : \{\downarrow, \uparrow, \downarrow, \uparrow, \uparrow, \downarrow\}$.

This assignment fulfills conditions of Corollary 5.1 p. 222, hence the subset of equations corresponding to the non-decisive arguments has always a solution. Such property can be detected automatically.

6.3   Verification of programs with respect to the unification semantics

We now apply the proof methods of Chapter 4 to the attribute grammars modelling the unification semantics of logic programs. For a given program P such a grammar $\mathcal{A}_{US}$ is obtained by the construction of Section 5.3.2.

The specifications to be considered are interpreted on the term domain $TERM$. A specification S defines a family of relations on the interpretation domain indexed by the predicates of P. As the interpretation is a term interpretation this family can be represented by a subset $\mathcal{M}(S)$ of the (nonground) term base. It describes the required properties of the unification semantics $US(P)$ defined in Chapter 2. The properties concern thus the exact form of the computed answers of P. Generally the unification semantics describes programs without goals. A goal $g(\bar{t})$ can be handled by adding to the program a clause of the form $answer(\bar{x}) \leftarrow g(\bar{t})$ where $\bar{x}$ is the vector of all variables occurring in the arguments $\bar{t}$ of the goal. In this case the specification formula S_{answer} describes properties of the answer substitutions.

The general notions of correctness and completeness of an attribute grammar with respect to a specification can now be restricted to a particular case of the attribute grammar $\mathcal{F}(P)$. Since this grammar is only an auxiliary construction for modelling the unification semantics we can directly consider correctness and completeness of a logic program with respect to a specification interpreted on the nonground term domain $TERM$.

Definition 6.5

Let S be a specification of a definite program P with an interpretation $\mathcal{T}$ on the term domain $TERM$ and let $\mathcal{M}(S)$ be the subset of $TERM$ representing the family of relations defined by S.

P is partially correct w.r.t. S iff $US(P)$ is a subset of $\mathcal{M}(S)$.

P is complete w.r.t S iff $\mathcal{M}(S)$ is a subset of $US(P)$.

$\square$

Recall that an atom a "is an element" of $US(P)$ iff $US(P)$ contains a variant of a. Hence "to be a subset" means that each element in the first set has a variant in the second.

We now reformulate the proof methods of Chapter 4 for the case of

unification semantics of logic programs. As the unification semantics is a
set of terms, the specification language has a term interpretation denoted
$\mathcal{T}$. The definitions concern logic programs and include no reference to
attribute grammars. A direct reformulation of the Definition 4.17 gives
the following:

Definition 6.6 Inductive specification

A specification $\langle S, \mathcal{T} \rangle$ of a definite program P is *inductive* iff for every
clause $c : p_0(\bar{t_0}) \leftarrow p_1(\bar{t_1}), \ldots, p_n(\bar{t_n})$ of P :

$$\mathcal{T} \models S_{p_1} \wedge \ldots \wedge S_{p_n} \wedge \sigma = mgu(\bigcup_{k>0}\{\bar{p_k} = \bar{t_k^u}\}) \rightarrow S_{p_0}(\bar{t_0}\sigma)$$

where $\bar{p_k}$ denotes the vector $\langle p_1(k), \ldots, p_{m_k}(k) \rangle$ of all argument variables of the predicate p_k for $k = 1, \ldots, n$ and $\bar{t_k^u}$ denotes the vector
of the corresponding standardized argument terms in k-th atom of c,
and $S_{p_0}(\bar{t_0}\sigma)$ is the formula obtained from S_{p_0} by substitution of the
variables in Var_{p_0} by the corresponding elements of the vector $\bar{t_0}\sigma$.
□

In other words, an inductive specification is such that whenever not
necessarily ground atoms $a_1, \ldots, a_n$ belong to $\mathcal{M}(S)$ and unify with the
body atoms $b_1, \ldots, b_n$ of a clause $c : h \leftarrow b_1, \ldots, b_n$ with the mgu σ then
$h\sigma \in \mathcal{M}(S)$.

We now reformulate the notion of co-inductive specification (Definition 4.6.1 p. 190) for the case of the unification semantics. In this case
the ordering functions map the term domain into a well-founded domain.
Instead of using families of ordering functions indexed by the predicates
we will use single ordering functions on the term base.

Definition 6.7 Co-inductive specification

Let P be definite program and let $\langle S, \mathcal{T} \rangle$ be a specification for P.
S is said to be *co-inductive* iff for some ordering function f, for every
atom $a \in \mathcal{M}(S)$ there exists a variant of a clause $c : h \leftarrow b_1, \ldots, b_n$ and
variants of atoms $a_1, \ldots, a_n \in \mathcal{M}(S)$ such that the a_i's, $i = 1 \ldots n$, a
and c do not share any variable and:

- the equations $a_1 = b_1, \ldots, a_n = b_n$ have an mgu σ,
- $h\sigma$ is a variant of a,
- $f(a) \succ f(a_i)$, for every atom a_i whose predicate is mutually recursive
  with the one of a.

□

Notice that in the special case of a unit clause σ is the identity substitution and the only nontrivial condition is a is a variant of h.

The proof methods for partial correctness and completeness can now be stated in the usual way, while their specificity is hidden in the above defined specific notions of inductive specification and co-inductive specification.

Theorem 6.2

A definite program P is partially correct w.r.t. a specification S if and only if S is weaker than some inductive specification.

A definite program P is complete w.r.t. a specification S if and only if S is stronger than some co-inductive specification.

$\square$

We now illustrate the method by some examples.

Example 6.4 The list reverse program

We consider the following list reverse program:

c_1: $rev(nil, L, L) \leftarrow$
c_2: $rev(A.L, R1, R2) \leftarrow rev(L, Q1, Q2), cd(Q1, Q2, A.M, M, R1, R2)$
c_3: $cd(L1, L2, L2, L3, L1, L3) \leftarrow$

We prove partial correctness and completeness of this program with respect to the following specification formulated in a natural language style and interpreted on the term domain $TERM$ including nonground terms.

S_{rev}:
rev_1 is a list of distinct variables and
$rev_2 - rev_3$ is a difference list representing the reverse of rev_1 and
rev_3 is a variable not occurring in rev_1.

S_{cd}:
$cd_1, cd_2, cd_3, cd_4, cd_5, cd_6$ are variables, respectively of the form
X, Y, Y, Z, X, Z.

Thus, rev_1, rev_2 and rev_3 are, respectively of the form
$A_1.A_2.\ldots.A_n.nil$, $A_n.\ldots.A_1.X$ and X, where X is different from

$A_1, A_2, \ldots, A_n$.

Partial correctness. We check that the specification is inductive:
For c_1 we obtain the following condition which obviously holds:

- *nil* is a list of distinct variables; this holds with $n = 0$ and
- $L - L$ is a difference list representing *nil* and
- L is a variable not occurring in *nil*.

For c_2 the condition is slightly more complicated but also easy to check:
Assume that x and y are in $\mathcal{M}(S)$ and unify with the body atoms of c_2. Hence

- $x\sigma$ is of the form $rev(A_1.\ldots.A_n.nil, A_n.\ldots.A_1.A.M, A.M)$,
- $y\sigma$ is of the form
$cd(A_n.\ldots.A_1.A.M, A.M, A.M, M, A_n.\ldots.A_1.A.M, M)$.

Consequently, σ applied to the head of the clause gives an atom of the form: $rev(A.A_1.\ldots.A_n.nil, A_n.\ldots.A_1.A.M, M)$, which obviously satisfies the specification.
For c_3 the verification condition holds trivially.

Completeness:
To prove completeness we show that S is co-inductive. As the ordering function we take the size of the first argument.
Let x be an element in $\mathcal{M}(S)$. Hence x is of the form $cd(X, Y, Y, Z, X, Z)$ or of the form $rev(A_1.\ldots.A_n.nil, A_n.\ldots.A_1.X, X)$, where $n \geq 0$. In the first case the verification condition is trivially satisfied by c_3. The second case splits into two disjoint sub-cases. If $n = 0$ the verification conditions are trivially satisfied by c_1. For $n > 0$ one can check that c_2 and the atoms $rev(A'_2.\ldots.A'_n.nil, A'_n.\ldots.A'_2.X', X')$ and $cd(U, Y', Y', Z', U, Z')$ satisfy the verification conditions. Indeed the mgu σ includes the bindings:
$L/A'_2.\ldots.A'_n.nil,$
$R1/A'_n.\ldots.A'_2.A.M,$
$Q1/A'_n.\ldots.A'_2.A.M,$
$X'/A.M,$

$R2/M$.

Hence the instance of the head under σ is $rev(A.A'_2.\ldots.A'_n.nil,$ $A'_n.\ldots.A'_2.A.M, M)$ which is a variant of x. The decreasing condition is also easy to check for the recursive predicate rev.

□

The program is both correct and complete with respect to the specification. This means that the specification is the strongest one, i.e. it describes exactly the unification semantics of the program.

In fact every element of $DEN_{TERM}(P)$ of a program P is an instance of an element of $US(P)$. Hence, the strongest specification concerning the unification semantics can be used for checking completeness (declarative and operational) of the program for particular goals.

As illustrated by the last example, proving properties of a program with respect to the unification semantics requires analysis of unification. This may be a rather difficult task. It turns out that proofs using declarative semantics on nonground term models can also give results concerning the unification semantics: if for some predicate p the specification $S_p(\bar{p})$ is valid for P in the ($TERM$-based) declarative semantics, then it is also valid in the unification semantics. The opposite implication does not hold. For example the specification $S_p : variable(p_1)$, with the natural interpretation of the predicate $variable$ on the term domain, is valid in the unification semantics of the program $p(X) \leftarrow$ but not valid in the denotation of P. An interesting point is that sometimes the operational properties of programs reflected by the unification semantics can be proved by referring only to the declarative semantics. In particular when the unification semantics is ground (see allowed programs in [Apt90]). In this case the proof may be simplified, since it does not require analysis of the unification process.

The concluding example of this section illustrates potential usefulness of the proof methods based on unification semantics in metaprogramming.

Example 6.5 The *vanilla* metainterpreter

Consider the following program ([Der88]).

c_1: $solve(true) \leftarrow$
c_2: $solve(A \text{ and } B) \leftarrow solve(A), solve(B)$

c_3: $solve(A) \leftarrow clause(A, B), solve(B)$

The program is a metainterpreter: it can be used for computing the unification semantics of a given definite program P. For this it should be augmented with a database of facts of the form $clause(A, B)$, representing all clauses of a program P. More precisely, for every clause $H \leftarrow B_1, \ldots, B_n$ of P the database should include a fact of the form $clause(H, B_1 \ and \ldots \ and \ B_n)$ if $n > 1$, of the form $clause(H, B_1)$ if $n = 1$ and of the form $clause(H, true)$ if $n = 0$, where and is a binary right associative operator. Terms constructed with the operator and will be called *conjunctions*.

We want to prove correctness and completeness of the metainterpreter with respect to a specification referring to the unification semantics of P. Notice that we are not specific about P which is used as a parameter of the following specification.

S_{solve}: $solve_1$ is an element of $US(P)$, the constant $true$,
          or a conjunction of such terms.
S_{clause}: $clause_1 \leftarrow clause_2$ is a renamed clause of P.

Partial correctness. Correctness can be proved by showing that S is inductive. We sketch the check of the verification conditions for each clause:

- For c_1 the condition holds trivially.
- For c_2, notice that if atoms $solve(t1), solve(t2)$ satisfy S_{solve} and unify with the body atoms, then the instance of the head of c_2 under the mgu has as its argument a conjunction including atoms in $US(P)$ or/and the atom $true$.
- To check verification condition for c_3 notice that if some atoms $clause(a, b), solve(b)$ satisfy S_{solve} and unify with the body of c_3 then their mgu σ applied to A must be an element of $US(P)$.

Notice, that P is a parameter of our proof and of our metainterpreter, so that the proof relies on the assumption that the actual database correctly represents P. This assumption appears as S_{clause} but cannot be checked without being specific about P.

Completeness. Completeness can be proved by showing that S is co-inductive. For checking the first part of the verification condition for the predicate *solve* one has to consider separately the following three disjoint cases, of the form of $solve_1$: (1) it is of the form *true*, (2) it is an element of $US(P)$ (3) it is a conjunction. These cases correspond to the use for verification, respectively, clauses c_1, c_3 and c_2. The check is relatively easy.

We now define a decreasing ordering function f_{solve}. There are three types of arguments of *solve*.

- $f_{solve}(solve(true)) = 0$.
- For the argument A which is an element of $US(P)$ $f_{solve}(solve(A))$ is defined to be the minimal depth of proof trees in P that produce A. Such trees exist by the definition of the unification semantics.
- For the argument of the form A *and* B where A and B are either elements of $US(P)$ or finite conjunctions of such elements $f_{solve}(solve(A \text{ and } B))$ is defined to be $max(f_{solve}(solve(A)), f_{solve}(solve(B))) + 1$.

On the clause c_1 the function is decreasing in a trivial way, since it is a unit clause. On the clause c_2 the function is decreasing since $f_{solve}(solve(A \text{ and } B)) > max(f_{solve}(solve(A)), f_{solve}(solve(B)))$. Consider clause c_3 with a substitution σ such that $A\sigma$ and $B\sigma$ are in $US(P)$. Then there is at least one proof tree in P producing $B\sigma$ and $f_{solve}(solve(A\sigma)) \geq f_{solve}(solve(B\sigma)) + 1$. Hence $f_{solve}(solve(A\sigma)) > f_{solve}(solve(B\sigma))$.
□

6.4   Verification of run-time properties

In this section we discuss a possibility of using attribute grammar techniques for proving so called "run-time properties" or "dynamic properties" of programs. Such properties concern atoms chosen at every step of the SLD-resolution, or more generally, properties of current subsets of equations solved in a step of resolution.

This section discusses two methods for proving run-time properties of a definite program P. Both can be derived from proof methods for attribute grammars applied to the grammars $A_{US}(P)$ and $A_{SLD}(P)$. However, to simplify the presentation the methods are introduced with little reference to the attribute grammars.

We will consider two kinds of run-time properties: the *answer specifications* and the *resolution invariants* for SLD-resolution.

Intuitively, an answer specification for certain kind of resolution describes a property of the answers obtained for a class of goals. As discussed in Section 2.2.3, the form of answers obtained for a goal is described by the unification semantics. Therefore, the notion of answer specification must be related to the unification semantics. However, an answer specification restricts the class of goals considered, hence also the class of obtained answers.

The other kind of specifications discussed in this section concerns properties of the atoms selected for resolution during the computation. Such properties will be called resolution invariants. Generally, it may be difficult to prove resolution invariants without referring to properties of answers.

6.4.1   Answer specifications and resolution invariants

We first give a formal definition of the notion of answer specification and resolution invariant. An answer specification relates goals to their answer substitutions. Resolution invariants concern the form of the calls during the computation. Therefore, in the specification language we will use special variables referring to the form of arguments of program predicates during call and upon the success of the computation. Let P be a definite program let p be an n-ary predicate of P. The specification language includes the set $Prevar_p$ consisting of the variables $\bullet p_1, \ldots, \bullet p_n$ and the set $Postvar_p$ consisting of the variables $p_1 \bullet, \ldots, p_n \bullet$.

The specification language is a logical language interpreted on the term domain $TERM$ of the program. We are not specific about its predicates; the interpretation of the predicates used in example specifications will be defined in the examples. The variables of the term domain play the role of constants in the specification language.

Definition 6.8

Let P be a definite program and let $Pred$ be the set of the predicates which occur in P. An *answer specification* of a program P is a family of pairs of formulae $\{\langle Pre_p, Post_p \rangle\}_{p \in Pred}$ such that the free variables of

Pre_p are in $Prevar_p$ and the free variables of $Post_p$ are in $Prevar_p \cup Postvar_p$.

A *resolution invariant* of a program P is a family of formulae $\{C_p\}_{p \in Pred}$ such that the free variables of C_p are in $Prevar_p$.

The preconditions of an answer specification A define a resolution invariant called the *associated resolution invariant*, denoted C_A.

The language of the formulae is interpreted on $TERM$-based term interpretation $\mathcal{T}$.
□

The interpretation $\mathcal{T}$ will be implicit for all the specifications in this section.

For given answer specification and predicate p the formula Pre_p will be called the *precondition* of p and the formula $Post_p$ will be called the *postcondition* of p.

For a goal atom $g = p(\bar{t})$ where $\bar{t} = \langle t_1, \ldots, t_n \rangle$ we denote by $Pre_p[\bar{t}]$ the formula obtained from Pre_p by replacing each free variable $\bullet p_i$ by the term t_i for $i = 1, \ldots, n$. Notice that $Pre_p[\bar{t}]$ is a closed formula of the specification language, hence it is either true or false in the considered interpretation $\mathcal{T}$. We say that g *satisfies its precondition* iff $Pre_p[\bar{t}]$ is true in the considered interpretation.

Let σ be an answer substitution of g. We denote by $Post_p[\bar{t}, \sigma]$ the formula obtained from $Post_p$ by replacing each free variable $\bullet p_i$ by the term t_i and each free variable $p_i\bullet$ by $t_i\sigma$. $Post_p[\bar{t}, \sigma]$ is also a closed formula of the specification language, hence it is either true or false in the considered interpretation. We say that g with σ *satisfies its postcondition* iff $Post_p[\bar{t}, \sigma]$ is true in the considered interpretation.

Example 6.6

Consider the append program:
$app(nil, X, X) \leftarrow$
$app(A.X, Y, A.Z) \leftarrow app(X, Y, Z)$

If a goal $\leftarrow app(t_1, X, Y)$ (whose second and third arguments are variables) succeeds, then the instance of Y upon success will be a list with a variable suffix bound to X. This can be described as the following answer specification:

Pre_{app}: $var(\bullet app_2)$
$Post_{app}$: $suffix(\bullet app_2, app_3\bullet)$.

The predicates *var* and *suffix* of the specification language have an interpretation on the terms of the object language that corresponds to the intuition discussed above.

In this interpretation the goal $app(nil, X, Y)$ satisfies its precondition and for the substitution $\{X/Y\}$ it also satisfies its postcondition. On the other hand the goal $app(nil, nil, nil)$ does not satisfy its precondition.

An example of invariant specification for this program is the precondition of the above answer specification. This invariant says that for the program called with the initial atomic goal satisfying the precondition every goal selected for the resolution also satisfies the precondition (i.e. its second argument is a variable).
□

An answer specification (a resolution invariant) may or may not give a proper description of the behaviour of the program. The first case is captured by the following formal definition.

Definition 6.9

A Horn program P is *partially correct* w.r.t. an answer specification A (or A is *valid* for P) iff for any atomic goal $\leftarrow g$ which satisfies its precondition, its computed answer substitution σ satisfies its postcondition.

A resolution invariant C is *valid* for P and a fixed computation rule iff in any SLD-tree whose initial goal satisfies C, the selected atom in the goal of every state satisfies C.
□

Notice that validity of the answer specification does not depend on a particular resolution scheme. So any full resolution scheme can be used to prove validity, in particular the SLD-resolution. On the other hand, validity of the resolution invariant depends on the computation rule, hence on the resolution scheme used in the computation.

6.4.2   Proving answer specification

By Proposition 2.4 p. 83 every answer substitution for given program and goal can be obtained by unification of the goal and an element of the unification semantics of the program. This gives the following idea for a proof method for answer specifications. Let S be a specification of P valid in the unification semantics. For a predicate p of P take a vector $\bar{t}$

of arguments satisfying the precondition of an answer specification. The
vector defines one of the atomic goals in the considered class of goals.
All answers for this goal are characterized by the unification semantics.
Hence, since the relation described by S is a superset of the unification
semantics, any answer to the goal $p(\bar{t})$ can be obtained by unification
of the argument vector $\bar{t}$ with a vector $\bar{u}$ of terms satisfying S_p. Consequently, if for every unifiable $\bar{t}$ and $\bar{u}$ the arguments $\bar{t}$ together with the
mgu obtained satisfy the postcondition then the answer specification is
valid. Thus, the proof method reduces to finding a specification which
is valid in the unification semantics and is related to the given answer
specification as explained above. The formal statement of the method
is given by the following theorem.

Theorem 6.3

An answer specification $\{\langle Pre_p, Post_p\rangle\}_{p\in Pred}$ of a Horn program P
is valid if and only if there exists a specification S of P valid with
respect to the unification semantics such that for every predicate p of
P the following formula is true in the considered interpretation of the
specification language:

$$\forall \bar{t} \forall \bar{p} Pre_p[\bar{t}] \wedge S_p \wedge unifiable(\bar{t} = \bar{p}) \rightarrow Post_p[\bar{t}, mgu(\bar{t} = \bar{p})]$$

where $\bar{p} = \langle p_1, \ldots, p_n\rangle$ is the vector of variables in Var_p and $\bar{t} = \langle v_1, \ldots, v_n\rangle$ is a vector of distinct variables not belonging to Var_p.
□

Proof. Assume that the condition is satisfied. We prove that the answer
specification is valid. Consider a goal $p(\bar{t})$ which satisfies the precondition and which is unifiable with some renamed atom $p(\bar{u})$ of $US(P)$. By
Proposition 2.4 p. 83 the mgu μ is an answer substitution for this goal.
Hence $S_p[\bar{u}]$ is true in the considered interpretation. It follows from
the fact that a specification valid in the unification semantics specifies
a superset of atoms of $US(P)$. Consequently, by the assumption, the
postcondition is satisfied, hence the answer specification is valid.

The only if case follows by Proposition 2.4 p. 83 and by the existence
of the strongest specification for $US(P)$ (provided that the specification
language is expressible enough).
□

Notice, that mgu is a partial operation, so that the truth value of the right hand side of the implication may not be defined. This happens, however, only in the case when the predecessor is false, since unifiability of the arguments is a condition of the predecessor. In this case we assume that the implication holds. A more formal treatment would be to define such a total extension of the mgu that non-unifiability would cause falsity of any postcondition.

We illustrate the method by two examples.

Example 6.7

The following program is considered in [DM88]:

c_1: $q(zero) \leftarrow$
c_2: $q(X) \leftarrow q(s(X))$

For this program to succeed with an atomic goal the goal must be of the form $q(t)$, where t unifies with $zero$. Any such goal would succeed with answer instantiating t to $zero$ if t is a variable. This intuition can be described by the following answer specifications:

$Pre_q : unifiable(\bullet q_1, zero)$ $Post_q : q_1\bullet = zero$
$Pre_q : \neg\ unifiable(\bullet q_1, zero)$ $Post_q : false$

It is easy to see that the strongest US-specification of the program is:
$S_q : q_1 = zero$

Applying the method for proving both answer specifications would reduce to proving the following assertions:

$unifiable(t_1, zero) \wedge q_1 = zero \wedge unifiable(q_1, t_1) \rightarrow t_1\sigma = zero$
where $\sigma = mgu(q_1, t_1)$, and
$\neg unifiable(t_1, zero) \wedge q_1 = zero \wedge unifiable(q_1, t_1) \rightarrow false$
which follow by the definition of unification.

The validity of a specification with the postcondition $false$ means that there is no answer substitution for the goals satisfying the precondition. Thus any computation defined by a full resolution scheme for this goal either finitely fails or does not terminate.

The behaviour of the example program can alternatively be described by the following answer specification:

Pre_q: $true$
$Post_q$: $(unifiable(\bullet q_1, zero) \rightarrow q_1\bullet = zero)\wedge$
$\qquad (\neg unifiable(\bullet q_1, zero) \rightarrow false)$

$\square$

In the previous example we used the strongest specification of the unification semantics. This is possible only in simple cases; in general weaker properties may be sufficient.

Example 6.8

The behaviour of the reverse program of Example 6.3 may not be immediately clear. Recall the program:

c_1: $rev(nil, L, L) \leftarrow$
c_2: $rev(A.L, R1, R2) \leftarrow rev(L, Q1, Q2),$
$\qquad\qquad\qquad cd(Q1, Q2, A.M, M, R1, R2)$
c_3: $cd(L1, L2, L2, L3, L1, L3) \leftarrow$

We describe it by an answer specification (expressed in the natural language). By a partial difference list we mean a term of the form $t_1 - t_2$ where

- either t_1 and t_2 are identical variables, or
- t_1 is of the form $e_1.....e_n.X$ and t_2 is either the variable X or it is of the form $e_k.e_{k+1}.....e_n.X$ for some $1 \le k \le n$, where $n > 0$, X is a variable and $e_1, \ldots, e_n$ are arbitrary terms. The terms e_i will be called elements of t_1 and t_2.

For the predicate cd we give the following answer specification:

Pre_{cd}: $\bullet cd_1 - \bullet cd_2$ and $\bullet cd_3 - \bullet cd_4$ are partial difference lists and
$\qquad \bullet cd_4$ is a variable and
$\qquad \bullet cd_4$ does not occur in $\bullet cd_1$ or in $\bullet cd_2$ and
$\qquad \bullet cd_4$ is not an element of $\bullet cd_3$.

$Post_{cd}$: $cd_5\bullet - cd_6\bullet$ is a partial difference list and
$\qquad cd_6\bullet$ is a variable and it is not an element of $cd_i\bullet$ for $i = 1, \ldots, 4$.

The validity of the answer specification can be proved using the following strongest specification of cd in the unification semantics:

S_{cd}: cd_1, cd_2, cd_3, cd_4, cd_5, cd_6 are variables and
$\quad cd_1 = cd_5$, $cd_2 = cd_3$, $cd_4 = cd_6$.

The predicate rev can be characterized by the following answer specification:

Pre_{rev}: $\bullet rev_2 - \bullet rev_3$ is a partial difference list and
$\quad \bullet rev_3$ is a variable and
$\quad \bullet rev_3$ does not occur in $\bullet rev_1$ and
$\quad \bullet rev_3$ is not an element of $\bullet rev_2$.

$Post_{rev}$: $rev_3 \bullet$ is a variable and
$\quad rev_3 \bullet$ does not occur in $\bullet rev_1$ or in $rev_1 \bullet$.

The strongest specification of rev in the unification semantics is the following one:

S_{rev}: $rev_1 = A_1.\ldots.A_n$ and $rev_2 = A_n.\ldots.A_1.X$ and $rev_3 = X$
$\quad$ for some variables $A_1, \ldots, A_n, X$ and some n.

But validity of the answer specification can be proved using the following weaker specification (obviously implied by S_{rev}):

S'_{rev}: $rev_2 - rev_3$ is a partial difference list and
$\quad rev_3$ is a variable and
$\quad rev_3$ does not occur in rev_1 nor in one of the elements of rev_2.

This shows that some results may be obtained without knowing the explicit form of $US(P)$.
□

6.4.3   Proving resolution invariant

We now present a sound and complete method for proving resolution invariants in the case of SLD-resolution with standard computation rule. It is based on the unification semantics. A resolution invariant describes the form of the atomic goals selected at every step of the computation. Such a goal originates from a body atom of some clause. It is selected iff all preceding body atoms have been already selected and the answers have been computed. These answers determine the actual form of the selected goal. On the other hand the form of the goal at call time together with the unification semantics of the program determines the answers which can be obtained for this goal. This gives the idea of proving validity of invariants by a kind of computational induction using the unification semantics. The method is formally stated by the following theorem.

Theorem 6.4

Let P be a Horn program and let C be a resolution invariant for the SLD-resolution with standard computation rule. C is valid if and only if there exists a specification S of P valid with respect to the unification semantics and such that for every non-unit clause c of P with n atoms in the body the following verification condition holds:

Let

- $\bar{u}_0$ be a vector of terms satisfying Pre_{p_0},

- $\bar{u}_j$, for $j = 1, \ldots, n-1$ be vectors of terms satisfying S_{p_j} (the $\bar{u}_j$'s, $0 \le j < n$ do not share any variable),

- $c' : p_0(\bar{t}_0) \leftarrow p_1(\bar{t}_1), \ldots, p_n(\bar{t}_n)$ be a variant of c sharing no variables with any $\bar{u}_j$, $0 \le j < n$,

- μ_j be mgu's of $\bar{u}_j$ and $\bar{t}_j \mu_0 \ldots \mu_{j-1}$ for $0 \le j < n$,

- For every k, $1 \le k \le n$, $Pre_{p_k}[\bar{t}_k \mu_0 \mu_1 \ldots \mu_{k-1}]$ holds.

□

Proof. One applies the annotation method of Section 4.5 on the attribute grammar $\mathcal{A}_{SLD}$ (Section 5.3.3) which models the SLD-resolution. There is only one inherited formula which corresponds to the resolution invariant: $I(Arg)$: $C(Arg)$. Validity of the resolution invariant is thus equivalent to the validity of this annotation in $\mathcal{A}_{SLD}$. Consider now the family of assertions (the index ranging over the predicate symbols is omitted)

$S_p(Arg, \sigma, \delta)$: $\exists \bar{u}, \mu\ S_p^{US}(\bar{u}) \wedge \mu = mgu(\bar{u} = Arg) \wedge \delta = \sigma\mu$, where S^{US} is the strongest specification with respect to the unification semantics and $\bar{u}$ is a vector of terms which don't share any variable with Arg. S is a valid specification of $\mathcal{A}_{SLD}$ by definition and Proposition 2.4 p. 83. Let S be a synthesized assertion in the annotation of $\mathcal{A}_{SLD}$ without incoming arrow in the logical dependency scheme (S being valid one may assume that there exists a purely synthesized dependency scheme and a sound annotation to prove it).

Let us consider an annotation for $\mathcal{A}_{SLD}$ with one inherited assertion I and one synthesized assertion S, and a logical dependency scheme in which all output assertions depend on all the previous input assertions according to the total order of the computation of Arg.

The LDS is non-circular (it is a L-LDS). The conditions of Theorem 6.4 imply soundness of the annotation for this LDS. In fact assume $I(Arg(0))$ and $S_{p_j}(Arg(j), \sigma(j), \delta(j))$, if $S_{p_j}(Arg(j), \sigma(j), \delta(j))$ for $j < k$, then the hypotheses in the conditions are satisfied (every atom specified by the strongest specification satisfies a valid specification too), hence their conclusions of the form $Pre_{p_k}(\bar{t}_k \mu_0 \mu_1 \ldots \mu_{k-1})$ which implies $Pre_{p_k}(Arg(k))$ using the substitutions of the hypotheses (the substitution $\sigma(0)$ does not influence the attribute values as it is already applied in $Arg(0)$).

The completeness of the method (only if part) follows from the fact that using the strongest specification in the conditions of the theorem, the substitutions μ correspond to the answer substitutions of the left subgoals, hence the conditions are equivalent to the definition of validity of the resolution invariant.
□

Notice that the proof method uses no explicit postconditions; they are hidden in the concept of unification semantics.

We now illustrate the method by an example.

Example 6.9

We consider the following quicksort program.

$$c_1: \quad qsort(nil, nil) \leftarrow$$
$$c_2: \quad qsort(A.L, R) \leftarrow partition(A, L, L1, L2),$$
$$qsort(L1, R1),$$

$$qsort(L2, R2),$$
$$append(R1, A.R2, R)$$

c_3: $partition(A, nil, nil, nil) \leftarrow$

c_4: $partition(A1, A2.L, A2.L1, L2) \leftarrow gt(A1, A2),$
$$partition(A1, L, L1, L2)$$

c_5: $partition(A1, A2.L, L1, A2.L2) \leftarrow le(A1, A2),$
$$partition(A1, L, L1, L2)$$

c_6: $append(nil, L, L) \leftarrow$

c_7: $append(A.L1, L2, A.L3) \leftarrow append(L1, L2, L3)$

The intention is to use the program for sorting lists. For sorting a list l one has to initialize a computation with the initial goal $qsort(l, X)$ where X is a variable. A successful computation would bind the sorted version of l to X. We want to prove that in every computation starting with such a goal every recursive "call" of quicksort will also have a list as its first argument and a variable as its second argument. Thus we want to prove a resolution invariant C such that $C_{qsort} : list(\bullet qsort_1) \wedge var(\bullet qsort_2)$. We impose no restriction on the form of other selected goals. Thus we put: $C_p : true$ for any other predicate p.

As the predicates gt and le are not specified in the program we assume that their unification semantics satisfies the following specification:

$S_{gt}: integer(gt_1) \wedge integer(gt_2) \wedge gt_1 > gt_2.$
$S_{le}: integer(le_1) \wedge integer(le_2) \wedge le_1 \leq le_2.$

Even without this assumption one can prove the following property of the unification semantics (this specification is inductive):

$S_{partition} : list(partition_2) \wedge list(partition_3) \wedge list(partition_4)$

We now verify the resolution invariant of quicksort. Actually it is a conjunction of two invariants and we verify them separately. We consider first the invariant $list(\bullet qsort_1)$.

The clause c_1 is a unit clause and no verification conditions are to be checked.

The body of clause c_2 includes two recursive calls, which give two verification conditions:

- $k = 2$

Let $\bar{u}_0$ be a vector of terms satisfying C_{qsort} and let u_{12}, u_{13}, u_{14} be terms satisfying $S_{partition}$. Thus, all these terms are lists. Consider the system of equations $\{u_{01} = A'.L', \ u_{02} = R', \ A' = u_{11}, \ L' = u_{12}, \ L1' = u_{13}, \ L2' = u_{14}\}$, where $A', L', L1', L2'$ are renamed variables of the clause. Clearly, if there exists an mgu σ_1, it must bind $L1'$ to a list, i.e. the verification condition holds.

- $k = 3$

For checking the verification condition according to the method one should now use a specification of the unification semantics of $qsort$. However, in this particular case the answer of the first recursive call of $qsort$ does not influence the form of the arguments of the second call. Formally, the specification $S_{qsort} : true$ is sufficient to verify the invariant. The system of equations to be considered is: $\{u_{01} = A'.L', \ u_{02} = R', \ A' = u_{11}, \ L' = u_{12}, \ L1' = u_{13}, \ L2' = u_{14}, \ L1' = u_{21}, \ R1' = u_{22}\}$, where u_{21} is an arbitrary term. Clearly, if there exists an mgu σ_2, it must bind $L2'$ to a list, i.e. the verification condition holds.

We now consider the invariant $var(\bullet qsort_2)$. We prove it without using information about unification semantics; formally this means that the weakest specification of the unification semantics is used. The verification condition for the first recursive call of $qsort$ in the body of c_2 concerns the mgu of the system of equations

$$\{u_{01} = A'.L', \ u_{02} = R', \ A' = u_{11}, \ L' = u_{12}, \ L1' = u_{13}, \ L2' = u_{14}\},$$

where u_{02} is a variable, $A', L', L1', L2', R'$ are renamed variables not appearing in the other terms, and no specific assumption is made about the remaining terms. Clearly, the renamed variable $R1'$ does not appear in these equations. If there exists an mgu σ of the set of equations then $R1'\sigma = R1'$, hence the verification condition $var(R1'\sigma)$ holds. The verification condition for the second recursive call can be proved in a similar way.

□

The method for proving resolution invariants given by Theorem 6.4 refers to the unification semantics. A proof of an invariant uses a specification describing properties of unification semantics. This specification has to be proved separately, using proof methods for unification semantics. An approach where both kinds of proofs are combined in one proof method has been proposed by Drabent and Maluszynski [DM87, DM88].

It can be stated as follows.

Theorem 6.5

Let P be a Horn program, $Pred$ be the set of all predicates of P, and let $A : \{\langle Pre_p, Post_p \rangle\}_{p \in Pred}$ be an answer specification of P and C_A the associated resolution invariant.

C is valid for P and C_A is valid for P and the standard computation rule if and only if for every clause c of P the following verification conditions hold:

Let

- $\bar{u}_0$ be a vector of terms satisfying Pre_{p_0},

- $c' : p_0(\bar{t}_0) \leftarrow p_1(\bar{t}_1), \ldots, p_n(\bar{t}_n)$ be a variant of c sharing no variables with $\bar{u}_0$,

- $\bar{u}_0$ and $\bar{t}_0$ be unifiable with an mgu ρ_0,

- ρ_k for $k = 1, \ldots, n$ be a substitution such that:
  the domain of ρ_k is a subset of the variables in the vector of terms $\bar{t}_k \rho_0 \ldots \rho_{k-1}$, and
  every variable in the range of ρ_k either appears in $\bar{t}_k \rho_0 \ldots \rho_{k-1}$, or is a new variable (i.e. it does not appear in $c', \bar{u}_0, \rho_0, \ldots, \rho_{k-1}$).

1. For every $i = 0, \ldots, n-1$, the conjunction of $Post_{p_j}[\bar{t}_j \rho_0 \ldots \rho_{j-1}, \rho_j]$ for $j = 1, \ldots, i$ implies $Pre_{p_{i+1}}[\bar{t}_{i+1} \rho_0 \ldots \rho_i]$.

2. The conjunction of $Post_{p_k}[\bar{t}_k \rho_0 \ldots \rho_{k-1}, \rho_k]$ for $k = 1, \ldots, n$ implies $Post_{p_0}[\bar{u}_0, \rho_0 \rho_1 \ldots \rho_n]$.

□

Proof. The theorem can be seen as a particular case of the annotation method of Section 4.5. Assume that the verification conditions are satisfied. The answer specification can be considered an annotation of the attribute grammar A_{SLD} (Section 5.3.3) using two families of assertions I (inherited) and S (synthesized) defined as follows:

$I(Arg)$: $Pre(Arg)$ because the precondition concerns argument values before calling.

$S(Arg, \delta)$: $Post(Arg, \delta)$ because the postconditon defines the relation between arguments before and after calling (hence applying the current answer substitution δ to Arg).

The dependencies are defined according to the conditions of Theorem 6.5 .

The validity of the answer specification and of the resolution invariant will follow from the validity of the annotation. We show now that the annotation is sound for a non-circular LDS, hence valid.

The LDS defined above is an L-LDS, hence it is non-circular. It remains to show that the verification conditions imply the soundness.

This can be concluded by the following observations:

- Proposition 5.7 p. 249 shows that every substitution $\delta(k)$ can be replaced by a composition of substitutions γ_j, and

- in every rule, the restriction of the substitutions $\gamma_j, j \geq 0$ to the variables of the clause and to the variables of $Arg(0)$ form a family of substitutions ρ_j.

The only if part follows by the completeness of the annotation method. If A and C_A are valid, then also the annotation constructed above is valid. In the annotation method one allows for weakening of the inherited assertions and for strengthening of the synthesized assertions. This would correspond to allowing for weakening of the preconditions and for strengthening of the postconditions of the answer specifications of Theorem 6.5 . The annotation used to show the completeness (see the of Theorem 4.3 p. 187) uses the same form of condition except that the post condition is stronger. Hence the existence of the substitutions $\delta(k)$, $k \geq 0$ (hence the substitutions γ_k), guarantees the existence of the substitutions ρ_k.
□

We now illustrate the method of Theorem 6.5 by an example.

Example 6.10

We consider again the quicksort program of Example 6.9 p. 303. We want to prove that the first argument of the selected atom of the actual goal at every step of the standard SLD-resolution is a list whose elements are non-variable terms (but they need not be ground terms). In our specification language we will denote this property by the predicate *nvelems*. In addition we want to prove that the second argument of every call is a variable. This can be expressed by the following precondition:

Pre_{qsort}: $nvelems({\bullet}qsort_1) \wedge var({\bullet}qsort_2)$

Furthermore, we want to prove that the variables of the sorted list (i.e. of the second argument of *qsort* upon a success of the computation) are those of the unsorted list (i.e. of the first argument of the call):

$Post_{qsort}$: ${\bullet}qsort_1 = qsort_1{\bullet} \wedge samevar({\bullet}qsort_1, qsort_2{\bullet}) \wedge$
$nvelems(qsort_1{\bullet})$

This is difficult to prove because one has to take into account the way the unification is performed.

As the predicates *gt* and *le* are not defined in the program some assumptions are made about their semantics. It is assumed that some ordering is defined on all terms, including variables, where the ordering on variables may be arbitrary. The predicates do not modify their arguments and just fail or succeed depending on the result of the comparison. Hence they satisfy the following answer specification (which is sufficient for our problem):

Pre_{gt}: *true*
$Post_{gt}$: ${\bullet}gt_1 = gt_1{\bullet} \wedge {\bullet}gt_2 = gt_2{\bullet}$

Pre_{le}: *true*
$Post_{le}$: ${\bullet}le_1 = le_1{\bullet} \wedge {\bullet}le_2 = le_2{\bullet}$

The remaining part of the quicksort answer specification is defined as follows:

$Pre_{partition}$:
$nonvar({\bullet}partition_1) \wedge nvelems({\bullet}partition_2) \wedge$
$$var({\bullet}partition_3) \wedge var({\bullet}partition_4)$$
$Post_{partition}$:

$samevar(\bullet partition_2, partition_3 \bullet \circ^8 partition_4 \bullet) \wedge$
$$nvelems(partition_3 \bullet) \wedge nvelems(partition_4 \bullet) \wedge$$
$$\bullet partition_1 = partition_1 \bullet \wedge \bullet partition_2 = partition_2 \bullet$$

Pre_{append}:
$nvelems(\bullet append_1) \wedge nvelems(\bullet append_2) \wedge var(\bullet append_3)$
$Post_{append}$:
$samevar(\bullet append_1 \circ \bullet append_2, append_3 \bullet) \wedge nvelems(append_3 \bullet)$

The proof consists in checking of the verification conditions for each of the clauses. For the clause c_1 there is only one verification condition. The easy proof is omitted. For the clause c_2 there are five verification conditions. The most interesting is the last one. It has the form of implication with five hypotheses (i1) - (i5). We now state it explicitly. A variable X in the condition originating from the clause is to be renamed; this is indicated by denoting it as X'.

(i1) $nvelems(s1) \wedge var(s2) \wedge \rho_0 = mgu(\{s1 = A'.L', s2 = R'\}) \wedge$
(i2) $samevar(L'\rho_0, L1'\rho_0\rho_1 \circ L2'\rho_0\rho_1) \wedge$
$$nvelems(L1'\rho_0\rho_1) \wedge nvelems(L2'\rho_0\rho_1) \wedge$$
$$A'\rho_0 = A'\rho_0\rho_1 \wedge L'\rho_0 = L'\rho_0\rho_1 \wedge$$
(i3) $samevar(L1'\rho_0\rho_1, R1'\rho_0\rho_1\rho_2) \wedge nvelems(R1'\rho_0\rho_1\rho_2) \wedge$
$$L1'\rho_0\rho_1 = L1'\rho_0\rho_1\rho_2 \wedge$$
(i4) $samevar(L2'\rho_0\rho_1\rho_2, R2'\rho_0\rho_1\rho_2\rho_3) \wedge nvelems(R2'\rho_0\rho_1\rho_2\rho_3) \wedge$
$$L1'\rho_0\rho_1\rho_2 = L1'\rho_0\rho_1\rho_2\rho_3 \wedge$$
(i5) $samevar(R1'\rho_0\rho_1\rho_2\rho_3 \circ A'.R2'\rho_0\rho_1\rho_2\rho_3, R'\rho_0\rho_1\rho_2\rho_3\rho_4) \wedge$
$$nvelems(R'\rho_0\rho_1\rho_2\rho_3\rho_4) \wedge$$

$\rightarrow$

$s1 = s1\rho_0\rho_1\rho_2\rho_3\rho_4 \wedge samevar(s1, s2\rho_0\rho_1\rho_2\rho_3\rho_4) \wedge$
$$nvelems(s2\rho_0\rho_1\rho_2\rho_3\rho_4).$$

For checking the verification condition a careful analysis of the computation of the first unifier ρ_0 is needed. Following (i1):

- it has the local variables A', L' and R' or variable $s2$ in its domain, and
- it binds A' to a compound term, and L' to a list of compound terms,

---

[8] $\circ$ denotes concatenation and is used in the assertion language only to simplify the notations for *samevar*.

- it does not affect the other variables of the clause.

By (i2) the set of the variables in $L1'\rho_0\rho_1$ and $L2'\rho_0\rho_1$ is the same as the set of variables in $L'\rho_0$ (tail of $s1$). Moreover $s1$ is identical to $s1\rho_0\rho_1$: ρ_0 does not affect $s1$ since $s1$ is a list with no variable elements. $L'\rho_0$ is the tail of $s1$. It is thus a list of compound terms and cannot be affected by ρ_1.

By (i3) ρ_2 does not affect $L2'\rho_0\rho_1$: any variable of $L2'\rho_0\rho_1$ that might be shared with $L1'\rho_0\rho_1$ remains unchanged by ρ_2.

By (i4), using a similar reasoning one can prove that, ρ_4 does not affect $R1'\rho_0\rho_1\rho_2\rho_3$, the first argument of *append*.

Thus by (i3) (i4) and (i5) one can conclude that $R'\rho_0\rho_1\rho_2\rho_3\rho_4$ has the same variables as $s1$, hence as $s2\rho_0\rho_1\rho_2\rho_3\rho_4$, since ρ_0 is the unifier of the variables R' and $s2$.

The fact that the variables of the initial call are preserved in the answer seems to be the most difficult aspect of the proof of the specification. The proof relies on the resolution invariant stating that the elements of the list to be sorted are non-variable terms.

For c_4 there are three verification conditions. The most interesting is the last one:

(i1) $nonvar(p1) \wedge nvelems(p2) \wedge var(p3) \wedge var(p4)\wedge$
$\quad \rho_0 = mgu(\{p1 = A1', p2 = A2'.L', p3 = A2'.L1', p4 = L2'\})\wedge$

(i2) $A1'\rho_0 = A1'\rho_0\rho_1 \wedge A2'\rho_0 = A2'\rho_0\rho_1$

(i3) $samevar(L'\rho_0\rho_1, L1'\rho_0\rho_1\rho_2 \circ L2'\rho_0\rho_1\rho_2)\wedge$
$\qquad\qquad nvelems(L1'\rho_0\rho_1\rho_2) \wedge nvelems(L2'\rho_0\rho_1\rho_2)\wedge$
$\qquad\qquad A1'\rho_0\rho_1 = A1'\rho_0\rho_1\rho_2 \wedge L'\rho_0\rho_1 = L'\rho_0\rho_1\rho_2$

$\rightarrow$

$samevar(p2, p3\rho_0\rho_1\rho_2 \circ p4\rho_0\rho_1\rho_2)\wedge$
$\qquad\qquad nvelems(p3\rho_0\rho_1\rho_2) \wedge nvelems(p4\rho_0\rho_1\rho_2)\wedge$
$\qquad\qquad p1 = p1\rho_0\rho_1\rho_2 \wedge p2 = p2\rho_0\rho_1\rho_2$

The proof is similar to the previous one. The main point is that by (i2) ρ_1 is the identity substitution: $A1'\rho_0$ is identical with $p1$, $A2'\rho_0$ is identical with the first element of $p2$ and the domain of ρ_1 may only

include the variables of $p1$ and $p2$. Since application of ρ_1 changes neither $p1$ nor $p2$, ρ_1 must be the identity substitution.
□

6.4.4   Proving universal termination

By *universal termination* of a definite program with a given goal and with a given computation rule we mean finiteness of the SLD-tree. Universal termination is practically important, e.g. in the context of using negation as failure: the positive answer to a query[9] of the form $not(q)$ is obtained in Prolog by checking that the SLD-tree for q is finite and has no success branches. It might be then desirable to know that the program universally terminates for all goals q such that $not(q)$ may be called.

In this section we discuss the universal termination problem for the standard computation rule. We first show that answer specifications can be used for proving universal termination. A valid resolution invariant describes the form of the actual calls. Together with the clauses of the program it provides an information about the form of the subsequent recursive calls for a given initial call. Termination can be proved if a given call and the subsequent recursive calls can be mapped into decreasing elements of a well-founded domain. Thus, to prove termination it suffices to find a family of ordering functions in the sense of Section 4.6.1 such that the functions are defined for every actual call and are decreasing on the subsequent recursive calls.

The question arises how to prove universal termination not for a single goal but for a class of initial goals. We focus our attention on the case of atomic goal. If it satisfies the precondition of the answer specification of the program, the technique outlined above is directly applicable. If the specification language is expressive enough, the answer specification of a program may exactly characterize the set of all actual goals and their form at the success for a class of the initial goals. In this case universal termination for every initial goal in the class implies existence of the ordering function with the required properties. This can be shown as follows. Every call satisfying the precondition of such an answer specification gives rise to a finite number of finite derivation trees; the ordering function can thus be defined as the maximal height of such a

---

[9] *query* is used here instead of "goal atom" because there is a negation.

tree. The method is formalized by the following proposition.

Proposition 6.1

Let P be a definite program, let $Pred$ be the set of all predicates of P and let g be an atomic goal satisfying a specification C. P universally terminates for g and the standard computation rule if and only if there exists a valid answer specification $\{\langle Pre_p, Post_p \rangle\}_{p \in Pred}$ for P with a valid associated resolution invariant for P and the standard computation rule, and a family f of ordering functions indexed by the predicates of P such that:

- Every atom with predicate p satisfying C_p also satisfies the precondition Pre_p and the function f_p is defined for the tuple of terms in atoms satisfying Pre_p.

- The following condition is satisfied for every non-unit program clause c:

  Let

  - $p_0(\bar{u}_0)$ be an atom satisfying Pre_{p_0},
  - $p_0(\bar{t}_0) \leftarrow p_1(\bar{t}_1), \ldots, p_n(\bar{t}_n)$ be a variant of c, sharing no variable with $\bar{u}_0$,
  - ρ_0 be an mgu of $\bar{t}_0$ and $\bar{u}_0$,
  - ρ_k for $k = 1, \ldots, n$ be a substitution such that:
    the domain of ρ_k is a subset of the variables in the terms $\bar{t}_k \rho_0 \ldots \rho_{k-1}$, and
    every variable in the range of ρ_k either appears in $\bar{t}_k \rho_0 \ldots \rho_{k-1}$, or is a new variable (i.e. it does not appear in $c', \bar{u}_0, \rho_0, \ldots, \rho_{k-1}$).

  Then the conjunction of all $Post_{p_j}(\bar{t}_j \rho_0 \ldots \rho_{j-1}, \rho_j)$, $j < k$, implies $f_{p_0}(\bar{u}_0) \succ f_{p_k}(\bar{t}_k \rho_0 \ldots \rho_{k-1})$ for every k such that p_0 and p_k are mutually recursive.

□

The soundness of the method can be proved using the same annotation as in the proof of Theorem 6.5 p. 6.5 . Its proof shows also that the depth-first left to right strategy of construction of the valid decorated trees of $A_{SLD}(P)$ guarantees termination. Thus, there is no infinite SLD-derivation starting from an initial goal in the class specified by C. The relative completeness was discussed above.

It may be worth noticing that the concept of ordering functions is applied both in proofs of existential completeness and in proofs of universal termination. In the first case one attempts to prove existence of an SLD-refutation such that the computed answer satisfies the specification. The ordering functions are used to show termination for some choice of the clauses used in the resolution. However, even for a goal having such a refutation there may exist an infinite derivation using other clauses. In universal termination proofs the ordering functions are used to prove termination for any choice of the clauses used in the resolution. In other words, in the completeness proofs one wants to show that every SLD-tree whose root satisfies some condition has at least one success branch. This is clearly different from proving that the SLD-tree is finite, i.e. that following the standard computation rule no infinite SLD-derivation can be produced.

The presented method for proving universal termination is very general but rather difficult. The reason is that it requires an answer specification, i.e. a description of the run-time behaviour of the program. The proof requires thus analysis of the substitutions that may be obtained during the computation. This is generally a very difficult task. We now present another approach to proving universal termination. It is based on the notion of proof tree and on the concept of annotation. The annotations discussed already in the context of attribute grammars can also be used for specifying and proving declarative properties of definite programs.

Our approach to universal termination assumes that a valid annotation of the program is given such that its dependency scheme is an L-LDS. Informally, this means that the dependency relation on the instances of assertions in every proof tree goes from left to right. Consequently, the left context of any node of the proof tree decides whether the inherited assertions of the node are satisfied in the tree or not. In other words the right context of the node is irrelevant for the truth value of its inherited assertions. Hence the truth value can be computed from a partial skeleton, not including the right context. We now want to use the annotation for proving universal termination of the program. The idea is, as usual, to use ordering functions. Consider an instance of a clause such that the head satisfies the inherited assertions of its predicate, k

first body atoms satisfy their synthesized assertions and the $k+1$ body atom satisfies the inherited assertion. To prove termination we want to find ordering functions which in all such cases are defined for the head and for the $k+1$ body atom with decreasing values. This, however, may not be sufficient for universal termination. The situation described corresponds to construction of a partial proof tree with the head labeled by the clause and such that the first k subtrees are complete proof trees. The extension of such a partial tree often results in further instantiation of the arguments of the atoms. Consequently, the ordering functions applied to the changed atoms may give new values. Thus, for proving universal termination we additionally require that the ordering functions do not change their values under instantiation of the atoms satisfying the inherited assertions. Now, if we find a valid L-annotation for a given program and ordering functions satisfying this requirement we can see that any proper partial skeleton has only a finite number of proper extensions constructed by the left-to-right strategy. This concerns in particular the initial skeleton, corresponding to the initial goal. As the branches of the SLD-tree represent extensions of this skeleton, the SLD-tree must be finite, i.e. the program universally terminates.

These ideas can be summarized by the following proposition stating the proposed proof method.

Proposition 6.2

Let P be a definite program, let $Pred$ be the set of all predicates of P and let g be a goal satisfying a specification C. Program P universally terminates for g and the standard computation rule if and only if there exists an L-annotation with one inherited and one synthesized assertion only, $\{Inh_p, Syn_p\}_{p\in Pred}$ [10], valid for P with respect to the declarative semantics (see Section 7.3), and a family f of ordering functions indexed by the predicates of P such that

- Every atom satisfying C_p also satisfies the assertion Inh_p.
- For every atom $p(\bar{t})$ satisfying the assertion Inh_p the domain of f_p includes all instances of $\bar{t}$ and $f_p(\bar{t}\sigma) = f_p(\bar{t})$ for every substitution σ.
- For every instance of a program clause
  $p_0(\bar{t_0}) \leftarrow p_1(\bar{t_1})\ldots p_k(\bar{t_k})\ldots p_n(\bar{t_n})$, for all k, $1 \le k \le n$, such that p_0

----

[10]i.e. $\Delta_I(p) = \{Inh_p\}$ and $\Delta_S(p) = \{Syn_p\}$.

and p_k are mutually recursive, if

- $\bar{t}_0$ satisfies the inherited assertion of p_0, and
- $\bar{t}_i$ satisfies the synthesized assertion of p_i for $i = 1, \ldots, k-1$, and
- $\bar{t}_k$ satisfies the inherited assertion of p_k,

then

$f_{p_0}(\bar{t}_0) \succ f_{p_k}(\bar{t}_k).$

All variables in the assertions are universally quantified.
□

The method defined by the proposition seems to be simpler than the previous one. It shows that the run-time property of universal termination can be proved by using only some auxiliary declarative properties. As usual, finding appropriate ordering functions may be the most difficult aspect of the proof. The relative completeness of the method can be shown as follows. Let P be a program universally terminating with any goal g satisfying a specification C. Hence, for every goal g there exists only a finite number of proper skeletons constructed with the top-down left-to-right strategy. The ordering functions can now be defined on the domain D of all atoms obtained by solving the equations associated with these skeletons. Every atom $p(\bar{t})$ in D is thus the head of some decorated skeleton. The number of such skeletons is finite. Hence the value of $f_p(\bar{t})$ can be defined as the maximum of their heights. Such a definition satisfies the conditions on the ordering functions imposed by the proposition.

Example 6.11

We prove the universal termination of the program *qsort* (Example 6.9 p. 303) with the class of goals of the form:

C_{qsort}: $list(qsort_1)$

Notice that there is no restriction on the elements of the list which is the first argument nor on the second argument. For proving universal termination of the program with the goals of this form we use the following L-annotation:

Inh_{qsort}: $\{list(qsort_1)\}$
Syn_{qsort}: $\{list(qsort_2)\}$

$Inh_{partition}$: $\{list(partition_2)\}$
$Syn_{partition}$: $\{list(partition_3) \land list(partition_4) \land$
   $length(partition_3) \leq length(partition_2) \land$
   $length(partition_4) \leq length(partition_2)\}$

Inh_{append}: $\{list(append_1) \land list(append_2)\}$
Syn_{append}: $\{list(append_3)\}$

It can be proved by the techniques of the next chapter that the annotation is valid; the proof is rather simple and we omit it.

For proving the universal termination we also define the following ordering functions:

$f_{qsort}(qsort_1, qsort_2) = length(qsort_1)$
$f_{partition}(partition_1, partition_2, partition_3, partition_4) =$
   $length(partition_2)$
$f_{append}(append_1, append_2, append_3) = length(append_1)$

We now check the verification conditions of the method:

- Inh_{qsort} includes only one inherited assertion which is identical with C_{qsort}, so that the first condition holds trivially.

- Each of the ordering functions when applied to its arguments results in the application of the function $length$ to a list argument x. Hence the second verification condition holds, as $f(x\sigma) = f(x)$ for every substitution σ.

- The last verification condition is to be checked separately for each clause of the program. The proofs are very simple. For example, in the case of the clause c_2 the check reduces to proving the following implications (the useless hypotheses are removed):

$(list(A.L) \land length(L1) \leq length(L)) \rightarrow (length(L1) < length(A.L))$
$(list(A.L) \land length(L2) \leq length(L)) \rightarrow (length(L2) < length(A.L))$.

$\square$

6.4.5 Proving finite failure

A program specification S such that S_p: *false* says that the success set of the program includes no atoms with the predicate p. If it is valid, the program cannot succeed; it must fail or loop. Using the proof methods of this chapter one can prove that the program is correct with respect to such a specification. Additionally one can prove the universal termination of the program for a class of goals. In this case the program finitely fails for every goal of this class.

6.5 Discussion and bibliographical comments

The chapter presents several proof methods for partial correctness, completeness and existential completeness aimed at proving different properties depending on the kind of semantics of definite programs which is considered (model-theoretic, unification or operational semantics). Results concerning properties related to the model-theoretic semantics are discussed in Chapter 7. All these methods are derived from the similar methods for attribute grammars, which are discussed in Chapter 4. Some parts of the proofs may sometimes be simplified. In the case of arguments which are terms built with any combination of given functors, proof of completeness may also be simplified using the kind of method studied in ([HH80, Bid82]).

The notion of dependency relation which originates from attribute grammars turns out to be a very useful concept also in proving properties of definite programs. It should be noticed that some of the methods discussed in this section (or their variants) have been introduced in the literature as specific for the field of logic programming. The objective of our presentation has been to show them in a broader perspective.

We considered properties of the model-theoretic semantics of programs, properties of the unification semantics and run-time properties. We noticed that proofs with respect to the unification semantics and proofs of run-time properties are significantly more difficult than proofs with respect to the model-theoretic semantics. This is due to the complexity of the operations performed by the unification.

The run-time properties of logic programs have been studied by sev-

eral authors. The papers [DM87] and [CM91], among others, consider
Hoare's proof method for partial correctness [Hoa69] as a source of inspiration for their work.

The generally accepted notion of partial correctness for algorithmic
programs is defined by the following condition. Whenever a program
is invoked by a call satisfying the precondition and the computation
terminates, the computed result satisfies the postcondition. In the case
of definite programs this kind of termination corresponds to construction
of one proof tree, but not to the universal termination.

The Hoare-like proof methods use a kind of computational induction.
This means that they are based on a kind of operational semantics,
also in the case of logic programs. The papers mentioned above refer
to the operational semantics based on SLD-resolution with the Prolog
computation rule. As SLD-resolution can be modelled by an L-attribute
grammar, the methods can be linked to the annotation proof method
for attribute grammars, as discussed in this chapter.

The problem of universal termination has also been studied by several
authors, see in particular [VP86], [ABK89], [AB90], [AP90], [Plü91].
Also in this case SLD-resolution with the Prolog computation rule is the
basis of analysis and the concepts originating from attribute grammars
can be useful, see e.g. [Plü89] and the discussion in Section 6.4.4.

Partial correctness and universal termination are well known examples of run-time properties. There are many other properties which are
less explored and might be of practical interest, e.g. non-floundering
([Llo87]), [Apt90]), uniqueness of solutions [Dev90b], absence of Prolog
system errors [DF88], determinism, operational completeness of logic
programs with external procedures [Boy91] and many others. The proof
methods for run-time properties discussed in this chapter give a conceptual basis for studying them.

As already pointed out, proof methods for run-time properties of
logic programs resemble proof methods for algorithmic languages, like
Floyd's inductive assertion method [Flo67] or Hoare's axiomatic approach [Hoa69]. As unification seems to be a more sophisticated operation than the assignment used in the imperative languages, the proofs of
run-time properties of logic programs may even be more complex than
proofs of algorithmic programs. The existence of model-theoretic semantics and its equivalence to the proof-theoretic semantics have been
considered as an advantage of logic programming. The observation that

the proof methods with respect to the declarative semantics are simpler than the other ones gives another argument in support of declarative style of programming.

7 Proof Methods for Partial Correctness of Definite Programs

Several approaches to proving partial correctness of definite programs have been proposed in the literature. Following the general idea of this book this chapter gives a unified view of the methods based on the notion of proof tree. Thus, correctness of programs is being related to properties of proof trees. As shown in Section 6.2.1 such methods can be derived from the methods of validation of attribute grammars presented in Chapter 4. The objective of this chapter is to discuss partial correctness of definite programs with respect to the declarative semantics with as little reference to attribute grammars as possible. This allows for independent reading of the material even if the methods presented have been obtained by combining results presented in Chapters 4, 5 and 6.

This chapter discusses preinterpreted definite programs. Thus the methods presented apply in particular to the usual case of definite programs with term interpretations, as well as to the special cases of logic programs with functions or constraints.

7.1 Introduction

As discussed in Chapter 2, different kinds of semantics of definite programs are equivalent in some well-defined sense. We now focus our attention on the proof-theoretic semantics which associates with a given program P the set of the heads of all its J-based proof trees, where J is the preinterpretation considered. In this chapter this set will be called the *actual* semantics of the program. Note that in the case of term interpretation the actual semantics coincides with the denotation of the program, i.e. it is the set of all atomic logical consequences of the program in the considered term base.

The problem to be described by a logic program can be thought of as a collection of relations on the domains of J. These relations are called the *intended* semantics. We assume that the intended semantics can be formalized as a set of J-atoms. The intention of the programmer is to write a program whose actual semantics coincides with the intended semantics. To fulfill this requirement the program must be partially correct and complete with respect to the intended semantics.

The proof methods presented in this chapter concern partial correctness of programs with respect to the intended semantics only. To compare the actual semantics with the intended one, it is necessary to specify the latter. A program is *partially correct* if its actual semantics is a subset of the intended semantics understood as a set of J-atoms. A specification is a formula in some logic language with an interpretation, and which defines this set. Generally it may be difficult to describe exactly the relations to be computed by the program. Instead the formula may describe their supersets, or in other words, some weaker properties of the program.

For example, consider the definite program:

$$plus(zero, X, X) \leftarrow$$
$$plus(s(X), Y, s(Z)) \leftarrow plus(X, Y, Z)$$

For the term preinterpretation of the program on some term domain H one may be interested whether the following properties hold:

1. All elements of the denotation have the form $plus(s^n(zero), t, s^n(t))$ where $n \geq 0$ and t is an arbitrary term.

2. For every atom in the denotation the first argument is of the form $s^n(zero)$.

3. For every atom in the denotation the second argument is ground iff the third argument is ground.

4. If x and y are of the form $s^n(zero)$ and an atom of the form $plus(x, y, z)$ is in the denotation then also the atom $plus(y, x, z)$ is in the denotation (this is commutativity of addition on integers represented by terms).

Our objective is to formulate methods for proving such properties. In particular, for the example above we will use induction on the structure of proof trees. As the example properties hold for the denotation they hold also for the actual semantics using any preinterpretation, e.g. the domain of natural numbers with *zero* interpreted as 0 and *s* interpreted as the successor function.

The structural induction mentioned above is a method for proving properties of the actual semantics, i.e. of the heads of the proof trees.

Let us consider now another kind of properties: properties holding inside the proof tree with some particular head. For example with the program above the following properties hold:

1. If the head of a proof tree has its second or third argument ground then the proof tree is ground.

2. If in the head of a proof tree the second or third argument has the form $s^n(zero)$ then all the arguments of all leaf atoms or of all heads of subtrees have the same form.

The motivation for studying such properties comes from the observation that logic programs are often used in some restricted way. For example, it may be expected that the quicksort program is used for sorting lists. In that case the first argument of every proof tree constructed is a list. This assumption restricts the class of proof trees considered and raises the question about the properties of the nodes of the proof trees in the restricted class.

For proving properties of the labels of arbitrary nodes of some specific proof trees another proof method, called the *annotation method* will be introduced.

The annotation method allows also for proving properties of the heads of proof trees, hence properties of the actual semantics. In contrast to the structural induction method the annotation method allows for proving properties holding inside suset of proof trees. Furthermore it facilitates modular proofs: instead of dealing with one complex assertion a number of simpler assertions is used related by a dependency scheme. Figure 7.1 shows such a scheme for a simple example.

Both methods are syntax directed but, although the first one can be viewed as a particular case of the second, it is studied separately. The reason is that the structural induction method can be presented without introducing additional concepts used in the annotation method. The structural induction is also better known and more often discussed in the literature. Its use is however restricted to proving properties of the actual semantics while the annotation method allows for proving properties of the proof trees.

The methods to be presented allow for proving of *partial correctness* of definite programs with respect to *specifications*. In Chapter 4 similar concepts have been discussed in the context of attribute grammars. We now discuss them in the context of definite programs.

Let P be a definite program. For an n-ary predicate p of P denote by Var_p the set of variables $\{p_1, \ldots, p_n\}$. A logic language $\mathcal{L}$ over the alphabet including the function symbols of P, the variables of Var_p for all predicates of P will be called a *specification language* for P. Unless explicitly stated we will also assume that a specification language does not include the predicates of P. We will use $\mathcal{L}$ with some J-based interpretation $\mathcal{I}$ to specify intended semantics of P. More precisely, what is to be specified is an interpretation of the predicates of P on the domains of $\mathcal{I}$. This will be called the interpretation of P defined by the specification. Consider a formula S_p of $\mathcal{L}$ whose only free variables are in Var_p. The interpretation $\mathcal{I}$ defines also a preinterpretation of P, which will be denoted by $J_{\mathcal{I}}$, or simply J. The intended semantics of P can be defined as the set of all J-atoms $p(v_1, \ldots, v_n)$ such that S_p is valid in $\mathcal{I}$ under the valuation that assigns p_i to the value v_i for $i = 1, .., n$ and for all predicates p of the program. We call this set the semantics of P *specified* by the family of formulae $\{S_p | p$ is a predicate of $P\}$ (or shortly $\{S_p\}_{p \in Pred}$) and by the J-based interpretation $\mathcal{I}$. Sometimes several instances of the same formula will be used together, for example in clauses in which the same predicate occurs more than once. In this case the instances differ only by a renaming of the free variables. The instance of a variable of Var_p, say p_i, occurring in a formula associated to the occurrence k of the predicate p^1 is denoted $p_i(k)$ and belongs to $Var_p(k)$.

Definition 7.1 Specification

A *specification* of a definite program P, whose set of predicate symbols is $Pred$, is a pair $\langle S, \mathcal{I} \rangle$ where S is a family of formulae $\{S_p\}_{p \in Pred}$ in a specification language $\mathcal{L}$, such that every free variables of S_p is in Var_p and $\mathcal{I}$ is an interpretation of $\mathcal{L}$. The intended semantics of P specified by S and $\mathcal{I}$ will be denoted $Spec(P, S, \mathcal{I})$.
□

A specification describes a required property of the program, more precisely of its actual semantics. Intuitively, a program is partially correct with respect to a given specification iff every element of its actual semantics, i.e. every atom which is the head of an I-based proof tree has this property. This is formalized by the following definition.

---

[1] The occurrence of the predicate is also usually denoted p_k.

Definition 7.2 Partial correctness

A definite program P is *partially correct* with respect to a specification $\langle S, \mathcal{I} \rangle$ iff the proof-theoretic semantics of P with respect to $\mathcal{I}$ is a subset of $Spec(P, S, \mathcal{I})$, i.e. $PT_J(P) \subseteq Spec(P, S, \mathcal{I})$.
$\square$

Note that the semantics specified may include atoms which are not present in the actual semantics of the partially correct program. In particular the program whose actual semantics with respect to $\mathcal{I}$ is empty is partially correct with respect to any specification $\langle S, \mathcal{I} \rangle$. Thus partial correctness does not say anything about the existence of solutions (completeness), termination of the computations or form of the selected goals during computations. Some methods for proving such properties are discussed in Chapter 6. From partial correctness one can only conclude that any computed atom (which belongs necessarily to the actual semantics) satisfies the specification.

We now give an introduction to the induction method already mentioned in Section 6.2.1. The method aims at proving properties of the heads of proof trees. The proof trees are constructed by combination of the program clauses as described in Chapter 2. The program clauses can be seen as operations on proof trees during the bottom-up construction. Assume that the arguments of such an operation are trees with the heads satisfying the specification. The question is whether the head of the tree resulting by the operation will also satisfy the specification. This question applies also to unit clauses which can be seen as nullary operations. The idea of the proof method is thus to show for every clause of the program that the answer for this question is positive. This is a structural induction on the proof trees, where the base case concerns the unit clauses and the induction assumption is used for non-unit clauses. Let P be a definite program and let $\langle S, \mathcal{I} \rangle$ be its specification. Following the idea stated above we have to examine every clause of P. Let $p_0(t_{01}, \ldots, t_{0n_0}) \leftarrow p_1(t_{11}, \ldots, t_{1n_1}), \ldots, p_k(t_{k1}, \ldots, t_{kn_k})$, where $k \geq 0$, be a clause of P. Let θ be the substitution with the domain $Var_{p_0}(0) \cup Var_{p_1}(1) \cup \ldots Var_{p_k}(k)$ [2] and such that $\theta(p_i(j)) = t_{ji}$ for $i =$

---

[2] corresponding to the union of the instances of the free variables occurring in the formulae associated to the occurrences of the predicates $p_0, \ldots, p_k$.

$0, \ldots, k$ and $j = 1, \ldots, n_i$. The structural induction proof for the clause considered will require proving that the formula $(S_{p_0} \leftarrow S_{p_1} \wedge \ldots \wedge S_{p_k})\theta$ is valid in $\mathcal{I}$. If this holds for all clauses of the program, the specification will be called an *inductive* specification of P. If a specification of P is inductive then P is partially correct with respect to it.

Example 7.1

The notion of inductive specification will be illustrated by the following program

$$plus(zero, X, X) \leftarrow$$
$$plus(s(X), Y, s(Z)) \leftarrow plus(X, Y, Z)$$
$$l(nil, zero) \leftarrow$$
$$l(A.L, N) \leftarrow l(L, M), plus(s(zero), M, N)$$

with the specification $\langle S, \mathcal{I} \rangle$:

$S = \{S_{plus}, S_l\}$, where
   $S_{plus} : plus_3 = plus_1 + plus_2,$
   $S_l : length(l_1) = l_2.$

The interpretation $\mathcal{I}$ is many-sorted; the domains considered are lists and natural numbers with usual operations; $+$ is interpreted as addition, s as the successor, $zero$ as 0, and $length$ as the operation length on lists; $=$ is the polymorphic identity on the corresponding domain.

The specification is inductive, hence the program is correct w.r.t. it. To show this one has to check that the following formulae obtained by the construction described above are valid in $\mathcal{I}$:

$$X = zero + X$$
$$Z = X + Y \rightarrow s(Z) = s(X) + Y$$
$$length(nil) = zero$$
$$(length(L) = M \wedge N = s(zero) + M) \rightarrow length(A.L) = N$$
□

Now we informally present the annotation method and illustrate its use on an example. Let $\langle S, \mathcal{I} \rangle$ be a specification of a program P. We now assume that every formula S_p of S has the form of implication $A_1^p \wedge A_2^p \wedge \ldots \wedge A_m^p \rightarrow B_1^p \wedge B_2^p \wedge \ldots \wedge B_n^p$ where $m, n \geq 0$. The formulae $A_1^p \ldots A_m^p$ are called the inherited assertions of p while the formulae

$B_1^p \ldots B_n^p$ are called the synthesized assertions of p. An alternative way of defining specification is thus to associate with each predicate p a finite set of formulae with free variables in Var_p and to divide the formulae into *inherited* assertions and *synthesized* assertions. The classified assertions associated to the predicates will be called *annotation*. Now the assertions can be thought of as attributes of the predicates.

The annotation proof method can be summarized as follows. For each clause create the assertion instances by replacing variables in predicate assertions by corresponding argument terms of the occurrences of predicates. They can be divided into input assertions and output assertions, as defined in the case of attributes in Section 4.5. The input assertions are the inherited assertions of the head and the synthesized assertions of the body atoms. The remaining assertions are output assertions. The idea of correctness proof is now to show for each clause that its output assertions are implied by the input assertions. Usually an output assertion of a clause can be proved with a (possibly empty) subset of the input assertions. This can be described by a local dependency relation imposed on the assertions of a clause.

It is required that the corresponding dependency scheme is non-circular. A program P is partially correct with respect to the specification given in the form of annotation if

- For every clause every output assertion is implied by the input assertions on which it depends.

- The dependency scheme is non-circular.

Example 7.2

We use the annotation method to prove that the program of Example 7.1 is well-typed. We consider the following annotation:

- The inherited assertions are: *is-integer*($plus_2$).

- The synthesized assertions are: *is-integer*($plus_1$), *is-integer*($plus_3$), *is-list*(l_1), *is-integer*(l_2).

The (many-sorted) interpretation $\mathcal{I}$ has the domains $\mathcal{I}_{Int} = \{integers\}$ and $\mathcal{I}_{List} = \{lists\}$ and the functors of the program are interpreted as follows: $zero_\mathcal{I}$ as 0, $s_\mathcal{I}$ as the increment function, $=_\mathcal{I}$ as the identity

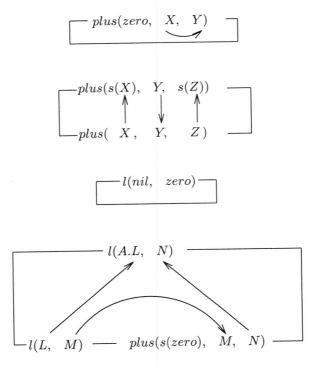

Figure 7.1
How the annotation describes type propagation

of integers, $nil_{\mathcal{I}}$ as the empty list and $._{\mathcal{I}}$ as the list constructor. Thus, the interpretation gives the signature of the function symbols. The formula is-$\alpha(v)$ is valid in the interpretation iff v is an object α. The local dependency relation in Figure 7.1 shows how the type information is propagated. This is the dependency relation which is used in the annotation proof.

The proof is performed by showing for each clause, each output assertion is implied in the interpretation by the input assertions on which it depends. For example, for the second clause of the program one has to prove validity of the following implications:

- is-$integer(X) \rightarrow is$-$integer(s(X))$
- is-$integer(Y) \rightarrow is$-$integer(Y)$
- is-$integer(Z) \rightarrow is$-$integer(s(Z))$

which follows immediately by the definition of the interpretation. The proofs for other clauses are also very easy.

The other component of the annotation proof is checking non–circularity of the dependency scheme used in the first part of the proof. This can be done automatically using the algorithms developed for attribute grammars. In our example the dependency scheme is non-circular hence the annotation is valid (see formal treatment in Example 7.11 p. 350).

Notice that the validity of the annotation implies the validity of the corresponding specification:

S_{plus}: is-$integer(plus_2) \rightarrow (is$-$integer(plus_1) \wedge is$-$integer(plus_3))$
S_l: is-$list(l_1) \wedge is$-$integer(l_2)$.

□

The rest of this chapter is organized as follows:

Section 7.2 discusses properties of the inductive proof method. The results of completeness, relative completeness (in the sense of Cook [Coo78]) and incompleteness are established. Relationships with fixpoint induction and structural induction on data are discussed.

Section 7.3 gives a formal presentation of the annotation method and discusses its properties.

Section 7.4 gives an example illustrating incremental construction of a proof by exploiting the modularity offered by the annotation method.

Finally a comparison with other results published in the literature is provided.

7.2 The inductive proof method

This section develops the inductive proof method outlined above. In particular soundness and completeness of the method will be discussed.

7.2.1 Soundness and completeness

For formal treatment of the inductive proof method we will use the notion of inductive specification defined in Section 6.2.1. We now recall this concept in a slightly modified notation: Let p be an n-ary predicate and let S_p be a formula with free variables in Var_p. For a vector of terms $\bar{t} = \langle t_1, \ldots, t_n \rangle$ we denote by $S_p[\bar{t}]$ the formula obtained from S_p by replacing each occurrence of p_i in S_p by t_i, for $i = 1, \ldots, n$.

Definition 7.3 Inductive specification
  A specification $\langle S, \mathcal{I} \rangle$ of a definite program P is *inductive* iff for every clause c: $p_0(\bar{t}_0) \leftarrow p_1(\bar{t}_1), \ldots, p_n(\bar{t}_n)$ of P the following holds:

$$\mathcal{I} \models S_{p_1}[\bar{t}_1] \wedge \ldots \wedge S_{p_n}[\bar{t}_n] \rightarrow S_{p_0}[\bar{t}_0].$$

□

  Thus, a specification is inductive iff in every clause, if the specification holds for the atoms of the body, it also holds for the head. Notice that the formula in the definition includes variables of the clause. These variables are universally quantified.
  For a given program it may be convenient to consider and to compare different specifications. In this case it is more natural to rephrase the problem of partial correctness of a program as the problem of *validity* of a specification with respect to a program.
  A specification $\langle S, \mathcal{I} \rangle$ is said to be *valid* with respect to a definite program P iff P is partially correct with respect to $\langle S, \mathcal{I} \rangle$.
  According to the Definition 7.2 p. 325, validity means that the set of heads of all J-based[3] proof trees of P is a subset of the set of J-based

---

[3] J stands for $J_{\mathcal{I}}$, the preinterpretation of P defined by $\mathcal{I}$.

atoms defined by the specification. In practice there is a more interesting definition of a valid specification which will be called *computational validity* to distinguish it from the previous one.

Definition 7.4

A specification $\langle S, \mathcal{I} \rangle$ is *computationally valid* with respect to P iff for every atom $p(\bar{t})$ in $DEN(P)$, $\mathcal{I} \models S_p[\bar{t}]$.

□

This definition refers to $TERM$-based proof trees. The heads of such proof trees preinterpreted in J are required to be among J-based atoms defined by the specification. Hence, by the results of Chapter 2 computationally valid specifications of a program are also valid. In fact $PT_J(P)$ (Definition 2.24 p. 79) is the set of all J-based proof trees, built with J-instances of clauses, hence all the J-instances of $TERM$-based proof tree roots are in $PT_J(P)$, but the converse does not hold necessarily.

Example 7.3 Fibonnacci

Consider the following definite program with non-term interpretation, defining Fibonnacci numbers. All function symbols used, including the constants, are interpreted on the domain of natural numbers in the usual way.

$$fib(0, 1) \leftarrow$$
$$fib(1, 1) \leftarrow$$
$$fib(N + 2, R1 + R2) \leftarrow fib(N + 1, R1), fib(N, R2)$$

The $TERM$-based denotation of this program contains only two atoms ($\{fib(0, 1), fib(1, 1)\}$). Hence this program is obviously correct w.r.t the intended meaning which is to define the (functional) relation "Fibonnacci". The (intended) specification is also obviously computationally valid. But $PT_J(P)$ where J is the preinterpretation on natural numbers contains many other atoms like $fib(2, 2), \ldots$. For this program the specification S_{fib}: $fib_2 = 1$ is clearly computationally valid, but not valid.

□

Both definitions of validity refer to the proof-theoretic semantics of the program and coincide in the case when $\mathcal{I}$ is a term interpretation.

The validity of the specification can be checked by using the notion of inductive specification.

Proposition 7.1
Every inductive specification of a definite program is valid.
□

Proof.

By induction on the size of the J-based proof trees. Let $PT_{J,N}(P)$ be the set of all J-based proof trees of size less than $N + 1$ and the size be the length of the longest path.

$PT_{J,N}(P) \subseteq Spec(P, S, \mathcal{I})$ by Definition 7.3 in the case $N = 0$.

Assume $PT_{J,n}(P) \subseteq Spec(P, S, \mathcal{I})$ for $n \leq N$, then $PT_{J,N+1}(P) \subseteq Spec(P, S, \mathcal{I})$ by the same definition.
□

Not all valid specifications are inductive.

Example 7.4 Fibonnacci (continued)
It is easy to check that the following specification is inductive, hence valid:

$fib_2 > 0$.

Note however, that the specification $fib_2 \geq fib_1$ is valid but not inductive since for $N = 0$ the verification condition for the third clause $R1 \geq (N + 1) \wedge R2 \geq N \rightarrow (R1 + R2) \geq N + 2$ is not satisfied.
□

Notice that if $\langle S, \mathcal{I} \rangle$ is a valid specification for P and S' is a family of formulae indexed by the predicates of P such that for every p the formula S'_p is a logical consequence of S_p then $\langle S', \mathcal{I} \rangle$ is also a valid specification of P. This gives an idea for comparing specifications which is formalized by the following definition.

Definition 7.5
Let $\langle S, \mathcal{I} \rangle$ and $\langle S', \mathcal{I} \rangle$ be specifications of a definite program P. S is said to be *weaker* than S' iff for every predicate p of P $\mathcal{I} \models (S'_p \rightarrow S_p)$. This will be denoted as follows: $\mathcal{I} \models S' \rightarrow S$. If S is weaker than S' then S' is said to be *stronger* than S.
□

For given specification language and its interpretation $\mathcal{I}$ the specification $\langle S, \mathcal{I} \rangle$ such that S_p is *true* for all $p \in Pred$ is the weakest specification of P. It is inductive in a trivial way. On the other hand, any specification $\langle S, \mathcal{I} \rangle$ such that $Spec(P, S, \mathcal{I})$ is exactly the set of all J-based proof tree roots is the strongest specification of P. Such a specification may or may not be expressible in the same language, depending on the expressiveness of the specification language. Assuming that there exists such a formula corresponding to the strongest specification, let us denote it $S_{P,\mathcal{I}}$. It is inductive, since the interpretation it defines corresponds to the set of the roots of the J-based proof trees. The following theorem gives a precise formulation of the inductive proof method and states its soundness and completeness.

Theorem 7.1 Soundness and completeness of the inductive proof method

A specification $\langle S, \mathcal{I} \rangle$ of P is valid iff it is weaker than some inductive specification $\langle S', \mathcal{I} \rangle$ of P.
□

Proof.

(Soundness). By the definition $Spec(P, S', \mathcal{I}) \subseteq Spec(P, S, \mathcal{I})$. Since the specification $\langle S', \mathcal{I} \rangle$ is inductive, by Proposition 7.1 it is valid, i.e. the actual semantics of P is a subset of $Spec(P, S', \mathcal{I})$. Thus, it is also a subset of $Spec(P, S, \mathcal{I})$, hence the specification $\langle S, \mathcal{I} \rangle$ is also valid.

(Completeness) If the specification $\langle S, \mathcal{I} \rangle$ is valid then it is weaker than the strongest specification of P, which by the assumption can be expressed in $\mathcal{L}$ and is inductive.
□

Thus, to prove that a program is correct with respect to a given specification it suffices to show that the specification is inductive, or that it is weaker than some other inductive specification. The method is complete if the specification language is expressive enough to describe the actual semantics of the program. In this case for every valid specification there exists a stronger specification which is inductive. Notice that it was not assumed that the specification language is a first order language. It will be shown in Section 7.2.3 that with this assumption the method may not be complete with a fixed language.

7.2.2   Examples of inductive proofs

We now illustrate the method by proofs of some properties of well-known
definite programs. The first example concerns groundness analysis. We
analyze toy examples, but the same approach would work also in the
case of large programs.

Example 7.5

For the program of Example 7.1 p. 326 we consider a specification
with a term interpretation $\mathcal{T}$. The specification language includes the
unary predicate *ground* with the obvious interpretation on terms. The
specification includes the following formulae:

$S_{plus} : ground(plus_1) \wedge (ground(plus_2) \rightarrow ground(plus_3))$
$S_l : ground(l_2)$

It is easy to check that this specification is inductive, hence valid.
□

The next example shows that a rich specification language makes a
specification relatively simple.

Example 7.6 Permutation

Consider the following well-known program:

$c_1 : p(nil, nil) \leftarrow$
$c_2 : p(A.L, B.M) \leftarrow p(N, M), ex(A.L, B, N)$
$c_3 : ex(A.L, A, L) \leftarrow$
$c_4 : ex(A.L, B, A.M) \leftarrow ex(L, B, M)$

This is the "permutation" program for lists and we want the specification language to be able to express this. For that we assume that
the language is many-sorted: the domains of interpretation include a
domain of elements and a domain of lists. A binary predicate *perm* of
the specification language is interpreted on the list domain: two lists
are in the relation denoted by this predicate iff they are permutations
of each other. The specification language uses also the binary function
symbols *append* and "." interpreted in the usual way. The specification
includes the following formulae

$S_p : perm(p_1, p_2)$

$S_{ex} : \exists x, y \; ex_1 = append(x, ex_2.y) \land ex_3 = append(x, y)$

To show that this specification is inductive one has to check that the following formulae are valid in the interpretation.

For c_1: $perm(nil, nil)$

For c_2: $perm(N, M) \land \exists x, y(A.L = append(x, B.y) \land N = append(x, y)) \to perm(A.L, B.M)$

For c_3: $\exists x, y \; A.L = append(x, A.y) \land L = append(x, y)$

For c_4: $\exists x, y \; (L = append(x, B.y) \land M = append(x, y))$
$\to \exists x', y'(A.L = append(x', B.y') \land A.M = append(x', y'))$

□

Similarly, a rich specification language may be used to prove properties of programs using difference lists. A difference list is a pair of lists $L1$ and $L2$, denoted $L1 - L2$, such that $L2$ is a suffix of $L1$. Such a pair represents the list which is the prefix of $L1$ obtained by removing the suffix $L2$. We now assume that the specification language has a predicate *is-dlist* which ranges over pairs of lists $L1 - L2$ and the atom *is-dlist*$(L1 - L2)$ is valid iff $L2$ is a suffix of $L1$. The language includes also the function symbol *list* which represents the function transforming difference lists into the lists they represent.

Example 7.7

Difference lists allow for efficient implementation of concatenation of lists. This is achieved by the following clause.

$cd(L1 - L2, L2 - L3, L1 - L3) \leftarrow$

The intended meaning of this program is captured by the following formula with the interpretation discussed above:

S_{cd}: *is-dlist*$(cd_1) \land$ *is-dlist*(cd_2)
$\to list(cd_3) = append(list(cd_1), list(cd_2)).$

This specification is inductive in a trivial way since in the interpretation considered the following formula associated with the only clause is valid:

$$is\text{-}dlist(L1 - L2) \land is\text{-}dlist(L2 - L3) \rightarrow$$
$$is\text{-}dlist(L1{-}L3) \land list(L1{-}L3) = append(list(L1{-}L2), list(L2{-}L3)).$$

□

The last example of this section concerns well-known problem of graph colouring. A natural specification of this problem is second-order.

Example 7.8

Given a (finite) graph and a finite set of colours we want to colour the nodes of the graph in such a way that no adjacent nodes of the graph have the same colour. A natural formalization of this problem would lead to a second-order formula since a solution of the problem is a function from nodes to colours. We will represent solutions as lists of pairs of the form ⟨*Node, Colour*⟩. The predicate *solution* of the specification language is interpreted on the domain of such lists. The *J*-atom *solution(l)* is valid in $\mathcal{I}$ iff the list l represents a mapping from nodes to colours satisfying the restrictions. The unary predicate *nonrepetitive* is interpreted on lists: a list is non-repetitive iff every two distinct elements of the list are different objects. The specification language includes also the predicates *is-node* and *is-colour* and the binary predicate *adjacent* on nodes interpreted as expected.

The definite program constructing a solution for a given graph and a given set of colours is assumed to include information about the graph structure and about the colours available. In the following example we refer to this information by the binary predicates *adj*, *nonadj* (for "adjacent" regions and "not adjacent" regions) and *dc* (for "different colours"), and by the unary predicates *node* and *colour*. The program includes the following clauses:

c_1: $p(nil) \leftarrow$

c_2: $p([\langle R, C \rangle]) \leftarrow colour(C), node(R)$

c_3: $p([\langle R1, C1 \rangle, \langle R2, C2 \rangle | S]) \leftarrow$
$\qquad adj(R1, R2), dc(C1, C2), p([\langle R1, C1 \rangle | S]), p([\langle R2, C2 \rangle | S])$

c_4: $p([\langle R1, C1 \rangle, \langle R2, C2 \rangle | S]) \leftarrow$
$\qquad nonadj(R1, R2), p([\langle R1, C1 \rangle | S]), p([\langle R2, C2 \rangle | S])$

The following specification of the program uses the predicates, whose interpretation was discussed above. It is inductive, hence valid:

S_p: $solution(p_1) \land nonrepetitive(p_1)$

S_{adj}: $is\text{-}node(adj_1) \land is\text{-}node(adj_2) \land adj1 \neq adj_2 \land$
$\quad adjacent(adj_1, adj_2)$

S_{nonadj}: $is\text{-}node(nonadj_1) \land is\text{-}node(nonadj_2) \land nonadj_1 \neq nonadj_2 \land$
$\quad \neg adjacent(nonadj_1, nonadj_2)$

S_{dc}: $is\text{-}colour(dc_1) \land is\text{-}colour(dc_2) \land dc_1 \neq dc_2$

S_{colour}: $is\text{-}colour(colour_1)$

S_{node}: $is\text{-}node(node_1)$

It remains to prove that that the specification is inductive. For this one has to check the conditions for every clause of the program.

For c_1 and c_2 the result holds trivially.

For c_3 we have to check that the list obtained is a solution and that it is nonrepetitive. We check these conditions separately. In the given interpretation the formula

$$solution([\langle R1, C1 \rangle | S]) \land solution([\langle R2, C2 \rangle | S]) \land C1 \neq C2 \land$$
$$R1 \neq R2 \land adjacent(R1, R2)$$

implies

$$solution([\langle R1, C1 \rangle, \langle R2, C2 \rangle | S])$$

so that the list obtained is a solution.

Similarly, the formula

$$nonrepetitive[\langle R1, C1 \rangle | S] \land nonrepetitive[\langle R2, C2 \rangle | S] \land C1 \neq C2$$
$$\land adjacent(R1, R2) \land R1 \neq R2$$

implies

$$nonrepetitive[\langle R1, C1 \rangle, \langle R2, C2 \rangle | S].$$

A similar check should be performed for c_4.

$\square$

7.2.3   Wand's incompleteness result

Theorem 7.1 p. 333 states the completeness of the proof method under the assumption that the specification language can express the strongest specification. We now discuss this requirement in some detail.

In [CD88] it is shown that Wand's incompleteness result established for Hoare's like deductive systems holds also for inductive proofs in attribute grammars. This result says that a fixed first order assertion language may not be rich enough to express the inductive properties needed for the correctness proof of a specification of a given program. For this reason we pointed out that the language should be strong enough to have completeness. However, as discussed in Chapter 5 definite programs can be seen as a special class of attribute grammars. Therefore the question arises, whether the incompleteness result obtained for all attribute grammars holds also for the particular case of definite programs. In this section we show that it is the case. We give a formal proof of this result by encoding Wand's example [Wan78, CD88] as a definite program. The example shows a specification language $\mathcal{L}$ with an interpretation $\mathcal{I}$, a definite program P and a valid specification for P such that there is no equivalent first order specification in $\mathcal{L}$.

Let $\mathcal{L}$ be the logic language over the alphabet consisting of the unary predicates p, q, r, the unary function symbol f and the equality predicate $=$. We choose the following interpretation $\mathcal{I}$: The domain is:

$I = \{a_n \mid n \geq 0\} \cup \{b_n \mid n \geq 0\}$.

The predicate $=$ is interpreted as the identity on the domain.

Functor f is interpreted as the following function:

$f(a_0) = a_0, f(b_0) = b_0,$
$f(a_n) = a_{n-1}, f(b_n) = b_{n-1}$ for $n \geq 1$.

The predicates are interpreted as follows:

$p(X)$ is true iff $X = a_0$,
$q(X)$ is true iff $X = b_0$,
$r(X)$ is true iff $X = a_{k(k+1)/2}$ for some k.

It has been shown by Wand ([Wan78], Theorem 2) that there is no first order formula ϕ in $\mathcal{L}$ with one free variable X such that for any valuation v in $\mathcal{I}$, $(\mathcal{I}, v) \models \phi$ iff $v(X) \in \{a_n \mid n \geq 0\}$. In other words, the language $\mathcal{L}$ is too weak to describe the set consisting of all elements a_i, for $i = 0, 1 \ldots$.

We now use this result in the context of definite programs. We construct a program P and we show that its actual semantics cannot be expressed in $\mathcal{L}$:

$$rec(X, Y) \leftarrow rec(f(X), Y)$$
$$rec(X, X) \leftarrow equal(f(X), X)$$
$$equal(X, X) \leftarrow.$$

Notice that the least Herbrand model of this program is empty but the proof tree semantics based on the preinterpretation $J_\mathcal{I}$ is not empty; the strongest specification of P corresponds to the J-based atoms defined for rec as
$$rec_1 \in \{a_n | n \geq 0\} \wedge rec_2 = a_0) \vee (rec_1 \in \{b_n | n \geq 0\} \wedge rec_2 = b_0$$
and for $equal$ as
$equal_1$ and $equal_2$ denote the same value.

Notice that S_{equal} can be expressed in this language: $equal_1 = equal_2$. It will be shown that S_{rec} cannot, i.e. no first order specification for P in $\mathcal{L}$ can describe the corresponding set.

The idea is as follows. We take an auxiliary valid specification of P, which is not inductive. If there exists a strongest specification of P in $\mathcal{L}$ it must be stronger than the auxiliary one and inductive. We show that these conditions imply a contradiction with Wand's result.

The auxiliary specification is defined as follows:

Q_{rec}: $r(rec_1) \rightarrow p(rec_2)$,
Q_{equal}: $true$.

It is valid: the relation $Spec(P, Q, \mathcal{I})$ is a superset of the strongest specification of P. In particular it includes the J-atom $equal(a_0, a_1)$. This atom is obtained by putting $X = a_1$ in the second clause of the program. With this valuation (as with any other) the body of the clause satisfies the new specification, but the head does not since $r(a_1)$ is true (with $k = 1$) and $p(a_1)$ is not. Hence the specification is not inductive.

Assume there is an inductive specification $\langle R, \mathcal{I} \rangle$ stronger than $\langle Q, \mathcal{I} \rangle$. By the definition, for such an interpretation the following formulae must be valid in $\mathcal{I}$:

1. $R_{rec}(rec_1, rec_2) \wedge r(rec_1) \rightarrow p(rec_2)$,

2. $R_{rec}(f(X), Y) \rightarrow R_{rec}(X, Y)$,

3. $R_{equal}(f(X), X) \rightarrow R_{rec}(X, X)$,

4. $R_{equal}(X, X)$.

Let now ϕ be the formula:
$\phi(x)$: $\forall y\ R_{rec}(x, y) \rightarrow p(y)$.
We will show that for every valuation v in $\mathcal{I}$ $(\mathcal{I}, v) \models \phi$ iff $v(X) \in \{a_n | n \geq 0\}$.

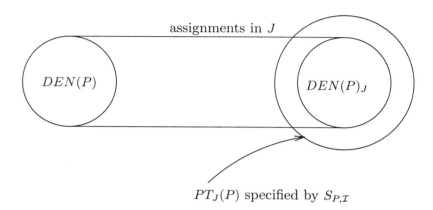

$PT_J(P)$ specified by $S_{P,\mathcal{I}}$

Figure 7.2
Relationships between the $TERM$-based denotation preinterpreted in $J_{\mathcal{I}}$ $(DEN(P)_J)$ of a program P and the $J_{\mathcal{I}}$-based proof tree semantics $(PT_J(P))$

If part: If $R_{rec}(a_n, y)$ holds for some $n \geq 0$ then by (2) $R_{rec}(a_m, y)$, holds for all $m > n$. Let us choose $m > n$ such that $r(a_m)$ holds. Then by (1), $p(y)$ also holds.

Only part: By (4) and (3), $R_{rec}(b_0, b_0)$ holds, hence by (2) $R_{rec}(b_n, b_0)$ holds for $n \geq 0$. Now consider $R_{rec}(b_n, y)$ with $y = b_0$; it holds, but since $p(b_0)$ does not then, $(\mathcal{I}, v) \models \phi$ does not hold if $v(X) \notin \{a_n | n \geq 0\}$. By Wand's result ϕ cannot be first order, hence R_{rec} cannot be a first order formula.

7.2.4 The incompleteness result for term interpretations

The incompleteness result of the previous section was obtained using a definite program with the empty denotation. This was the limit case of the common situation illustrated on Figure 7.2 in which the set of J-based atoms obtained by preinterpretation of the denotation is a subset of the actual semantics [4].

If $\mathcal{I}$ is a term interpretation then the denotation coincides with the actual semantics. In this case validity and computational validity coincide and every element of the actual semantics is the head of a proof tree of P. The question arises, whether in this specific situation the incom-

---

[4]See also Example 7.3 p. 331.

pleteness result still holds. We now show that it is the case. Let P be a definite program with term interpretation. Consider the specification language $\mathcal{L}$ whose only predicate symbol is the equality (interpreted as the identity on the term domain). Clearly, the denotation can be expressed in $\mathcal{L}$ by a (possibly infinite) disjunction of formulae of the form $p_1 = t_1 \wedge \ldots \wedge p_n = t_n$ where p is an n-ary predicate of P and $p(t_1, \ldots, t_n)$ is in the denotation of P. Now the problem is whether there exists a finite first order formula F_P in $\mathcal{L}$ describing the elements of the denotation.

It is shown in [CL88] that there exists a decision procedure for the validity in the Herbrand universe of any first order formula with the only predicate symbol $=$. Hence existence of F_P for every program P would mean that the denotation of every program is recursive.

This is not true, since it is known that definite programs can simulate Turing machines (see also Section 8.4). Hence the incompleteness result. The incompleteness of the method does not come from the nature of the interpretation but rather is relative to the nature of the language.

7.2.5   Proving properties of the denotation

Let us now consider the case where the specification language uses only predicates of a definite program P. This corresponds to the study of properties of a program expressed in the same language. In this case the domain of interest is the $TERM$-based denotation of P. The inductive proof method can be used for proving such properties. As discussed above, in this case the concept of validity coincides with the concept of computational validity. Thus, for a given program P a specification $\langle S, DEN(P) \rangle$ is valid with respect to P iff for every atom $p(x_1, \ldots, x_n)$ where $x_1, \ldots, x_n$ are distinct variables

$$DEN(P) \models p(x_1, \ldots, x_n) \rightarrow S_p[x_1, \ldots, x_n].$$

This holds if the specification is inductive.

Now, validity of a formula F in the denotation of P may proved using the following observations:

1. If F is an atom it is valid iff it belongs to $DEN(P)$. This can be established if an interpreter with a complete strategy terminates on the goal $\leftarrow F$. Similarly, to check validity of $\forall(F)$ in the denotation one has to run the goal $\leftarrow F'$ obtained from $\leftarrow F$ by replacing the universally

quantified variables of F by new constants.

2. If F is an instance of a clause of P it is valid.

3. The equality axioms of the Clark's equality theory (cf. Section 2.2.6) can be used to transform F. For example, if t is a term and p is a unary predicate, then $DEN(P) \models p(t)$ is equivalent to $DEN(P) \models \forall(\exists x\; x = t \wedge p(x))$.

4. If F is of the form $\forall(p(x_1, \ldots, x_n) \to S_p[x_1, \ldots, x_n])$, where p is an n-ary predicate and $x_1, \ldots, x_n$ are distinct variables, and if the family S_p for all predicates of P is a specification S according to Definition 7.1 p. 324, then F is valid if the specification $\langle S, DEN(P) \rangle$ is valid. It is the case, in particular, if S is inductive.

5. If $COMP(P) \models F$ then $DEN(P) \models F$. This follows by the fact that $DEN(P)$ is a model of $COMP(P)$ (cf. Section 2.2.6). This observation may be used in the case of non-inductive specifications.

These observations give rise to proof techniques, which may be used for automatic support of proof construction. We now give two examples of proofs where these techniques are used.

Example 7.9 Commutativity of addition in the least Herbrand model
Consider the following program P:

c_1: $int(zero) \leftarrow$
c_2: $int(s(X)) \leftarrow int(X)$
c_3: $plus(zero, X, X) \leftarrow$
c_4: $plus(s(X), Y, s(Z)) \leftarrow plus(X, Y, Z)$

We want to prove the commutativity of $plus$ in the denotation of P, i.e. to prove

(1) $DEN(P) \models (int(X) \wedge int(Y) \wedge int(Z) \wedge$
$$plus(X, Y, Z)) \to plus(Y, X, Z)$$

First of all notice that:
(2) $DEN(P) \models plus(X, Y, Z) \to int(X)$
as the specification $\langle S1_{plus}, DEN(P) \rangle$ where $S1_{plus}$: $int(plus_1)$ is inductive. Indeed,
$$DEN(P) \models int(zero) \text{ and } DEN(P) \models int(X) \to int(s(X)).$$

Moreover:

(3) $DEN(P) \models plus(X, Y, Z) \wedge int(Y) \to int(Z)$.

To check this, notice that the specification $\langle S2_{plus}, DEN(P) \rangle$, where $S2_{plus} : int(plus_2) \to int(plus_3)$ is inductive, i.e.:

$DEN(P) \models int(X) \to int(X)$, trivially and

$DEN(P) \models (int(Y) \to int(Z)) \to (int(Y) \to int(s(Z)))$

as $int(Z) \to int(s(Z))$ is a variant of the clause c_2. Thus for proving (1), in view of (2) and (3), it suffices to prove:

(4) $DEN(P) \models plus(X, Y, Z) \wedge int(Y) \to plus(Y, X, Z)$.

Notice that (4) can be reformulated as the problem of validity of the specification $\langle S4_{plus}, DEN(P) \rangle$ where

$S4_{plus} : int(plus_2) \to plus(plus_2, plus_1, plus_3)$.

We show that this specification is inductive, i.e. that

(5) $DEN(P) \models int(X) \to plus(X, zero, X)$ and

(5') $DEN(P) \models (int(Y) \to$
$$plus(Y, X, Z)) \to (int(Y) \to plus(Y, s(X), s(Z))).$$

To prove (5) it suffices to show that the specification $\langle S_{int}, DEN(P) \rangle$, where $S_{int} : plus(int_1, zero, int_1)$ is valid. Indeed, it can be checked that it is inductive since the formulae

$plus(zero, zero, zero)$ and $plus(X, zero, X) \to plus(s(X), zero, s(X))$

are instances of clauses.

To prove (5') it suffices to show

(6) $DEN(P) \models plus(X, Y, Z) \to plus(X, s(Y), s(Z))$,

obtained from (5') by removing the hypotheses $int(Y)$ of the component implications and by renaming of the variables. Notice that (5') is implied by (6). Notice also that (6) can be seen as the statement that the specification $\langle S5_{plus}, DEN(P) \rangle$, where

$S5_{plus} : plus(plus_1, s(plus_2), s(plus_3))$, is valid.

This specification is inductive since the formulae

$plus(zero, s(X), s(X))$ and

$plus(X, s(Y), s(Z)) \to plus(s(X), s(Y), s(s(Z)))$

are instances of clauses.

This concludes the proof of (1).

Notice that in contrast to (5) the formula $plus(X, zero, X)$ is not valid in $DEN(P)$ (as it does not belong to $DEN(P)$).
□

The steps of the example proof employ nondeterministically the observations 1 to 4 discussed above, so that some automatic support for its construction could be provided.

The following example shows that these steps may not be sufficient.

Example 7.10 List permutation
We consider the following program:

c_1: $p(nil, nil) \leftarrow$,
c_2: $p(A.L, B.M) \leftarrow p(N, M), ex(A.L, B, N)$
c_3: $ex(A.L, A, L) \leftarrow$
c_4: $ex(A.L, B, A.M) \leftarrow ex(L, B, M)$
c_5: $list(nil) \leftarrow$
c_6: $list(A.L) \leftarrow list(L)$

We claim that in $DEN(P)$ all arguments of p are lists. To prove this we show the following property of the denotation:

$$DEN(P) \models \forall(p(X, Y) \rightarrow (list(X) \land list(Y)))$$
$$\land \forall((ex(X, Y, Z) \land list(Z)) \rightarrow list(X))$$

Following the general technique, it suffices to show that the specification $\langle S, DEN(P) \rangle$ is inductive where S is defined as follows:

$S_p : list(p_1) \land list(p_2)$
$S_{ex} : list(ex_3) \rightarrow list(ex_1)$

Thus the following conditions are to be checked:

for c_1: $DEN(P) \models list(nil) \land list(nil)$
for c_2: $DEN(P) \models (list(N) \rightarrow list(A.L))$
$\qquad\qquad \land (list(N) \land list(M)) \rightarrow (list(A.L) \land list(B.M))$
for c_3: $DEN(P) \models list(L) \rightarrow list(A.L)$
for c_4: $DEN(P) \models (list(M) \rightarrow list(L)) \rightarrow$
$\qquad\qquad\qquad\qquad\qquad (list(A.M) \rightarrow list(A.L))$

The conditions for c_1 c_2 and c_3 can be checked using the four first observations. The condition for c_4 is obtained by the following property :
$$DEN(P) \models list(A.M) \rightarrow list(M)$$
The latter holds as a consequence of the axioms of the completion, but it cannot be proven with these observations only.
□

The question arises when the properties of denotation carry over to other models of the program. This happens for the least J-based model of the program if the domain of the preinterpretation J is isomorphic to the term domain used for construction of the denotation. For example, as the Herbrand universe of the addition program is isomorphic to the domain of natural numbers with successor function, the proof of (1) shows that the predicate *plus* is commutative in the least model of the program with the standard preinterpretation of *zero* and s on the domain of natural numbers. Take as another example the following preinterpretation ([Bid81]). The domain is the product of the domain of natural numbers and the finite set $\{+1, -1\}$; *zero* is interpreted as $\langle 0, +1 \rangle$, and s is interpreted as the function which for a given pair $\langle n, s \rangle$ returns the pair $\langle n', s \rangle$, where n' is the successor of n. With this preinterpretation J, the least J-model of the addition program includes no J-atom of the form $int(\langle n, -1 \rangle)$ and *plus* is still commutative in this model. For the same preinterpretation J, the set consisting of all J-atoms of the form $int(\langle n, s \rangle)$ and all J-atoms of the form $plus(\langle m, r \rangle, \langle n, s \rangle, \langle m + n, s \rangle)$, where m, n are natural numbers and r, s are in the two-element set $\{+1, -1\}$, is also a model of the program. However, in this model *plus* is not commutative, since e.g. the atom $plus(\langle (2, -1) \rangle, \langle 2, +1 \rangle, \langle 4, +1 \rangle)$ is in the model but the atom $plus(\langle (2, +1) \rangle, \langle 2, -1 \rangle, \langle 4, +1 \rangle)$ is not in the model.

7.2.6   Summary of results on the inductive proof method

We now summarize the results presented in this section. We introduced a notion of specification. It is given as a family of formulae indexed by the predicates of the program. The formulae are written in a specification language with some interpretation. Assuming that an interpretation of the specification language is given, we introduced:

- The notion of validity of a specification with respect to a program (Definition 7.2 p. 325).

- The notion of computational validity of a specification with respect to a program (Definition 7.4 p. 331).

- A condition for validity which requires existence of an inductive specification stronger than given one, and gives rise to the inductive proof method of Theorem 7.1 p. 333.

The computational validity follows from validity, but not vice versa, and the proof method is sound and relatively complete, i.e. complete under the assumption that the specification language is expressive enough to define the J-based proof-theoretic semantics of the program.

In the case of term interpretation the notions of computational validity coincides with the notion of validity.

7.3   Proof method with annotation

We now give a more formal presentation of the annotation method.

7.3.1   Valid annotation

Definition 7.6 Annotation of a definite program

Let P be a definite program and let $\mathcal{L}$ be a specification language for P with an interpretation $\mathcal{I}$. An *annotation* of P is a mapping Δ assigning to every predicate p of P two finite sets of formulae of $\mathcal{L}$, denoted $\Delta_I(p)$ and $\Delta_S(p)$ such that every free variable of a formula is in Var_p. The formulae are called *assertions*: the elements of $\Delta_I(p)$ are called *inherited assertions* of p, while the elements of $\Delta_S(p)$ are called *synthesized assertions* of p. The union of the sets is denoted $\Delta(p)$.
□

The specification *associated with an annotation* Δ is the specification $\langle S_\Delta, \mathcal{I} \rangle$, where for every predicate p the formula $S_{\Delta p}$ is of the form $\bigwedge \Delta_I(p) \to \bigwedge \Delta_S(p)$.

Intuitively, an annotation is expected to describe properties of node labelling in any J-based proof tree of the program. This is done by the associated specification. Notice that the formulae of these specification have the form of implications with inherited assertions used as hypotheses. The inherited assertions associated with the head of the tree can be seen as a precondition describing a subclass of proof trees whose properties are described. Intuitively, a proof tree in this class satisfies the specification if all assertions concerning its nodes are satisfied. This means in particular that whenever the head of the tree satisfies the inherited assertions of its predicate then also the head of every subtree of this tree satisfies the inherited assertions of its predicate. This means also that the head of every subtree (including the tree itself) satisfies all its synthesized assertions.

This is formalized by the following definition.

Definition 7.7 Validity of an annotation

Let Δ with a J-based interpretation $\mathcal{I}$ be an annotation of P and let T be a J-based proof tree of a program P. Let $p(v_1, .., v_n)$ be the head of T.

The annotation Δ is valid for T iff $\mathcal{I} \models \bigwedge \Delta_I(p)[v_1, \ldots v_n]$ implies that $\mathcal{I} \models \bigwedge \Delta(q)[u_1, \ldots u_k]$ for every J-based atom $q(u_1, \ldots, u_k)$ which is the head of a subtree of T. The annotation of P is valid iff it is valid for every J-based proof tree.

□

In other words, an annotation is valid for P if in every proof tree whose head satisfies the inherited assertions, all assertions are satisfied at every of its nodes. This concerns in particular, the synthesized assertions of the head.

The notion of computational validity introduced for the inductive proof method extends to annotations by restricting the hypotheses to the elements of $DEN(P)$.

Definition 7.8 Computational validity of an annotation

Let Δ with an interpretation $\mathcal{I}$ be an annotation of P, T be a proof tree of a program P and let $p(t_1, .., t_n)$ be the head of T. Δ is *computationally valid* for T iff for every valuation ν of T,

$$(\mathcal{I}, \nu) \models \bigwedge \Delta_I(p)[t_1, \ldots t_n]$$

implies that

$$(\mathcal{I}, \nu) \models \bigwedge \Delta(q)[u_1, \ldots u_k]$$

for every atom $q(u_1, \ldots, u_k)$ which is the head of a subtree of T. The annotation of P is computationally valid iff it is computationally valid for every proof tree.

□

While the definition of validity concerns J-based proof trees, the computational validity concerns $TERM$-based proof trees whose labels are interpreted in $\mathcal{I}$. Both definitions coincide in case of term interpretation [5].

The following propositions summarize relations between various notions of validity. They follow directly from the definitions.

Proposition 7.2

   If Δ is a valid annotation of P then

1. it is also a computationally valid annotation for P, but the converse does not hold;

2. the associated specification S_Δ is valid for P.

   □

An interesting observation is that the associated specification of a valid annotation need not be inductive. This fact will be illustrated by an example later in this chapter (Example 7.15 p. 7.15).

7.3.2   Logical dependency scheme

We now formulate sufficient conditions for the validity of an annotation as a basis for the proof method with annotation. Our approach will be based on the notion of attribute dependency scheme discussed in Section 4.3. For a given definite program P with annotation Δ we construct an attribute dependency scheme called the *logical dependency scheme* of Δ, which will be denoted LDS_Δ. The idea of the construction is as follows.

The annotation Δ associates with each predicate of the program the inherited assertions and the synthesized assertions. With each assertion in Δ we now associate a name. The names can be seen as attributes of the predicate, while the assertions are attribute values. We will denote by A_Δ the set of all such attributes. For a clause of the program instances of the assertions are produced by instantiation of the free variables by corresponding argument terms. Thus the skeleton of the clause is decorated by the attribute occurrences. Following the terminology of

---

[5]See the discussion after Definition 7.4 p. 331.

Chapter 4 we can now use attribute occurrences in the clauses and in proof trees as names of instances of the assertions. The main question is about proving validity of these assertions. Following the standard approach of attribute grammars we distinguish the *input assertions* of the clause. They are the inherited assertions of the head of the clause and the synthesized assertions of the body atoms. The remaining assertions of the clause are *output assertions*. We want to be able to prove validity of the output assertions assuming the validity of the input assertions. When constructing such proofs we notice that the validity of an output assertion is proved referring to a validity of certain subset of the input assertions. In this sense the output assertion depends on some input assertions. This information can be abstracted as the notion of local dependency relation on attribute occurrences. It can be given in the form of an attribute dependency scheme defined as follows.

Definition 7.9 Logical dependency scheme (ADS)

Let P be a definite program with an annotation Δ. A *logical dependency scheme* for Δ is an attribute dependency scheme $\langle N, R, A_\Delta, D \rangle$ such that:

- N is the set of predicates of P.

- R is the N-sorted signature: $r_c : \langle p_1 \ldots p_m, p_0 \rangle$ is in R iff

  $c : p_0(t_{01}, \ldots, t_{0n_0}) \leftarrow p_1(t_{11}, \ldots, t_{1n_1}), \ldots, p_m(t_{m1}, \ldots, t_{mn_m})$

  is a clause of P. Thus, the elements of the signature correspond to clause rules of P. The signature can also be seen as context-free grammar with the empty terminal alphabet.

- A_Δ is the set of attributes. Each attribute denotes one assertion in the range of Δ. Inherited (synthesized) attributes correspond to the names of inherited (synthesized) assertions. Each nonterminal has the attributes corresponding to the assertions associated by Δ.

- D is a family of local dependency relations relating the input attribute occurrences and the output attribute occurrences of each r in R.

□

We illustrate the notion of a logical dependency scheme by an example and then we give a formal presentation of the annotation proof method. The notation used follows that of Chapter 4. In particular, if $p_0 \rightarrow$

$p_1, \ldots, p_n$ is the rule r_c corresponding to a clause c and ψ is a name of an assertion of a predicate p_i then we denote by $\psi(i)$ the instance of ψ in this rule[6]. We will also use the following notation for referring to the assertion instances in the clauses.

Let ψ be a name of the assertion Ψ of the predicate p_i occurring at node i. Then by $\psi_i(r_c)$ we denote the formula $\Psi[t_{i1}, \ldots, t_{i,n_i}]$ in which every free variable $p_k(i)$ in $Var_{p_i}(i)$ is replaced by the term t_{ik} of clause c. The set of input attribute occurrences of a production rule r will be denoted $Hyp(r)$, since the input attribute occurrences are names of hypotheses, i.e. the assertions assumed to be valid. The set of output attribute occurrences of a production rule r will be denoted $Conc(r)$, since the output attribute occurrences are names of conclusions, i.e. the assertions whose validity is to be proved. For an output attribute occurrence $\psi(i)$ in a rule r we denote by $hyp(r, \psi(i))$ the set of all attribute occurrences of r on which $\psi(i)$ depends.

Example 7.11

For the addition program of Example 7.2 p. 327:

c_1: $plus(zero, X, X) \leftarrow$
c_2: $plus(s(X), Y, s(Z)) \leftarrow plus(X, Y, Z)$

We define the following annotation Δ.

The assertions of the annotation are specified with names which are then used to defined a logical dependency scheme.

$\Delta(plus) : \Delta_I(plus) \cup \Delta_S(plus)$
$\Delta_I(plus) : \{\phi : ground(plus_2)\}$
$\Delta_S(plus) : \{\psi : ground(plus_1), \delta : ground(plus_3)\}$
$S_{\Delta plus}: ground(plus_2) \rightarrow (ground(plus_1) \wedge ground(plus_3))$
$R : \{r_1 : plus \rightarrow \varepsilon, r_2 : plus \rightarrow plus\}$
$D : \{D(r_1) : \{(\phi(0), \delta(0))\},$
$\qquad D(r_2) : \{(\phi(0), \phi(1)), (\psi(1), \psi(0)), (\delta(1), \delta(0))\}$
$Hyp(r_1) : \{\phi(0)\}, \qquad\qquad Conc(r1) : \{\psi(0), \delta(0)\}$
$Hyp(r_2) : \{\phi(0), \psi(1), \delta(1)\}, \quad Conc(r_2) : \{\phi(1), \psi(0), \delta(0)\}$
Using the notation introduced we have
$\phi_0(r_2) = ground(Y), \phi_1(r_2) = ground(Y)$

---

[6]It corresponds to the occurrence i of the attribute ψ in r_c.

r_1 :

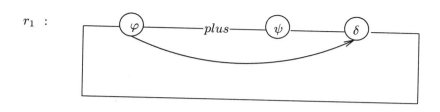

r_2 :

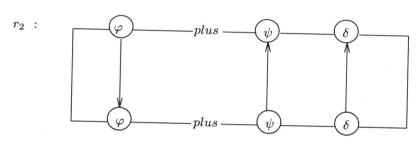

Figure 7.3
Graphical representation of the example logical dependency scheme of
Example 7.12 p. 352

$hyp(r_2, \psi(0)) = \{\psi(1)\}$

In order to simplify the presentation of logical dependency schemes
we will use the graphical representation of Chapter 4. It is illustrated in
Figure 7.3.

Notice that the formulae ψ alone define a purely synthesized annotation, hence (provided the restricted dependency scheme is sound) they
hold in all proof trees independently from any other condition. A formula
stronger than S_Δ consists of the conjunction of the two valid specifications $ground(plus_1)$ and $ground(plus_2) \rightarrow ground(plus_3)$.
□

Since a logical dependency scheme is an attribute dependency scheme
the results on ADS's discussed in Section 4.3.8 carry over for the case of
LDS's. In particular:

- Non-circularity of an LDS is decidable.

- Non-circularity test is intrinsically exponential.

- Some nontrivial non-circular subclasses of LDS can be decided in polynomial time.
- A purely-synthesized LDS is (trivially) well-formed.

On the other hand, an LDS is connected with an annotation of a definite program. We will use this connection for proving validity of the annotation. The following auxiliary notion is important for that purpose.

Definition 7.10 Soundness of an annotation for an LDS

Let Δ with an interpretation $\mathcal{I}$ be an annotation for a definite program P and let $L : \langle N, R, A_\Delta, D \rangle$ be a logical dependency scheme for Δ. Δ is *sound* for L iff for every $r \in R$ and for every $\psi \in Conc(r)$ the following condition is satisfied:

$$\mathcal{I} \models (\bigwedge_{\xi \in Hyp(r,\psi)} \xi(r)) \rightarrow \psi(r)$$

□

Thus, the definition specifies for every clause rule r of the program (i.e. for every element of the signature of the LDS) a finite number of verification conditions. They are simple implications on the assertion occurrences (recall that the assertion occurrences are obtained from the assertions by replacing their free variables by the corresponding terms of the clause). For every output assertion occurrence b in r a verification condition of the form $a_1 \wedge ... \wedge a_k \rightarrow b$ is created, where $a_1, ..., a_k$ are all input attribute occurrences of r on which b depends in the local dependency relation D_r.

Example 7.12

The annotation in Example 7.11 is sound for the LDS shown in Figure 7.3. The definition of soundness results in this case in the following conditions which can be easily verified in $\mathcal{T}$:

for r_1: $\{ground(X) \rightarrow ground(X), ground(zero)\}$

for r_2: $\{ground(X) \rightarrow ground(s(X)), ground(Y) \rightarrow ground(Y),$
$ground(Z) \rightarrow ground(s(Z))\}$

□

7.3.3   Proof method with annotation: soundness and completeness

We now reformulate Theorem 4.3 p. 187 in the context of definite programs. It gives a sound and complete method for proving validity of annotations of programs. Denote by $\iota_\Delta(p)$ the conjunction of all assertions in $\Delta_I(p)$ and by $\sigma_\Delta(p)$ the conjunction of all assertions in $\Delta_S(p)$.

Theorem 7.2

Let P be a definite program and let Δ be an annotation of P with an interpretation $\mathcal{I}$. Δ is valid for P if and only if there exists an annotation Δ' for P and a non-circular logical dependency scheme L' for Δ' such that

- Δ' is sound for L',

- for every predicate symbol p of P,

$\mathcal{I} \models \iota_\Delta(p) \leftrightarrow \iota_{\Delta'}(p)$, and

$\mathcal{I} \models \sigma_{\Delta'}(p) \to \sigma_\Delta(p)$.

□

The proof is analogous to that of Theorem 4.3 p. 187 and it is omitted. The completeness of the method relies on the fact that the strongest specification of the program can be formalized as the annotation Δ' provided that the specification language is expressive enough to describe it. This is known as relative completeness of the proof method. We now illustrate the method by some examples.

Example 7.13

As is it was discussed in Example 7.12 the LDS introduced for the considered annotation Δ of the addition program is non-circular and Δ is sound for it. Hence by Theorem 7.2 the specification $\langle S_{\Delta plus}, \mathcal{I} \rangle$ is valid.

□

We now show the use of the annotation for structuring inductive definitions.

Example 7.14

We reformulate as definite program the attribute grammar example

of Katayama and Hoshino (cf. Example 4.4 p. 153)[7]. The program
will be considered together with the preinterpretation on the domain of
natural numbers where *zero* and *s* denote the constant "0" and the function "successor", respectively. With this preinterpretation the program
"computes" the set of all multiples of number 4.

c_1: $fourmultiple(K) \leftarrow p(zero, H, H, K)$
c_2: $p(F, F, H, H) \leftarrow$
c_3: $p(F, s(G), H, s(K)) \leftarrow p(s(F), G, s(H), K)$

The interpretation $\mathcal{N}$ of the specification language is defined on the
domain of natural numbers in the usual way. The informal statement
about the meaning of the program can be expressed by the following
formula of the specification language:

$S_{fourmultiple}$: $\exists n \; fourmultiple_1 = 4 * n$

We now reformulate the specification of the attribute grammar in Example 4.4 as the following annotation Δ (used in Example 4.9 p. 185) :

$\Delta_I(fourmultiple) = \emptyset, \Delta_S(fourmultiple) = \{\delta\}$
$\Delta_I(p) = \{\beta\} \; , \Delta_S(p) = \{\alpha, \gamma\}$
α: $\exists n \; p_2 = p_1 + 2 * n$
β: $p_3 = p_2 + 2 * p_1$
γ: $p_4 = 2 * p_2 + p_1$
δ: $S_{fourmultiple}$

The assertions can be easily understood if we observe that such a
program describes the construction of a "path" of length $4 * N$ and that
p_1, p_2, p_3 and p_4 are lengths at different steps of the path as shown in
Figure 7.4.

For Δ we consider the logical dependency scheme presented in Figure 7.5.

Δ is sound for this LDS which is non-circular. For example it is easy
to check that the following verification conditions are valid in $\mathcal{N}$:

for c_1:

- $(\alpha(1) \wedge \gamma(1) \rightarrow \delta(0))$ [8]:
  $\exists n \; H = 0 + 2 * n \; \wedge K = 2 * H + 0 \rightarrow \exists n \; K = 4 * n$
- $\beta(1)$: $H = H + 2 * 0$

---

[7]Where *fourmultiple* is denoted by X and p by Y.
[8]The formula is built as $\alpha_1(r_1) \wedge \gamma_1(r_1) \rightarrow \delta_0(r_1)$.

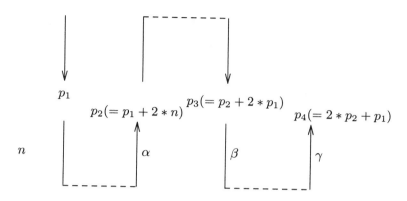

Figure 7.4
Intuition of the program of Example 7.14 p. 353

for c_2:

- $\beta(0) \to \gamma(0))$ [9]:
  $H = F + 2 * F \to H = 2 * F + F$
- $\alpha(0)$: $\exists n \; F = F + 2 * n$

  etc . . . .

It can be checked that the specification $\langle S_\Delta, \mathcal{N} \rangle$ is inductive. However, the verification condition needed to check this are somewhat complicated (it is not the same as the inductive and simpler specification given in Example 4.7 p. 179). On the other hand, the verification conditions of soundness of the annotation for the considered LDS are relatively simple. Thus, the annotation method in this case allows for modularization and simplification of the proof of an inductive specification.
□

We now show that the annotation method can be used for proving validity of specifications which are not inductive.

Example 7.15 A non-inductive valid specification
Consider again the program of the previous example. The specification language is interpreted on the domain of all terms and includes the

---
[9]The formula is built as $\beta_0(r_2) \to \gamma_0(r_2)$.

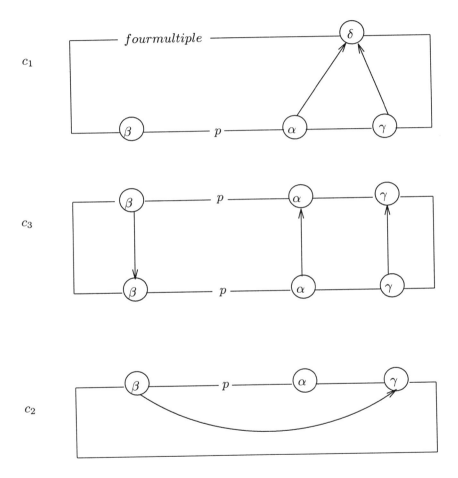

Figure 7.5
The logical dependency scheme of the program of Example 7.14 p. 353 (also
Example 4.9 p. 185)

unary predicate *ground* interpreted in the natural way as a groundness test for terms. Consider the specification $\langle S1, \mathcal{T} \rangle$ defined as follows:

$$S1_{fourmultiple} : ground(fourmultiple1),$$
$$S1_p : (ground(p_1) \wedge ground(p_3)) \rightarrow (ground(p_2) \wedge ground(p_4)).$$

The specification is clearly valid but it is not inductive since in the interpretation considered the verification condition for clause c_1:

$$((ground(zero) \wedge ground(H)) \rightarrow (ground(H) \wedge ground(K)))$$
$$\rightarrow ground(K)$$

is not satisfied. The verification conditions for the remaining clauses are satisfied.

We now consider an annotation Δ such that $S_\Delta = S1$ and we associate with it the logical dependency scheme of Figure 7.6.

The annotation is defined as follows:

$$\Delta_I(fourmultiple) : \emptyset, \Delta_S(fourmultiple) : \{\xi : S1_{fourmultiple}\}$$
$$\Delta_I(p) : \{\alpha, \gamma\}, \Delta_S(p) : \{\beta, \delta\}, \text{ where}$$
$$\alpha : ground(p_1), \beta : ground(p_2), \gamma : ground(p_3), \delta : ground(p_4).$$

It is easy to show that the annotation is sound for the LDS of Figure 7.6. The LDS is non-circular, as shown by the dotted lines.
□

The annotation of this example describes the groundness property of the proof trees and the LDS allows for its verification. This kind of groundness analysis can be automatized for the class of simple programs discussed in Section 5.2.3.

7.4   An extended example

The examples of the previous sections were used to illustrate the notions introduced and were therefore as simple as possible. The objective of this section is to illustrate potential practical usefulness of the annotation method as opposed to the induction method which could be rather seen as providing theoretical foundations for proving declarative properties of interpreted definite programs. For this purpose we have to present a more realistic example. The example chosen concerns correct-

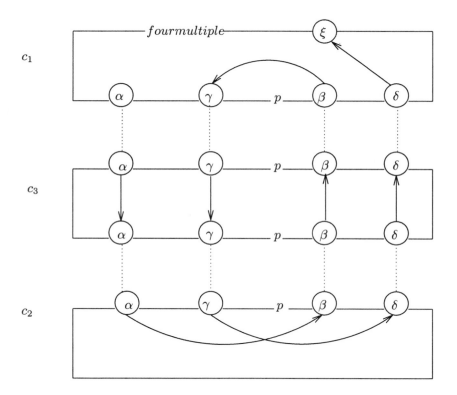

Figure 7.6
The annotation corresponding to a non-inductive specification (Example 7.15
p. 355)

ness of a compiler of a toy language. It illustrates also the versatility of logic programming in handling of symbol tables with partially known references.

The program, its specification and the correctness proof will be developed by stepwise refinement, starting from a context-free grammar describing the source language. The refinement steps consist in enriching predicates with new arguments and new assertions concerning: the source program, the symbol table, the addresses and the generated code. The program constructed corresponds to a DCG based on the initial context-free grammar. Some auxiliary predicates are used to describe manipulations of the symbol table. The proof of partial correctness of these additional predicates will be omitted as their specification is inductive and easy to prove.

7.4.1   The source language

The syntax of the language is defined by the following (ambiguous) context-free grammar G, with the nonterminal symbols *prog* (program), *li* (list of instructions), *lins* (labeled instruction) and *ins* instruction. The grammar abstracts from further details of the syntax by using "generic" terminal symbols *lab*, *ins*, *expr* which should be extended to specify the syntax of labels, instructions and expressions.

$$prog \rightarrow li$$
$$li \rightarrow li; li$$
$$li \rightarrow lins$$
$$lins \rightarrow \underline{lab} : ins$$
$$lins \rightarrow ins$$
$$ins \rightarrow \underline{ins}$$
$$ins \rightarrow \underline{if}\ expr\ \underline{thengoto}\ \underline{lab}$$

The following string *Prog0* belongs to the language $L(G)$:

$a : \underline{ins};\ \underline{if}\ expr\ \underline{thengoto}\ d;\ \underline{if}\ expr\ \underline{thengoto}\ a;\ \underline{d} : \underline{ins}$

Notice that some concrete terminal symbols are used as labels, instead of the generic label symbol of the grammar.

7.4.2   The idea of the compilation

The programs in the example language are sequences of possibly labeled instructions. Some of the instructions are conditional jumps. The purpose of the compiler is to number the consecutive instructions of a program starting from 1, to assign labels to numbers, and to replace the address labels of the jump instructions by corresponding numbers. Thus, the source instruction sequence is to be transformed into a list of the same length, whose elements are pairs or triples of the form [10]:

$[number, \underline{ins}]$ or $[number, \underline{expr}, number]$.

Such a compiler is a (partial) function, to be denoted *trans*. For the example source program *Prog0* we see that

$$trans(Prog0) = [[1, \underline{ins}], [2, \underline{expr}, 4], [3, \underline{expr}, 1], [4, \underline{ins}]]$$

In the annotation the function *trans* will be used as a binary relation.

The assignment of program labels to numbers can be represented as a list of label-number pairs, to be called the *label-table*. The label-table represents an assignment, so that every label of a program appears in the list exactly once. A list of label-number pairs with this property will be called *nonrepetitive*. The notion of label table can be extended to cover the case of programs including jumps to undefined labels. The undefined labels can be represented in the table as label-variable pairs. For example the source program:

$a : \underline{ins}; \; \underline{if} \; \underline{expr} \; \underline{thengoto} \, d; \; \underline{if} \; \underline{expr} \; \underline{thengoto} \, e$

gives rise to the label-table:

$[[a, 1], [d, X], [e, Y]]$.

Thus, we can define a partial function *table* from source programs to label-tables. The function is undefined on the programs with ambiguous labels, like e.g.

$a : \underline{ins}; \; a : \underline{ins}$.

Incremental construction of a label-table would involve checking whether a given pair is already included in the table and inserting it if it is not the case. The corresponding relation *incl* can be defined as

---

[10]Lists are denoted with usual Prolog syntax.

follows:

$$incl(T, I, T) \leftarrow isin(T, I)$$
$$incl(T, I, [I|T]) \leftarrow isnotin(T, I)$$

$$isin([I|T], I) \leftarrow$$
$$isin([I1|T], I2) \leftarrow isin(T, I2)$$

$$isnotin([], I) \leftarrow$$
$$isnotin([I1|T], I2) \leftarrow diffI(I1, I2), isnotin(T, I2)$$

$$diffI([E1, A1], [E2, A2]) \leftarrow diff(E1, E2)$$

Notice that the predicate $diff$ has no defining clauses. One may assume, that its definition consists of all unit clauses $diff(a, b) \leftarrow$ such that a and b are different labels in a source program.

The intuition behind the program can be formalized as a specification $\langle S, \mathcal{I} \rangle$ on a (many-sorted) specification language, where S is as follows:

$$S_{diff} : diff_1 \neq diff_2,$$
$$S_{diffI} : car(diffI_1) \neq car(diffI_2),$$
$$S_{isin} : \exists I \ I \in set(isin_1) \wedge I = isin_2,$$
$$S_{isnotin} : \neg(\exists I \ I \in set(isnotin_1) \wedge car(I) = car(isnotin_2)),$$
$$S_{incl} : \forall I \ I \in set(incl_3) \leftrightarrow (I \in set(incl_1) \vee I = incl_2).$$

The final program will use a system predicate is with two arguments whose sppecification is:
$$S_{is} : is_1 = value(is_2),$$

where $value$ is a function whose result is the value of the arithmetic expression given as argument.

The equality is interpreted as (many-sorted) identity on the domains. The function symbols are interpreted in the usual way: set transforms a list into the set consisting of the elements of the list, car returns the head of the list.

The example specification is inductive but not the strongest one. As the program gives no explicit typing of variables, correctness proof with respect to this specification should be complemented by well-typedness proof. This means that the specification should be augmented with

information about types. For example the ternary relation *incl* should
also satisfy the requirement that whenever the first component of its
element is a table and the second one is a label-number pair then the
third component is also a table. Such a requirement can be formalized as
an additional specification and then combined with the present one. In
this way we would be able to modularize the specification and its proof.
The proof of well-typedness of our toy compiler will be done separately
in Section 7.4.9.

7.4.3 The parser

We start development of our compiler by constructing a parser and
proving its correctness. The syntax of the language is defined by the
context-free grammar, which can be seen as a definite clause grammar.
The parser can be obtained by transformation of the grammar into a
definite program, as described in Section 3.2.2. The source program for
parsing is to be represented by a difference list in which each element
is a terminal symbol of the grammar. The transformation is defined by
the following cases.

- A grammatical rule of the form:

$$x \rightarrow t_1, t_2, \ldots, t_n$$

where $n \geq 0$ and t_i for $i = 1, \ldots, n$ is a terminal symbol gives rise to the
clause:

$$c_1: x([t1, \ldots, tn|L] - L) \leftarrow$$

- A grammatical rule of the form:

$$x_0 \rightarrow w_0 x_1 w_1 \ldots x_k w_k \ldots x_n w_n$$

where $n > 0, x_1, \ldots, x_n$ are nonterminal symbols and $w_0, \ldots, w_n$ are
terminal strings is transformed into the clause

$$c_2: x_0([w_0|L_0] - L_n) \leftarrow x_1(L_0 - [w_1|L_1]), \ldots, x_k(L_{k-1} - [w_k|L_k]), \ldots,$$
$$x_n(L_{n-1} - [w_n|L_n])$$

where $L_0, \ldots, L_n$ are distinct variables and $[w_k|L_k]$, for $0 \leq k \leq n$ stands
for $[t_1, \ldots, t_m|L_k]$ if $w_k = t_1 \ldots t_m$ for some terminal symbols $t_1, \ldots, t_m$
and for L_k if w_k is the empty string.

As discussed in Section 3.2.2, the intuition of this transformation is
to consider each nonterminal of the grammar as a predicate of a definite

program with the argument representing the terminal string derived. This observation can be formalized as a specification, which can be used for correctness proof.

Let X be a difference list with elements being terminal symbols of the grammar. Denote by $repr(X)$ the string represented by such a list. Hence the specification $\langle S1, \mathcal{I} \rangle$ formalizing the intuition includes the formulae

$$S1_x : x \to^+ repr(x_1)$$

for every nonterminal x of the grammar (i.e. for every predicate symbol of the DCG obtained by the transformation). It can be proved that the specification is inductive (hence a purely synthesized LDS is associated with assertion $S1$). The proof is analogous to the one presented in Section 3.2.2.

The specification is also complete. It follows from the one-one correspondence between the rules of the grammar and the clauses of the constructed program.

Notice that our correctness proof does not refer to our particular example but it is generic.

The application of the construction discussed above to our example grammar yields the following definite program $P1$ [11]:

$$prog(L) \leftarrow li(L)$$

$$li(L0 - L2) \leftarrow li(L0 - [;|L1]), li(L1 - L2)$$
$$li(L) \leftarrow lins(L)$$

$$lins([\underline{lab}, : |L0] - L1) \leftarrow ins(L0 - L1)$$
$$lins(L) \leftarrow ins(L)$$

$$ins([\underline{ins}|L] - L) \leftarrow$$
$$ins([\underline{if}, expr, thengoto, \underline{lab}|L] - L) \leftarrow$$

From now on we will enrich the "parser" with additional semantic arguments in a stepwise manner. For every refinement we will also introduce and prove correct new annotations formalizing the intuitions behind the refinement.

---

[11] Strictly speaking this program is obtained by a straightforward simplification of the program obtained by the construction: for example the first clause should read $prog(L0 - L1) \leftarrow li(L0 - L1)$

7.4.4   Adding an argument for the prefixes

The first refinement consists in introducing a new auxiliary argument which will be removed at the end. In the program $P1$ the argument of each predicate represents the terminal string derivable from the corresponding nonterminal. We now want to keep the information about the prefix preceding this string in the program. For this purpose a new argument is added to each predicate with except of *prog*. Since the nonterminal *prog* is the root of the parse trees, the terminal string derived from it has always empty prefix in the program derived. The prefix of a given string will be modelled by a difference list. This idea gives rise to the following definite program, denoted $P2$:

$$prog(M - L) \leftarrow li(M - M, M - L)$$

$$li(M - L0, L0 - L2) \leftarrow li(M - L0, L0 - [; |L1]), li(M - L1, L1 - L2)$$
$$li(M, L) \leftarrow lins(M, L)$$

$$lins(M - N, [\underline{lab}, : |L0] - L1) \leftarrow ins(M - L0, L0 - L1)$$
$$lins(M, L) \leftarrow ins(M, L)$$

$$ins(M, [\underline{ins}|L] - L) \leftarrow$$
$$ins(M, [\underline{if}, expr, thengoto, \underline{lab}|L] - L) \leftarrow$$

This idea can be generalized for arbitrary context-free grammar with a distinguished start nonterminal *axiom* (like *prog* in our example). Instead of the previously defined transformation to a DCG we have now the transformation defined by three cases:

- Every rule of the form $axiom \to x$ is transformed to the clause

  c_0': $axiom(M - L) \leftarrow x(M - M, M - L)$

- Every rule of the form $x \to w$, where w is a terminal string is transformed into the clause

  c_1': $x(M, [w|L] - L) \leftarrow,$

  where the notation $[w|L]$ is as in c_2 of the previous transformation.

- Every rule of the form

  $$x_0 \to w_0 x_1 w_1 \ldots x_k w_k \ldots x_n w_n$$

where $n > 0, x_1, \ldots, x_n$ are nonterminal symbols and $w_0, \ldots, w_n$ are terminal strings is transformed into the clause

$$c_2': x_0(M - N, [w_0|L_0] - L_n) \leftarrow x_1(M - L_0, L_0 - [w_1|L_1]), \ldots,$$
$$x_k(M - L_{k-1}, L_{k-1} - [w_k|L_k]), \ldots, x_n(M - L_{n-1}, L_{n-1} - [w_n|L_n]).$$

The first argument of a non-axiom predicate represents the prefix of the string derived, i.e. the string derived from the axiom to the left of the nonterminal x (or x_k in the rule c_2'). The second argument of every non-axiom predicate plays the same role as the first argument of this predicate in the program $P1$. Now we can formalize our intuition as two assertions associated with every nonterminal x different from *axiom*. The synthesized assertion is unchanged:

$S1_x : x \rightarrow^+ repr(x2)$.

The inherited assertion is:

$I1_x : \exists L\ cd(x_1, x_2, L) \wedge repr(x_1)$ is the prefix of x,

assuming that $x1$ and $x2$ are difference lists (proved in Section 7.4.9) and cd is the concatenation of difference lists defined as usual (see Example 7.7 p. 335).

For $x = axiom$ we have only the synthesized assertion. With this annotation we associate the logical dependency scheme shown in Figure 7.7: in the rule c_2', all output assertions $I1(k), k > 0$, depend on all input assertions $S1(k), k > 0$ and on the assertion $I1(0)$. $S1$ is purely synthesized.

The LDS of Figure 7.7 is non-circular. This can be proved by methods of Chapter 4: the indicator D_0 (Section 4.1) is a singleton with the empty relation, and the LDS is in normal form, hence it is non-circular.

We now discuss soundness of the annotation for the LDS. By the correctness of the specification based on $S1$ it suffices to check the verification conditions for the inherited assertion.

For the axiom rule (c_0') we have to check that

$$\exists L'\ cd(M - M, M - L, L') \wedge repr(M - M) \text{ is the prefix of } x.$$

This holds since $L' = M - L$ by definition of cd, and the prefix of the axiom is empty.

Axiom rule c_0'

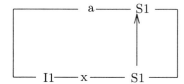

Terminal rule c_1'

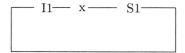

General rule c_2'

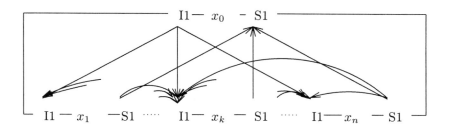

Figure 7.7
LDS for the clauses modelling prefixes (Section 7.4.4)

For the general rule c_2' we have the situation illustrated in Figure 7.8. Thus the verification condition for the inherited assertion of every nonterminal x_k is to be checked for $k = 1, \ldots, n$.

The hypotheses are

$I1(0)$: $\exists L^0 \, cd(M - N, [w_0|L_0] - L_n, L^0) \wedge repr(M - N)$ is the prefix of x and

$S1(j)$, $0 < j \leq n$: $x_j \rightarrow^+ repr(L_{j-1} - [w_i|L_i])$) (which implies $S1(0)$ has already been proved in the previous section).

The conclusions are:

$I1(k)$, $1 \leq k \leq n$: $\exists L^k \, cd(M - L_{k-1}, L_{k-1} - [w_k|L_k], L^k) \wedge repr(M - L_{k-1})$ is the prefix of x_k.

The conclusions follow from $L^k = M - [w_k|L_k]$ by definition of cd and by construction. Figure 7.8 shows the informations provided by the hypotheses and may facilitate proving the conlusions.

In this way we proved correctness of a general construction. The program $P2$ has been obtained from the example grammar by this construction and by the additional simplification used also in construction of P_1 (variables replace identical difference-lists). Adaptation of the logical dependency schemes to the case of $P2$ is straightforward.

7.4.5 Adding information about the number of instructions

According to our intention the number of instructions of the generated code equals the number of instructions in the source program. Thus the address of an instruction in the code is determined by the number of instructions in the prefix preceding this instruction in the program: the address of the first instruction of the code generated for a nonterminal x is $nbofins(x_1) + 1$. To avoid the explicit use of the first argument which will be removed later, we add two arguments to each nonterminal $x \in \{li, lins, ins\}$, which models the numbers of instructions. We now formalize our intuition by the following assertions:

$I2_x : x_3 = nbofins(repr(x_1)) + 1$
$S2_x : x_4 = nbofins(repr(x_1) \circ {}^{12} repr(x_2)) + 1$

---

[12]$\circ$ denotes binary functional concatenation of lists.

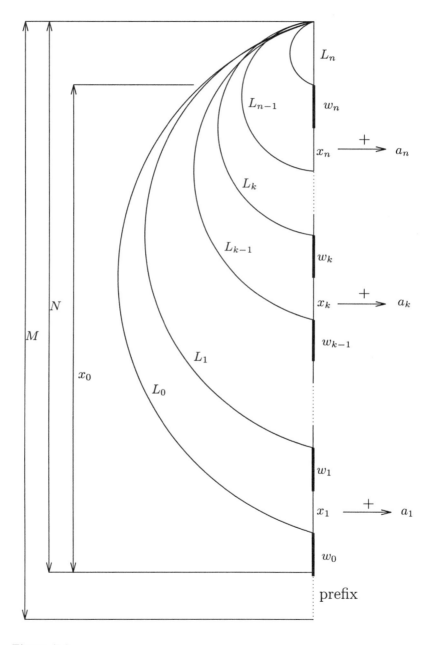

Figure 7.8
Proof of correctness of the transformation rule c_2' (Section 7.4.4)

for all $x \in \{li, lins, ins\}$.

The intuition is that x_3 denotes the address of the first instruction of the generated code for the nonterminal x (it is the number of instructions in its prefix plus 1).

In this way we obtain the following program $P3$ enriched with the additional arguments:

$$prog(M - L) \leftarrow li(M - M, M - L, 1, A2)$$

$$li(M - L0, L0 - L2, A1, A2) \leftarrow li(M - L0, L0 - [; |L1], A1, A3),$$
$$li(M - L1, L1 - L2, A3, A2)$$
$$li(M, L, A1, A2) \leftarrow lins(M, L, A1, A2)$$

$$lins(M - N, [\underline{lab},: |L0] - L1, A1, A2) \leftarrow ins(M - L0, L0 - L1, A1, A2)$$
$$lins(M, L, A1, A2) \leftarrow ins(M, L, A1, A2)$$

$$ins(M, [\underline{ins}|L] - L, A1, A2) \leftarrow A2 \ is \ A1 + 1$$
$$ins(M, [\underline{if}, \underline{expr}, \underline{thengoto}, \underline{lab}|L] - L, A1, A2) \leftarrow A2 \ is \ A1 + 1$$

The annotation is proven sound by checking the verification conditions for the dependency schemes of Figure 7.9.

Notice that, in the clauses c_4, c_5 and c_6, the LDS involves the annotation $I1$ introduced in the proof of program P_2. For example, in c_4 one needs $I1$ to know that $N = [\underline{lab},: |L0]$, thus $M - N$ has the same number of instructions as $M - L0$. This information is also needed for $S2$.

7.4.6 Adding a label-table

We now enrich the program $P3$ with a mechanism for label handling. For this two arguments are added to each nonterminal symbol with except of $prog$. Two additional assertions, one synthesized and one inherited specify these arguments: for a nonterminal x in $\{li, lins, ins\}$

$$I3_x : ltable(repr(x_1), x_5),$$
$$S3_x : ltable(repr(x_1) \circ repr(x_2), x_6),$$

where $ltable$ is a relation that holds between z and y iff z is a sequence of instructions and y is a list of pairs $\langle l, n \rangle$ such that l is a label in z and n is either the address of l in z or a distinct variable and y contains all and

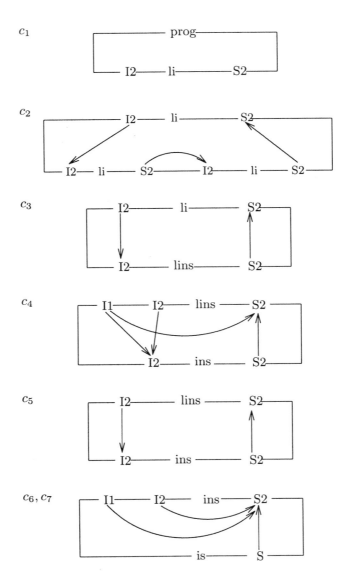

Figure 7.9
LDS for proving the correctness of the number of instruction definitions
(Section 7.4.5)

only the labels of z (it is called *non-repetitive*, see Section 7.4.9 where this property is proved). Informally, x_5 is the label-table corresponding to the prefix of x and x_6 to the prefix and the string derived from x.

Using two arguments instead of one makes it possible to describe symbol tables in a simple way without reference to a more complicated functions like merging of two label-tables.

The program $P4$ describing handling of label-tables is built by adding two extra arguments to every predicate (except *prog*) of the program $P3$.

$$prog(M - L) \leftarrow li(M - M, M - L, 1, A2, [], T2)$$

$$li(M - L0, L0 - L2, A1, A2, T1, T2) \leftarrow$$
$$\quad li(M - L0, L0 - [; |L1], A1, A3, T1, T3),$$
$$\quad li(M - L1, L1 - L2, A3, A2, T3, T2)$$
$$li(M, L, A1, A2, T1, T2) \leftarrow lins(M, L, A1, A2, T1, T2)$$

$$lins(M - N, [\underline{lab}^{13}, : |L0] - L1, A1, A2, T1, T2) \leftarrow$$
$$\quad incl(T1, [\underline{lab}^{13}, A1], T3),$$
$$\quad ins(M - L0, L0 - L1, A1, A2, T3, T2)$$
$$lins(M, L, A1, A2, T1, T2) \leftarrow ins(M, L, A1, A2, T1, T2)$$

$$ins(M, [\underline{ins}|L] - L, A1, A2, T, T) \leftarrow A2 \ is \ A1 + 1$$
$$ins(M, [\underline{if}, \underline{expr}, \underline{thengoto}, \underline{lab}^{13}|L] - L, A1, A2, T1, T2) \leftarrow$$
$$\quad A2 \ is \ A1 + 1, incl(T1, [\underline{lab}^{13}, X], T2)$$

The soundness of the annotation can be checked using the logical dependency schemes of Figure 7.10. It is a L-LDS.

7.4.7 Adding the generated code

In order to avoid the use of concatenation of lists, the generated code will be represented by a difference-list. Thus we will add one more argument specified by the following synthesized assertion:

$S4_x : repr(x_7) = trans(repr(x_2))$ for all $x \in \{prog, li, lins, ins\}$.

The new program $P5$ is the following:

---

[13]Labels must be the same in one clause.

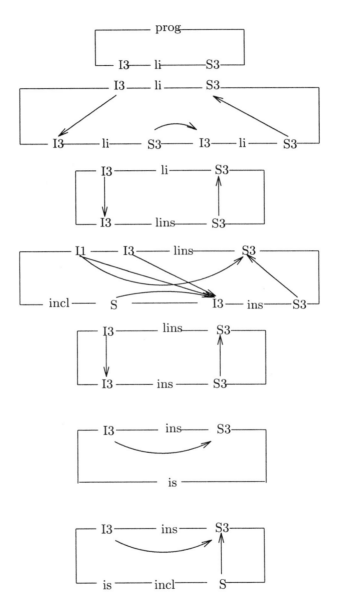

Figure 7.10
LDS for proving the correctness of the label-table definitions (Section 7.4.6)

$$prog(M - L, C) \leftarrow li(M - M, M - L, 1, A2, [], T2, C)$$

$$li(M - L0, L0 - L2, A1, A2, T1, T2, C1 - C3) \leftarrow$$
$$li(M - L0, L0 - [; |L1], A1, A3, T1, T3, C1 - C2),$$
$$li(M - L1, L1 - L2, A3, A2, T3, T2, C2 - C3)$$
$$li(M, L, A1, A2, T1, T2, C) \leftarrow lins(M, L, A1, A2, T1, T2, C)$$

$$lins(M - N, [\underline{lab}, : |L0] - L1, A1, A2, T1, T2, C) \leftarrow$$
$$incl(T1, [\underline{lab}, A1], T3),$$
$$ins(M - L0, L0 - L1, A1, A2, T3, T2, C)$$
$$lins(M, L, A1, A2, T1, T2, C) \leftarrow ins(M, L, A1, A2, T1, T2, C)$$

$$ins(M, [\underline{ins}|L] - L, A1, A2, T, T, [[A1, \underline{ins}]|C] - C) \leftarrow A2 \text{ is } A1 + 1$$
$$ins(M, [\underline{if}, expr, \underline{thengoto}, \underline{lab}|L] - L, A1, A2, T1, T2,$$
$$[[A1, expr, X]|C] - C)) \leftarrow$$
$$A2 \text{ is } A1 + 1, incl(T1, [\underline{lab}, X], T2)$$

The soundness of the annotation can be checked using the logical dependency schemes of Figure 7.11.

Note that a label in the generated code may remain a variable if it is not defined in the source program, and, if a label is defined twice (i.e. with different addresses), there will not be object code as in this case there exists no proof tree for $P5$.

7.4.8 Complete dependencies

We have completed development of the example program together with the following annotation:

The inherited assertions are given for every nonterminal $x \in \{li, lins, ins\}$.

$I1_x : \exists L\ cd(x_1, x_2, L) \wedge repr(x_1)$ is the prefix of x
$I2_x : x_3 = nbofins(repr(x_1)) + 1$
$I3_x : ltable(repr(x_1), x_5)$

The synthesized assertions are:

$S1_x : x \rightarrow^+ repr(x_2)$ for all $x \in \{prog, li, lins, ins\}$
$S2_x : x_4 = nbofins(repr(x_1) \circ repr(x_2)) + 1$ for all $x \in \{li, lins, ins\}$
$S3_x : ltable(repr(x_1) \circ repr(x_2), x_6)$ for all $x \in \{li, lins, ins\}$

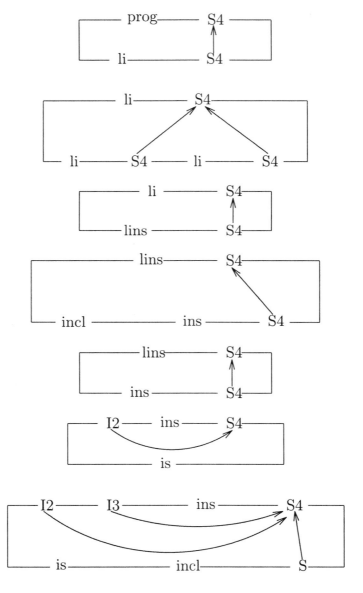

Figure 7.11
LDS for proving the correctness of the generated code definitions (Section 7.4.7)

$S4_x : repr(x_7) = trans(repr(x_2))$ for all $x \in \{prog, li, lins, ins\}$
$S_{diff} : diff_1 \neq diff_2$
$S_{diffI} : car(diffI_1) \neq car(diffI_2)$
$S_{isin} : \exists I\ I \in set(isin_1) \wedge I = isin_2$
$S_{isnotin} : \neg(\exists I\ I \in set(isnotin_1) \wedge car(I) = car(isnotin_2))$
$S_{incl} : \forall I\ I \in set(incl_3) \leftrightarrow (I \in set(incl_1) \vee I = incl_2)$
$S_{is} : is_1 = value(is_2)$

The logical dependency schemes are obtained by merging the previously considered dependency schemes. It is shown in Figure 7.12.

The annotation has been constructed in a modular way. Its soundness follows by the soundness of its components. The LDS is non-circular. Proving non-circularity of the merged LDS may be non-trivial. The sufficient conditions of Section 4.3 may be used to achieve this task by an automatic test. In the case of our example we note that every new introduced scheme was non-circular and used only the assertions introduced at the previous stages. This illustrates a modular approach to construction of non-circular dependency schemes.

We now notice that the first arguments of the predicates $li, lins$ and ins in $P5$ are not used for computation of number of instructions, symbol table or code associated with these predicates and we remove them. This results in the following final program $P6$:

$prog(L, C) \leftarrow li(L, 1, A2, [], T2, C)$

$li(L0 - L2, A1, A2, T1, T2, C1 - C3) \leftarrow$
$\qquad\qquad li(L0 - [; |L1], A1, A3, T1, T3, C1 - C2),$
$\qquad\qquad li(L1 - L2, A3, A2, T3, T2, C2 - C3)$
$li(L, A1, A2, T1, T2, C) \leftarrow lins(L, A1, A2, T1, T2, C)$

$lins([\underline{lab}, : |L0] - L1, A1, A2, T1, T2, C) \leftarrow$
$\qquad\qquad incl(T1, [\underline{lab}, A1], T3),$
$\qquad\qquad ins(L0 - L1, A1, A2, T3, T2, C)$
$lins(L, A1, A2, T1, T2, C) \leftarrow ins(L, A1, A2, T1, T2, C)$

$ins([\underline{ins}|L] - L, A1, A2, T, T, [[A1, \underline{ins}]|C] - C) \leftarrow A2\ is\ A1 + 1$
$ins([\underline{if}, expr, thengoto, \underline{lab}|L] - L, A1, A2, T1, T2,$
$\qquad\qquad\qquad\qquad [[A1, \underline{expr}, X]|C] - C)) \leftarrow$

$$A2 \ is \ A1 + 1, incl(T1, [\underline{lab}, X], T2)$$

By the validity of the annotation of $P5$, $S4_{prog}$ is a valid specification of $P6$, because $prog$ has no inherited attribute. It follows that the code generated by the compiler for a syntactically correct program p is defined by the function $trans$, i.e if $prog(p, c) \in DEN(P6)$ then $\mathcal{I} \models repr(p) = trans(repr(c))$.

7.4.9   Checking well-typedness

In the previous sections we informally discussed the form of the arguments of the predicates. We now formalize this as an annotation of the program $P6$, which can be seen as a specification of types of the predicates. The annotation method allows us to prove well-typedness of the program, i.e. to show that the arguments of the predicates in every proof tree of the program have the required form.

In the assertions we will use the following unary predicates:

- $atom(X)$ holds iff X is an integer or a sequence of characters,

- $item(X)$ holds iff X is a pair $\langle s, k \rangle$ where $atom(s)$ holds and k is either an integer or a variable,

- $itemlist(X)$ holds iff X is a list $[a_1, \ldots, a_n]$, $n \geq 0$ such that $item(a_i)$ holds for $i = 1, ..n$,

- $dlist(X)$ holds iff X is a difference list, i.e. a term of the form $l - p$, where l is a list $[a_1, \ldots, a_n]$ for some $n \geq 0$ and p is the list $[a_k, \ldots, a_n]$, tail of l, for some $1 \leq k \leq n$, or the empty list,

- $code(X)$ holds iff X is a list whose elements are pairs $\langle l, a \rangle$ or triples $\langle l, a, l' \rangle$, where l and l' are integers, a an instruction,

- $nonrepetitive(X)$ holds iff $itemlist(X)$ holds and for every two different items $\langle s, k \rangle$ and $\langle s', k' \rangle$ of the list s is different from s'.

The annotation includes the following assertions:

- The inherited assertions:

  $T1_x$: $itemlist(x_4) \wedge nonrepetitive(x_4)$ for $x \in \{li, lins, ins\}$

  $T3_{incl}$: $itemlist(incl_1) \wedge nonrepetitive(incl_1) \wedge item(incl_2)$

  $T4_x$: $itemlist(x_1) \wedge item(x_2)$, for $x \in \{isin, isnotin\}$

$T5_{diffI}$: $item(diffI_1) \land item(diffI_2)$

$T6_{diff}$: $atom(diff_1) \land atom(diff_2)$

$T7_x$: $integer(x_2)$, for $x \in \{li, lins, ins, is\}$

- The synthesized assertions:

$U1_x$: $dlist(x_1)$, for $x \in \{prog, li, lins, ins\}$

$U2_{prog}$: $dlist(prog_2) \land code(repr(prog_2))$

$U2_x$: $dlist(x_6) \land code(repr(x_6))$, for $x \in \{li, lins, ins\}$

$U3_x$: $itemlist(x_5) \land nonrepetitive(x_5)$, for $x \in \{li, lins, ins\}$

$U3_{incl}$: $itemlist(incl_3) \land nonrepetitive(incl_3)$

$U5_x$: $integer(x_3)$, for $x \in \{li, lins, ins, is\}$

$U6_{is}$: $integer(is_2) \rightarrow integer(is_1)$

The validity of the annotation can be checked using the dependency scheme of Figure 7.13: the LDS is non-circular and the annotation is sound for this LDS.

7.5   Discussion and bibliographical comments

A method similar to our iductive proof method was originally proposed by Clark [Cla79]. The method was formulated for proving the computational validity of specifications in classes of interpretations characterized by axioms. The method uses two kinds of induction:

- The *structural induction* in the sense of Burstall and Darlington [BD75]. This is an induction on the data structures defined by the axioms characterizing the class of interpretations.

- The *computational induction* in the sense of Manna [Man74], where the induction follows the steps of the computation and uses loop invariants.

In the case of logic programs with term interpretations the distinction between the two kinds of induction mentioned above may not be so sharp. If the data structures are described by definite programs, the structural induction may reduce to induction on proof trees. On the other hand, properties of the denotation of any definite program can also be proved by induction on proof trees. Finally, a computation of a definite program can be seen as construction of a proof tree. If the tree is

built bottom-up, the computational induction also reduces to induction
on proof trees.

The inductive proof method is also related to fixpoint induction (see
e.g. [BS69, Par69], or [LS87] for a tutorial presentation). This is a direct
consequence of the equivalence of the proof-theoretic semantics, denoted
by the set of the heads of the J-based proof trees $(PT_J(P))$, and the
fixpoint semantics, as $PT_J(P)$ is also the least fixpoint of the immediate
consequence operator $T_{P,J}$, where J is a preinterpretation for P.

For a given definite program P and a preinterpretation J of P, the J-
based models of P form a lattice with inclusion ordering. A specification
$\langle S, \mathcal{I} \rangle$ defines an $J_{\mathcal{I}}$-based interpretation $\mathcal{I}_S$ of P. On the other hand, the
operator $T_{P,J}$ is a continuous function on the lattice and its least fixpoint
defines the actual semantics of the program. The specification is valid
if the actual semantics is a subset of $\mathcal{I}_S$. By Park's theorem [Par69], to
show this it suffices to show that for every $i = 0, 1, \ldots, T_{P,J} \uparrow i \subseteq \mathcal{I}_S$. A
sufficient condition for that is the verification condition of the induction
method, which can be stated as $T_{P,J}(\mathcal{I}_S) \subseteq \mathcal{I}_S$. Thus, soundness of the
induction method can be seen as a corollary of Park's theorem.

The proof methods of this chapter require that a specification is given
with some interpretation. Extensions can be considered, when the interpretation is not given but only characterized by axioms. The proofs
constructed by such extended methods would concern validity with respect to every interpretation in the class of interpretations satisfying the
axioms. Such extended proof methods are discussed in [Der93], where
it is also shown that they are incomplete. Notice that the axioms may
be themselves definite clauses.

Hogger [Hog81, Hog84] uses definite clauses for specification of the
predicates defined by the program and also for characterizing the interpretation. For a set S of such axioms the correctness of a program P
with respect to S is stated by the condition $S \models P$, i.e. the clauses of
the program are to be logical consequences of the specification. This is
very similar to our inductive proof method: Theorem 7.1 p. 333 is a reformulation of the sufficient criterion given by Hogger, in this particular
case.

The same idea is used in [Hun90] to prove the equivalence of definite
programs. Assuming for simplicity that both programs define (in a different manner) the same predicate, then two programs P and P' are

equivalent (called *CAS equivalence*) iff $DEN(P) = DEN(P')$. One way
to obtain the result is to prove by some method that the denotation of
one program is a model of the other and conversely, i.e. $DEN(P) \models P'$
and $DEN(P') \models P$.

In Shapiro and Sterling's book [SS86] the inductive proof method
is used to validate specifications (computational validity) expressed on
Herbrand interpretations, but the method itself is not investigated.

Execution of a definite program is construction of a proof. Proof techniques used for that purpose may also be used for showing that a general
formula is a logical consequence of the completion of a given program,
or that it is valid in the denotation of the program. Several researchers
studied this idea. An early paper is [HS84]. Kanamori [Kan86, KS86]
explored extensively this idea. His work is restricted to definite pro-
grams and to formulae called S-formulae (of the form $\forall \bar{x} \exists \bar{y} F(\bar{x}, \bar{y})$. In
[Kan86] the *extended execution deduction rule*, which is an extension of
the SLDNF resolution, is defined and proved sound and, for a restriction
of the S-formulae, complete; i.e. given a DCP P and a S-formula F,
$COMP(P) \models F$ if and only if starting with F, the extended execution
deduction rules permit to derive the goal atom *true*. This deduction
rule is implemented in the system ARGUS [KFHM86] with the induction proof method which is used to prove S-formulae valid in $DEN(P)$.
A substantial contribution to this direction of research is the work of
Fribourg [Fri88, Fri90].

The first presentation of the annotation proof method appears in
[CD88] as a method for proving validity of specifications. The version of
the method described in this chapter allows also for proving properties
of internal labels in subsets of proof trees and some dynamic properties
of definite programs.

In Bossi and Cocco [BC89] an annotation based on a L-LDS is used to
prove partial correctness of *modules* w.r.t. a specification (computational
validity).

Finally observe that the results concerning the proof methods have
been obtained without any particular assumptions about the domains
of interpretations. They hold for term interpretations as well as for
non-term interpretations. This makes it possible to use the method
for functional extensions of logic programs, where the function symbols
represent functions different from term constructors, or constraint logic

programming. The method can also be extended to handle programs with some Prolog system predicates. For such predicates a given specification is assumed valid.

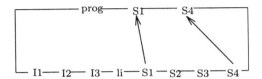

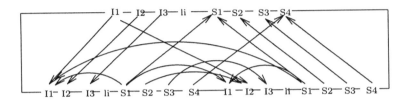

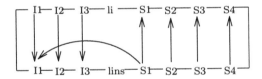

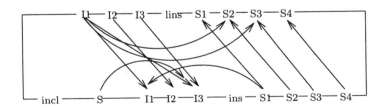

Figure 7.12
The merged LDS for the annotation used to prove the example compiler
(Section 7.4.8) (part1)

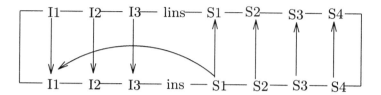

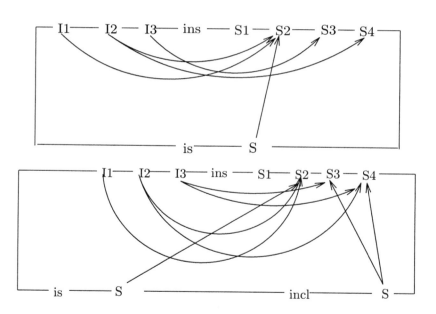

Figure 7.12

The merged LDS for the annotation used to prove the example compiler (Section 7.4.8) (part 2)

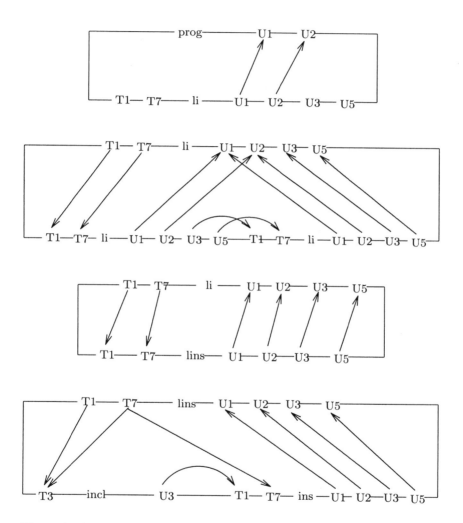

Figure 7.13
A sound LDS for proving the well-typedness of the compiler (Section 7.4.9) (part 1)

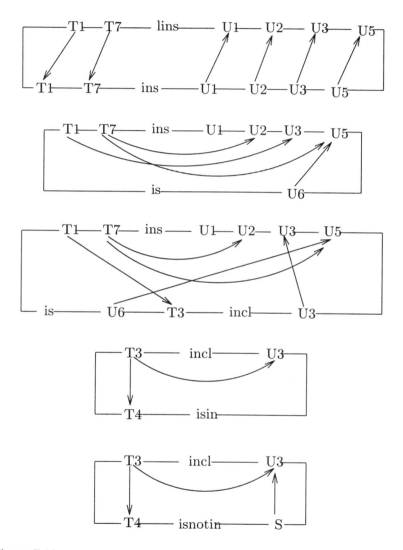

Figure 7.13

A sound logical dependency scheme for proving the well-typedness of the compiler
(Section 7.4.9) (part 2)

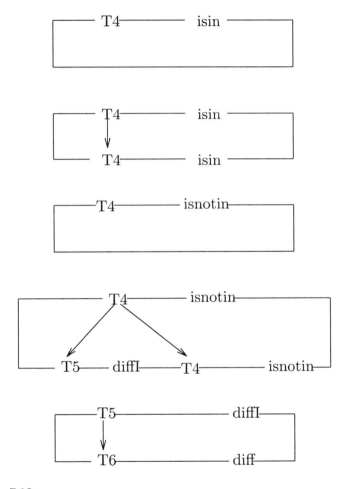

Figure 7.13

A sound logical dependency scheme for proving the well-typedness of the compiler (Section 7.4.9) (part 3)

8 The Occur-check Problem

This chapter discusses an important problem related to the use of unification in practical implementations of SLD-resolution. The unification algorithm of Section 1.6.3 constructs an mgu of a set of equations by nondeterministic application of a number of transformations and tests. One of the tests is called the *occur-check*. It checks whether a given equation is of the form $x = t$, where x is a variable and t is a term including x. Such an equation has no unifier and the positive occur-check terminates unification and reports the failure. For the efficiency reasons many Prolog systems implement unification without occur-check. Such algorithms may erroneously report success of unification for non-unifiable terms. This would lead to construction of unsound answers. Consider for example the goal $\leftarrow plus(zero, s(X), X)$ for the definite program describing addition in the usual way (see Example 5.1 p. 208). The first clause of the program is the fact $plus(zero, X, X) \leftarrow$. The attempt to unify the atom of the goal with the fact would normally fail by occur-check but may succeed if the occur-check is not included in the implementation. On the other hand, for many programs and goals the positive occur-check will never occur during the computation. For such programs and goals Prolog implementations without occur-check give correct answers. The question arises how to check that the computations of a program can be safely performed without occur-check. This chapter gives a precise statement of the problem, discusses its decidability and presents some solutions. The material concerning decidability assumes familiarity with some basic concepts of computability theory, as presented e.g. in [HU79]. However, this part of the chapter is relatively independent and can be skipped by the reader not interested in this aspect of the problem.

8.1 The problem

Our first objective is to formulate the problem in a rigorous way. The logic programming systems may implement unification in a different way. The design decisions may or may not influence the answer to the question whether a program can be safely executed without occur-check or not. Let us illustrate this by a number of examples.

- *Eager and lazy occur-check.* In a particular implementation the occur-check test may be performed as soon as an equation of the form $x = t$, where x is a variable, is selected for processing. Alternatively, the occur-check may be delayed until a normal form of the set of equations is reached, where no transformation is applicable (the algorithms of this kind apply special techniques for handling the equations to avoid looping on variable elimination). Clearly, if a unification algorithm of the second kind reports the positive occur-check for a set of equations then also any algorithm of the first kind will do that. Therefore we restrict our considerations to unification algorithms with eager occur-check.

- *The unification strategies.* The unification algorithm of Section 1.6.3 is nondeterministic. Its deterministic versions would use some fixed strategies for application of the transformation rules. This may influence the computations. Consider for example unification of the equation

  $f(X, g(X), X) = f(Y, Y, a)$. In the first step of unification it splits to the set of equations:

  $\{X = Y, \ g(X) = Y, \ X = a\}$. Considering the equations in the above textual ordering apply a rule or a test of the unification algorithm to the first possible equation. Following this strategy we get

  $\{X = Y, \ g(Y) = Y, \ Y = a\}$ and the positive occur-check in the next step.

  However, if in the next step the equation $Y = a$ is selected instead, we get $\{X = a, \ g(a) = a, \ Y = a\}$. Thus we obtain the disagreement $g(a) = a$ and the unification fails without application of the occur-check.

- *The resolution strategies.*

  The equations unified at every step of computation of a logic program depend on the resolution scheme used. Thus, with different resolution schemes, the computations of the same program may or may not use the occur-check. For example the goal clause $\leftarrow X = f(X), X = a$. executed by the SLD-resolution scheme with the standard computation rule fails with the positive occur-check. The same goal clause executed from right to left fails without using the occur-check. Another example is the following program:

  $\leftarrow p(a)$
  $p(X) \leftarrow q(X, X)$
  $q(X, f(X)) \leftarrow$

A top-down resolution scheme applied to the program would not employ any positive occur-check, but a bottom-up scheme would do.

Let us summarize the discussion. For efficiency reasons Prolog systems employ unification without occur-check. Generally this may lead to unsound behaviour. Soundness is guaranteed if positive occur-check cannot happen during computations of a given program. To avoid occur-check in run-time and preserve soundness one has to develop static tests for absence of positive occur-check during computations of a given program. Two approaches are possible:

- Finding dangerous points in the program where positive occur-check cannot be excluded by the analysis method, and re-introducing the occur-check at these points only. As the above examples show, such points depend on the particular unification strategy and on the resolution scheme used. In modern systems employing delays or parallel execution such analysis becomes very complicated, if at all possible.

- Identifying a class of programs for which the positive occur-check cannot happen regardless of the used resolution scheme.

The rest of the chapter presents the second approach.

8.2   The occur-check problem for a system of equations

This section defines the notion of a set of equations which is not subject to occur-check during unification. As discussed above, positive occur-check may depend on the used unification strategy. We want to characterize sets of equations such that the positive occur-check does not happen during unification, regardless of the strategy used. Thus, our considerations will be based on the nondeterministic unification algorithm of Section 1.6.3. We now recall this algorithm in a slightly changed formulation.

Definition 8.1 The unification algorithm
   Given a system of equations apply in any order one of the following rules:

a- *splitting*: if there is an equation of the form $f(t_1, \ldots, t_n) = f(t'_1, \ldots, t'_n)$, where $n \geq 0$, then replace it by the system of equations $\{t_1 = t'_1, \ldots, t_n = t'_n\}$, or suppress it if $n = 0$.

b- *identity removal*: if there is an equation of the form $X = X$, where X is a variable, then remove it.

c- *swapping*: if there is an equation of the form $t = X$, where X is a variable and t is a non-variable term, then replace it by the equation $X = t$.

d- *variable elimination*: if there is an equation of the form $X = t$ where (1) X is a variable and t a term in which the variable X does not occur, and (2) the variable X occurs in some other equation, then substitute in all other equations every occurrence of the variable X by the term t.

e- *disagreement*: if there is an equation of the form $f(s_1, \ldots, s_n) = g(t_1, \ldots, t_m)$, where f and g are different functors $(n, m \geq 0)$, then halt with *failure*.

f- *positive occur-check*: if there is an equation of the form $X = t$, where X is a variable and t is a non-variable term in which this variable occurs then halt with *failure*.

g- if none of the above rules applies, then halt with *success*.

□

Notice that the system of equations dealt with by the algorithm is a bag, not a set, i.e. two different equations may be the same. However such duplicate equations do not modify the unifier of the whole set. It has been shown in Section 1.6.3 that for a given set of equations E the algorithm always terminates, and if it terminates with success the remaining system of equations is an idempotent mgu of E.

Example 8.1

We show examples of the computations of the unification algorithm. The equations selected for application of a rule are indicated by the stars.

$^*f(X, Y) = f(g(Y), a)$
rule **a** $X = g(Y)$ $,^*$ $Y = a$
rule **d** $X = g(a)$, $Y = a$
rule **g** success

* $f(X, X, X) = f(Y, g(Y), a)$
rule **a** $X = Y$, $X = g(Y)$ $,^*$ $X = a$

rule **d** $a = Y$, * $a = g(Y)$
rule **e** failure (disagreement).

But the behaviour of the algorithm is not unique. Another computation is:

* $f(X, X, X) = f(Y, g(Y), a)$
rule **a** * $X = Y$, $X = g(Y)$, $X = a$
rule **d** $X = Y$, * $Y = g(Y)$, $Y = a$
rule **f** failure (positive occur-check).
□

Definition 8.2 NSTO, STO

A system of equations is *Not Subject To Occur-check* (NSTO) iff no computation of the unification algorithm includes an application of rule **f** (positive occur-check). A system of equations is *Subject To Occur-check* (STO) if it is not NSTO, i.e. iff there exists a computation of the unification algorithm including an application of rule **f**.
□

Notice that NSTO and STO are decidable properties of sets of equations. This follows by the termination of the unification algorithm. For a given set of equations every computation terminates. The number of possible computations is finite, since the original set of equations is finite, application of any rule to a finite set of equations gives a finite set of equations, and the algorithm consists of a finite number of rules. Thus, to check whether a given set of equations is NSTO it suffices to construct all computations of the unification algorithm. If one of them includes the positive occur-check, the set is STO, otherwise it is NSTO.

8.3   The occur-check problem for a program

As already illustrated by examples, the positive occur-check during the computation of a given Horn program may depend on the resolution scheme used. Our objective is to find classes of programs for which positive occur-check does not appear in any computation, regardless of the resolution scheme. This is formalized by the following definitions, where the notion of resolution scheme is as defined in Chapter 2.

Definition 8.3

A Horn program P is said to be *Not Subject To Occur-check* (NSTO) with respect to a resolution scheme $\mathcal{R}$ iff at any equation solving step of $\mathcal{R}$ applied to P the system of equations to be solved is NSTO.

A Horn program P is said to be *Subject To Occur-check* (STO) with respect to a resolution scheme $\mathcal{R}$ iff it is not NSTO with respect to $\mathcal{R}$.
□

Definition 8.4 NSTO programs and STO programs

A Horn program is said to be *Not Subject To Occur-check* (NSTO) iff it is NSTO with respect to any resolution scheme. It is said to be *Subject To Occur-check* (STO) iff it is STO with respect to some resolution scheme.
□

By the *occur-check problem* we mean the problem whether a given Horn program is NSTO or STO.

Remark 3 Equivalent definitions

To say that a program is NSTO is equivalent to say that it is NSTO w.r.t. the general resolution scheme.

A more important observation is that a program is NSTO iff *in every partial skeleton the system of the associated equations is NSTO*.

In fact, some resolution scheme may start with any partial skeleton and try to solve all the associated equations in one step. Hence this property.

Conversely, every step of a resolution scheme consists of solving a subset of the associated equations of a partial skeleton which may have been instantiated by some previous current unifier. So if, by hypothesis, the set of associated equations in the partial skeleton is NSTO, this step must be NSTO too.

Similarly, a program is STO iff *there exists a partial skeleton in which a subset of the associated equations is STO*.

This characterization of the NSTO/STO programs is used to obtain decidability results.

8.4   Undecidability of the occur-check problem for a program

This section presents some undecidability results related to the occur-check problem.

We first prove undecidability of the NSTO property with respect to the SLDT-resolution scheme. This result gives as an immediate corollary the undecidability of the NSTO property with respect to the SLD-resolution.

The theorem which follows can be obtained from a more general result presented in this section (Corollary 8.1 p. 402). However, we also give an independent proof. The objective is to demonstrate an encoding of Turing machines into Horn clauses which may be useful for proving undecidability of various dynamic properties of Horn programs executed by SLD-resolution with the standard strategy. Such properties include groundness of selected predicate arguments at call, and many others. The encoding is relatively simple and may also facilitate understanding of the more elaborate construction in the proof of Theorem 8.2 p. 396. For the definition and terminology concerning Turing machines the reader is referred to [HU79].

Theorem 8.1 [DM85b]
It is undecidable whether a program is NSTO (or STO) w.r.t. the SLDT-resolution scheme.
□

Proof. We describe a construction which for an arbitrary Turing machine M with two-way infinite tape gives a definite program C that "simulates" the computations of M by proof trees of C. The construction will be then augmented for relating the halting problem for Turing machines with the occur-check problem for a class of definite programs.

The construction goes as follows. Any instantaneous description of M is modelled by a ground term of the form $id(l, r, q)$, where l is a list describing the tape of M to the left of the head in reverse order, r is a list describing the tape of M to the right of the head, including the scanned symbol, and q is the actual state of M. Thus, the instantaneous description $abqcd$, where a, b, c, d are tape symbols and q is a state, will

be represented by the term $id([b,a],[c,d],q)$ [1]. It is assumed, as usual,
that the remaining cells of the infinite tape are empty. More precisely,
this means that they contain a special symbol, say for example $\sharp$. A
move of M in the state q for a scanned symbol x is determined by the
transition function; q is replaced by some q', x by some symbol x', and
the head may be moved one cell to the left or to the right. Thus, each
move can be represented by a pair of terms. The move to the left can
be represented by the pair:)) $\langle id([Z|L],[x|R],q), id(L,[Z,x'|R],q')\rangle$
    or by the pair:
$\langle id([],[x|R],q), id([],[\sharp,x'|R],q')\rangle$ if the tape to the left of the head is
empty.
    The move to the right can be represented by the pair:
$\langle id(L,[x,Z|R],q), id([x'|L],[Z|R],q')\rangle$
    or by the pair:
$\langle id(L,[x],q), id([x'|L],[\sharp],q')\rangle$ if the tape to the right of the head is
empty.
    Clearly, all moves of M can be represented by a finite set of pairs of
terms.
    The machine M, when started in some initial instantaneous descrip-
tion i_0, continues moving until it reaches a final state q_f (it may also
interrupt the computation if the next move is undefined). The result
of a successful computation is the final instantaneous description. To
simulate operation of M we introduce a ternary predicate *machine*. Its
intended interpretation is the relation on instantaneous descriptions defined as follows: $machine(i_1,i_2,i_3)$ holds iff the machine M when started
in i_1 reaches i_2 in one move and the computation terminates in i_3. The
computations are to be simulated by derivation trees. If the final state
q_f is reached by M, the derivation tree corresponding to the computation should be completed. This can be achieved by introducing the
clause
    (i) $machine(id(L,R,q_f),S,id(L,R,q_f)) \leftarrow$

    where L, R and S are variables. The remaining clauses of the program
correspond to the moves of the machine. For each move of M characterized by a pair $\langle a,b\rangle$ of terms, as discussed above, we introduce the
clause

---

[1]Lists are denoted with usual Prolog syntax.

(ii) $machine(a, b, F) \leftarrow machine(b, N, F)$

where N and F are variables not occurring in the terms a and b.
The program C consists of all clauses of type (i) and (ii).
To simulate computations of M we call C with the goal clause:
$\leftarrow machine(i_0, N, F)$
where i_0 is the ground term representing the initial instantaneous
description of the computation while N and F are variables.

It is easy to see that any derivation tree T with the root labeled by
such a goal clause has the following properties:

- Each of the nodes of T has at most one child.
- Let $T_0, T_1, \ldots, T_k$ be the sequence of subtrees of T such that $T_0 = T$ and
  T_{j+1} is the child subtree of T_j for $j = 0, 1, \ldots k-1$. Let a_j for $j = 1, \ldots, k$
  be the first argument of the head of T_j. Then a_j is a ground term representing an instantaneous description of M. Furthermore, $a_1 = i_0$ and
  for each $j = 1, \ldots, k - 1$, a_{j+1} represents the instantaneous description
  obtained by a move of M from the instantaneous description represented
  by a_j. Thus, the sequence $a_1, a_2, \ldots, a_k$ represents a computation of M.

It follows by these properties, that at every step of the SLDT-
resolution the equations to be solved are NSTO. Hence the program
is NSTO w.r.t. the SLDT-resolution, and also w.r.t. SLD-resolution.
Notice also that every terminating computation of M is represented by
a unique proof tree of C.

Consider now the definite program C' obtained from C by replacing
the clause (i) by the following clauses:

(iii) $machine(id(L, R, q_f), S, id(L, R, q_f)) \leftarrow equal(U, g(U))$

(iv) $equal(X, X) \leftarrow$

Call C' with the same goal clause g: $\leftarrow machine(i, N, F)$. Let T be
an incomplete derivation tree of this goal. Two cases are possible:

Case 1. The node atom of the only leaf of T is of the form
$machine(r, s, t)$. In this case T represents a sequence of consecutive
moves of M, as discussed above, and the set of equations associated
with the skeleton of T is not subject to occur-check.

Case 2. The node atom of the only leaf of T is of the form $equal(U, g(U))$ and any attempt to extend T produces a set of equations subject to occur-check. Notice that T represents a terminating computation of M in the sense discussed above. Notice also that any terminating computation of M can be represented by such a tree.

Thus, the Horn program $C' \bigcup \{g\}$ is subject to occur-check w.r.t. SLDT-resolution iff the machine M halts on the input determined by the goal clause g. If the problem whether a Horn program is STO w.r.t. SLDT-resolution were decidable, we could decide whether a given Turing machine halts on a given input, what is known to be undecidable. Hence the problem considered is undecidable.
□

The undecidability result obtained above concerns SLDT-resolution scheme. The following theorem states that also the general occur-check problem is undecidable.

Theorem 8.2
It is undecidable whether a program is NSTO (or STO).
□

Proof. By Remark 3 p. 392, the program describing the Turing machine used in the proof of Theorem 8.1 is STO. This is because the set of equations associated to the partial skeleton built with the two last clauses is STO. Hence another construction is needed for proving undecidability of the occur-check problem.

The construction used in this proof combines two independent ideas:

- A coding of Turing machine by definite programs, different from that discussed above.

- A property of a specific set of equations.

The construction produces a definite program simulating computations of a given Turing machine by the derivation trees of the program. The trees can be constructed by any resolution scheme. The program is NSTO iff for every skeleton the associated set of equations is NSTO. The construction makes it possible to reduce the halting problem of the Turing machine to the occur-check problem of the program. To achieve this, one has to be sure that an STO set of equations is produced whenever a terminating computation is simulated by the program and only in this case.

We first discuss the coding of Turing machines by definite programs used by the construction. We consider Turing machines with two-way infinite tape. Additionally we assume that the tape is never empty and that the nonempty portion of the tape is placed between the left end-marker l and the right end-marker r. The halting problem for this kind of Turing machine is still undecidable.

The machine is now coded as follows. An instantaneous description of the machine is represented by an atom of the form $q(left, right)$, where q is a state, $left$ and $right$ are lists of tape symbols. The list $left$ represents the nonempty portion of the tape to the left of the actual position of the head of the Turing machine. The symbols are placed on the list in the reverse order. The list $right$ represents the nonempty portion of the tape to the right of the actual position of the head. The first symbol of the list is that scanned by the head. The moves of the machine are described by the definite clauses of the following form [2].

Moves to the left:

$m1$: $q([Z|L], [x|R]) \leftarrow q'(L, [Z, x'|R])$ if x is different from l and r.

$m2$: $q([Z|L], [r|R]) \leftarrow q'(L, [Z, r])$ (R is for sake of generality. It will always be bound to the empty list in this case). Note that the read symbol is not modified in this move (x' is r).

$m3$: $q(L, [l|R]) \leftarrow q'(L, [l, x'|R])$ (similarly L will always be empty).

Moves to the right:

$m4$: $q(L, [x, Z|R]) \leftarrow q'([x'|L], [Z|R])$ if x is different from l and r.

$m5$: $q(L, [r|R]) \leftarrow q'([x'|L], [r])$

$m6$: $q(L, [l, Z|R]) \leftarrow q'([l], [Z|R])$ (L is empty in this case). Note also that the read symbol is not modified in this case.

The initial state of a computation is described by a goal clause of the form

$\leftarrow q_0(left, right)$, where q_0 is the initial state of the machine, while $left$ and $right$ represent the initial contents of the tape and the initial placement of the head; usually the head is initially placed at the left end of the nonempty portion of the tape, so that $left$ is the empty list.

---

[2]Lists are denoted with usual Prolog syntax.

For the final state of the Turing machine the following clauses (*final state facts*) are added: $q_f(L, [x, R]) \leftarrow$ for all symbols x of the alphabet including l and r.

Clearly, any proper skeleton represents a computation of the Turing machine. The final state facts make it possible to complete any proper skeleton representing a terminating computation. It is not difficult to see that the program constructed is NSTO, since all clause heads are linear[3].

We want to modify the construction in order to reduce the halting problem of Turing machine to the occur-check problem. Such a reduction will be based on the properties of the equation systems associated with the skeletons of the definite programs constructed.

Let us characterize first the systems of equations associated with skeletons of the programs constructed so far. Every equation associated with such a skeleton is of the form

$q(left, [s|right]) = q(left', [s'|right'])$

where s and s' are tape symbols or variables. Assume that the equations are solved in a top-down way starting from the equation associated with the goal. It can be shown by induction on the number of solved equations that in the next equation solved s and s' will be instantiated to tape symbols, and that a skeleton is not proper iff there is a disagreement of s and s' on some step of the equation solving. Clearly, the Turing machine halts on a given input iff there exists a proper complete skeletons of the constructed program starting with the goal clause representing the input.

We now modify the program constructed in order to reduce the halting problem of Turing machine to the occur-check problem. The modification employs a property of the following system of $n+1$ equations (where $n \geq 1$):

$$X_1 = U$$
$$X_2 = X_1$$
$$X_3 = X_2$$
$$\ldots$$
$$X_{n-1} = X_{n-2}$$
$$X_n = X_{n-1}$$

---

[3]This is a well-known sufficient condition for a program to be NSTO. It is formally stated by Proposition 8.3 p. 411.

$X_n = f(U)$.

This system is STO. But if one equation is removed or if one occurrence of X_n is replaced by a new variable which does not occur already in the equations, the system becomes NSTO. In the modified construction every complete proper skeleton will generate an STO system of equations of this kind. On the other hand, every incomplete proper skeleton will be NSTO since some of the above equations will be missing.

This idea is implemented by adding a variable argument to each tape symbol and an extra argument to each atom in the program. The new coding of the Turing machine is as follows:

The initial state of the computation is represented as a goal clause of the form

$\leftarrow q_0(left, [c(X)|right], f(X))$, where:

- *left* is a list representing the content of the nonempty portion of the tape to the left of the head of the machine; each occurrence of a tape symbol a on this list is represented by the term $a(Y)$ where Y is a variable different from other variables occurring in the goal.

- *right* is a list representing the content of the nonempty portion of the tape to the right of the head of the machine; each occurrence of a tape symbol b on this list is represented by the term $b(Z)$ where Z is a variable different from other variables occurring in the goal.

- c is the tape symbol scanned by the head and X is a variable different from all variables occurring in the terms *left* and *right*.

- $f(X)$ is the additional argument used to achieve the objectives of the construction.

For example, the initial state, where the string on the tape is abc and the head is scanning the first symbol of the string, will be represented (modulo renaming of the variables) as:

$\leftarrow q_0([l(Y)], [a(X), b(U), c(V), r(Z)], f(X))$.

The moves of the considered Turing machine are coded by clauses modifying the clauses of type $m1$-$m6$.

Moves to the left:
For every clause

$m1$: $q([Z|L], [x|R]) \leftarrow q'(L, [Z, x'|R])$
and for every tape symbol a different from r we introduce the clause:
$q([a(Y)|L], [x(X)|R], U) \leftarrow q'(L, [a(X), x'(Z)|R], U)$.

For every clause
$m2$: $q([Z|L], [r|R]) \leftarrow q'(L, [Z, r])$
and for every tape symbol a different from r,
we introduce the clause:
$q([a(Y)|L], [r(X)|R], U) \leftarrow q'(L, [a(X), r(Z)], U)$.

For every clause
$m3$: $q(L, [l|R]) \leftarrow q'(L, [l, x'|R])$
we introduce the clause:
$q(L, [l(X)|R], U) \leftarrow q'(L, [l(X), x'(Y)|R], U)$.

Moves to the right:
For every clause
$m4$: $q(L, [x, Z|R]) \leftarrow q'([x'|L], [Z|R])$
and for every tape symbol a different from l,
we introduce the clause:
$q(L, [x(X), a(Y)|R], U) \leftarrow q'([x'(Z)|L], [a(X)|R], U)$.

For every clause
$m5$: $q(L, [r|R]) \leftarrow q'([x'|L], [r])$,
we introduce the clause:
$q(L, [r(X)|R], U) \leftarrow q'([x'(Y)|L], [r(X)], U)$.

For every clause
$m6$: $q(L, [l, Z|R]) \leftarrow q'([l], [Z|R])$
and for every tape symbol a different from l,
we introduce the clause:
$q(L, [l(X), a(Y)|R], U) \leftarrow q'([l(Z)], [a(X)|R], U)$.

The final state: for every tape symbol a (including l and r),
we introduce the clause:
$q_f(L, [a(X)|R], X) \leftarrow$.

Consider the Horn program P consisting of all clauses defined above, including the goal clause. Let P' be the program obtained from P by removing the third argument of every atom. Notice that the heads of the clauses of P' are linear. Thus P' is NSTO, and the set of equations associated with any skeleton of P' is NSTO.

Let P_0 be the program describing the same Turing machine by the clauses of type $m1$-$m6$ according to the first construction (beginning of the proof). Every clause of P (and P') originates from one particular clause of P_0. Thus, every skeleton S of P (and the corresponding skeleton S' of P') can be linked to one particular skeleton S_0 of P_0. This mapping is many-to-one since one clause of P_0 gives rise to a finite number of clauses of P (and P').

Let S' be a proper skeleton. Then, by construction of P', S_0 must also be a proper skeleton. The derivation tree T' based on S' can be considered as a description of the computation of Turing machine represented by the decorated tree T_0 based on S_0. The difference is that every term representing a tape symbol s in T' is of the form $s(X)$, where X is a variable. It can be checked that for every step of the computation the representation of the symbol scanned by the head has in T' the same variable as its argument. It can also be proved that for every proper skeleton S of P the set of the skeletons of P' which are linked to S includes only one proper skeleton.

This allows us to conclude that there is one-one mapping between terminating computations of Turing machines and the proper complete skeletons of P'.

Let S' be a proper complete skeleton of P' and let S be the corresponding skeleton of P. The third arguments of the clause atoms of P give rise to the equations:

$f(X_0) = U_0$

$U_0 = U_1$

$\ldots$

$U_k = X_{k+1}$

where k is the depth of the complete skeleton. Notice that only the first and the last equations share variables with equations originating from the first two arguments of program atoms. On the other hand, as discussed above, the solution of the equations associated with the first two arguments will bind to each other all variables attached to the representations of the scanned symbols. This will give the equation $X_0 = X_{k+1}$. Hence the set of equations associated with every complete skeleton of P is STO.

Consider now any incomplete skeleton of P. As discussed above, the

equations associated with the first two arguments of program atoms are always NSTO. The only possibility to obtain an STO set of equations is thus related to equations originating from the third arguments of the atoms. As the skeleton is incomplete, the set of equation originating from the third arguments is a subset of the above considered set for a complete skeleton. This is not sufficient to obtain positive occur-check, thus the set of equations associated to any incomplete skeleton of P is NSTO. Consequently P is STO iff the Turing machine described by P halts on the input described by the goal clause. As the halting problem is undecidable, the occur-check problem must also be undecidable.
□

The proof was done by analysis of the properties of equations associated with the derivation trees of the programs describing given Turing machines. The assumption that the programs constructed are executed by some particular resolution scheme would not change the conclusions. Thus we obtain the following corollary, which is not an instance of Theorem 8.2 p. 396, but follows from the fact that the constructions of the proof apply as well to the case of any particular full resolution scheme.

Corollary 8.1
It is undecidable whether a program is NSTO w.r.t. a given resolution scheme.
□

Although the STO problem is undecidable, it is semi-decidable. This means that there exists an algorithm, which for a given program terminates with answer "yes", if the program is STO but does not terminate if the program is NSTO.

Proposition 8.1
It is semi-decidable whether a program is STO or whether a program is STO w.r.t. a given resolution scheme.
□

Proof. It is possible to construct an algorithm that enumerates all partial skeletons of a given program. For each constructed skeleton the associated set of equations is finite and it can be checked whether it is STO. The algorithm stops with "yes" after having found the first skeleton with such property. If the STO property with respect to a particular resolu-

program :

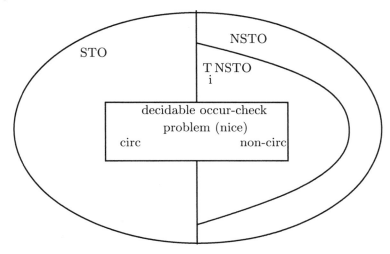

Figure 8.1
Decidable occur-check problem class

tion scheme is to be examined one has to apply this particular scheme
to the program in question. A positive occur check after a finite number
of steps results in termination with answer "yes".
□

The NSTO problem is undecidable. However, there exist subclasses
of definite programs for which the problem is decidable, as illustrated
by the following result.

Theorem 8.3
Let P be a program P for which there exists a nice d-assignment such
that in every clause of P all the output positions are non-variable terms.
The program P is NSTO iff the d-assignment is non-circular.
□

Proof. If there is a nice d-assignment with the required properties then
every equation associated to a skeleton has the form $X = t$, where t
is a non-variable term (or is a swapped version of such an equation).

Furthermore, the variable sides of all equations are distinct. This is
because the variables originate from the input positions of clauses. If two
of them originate from the same clause, they are distinct by the niceness
condition, otherwise by the fact that distinct clauses are standardized
by renaming.

The only transformations of the unification algorithm applicable to
such equations are *variable elimination* or *swapping*. These transformations follow the dependency relation of the ADS and lead to new sets of
equations of the same form. It follows that the positive occur-check case
does happen if and only if in some partial skeleton there is a circularity
in the dependency relation, i.e. iff the d-assignment is circular.
□

A program satisfies the conditions iff it is an image of an attribute
grammar without copy rules under the transformation defined in Section 5.4.1 (notice that a copy rule of the form $X = Y$, where X and
Y are variables can be replaced by the rule $X = id(Y)$, where id is
interpreted as the identity function). Hence the theorem reduces the
occur-check problem for this class of programs to the non-circularity
problem of attribute grammars, which is decidable but intrinsically exponential. However, as mentioned in Chapter 4, for practical attribute
grammars checking non-circularity is often not so expensive. There exist sub-categories of attribute grammars whose non-circularity can be
checked in polynomial time. This holds in particular when the condition of the theorem is restricted to nice L-d-assignments (corresponding
to an L-AG), which are non-circular by the definition. The existence
of such d-assignment can be decided polynomially (see the discussion in
Section 8.7).

Figure 8.1 summarizes the discussion. Each definite program is either
STO or NSTO but the properties are undecidable. They are however
decidable for a restricted class of nice programs, as indicated in the
figure. For these programs the occur-check problem reduces to the non-
circularity problem of the attribute dependency scheme defined by the
nice d-assignment. If the scheme is circular, the program is STO, otherwise it is NSTO. In the remaining sections of this chapter we will develop
a family of the sufficient conditions for a program to be NSTO (this is
illustrated in the figure by the subset T_i $NSTO$ of the NSTO area).

8.5   A sufficient NSTO condition for a system of equations

All the NSTO sufficient conditions will be based on a fundamental property of a system of equations. This section presents the property.

As discussed in Section 1.6,1, an *equation* is a pair of terms denoted
$t = t'$. The terms t and t' are called, respectively, the *left member* and
the *right member* of the equation.

Definition 8.5 Relations on equations

Let E be a system of equations. We denote by R_E the relation on E
defined as follows:

- For distinct equations e_1 and e_2 e_1 R_E e_2 iff a variable of the left member
  of e_1 has an occurrence in e_2.

- e_1 R_E e_1 iff a variable of the left member of e_1 has at least two occurrences in e_1.

□

We will also use the notation $e_1 \rightarrow e_2$ (or $e_1 \rightarrow_E e_2$ if one needs to
specify the system of equations) to denote e_1 R_E e_2.

For example, for the system of equations $\{e_1 : X = f(Y), e_2 : Z = f(X)\}$ one gets $e_1 \rightarrow e_2$. For the singleton systems $\{e_1 : f(X,X) = Y\}$
or $\{e_1 : f(X) = X\}$ the relation consists of the cycle $e_1 \rightarrow e_1$.

For a system of equations such that every left member is a variable,
the dependencies between the equations induced by the relation R_E indicate possible order of variable elimination. If the relation has no cycle,
the successive replacements produce equations having distinct variables
as left members. None of the produced equation has its left member
variable included in the right member. We now use this observation to
develop a sufficient condition for arbitrary sets of equations to be NSTO.

A positive occur-check during unification of a system of equations E
is caused by an equation in a system E' obtained by transformations of
E. This equation originates thus from some equations in E. Let e be
an equation in E. In the following cases no equation obtained from e by
transformations of the set E can give rise to positive occur-check:

- One of the members of e is a ground term.

- e is of the form $t = t$.

- The main function symbol of the left member of e is different from the main function symbol of the right member of e.

Notice that these conditions do not depend on E. Call a *candidate* equation, any equation satisfying none of the above conditions. We now define a sufficient NSTO condition for a set of equations. The idea is to analyze dependencies of the subset consisting of the candidate equations.

Definition 8.6

A system E of equations is *well-oriented* iff the relation R_E is cycle free. It is *safe* iff there exists an orientation of the equations such that it is well-oriented.
□

Theorem 8.4

If the set E_c of all candidate equations of a system E is safe then E is NSTO.
□

Proof. The property required by the theorem is that for a given set E of equations the subset E_c of candidate equations is safe. We prove that this property is an invariant of the transformations used by the unification algorithm. In other words, if E_c is safe and E' is obtained from E by application of one of the transformations then E'_c is safe.

First of all observe that a safe system of equations has no equation such that the rule **f** (*positive occur-check*) of the unification algorithm applies. On the other hand, as discussed above, transformations performed on non-candidate equations never generate equations to which rule **f** is applicable. Thus, it suffices to show that safeness is preserved when transforming candidate equations.

It remains to consider the two nontrivial transformations applied to a candidate equation: *splitting* (rule **a**) and *variable elimination* (rule **d**).

1. Rule **a**: An equation e in E is split into a number of equations $e_1, \ldots, e_n$, $n \geq 1$ to obtain the set E'. By the safeness assumption there is no cycle including e. Thus, in particular, the left member of e is linear and shares no variable with the right member. Otherwise we would have $e \to_E e$. It follows that for no $1 \geq i, j \geq n$ $e_i \to_{E'} e_j$. On the other hand, if, for

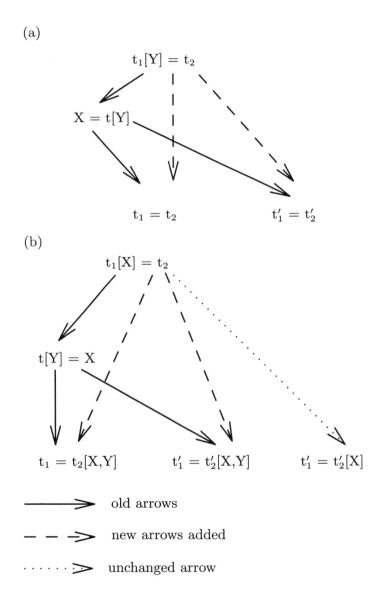

Figure 8.2
Modification in the arrows by performing reduction steps

some $1 \geq i \geq n$ and for some equation h, $h \to_{E'} e_i$ (or $e_i \to_{E'} h$) then $h \to_E e$ (or respectively $e \to_E h$). Intuitively this means that the new nodes are independent and the arcs connecting e with other equations of E are split to connect (some of) e_i's with the same equations. Such a splitting cannot introduce new cycles.

2. Rule **d**: An equation e of the form $X = t$, where the variable X does not occur in t, but occurs in some other equations of E is selected. The set E' is obtained from E by replacing all occurrences of X in $E - \{e\}$ by t.

   By the assumption E is safe, hence it is well-oriented under some orientation. We consider separately two cases:

   - The orientation of e is unchanged for the analysis, i.e. we consider the equation $X = t$. In this case X cannot occur in the left member of another candidate equation. Otherwise the candidate equations would not be well-oriented. By the same reason any variable Y of the right member of e can occur in the left member of only one equation. This situation is depicted in Figure 8.2(a). So the replacement of the variable X by a term in which Y occurs may introduce new arrows, but these arrows correspond to the closure of already existing paths (traversing e). Some arrows may disappear, as new non-candidate equations may appear. Hence the new candidate equations are safe.

   - The orientation of e is changed for the analysis, i.e. we consider the equation of the form $t = X$. The variable X can occur in the left member of only one equation, say e'. This situation is depicted in Figure 8.2(b). Analogous reasoning leads to the same result: the set of the candidate equations of E' is safe. The only difference concerns the arrows connecting e' with the equations having occurrences of X in their right members. Such arrows are preserved by the transformation.

   As the computation of the unification algorithm for the initial set E terminates after a finite number of steps with a set E_f which has a safe set of candidate equations, the positive occur-check cannot happen. Thus E is NSTO.
   □

   The following direct corollary gives a simple sufficient NSTO condition for a single equation.

Corollary 8.2

A pair of nonground terms with no common variable and such that one of them is linear is NSTO.

□

Recall that a term t is called linear iff each variable occurs in t at most once. Notice that the notion of safe system of equations is also related to linearity of terms: each equation in a safe system has a linear member which does not share variables with the other member. Furthermore, if the safe system is well oriented, all the left members are linear together, i.e. every variable appears at most once in at most one left member.

The condition of Theorem 8.4 is not necessary for a system of equations to be NSTO. For example the equation: $f(h(X), g(X), h(Z)) = f(Y, g(T), Y)$ is not safe but it is NSTO. The only transformation applicable to it is splitting. As a result one gets the system $\{Y = h(X), X = T, h(Z) = Y\}$ which is safe and well-oriented. This leads to the idea of weakening the NSTO condition by application of transformations to the original set of equations. However, one can only apply transformations preserving the STO property. Clearly if a system E of equations is NSTO, then the new system obtained after an arbitrary number of transformation steps is still NSTO (by definition). But if E is STO the new system may be NSTO (consider for example the system $\{X = f(X), X = a\}$). We now prove that the only transformation able to change an STO system to an NSTO system is variable elimination. We first prove a lemma.

Lemma 8.1

The STO property (hence the NSTO property) of a system of equations does not depend on the orientation of the equations.

□

Proof. It is sufficient to make the proof with one permuted equation. Let E be a system of equations such that the system $E' = E \cup \{t_1 = t_2\}$ is STO. We want to prove that the system $E'' = E \cup \{t_2 = t_1\}$ is also STO.

Since E' is STO there exists a sequence of transformations applied to E' giving systems $E'_1, \ldots, E'_n$ and such that an equation in E'_n is of the form $X = t$, where X is a variable occurring in t (positive occur-check).

Notice that there is one-one correspondence between the equations of E' and E''. If the variable elimination is not involved, the same transformations are applicable to the corresponding equations in E' and E'' and give the same results modulo swapping. Denote the longest sequence obtained in that way by $E_0'' = E'', E_1'', \ldots, E_k''$, where $0 \leq k \leq n$. Notice that for every $i = 1, \ldots k$ there is one-one correspondence between equations of E_i' and equations of E_i'' such that the corresponding equations are identical modulo swapping. Now, if $n = k$ then E_n'' includes an equation which gives directly positive occur-check. If $k < n$ then the transformation of E_k' is variable elimination using an equation of the form $X = t$. The corresponding equation of E_k'' may be of the form $t = X$ or $X = t$. Now applying swapping and variable elimination, or simply variable elimination, to E_k'' we obtain the system E_{k+1}'' which consists of the same equations as E_{k+1}', possibly swapped. The iteration of this construction gives a set E_n'' including an equation that gives directly positive occur-check. Hence E'' is STO.
□

The lemma allows us to prove the following refined sufficient condition for a system of equations to be NSTO.

Proposition 8.2 Sufficient NSTO condition refined
Let E' be a system of equations obtained from a system E by a finite number of transformations not including variable elimination. E is NSTO iff E' is NSTO.
□

Proof. If E is NSTO then E' is also NSTO by the definition of NSTO property.

Now it suffices to prove that STO property is invariant under any single transformation other than variable elimination that transforms E into a system E_1 assuming E has no equation corresponding to a positive occur-check. We consider each of them:

- *Identity removal*: if E is STO then E_1 must also be STO since the removed equation cannot lead to the positive occur-check.

- *Swapping*: The result follows by Lemma 8.1.

- *Splitting*: Let E be STO. Let e be an equation in E such that splitting is applicable to e and let E_1 be the system obtained from E by splitting *e.* We prove that E_1 is STO. Let E' be the system of equations obtained from E by a finite number of transformations and including an equation subject to direct positive occur-check. The equation e may or may not be selected by the transformations leading to E'. In the second case E_1 is clearly STO since the positive occur-check is obtained without involving e.

Consider now the case when e is involved in the transformations. The transformations that may affect e are variable elimination and splitting. If the transformations leading to E' affect e only by variable elimination then the transformed version of e does not contribute to the positive occur-check. In this case E_1 is clearly STO.

Assume now that some step of the transformation process leading to E' is splitting of e (or of its version obtained by variable elimination). Denote by E'' the intermediate system obtained in that way. Notice that all transformations before the splitting step originate from other equations than e. Thus, E'' could have been obtained by splitting e at the beginning and then applying the other transformations. In other words E_1 can be transformed to E''.

Thus E_1 is STO. This completes the proof.
□

8.6 Sufficient NSTO conditions for a program

We now present some sufficient conditions for programs to be NSTO. Corollary 8.2 implies that top-down resolution of a Horn program with linear heads of the clauses will never lead to a positive occur-check. We now prove that the same holds for any resolution scheme.

Proposition 8.3 Linear heads

A Horn program consisting of clauses with linear heads is NSTO.
□

Proof. Consider a partial standardized derivation tree such that $\langle c_n, \sigma_n \rangle$ is the instance name labelling a complete node n. For every non-root node n construct the equations $head_n \sigma_n = atom_{n'} \sigma_{n'}$, where $head_n$ is the head of the clause labelling n and $atom_{n'}$ is the appropriate body

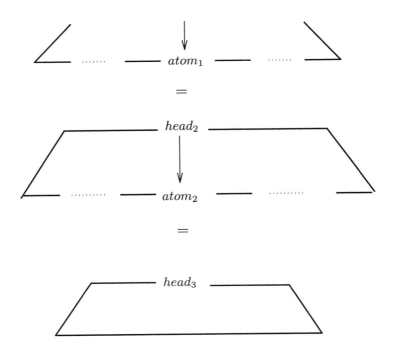

Figure 8.3
Well-oriented equations of a program with linear heads

atom of the clause labelling the parent n' of n. The system obtained in
that way is well-oriented if every $head_n$ is defined as the left member of
the equation. Thus it is NSTO. Notice that the system constructed is
very similar to that associated with a given skeleton by construction of
Section 2.1.3. The latter can be obtained from the former by applying
the splitting transformation to every equation. Hence also the latter
system is NSTO. Consequently, the program is NSTO, since any computation of any resolution scheme consists in solving the latter system
of equations. This situation is depicted in Figure 8.3.
□

The programs used in practice seldom satisfy the above condition.
A first refinement of the condition has been presented by the authors
in [DM85b] in the context of the SLD-resolution. They did not notice
at that time that the result was independent from the strategy. The

condition uses the following auxiliary notion.

Definition 8.7

A set of terms is said to be *co-linear* iff every term is linear and does not share variables with other terms in the set.

□

Theorem 8.5 First refined sufficient condition

A Horn program is NSTO if there exists a non-circular d-assignment such that in every clause all the input positions are co-linear.

□

Proof. We will prove that if the conditions are fulfilled, the equation system associated to any partial skeleton is safe. First of all notice that the equation system does not contain any equation of the form $X = X$ because of the "renaming" of the clauses used to build the proof trees.

Now consider all the nodes with the system of their associated equations. Only defined nodes with a parent node may have equations. Each member of an equation comes from a unique clause only. As the d-assignment is given, one member of every equation is an input position of a clause and the other member is an output position of another clause. Consider the orientation of the equations such that the left member of every equation is the member which is an input position of a clause. To conclude the proof one has to show that the system is well-oriented.

We show first that all left members of the system are co-linear. Two left members could share a variable only if they came from the same clause variant. But all left members originating from the same clause variant are input positions of the same clause. Hence they are co-linear by the condition imposed.

We now show that the system is non-circular. By definition of the relation on the equations, an arrow goes from the equation $t_1 = w_1$ to the equation $w_2 = t_2$ iff t_1 is an input position and t_2 is an output position of the same clause variant. This is because only subterms of the same clause variant may share a variable. This situation is shown in Figure 8.4. In other words, any arrow connects the equations whose members come from the same clause and are respectively input and output arguments sharing a variable. Consider now the ADS defined for the program with the given d-assignment, as discussed in Section 5.2.1. For

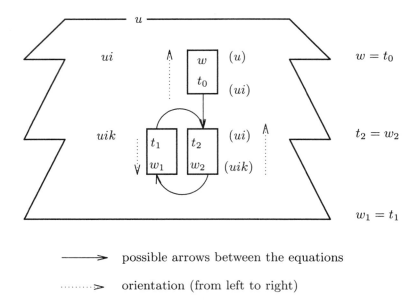

$\longrightarrow$ possible arrows between the equations

$\cdots\cdots\!\!>$ orientation (from left to right)

Figure 8.4
Well-oriented equations associated to a directed program skeleton. Variables of w, t_j, w_j are standardized respectively at nodes u, ui, uik.

a given skeleton there is one-one correspondence between the equations created and the attribute occurrences of the ADS. By the definition, the dependency relation on the equations corresponds to the dependency relation on the attribute occurrences defined by the ADS. As the ADS is non-circular, the dependency relation on the equations is well-formed.

This completes the proof.

$\square$

The head-linearity criterion can be viewed as a particular case of Theorem 8.5 . For a program with linear heads of all clauses and for the d-assignment in which all the arguments are inherited, the conditions of Theorem 8.5 are trivially satisfied.

Example 8.2

Consider the following program:

c_1: $\leftarrow conc(L, L, [A, B])$

c_2: $conc([], L, L) \leftarrow$

c_3: $conc([E|L_1], L_2, [E|L_3]) \leftarrow conc(L_1, L_2, L_3)$

The program is NSTO since the d-assignment

$conc \rightarrow \{\downarrow, \downarrow, \uparrow\}$

is non-circular and such that all input positions in every clause are co-linear (see Figure 8.5).

$\square$

Theorem 8.5 is too weak to show that the program of Example 8.2 with the new goal clause $\leftarrow conc([a, B|L], M, [B, N])$ is NSTO. This is caused by the two occurrences of the variable B which, under any d-assignment, cause the violation of the conditions of the theorem. We now define a family of refined NSTO tests based on Proposition 8.2 p. 410. The idea is to transform the equations matching head arguments to the body atom arguments before applying the well-formedness criterion. The transformations allowed will be the STO-preserving ones: splitting and removal of non-candidate equations. We first introduce some auxiliary notions.

Let e be an equation such that its members are atoms with the same predicate symbol.

Apply in any order the following transformations a finite number n of times:

- equation splitting,
- remove an equation having a ground member,
- remove an equation satisfying the disagreement test.

The system we get is called *reduced system* of e.

By the definition the members of every equation in the reduced systems are corresponding subterms of the members of e. To be more precise, consider an equation $t = t'$. If $r = r'$ is an equation of the reduced system then there exists a functor s such that $s(t)$ is r and $s(t')$ is r'. In this section we will denote position of a subterm in a term by indices in the form of natural numerals separated by points. For example, in the term $f(t_1, \ldots, t_n)$ the position of the subterm t_i is denoted by i and the position of the k-th direct subterm of t_i is denoted by $i.k$. Now one can characterize any reduced system E of e by a set of indices localizing the members of the equations of E in the members of e. Such

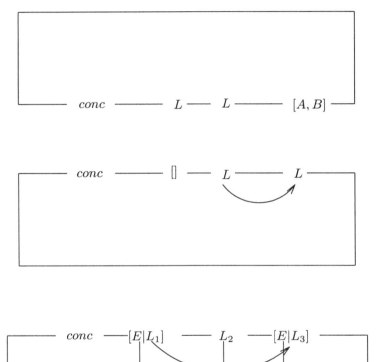

Figure 8.5
Relations between potential equations of Example 8.2 p. 414

a set of indices will be called *a set of attributes* of e. The root position is denoted 0.

We will only consider the following special cases of reduction:

- $n = 0$. The reduced set of e is the singleton $\{e\}$ and the set of attributes is $(\{0\})$.

- $n = 1$. The only applicable transformation is splitting. The reduced set of the equation $f(t_1, ..., t_n) = f(t'_1, ..., T'_n)$ is $\{t_1 = t'_1, ..., t_n = t'_n\}$ and the set of attributes is $\{1, ..., n\}$.

- n is the maximal number of applicable transformations. This case will be denoted $n = \omega$. The reduced set and the set of attributes depend on the original equation. Notice that in the reduced system one member of every equation is a variable while the other member is a nonground term. Notice also that the reduced system may be empty.

The corresponding set of attributes will be denoted 0-attributes, 1-attributes, ω-attributes.

Example 8.3

We will reduce the equation:

$p(X, g(X, a), h(X)) = p(Y, g(h(U), b), h(h(a)))$.

- For $n = 1$ we get the reduced system

$X = Y, \ g(X, a) = g(h(U), b), \ h(X) = h(h(a))$.

The set of attributes is $\{1, 2, 3\}$.

- For $n = \omega$ we get the reduced system:

$X = Y, \ X = h(U)$.

The attributes characterizing these equations are: $\{1, 2.1\}$.

□

The refined NSTO condition for a Horn program P will be formulated as application of Theorem 8.5 to the program P' obtained by transformation of P. The idea of the transformation is as follows. The derivation trees of P are obtained by pasting together clause skeletons of P and unifying the resulting equations. The condition for pasting together clause skeletons of some clauses c and c' is that the head of c' and some, say i-th body atom of c have the same predicate symbol. Clearly, for fixed c and i there may be many clauses c' satisfying this condition, and every such combination gives rise to a different equation. However, the number of combinations is finite. Thus all the cases of combining clause skeletons of P can be described by the context-free grammar G_P defined as follows:

Definition 8.8

Let P be a Horn program. We denote by G_P the context-free grammar such that:

- The terminal alphabet is empty.
- The nonterminal alphabet includes only the following elements:

  – All triples $\langle c, i, c' \rangle$ such that c and c' are clauses of P and the i-th body atom of c has the same predicate as the head of c'. They will be called *proper nonterminals* of the grammar.

  – If for some c (or c') there is no i and c' (no c and i) with the required property, then the alphabet includes the triple $\langle c, *, * \rangle$ ($\langle *, *, c' \rangle$). They will be called *improper nonterminals* of the grammar. The improper nonterminals originate from the predicates which either do not have defining clauses in P or are not used in the bodies, or from goal clauses.

- The set of production rules is defined as follows:

  Let c be a clause of P of the form whose body has n atoms ($n \geq 0$). A *rule generated by* c is any rule of the form:

  $$\langle c_0, i_0, c \rangle \rightarrow \langle c, i_1, c_1 \rangle, \ldots, \langle c, i_n, c_n \rangle$$

  where c_k, i_k for $k = 0, \ldots, n$ is any clause and any number such that the k-th triple is a nonterminal.

  □

By this definition every production rule of G_P corresponds to a clause skeleton of P but every clause skeleton may be represented by many production rules of G_P. The same holds for incomplete skeletons and incomplete parse trees.

We now define a Horn program P', whose clause skeletons are the production rules of G_P. Thus, the nonterminal symbols of G_P become the predicates of P'. We first define the arity of each predicate. The predicates obtained from the improper nonterminals are defined to be nullary. Consider a proper terminal $\langle c, i, c' \rangle$. Let $t_1 = t_1', \ldots, t_m = t_m'$ be a reduced sequence of equations obtained from the equation $t = t'$ where t is the i-th (renamed) body atom of c and t' is the (renamed) head of c', and the equations are ordered according to the top-down left to right traversal order of the terms[4]. By the definition of the reduced sequence each t_i is a subterm of t and each t_i' is a subterm of t, and $m \geq 0$.

For every production rule r of G_P we now construct a clause c_r of P'. This is done by augmenting every occurrence of a proper nonterminal $\langle c, i, c' \rangle$ in r with m arguments:

- If it is the head occurrence, the arguments are $t_1', \ldots, t_m'$.
- If it is a body occurrence, the arguments are $t_1, \ldots, t_m$.

The construction is thus defined as follows.

Definition 8.9

Let P be a Horn program. The Horn program P' consisting of all clauses c_r such that r is a production rule of G_P will be called a *derived* program of P.

□

Notice that the constructed program depends on the number of transformations used in the reduction process. In the sequel we will only consider the maximally reduced sets (ω-attributes).

We illustrate the construction by the following example:

Example 8.4

The Horn program P^5 is:

c_1: $\leftarrow conc([a, B|L], M, [B|N])$

c_2: $conc([], L, L) \leftarrow$

c_3: $conc([E|L_1], L_2, [E|L_3]) \leftarrow conc(L_1, L_2, L_3)$

We now construct the nonterminals of the grammar G_P. For every nonterminal we perform the ω-reduction of the corresponding equation and we characterize the result of this operation by the attributes.

---

[4]In principle any order can be used.
[5]The usual Prolog list notation is used.

$$\langle c_1, 1, c_2 \rangle \ \{2, 3\}$$
$$\langle c_1, 1, c_3 \rangle \ \{1.2, 2, 3.1, 3.2\}$$
$$\langle c_3, 1, c_2 \rangle \ \{2, 3\}$$
$$\langle c_3, 1, c_3 \rangle \ \{1, 2, 3\}$$

The rules of G_P are:

- From c_1:

$$\langle *, *, c_1 \rangle \rightarrow \langle c_1, 1, c_2 \rangle$$
$$\langle *, *, c_1 \rangle \rightarrow \langle c_1, 1, c_3 \rangle$$

- From c_2:

$$\langle c_3, 1, c_2 \rangle \rightarrow \varepsilon$$
$$\langle c_1, 1, c_2 \rangle \rightarrow \varepsilon$$

- From c_3:

$$\langle c_1, 1, c_3 \rangle \rightarrow \langle c_3, 1, c_2 \rangle$$
$$\langle c_1, 1, c_3 \rangle \rightarrow \langle c_3, 1, c_3 \rangle$$
$$\langle c_3, 1, c_3 \rangle \rightarrow \langle c_3, 1, c_2 \rangle$$
$$\langle c_3, 1, c_3 \rangle \rightarrow \langle c_3, 1, c_3 \rangle$$

We get thus the following derived program:

$$\langle *, *, c_1 \rangle \leftarrow \langle c_1, 1, c_2 \rangle (M, [B|N])$$
$$\langle *, *, c_1 \rangle \leftarrow \langle c_1, 1, c_3 \rangle ([B|L], M, B, N)$$
$$\langle c_3, 1, c_2 \rangle (L, L) \leftarrow$$
$$\langle c_1, 1, c_2 \rangle (L, L) \leftarrow$$
$$\langle c_1, 1, c_3 \rangle (L_1, L_2, E, L_3) \rightarrow \langle c_3, 1, c_2 \rangle (L_2, L_3)$$
$$\langle c_1, 1, c_3 \rangle (L_1, L_2, E, L_3) \rightarrow \langle c_3, 1, c_3 \rangle (L_1, L_2, L_3)$$
$$\langle c_3, 1, c_3 \rangle ([E|L_1], L_2, [E|L_3]) \rightarrow \langle c_3, 1, c_2 \rangle (L_2, L_3)$$
$$\langle c_3, 1, c_3 \rangle ([E|L_1], L_2, [E|L_3]) \rightarrow \langle c_3, 1, c_3 \rangle (L_1, L_2, L_3)$$

□

As already pointed out, and illustrated by the example, every production rule of G_P maps into a unique clause skeleton of P. Thus, every skeleton S' of P' maps into a unique skeleton of P. On the other hand for every skeleton S of P there exists a skeleton S' of P', such that S' maps into S. We now show the relation between the set of equations associated to the corresponding skeletons.

Proposition 8.4

Let P be a Horn program and let P' be its derived program. Let S be the skeleton of P corresponding to a skeleton S' of P'. Then the set of equations of $E(S')$ is the ω-reduced set of $E(S)$.
$\square$

Proof. The proof is done by induction on the number n of clause skeleton copies occurring in S.

Base case: $n = 1$. The corresponding sets $E(S)$ and $E(S')$ are empty. Thus the condition holds trivially.

Assume that the theorem holds for every S obtained by combination of n clause skeletons. Let S_1 be a skeleton obtained by grasping $n + 1$ clause skeletons. Thus there exist a skeleton S and a clause c such that S_1 is obtained by attaching the skeleton of c at some node u of S. Clearly, S is obtained by grasping n clause skeletons. The set of equations $E(S_1)$ consists thus from the equations of $E(S)$ and the equations $E(c)$ originating from c. The latter are obtained by splitting of an equation e such that,

- One member of e is the renamed head of c.

- The other member is a variant of an i-th body atom of a clause c_0 labelling a node of S.

Let S_1' be a skeleton of P' that maps into S_1. Clearly, S_1' is obtained by composition of a skeleton S' that maps into S with a skeleton of a clause c' originating from c. The clause skeleton of c' is attached to S' at the node corresponding to the node u of S. The system $E(S_1')$ consists of the equations of $E(S')$ and of the equations $E(c')$ obtained by attaching c' to S'. The new equations are obtained by splitting of an equation e', whose one member is the (renamed) i-th body atom of c_0' and the other is the (renamed) head of c'. By the construction, the predicate of the members of e' is $\langle c_0, i, c \rangle$ and the arguments of these predicates are obtained by ω-reduction of e. Hence $E(c')$ is the ω-reduced version of $E(c)$. By the induction hypothesis $E(S')$ is the ω-reduced version of $E(S)$. Hence, by the definition of ω-reduction $E(S_1')$ is the ω-reduced version of $E(S_1)$.

□

It follows that for every skeleton S of P if $E(S)$ is STO, then in the derived program any skeleton S' that maps to S must be STO. Consequently, if P is STO then the derived program of P is also STO. We can now apply Theorem 8.5 p. 413 to the derived program to obtain a sufficient NSTO condition for P.

Corollary 8.3

A Horn program P is NSTO iff there exists a non-circular d-assignment such that in every clause of its derived program P' all the input positions are co-linear.

□

We illustrate application of the condition by an example.

Example 8.5

Consider the program of Example 8.4 . For the following d-assignment the input positions of every clause of the derived program (constructed in Example 8.4) are co-linear.

$$\langle c_1, 1, c_2 \rangle \ \{ \downarrow, \uparrow \}$$
$$\langle c_1, 1, c_3 \rangle \ \{ \downarrow, \downarrow, \uparrow, \uparrow \}$$
$$\langle c_3, 1, c_2 \rangle \ \{ \downarrow, \uparrow \}$$
$$\langle c_3, 1, c_3 \rangle \ \{ \downarrow, \downarrow, \uparrow \}$$

The local dependency relations are shown in Figure 8.6. It can be shown that the d-assignment is non-circular. Hence the program is NSTO.

□

In this section we formulated three conditions for a program to be NSTO. All of them can be seen as special cases of the same technique based on checking co-linearity of input attribute occurrences under a non-circular d-assignment for a transformed version of the program. In the base case 0-attributes are used and the considered d-assignment has only inherited positions. Thus, non-circularity is achieved in a trivial

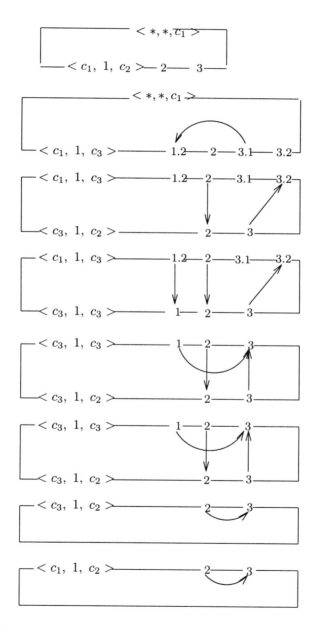

Figure 8.6
Well-founded relation between potential equations of Example 8.4 p. 419

way and the co-linearity condition reduces to the head linearity of every clause. The first refinement is to use 1-attributes and to search for a d-assignment satisfying input co-linearity. The second refinement is to use ω-attributes. For this a substantial transformation of the program is needed and a search for d-assignment satisfying input co-linearity of the transformed program.

8.7 Discussion

8.7.1 Complexity

In the section 8.3 we suggested that most of the interesting NSTO tests must be of exponential complexity, hence intractable in general. In fact it is easy to observe the increasing complexity of the test each time a new refinement is introduced: linearity of the heads has a linear complexity in the size of the program. The test using simply the arguments has two exponential factors (the number of d-assignments to be tried and the non-circularity test). The last improvement has a third exponential factor (the number of rules in the constructed grammar). Notice also that the two last tests contain the non-circularity test of attribute grammar, hence they are intrinsically exponential.

There are many ways to overcome these limits, but at the cost of a reduction of the power of the tests. A way to reduce the first factor consists in choosing arbitrarily one d-assignment only. There exists polynomial algorithms to find a d-assignment such that all input positions are co-linear in all clauses of the derived program [Bou92b]. The second factor can be reduced by considering simply subclasses of ADS. For example they can be restricted to strongly non-circular ADS which is the largest class which can be tested polynomially. Although some simplifications are possible we do not know how to reduce the worst complexity of the last factor.

8.7.2 Improving the NSTO test

We have presented a well known NSTO condition with two refinements (to be referred to in the following discussion as C_0, C_1 and C_ω). The question arises how large are the classes of NSTO programs satisfying the conditions (the classes are obviously strictly increasing).

The first condition C_0 (linearity of the heads) is satisfied by most of the

clauses in most of the programs. But violation of the condition even by
one clause makes the test inapplicable to a given program. Elimination
of non-linearity by flattening is not a remedy, since the definition of
equality is itself a non-linear fact ($X = X \leftarrow$).

Some experiments show that the class of NSTO programs defined by
the last condition C_ω is significantly larger than the one defined by the
condition C_0 [Tég90].

Further refinement of the test C_ω seems difficult to achieve. This is
because ω-reduction seems to be the limit of the transformations preserving STO property. An improvement could be achieved by transformations based on variable elimination. But this requires assumptions
on the resolution and/or unification strategies. As already illustrated
by examples, application of variable elimination may change an STO
system into an NSTO system.

Another kind of refinement has been considered in [Tég90]. Programs
including only variables and constants are NSTO: there is no compound
term, hence positive occur-check is not possible. This observation shows
that also in other programs cycles involving variables only can be ignored
in the NSTO tests.

The notion of multi d-assignment of Section 5.2.4 can also be used
for refinement of the NSTO tests. The transformation of the program
connected with a multi d-assignment may result in an equivalent program to which our tests are applicable. This, however, introduces a new
exponential factor.

The proposed tests are based on the concepts of co-linearity and non-
circularity. Both properties are required by the sufficient tests. However,
some NSTO programs do not satisfy the properties. For example the
following NSTO program (as well as its derived program) does not have
co-linear input positions under any multi d-assignment.

$$p(f(X), f(X)) \leftarrow p(X, X)$$
$$p(a, a) \leftarrow$$

For some other programs the non-circularity cannot be reached (although for some d-assignment the input positions are co-linear). An
example is the following NSTO program:

$$\leftarrow p(X, X)$$

$$p(X,Y) \leftarrow p(X,Y)$$
$$p(f(X), f(X)) \leftarrow$$

The co-linearity is the most restrictive criterion. Indeed any non-circular d-assignment makes the equations non-circular in any skeleton, but seldom satisfies the input co-linearity condition for all clauses.

8.7.3 Comparison with tests based on abstract interpretations

The literature on the occur-check problems presents many NSTO tests based on abstract interpretation or partial evaluation [Pla84, Søn86, Cor89, Cod89]. All of them assume some resolution scheme (usually the standard SLD-resolution) and use an abstract representation of the effects of the unification (some abstract representation of the solutions of a system of equations). These tests are incomparable with ours. The reason is that the problems studied are different. Clearly, an NSTO program in our sense is also NSTO with respect to any given resolution scheme, but not necessarily vice-versa. Figure 8.7 may help to understand this point. The set of all NSTO programs (denoted NSTO) is, as illustrated by the examples in this chapter, properly included in the set of programs which are NSTO w.r.t. some fixed resolution scheme (e.g. RS1 or RS2). A test proposed for a given strategy identifies a proper (by the undecidability results) subset of such programs, possibly including also some, NSTO programs. The best test we proposed (denoted in the figure $T_\omega NSTO$) identifies a proper subset of NSTO programs.

The tests based on a specific resolution scheme may analyze also the execution of the variable-elimination step of the unification, thus may collect more information about the actual form of arguments during computation. Therefore, one could expect existence of tests which subsume the methods presented here, i.e. that $T_\omega NSTO$ may be also included into some set "TNSTO w.r.t. RS2". The existing tests based on SLD-resolution are usually not comparable with our tests. For example, it can be checked by our second method that the following program is $NSTO$ but the test of [Cor89] fails to show that it is NSTO w.r.t. SLD-resolution:

$$\leftarrow p(X, Z, Y), q(X, Y)$$
$$p(A, f(A, B), B) \leftarrow$$

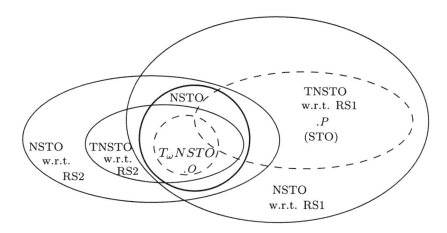

Figure 8.7
Comparison of the approaches

$$q(X, X) \leftarrow$$

Nevertheless there are reasons to believe that some improved method based on abstract interpretation could detect this.

8.7.4 Comparison with other work based on d-assignments

The papers [AP92b] propose tests for NSTO w.r.t. SLD-resolution using a technique based on a similar to ours dependency analysis, but with a different terminology.

In [AP92b] three classes of directed Horn programs are defined: well-moded, nicely moded and strictly moded programs.

A *well-moded program* is, in the terminology of this book, a directed program with a simple, L- d-assignment. It is called simple in [Dra87] and also well-moded in [Ros90] where this terminology is introduced. The work [Dra87] has been discussed in Section 5.2.3. We pointed out that for any directed program with a simple and non-circular d-assignment resolution without occur-check is sound but may not terminate in some cases when it would terminate with occur-check. However, such programs may not be NSTO, even in the case of a top-down strategy. The test of [AP92b] for a program to be NSTO w.r.t. the SLD-resolution requires that the program is well-moded and all the synthesized positions of the head of the clauses are co-linear (thus, as the input positions of the chosen atom at each step of the SLD-resolution are ground, the equation to be solved is trivially NSTO). Notice that not all programs can be well-moded.

A *nicely moded* program [AP92b] is a directed program with an L-d-assignment which furthermore satisfies the following property: all the input terms (called "output" in [AP92b]) in the body of the clauses (hence also in a goal) are co-linear and do not share any variable with the input terms of the head. In that case if additionally the input positions of the heads are co-linear, the program fulfills the second condition of Corollary 8.3 p. 422 and is NSTO (hence, in particular it is NSTO w.r.t. the SLD-resolution). Notice that all programs are nicely moded under a purely inherited d-assignment. But there exist better d-assignments. It is easy to find polynomial algorithms which compute such better d-assignments.

A *strictly moded* program is a directed program with a simple, L-d-assignment (well-moded) such that all the input terms of the body of the clauses are co-linear. Thus, in any clause a variable of an input position of the body may occur only in an output position of another body atom or of the head. A simple induction on the resolution steps shows that the synthesized positions of the goal atom chosen for resolution are co-linear. On the other hand, the inherited positions of the head of every clause are co-linear. Hence unification of the chosen atom with the head of a renamed clause is trivially NSTO. A strictly moded program is thus NSTO w.r.t. the standard SLD-resolution.

It turns out that the above tests are often sufficient for the programs published in the literature. For example, as demonstrated in [AP92a], they are sufficient to show the NSTO property w.r.t. the standard SLD-resolution for all but two of the programs in the textbook [SS86]. The same paper gives also an interesting example of logic program where the use of occur-check is essential for proper solution of the typing problem for λ-expressions.

8.7.5   Towards insertion of occur-check points

In practice it may be convenient to have programs which are STO w.r.t. the used resolution scheme. On the other hand, the complexity of a test which can show that a program is NSTO w.r.t. a given resolution scheme may be prohibitive. A practical solution would be thus to perform occur-

check only at some steps of resolution and to skip it whenever it is known
that the actual arguments of unification are NSTO.

In the case of a top-down resolution scheme (the SLD-resolution is
a particular, but not only, case) Corollary 8.2 p. 409 gives an obvious
solution: perform occur-check only if the clause used has a non-linear
head. As most of the programs have most of their heads linear and
are interpreted with a top down strategy, one may expect that such
a solution is satisfactory in most of the cases. The following simple
transformation techniques may allow for separation and minimization
of the number of occur-checks. If a variable occurs n times in the head
of a clause (except the unit-clause defining the identity), replace $n - 1$
occurrences by new variables not occurring in the clause, say X replaced
by X_i (hence the head become linear) and add in the body of the clause
$n - 1$ additional atoms of the form $X = X_i$. The equality is supposed
to be defined by the unit clause $X = X \leftarrow$. In the transformed program
occur-check is needed only when resolving the equalities.

The non-linearity criterion for insertion of occur-check can be combined with the concepts of moding discussed above. In the standard
SLD-resolution the resolvents of a strictly moded program are strictly
moded, regardless of the unification algorithm used. The same holds for
nice moding. Hence in the case of nicely moded programs it is sufficient
to perform occur-check when using a clause with non-co-linear inherited
positions of the head. Also in this case restoring co-linearity of these
positions by introduction additional equalities in the body is possible.
The transformation techniques used in our refined NSTO test, as the
use of d-assignment, can be applied and may lead to minimization of
the number of occur-checks as well.

The problem of insertion of the occur-checks into compiled logic programs should be studied in connection with the compilation techniques
used. For example, compilers based on the Warren Abstract Machine
collect some information about groundness, distinguish between occurrences of the same variable, etc. As discussed in [Bee88] this kind of
information already present in WAM can be used to avoid some unnecessary occur-checks.

The concepts used in our NSTO tests are applied in [Dum92] for combining resolution schemes and occur-check tests. This paper introduces
a notion of *partially NSTO* system of equations. It is a system S partitioned into two subsystems S_1 and S_2. In S_1 equations are unified with

occur-check, in S_2 without occur-check. A partial order on the equations is considered which formalizes the strategy used for equation solving in the resolution scheme. A compatibility condition on this order is introduced to guarantee sound unification of S. The compatibility condition applies the notion of ω-reduction discussed in this chapter. Our NSTO conditions can be seen as a particular case of this technique, where S_1 is empty ($S = S_2$). The paper gives a conceptual framework for studying various criteria for NSTO w.r.t. arbitrary resolution schemes. For example, consider nicely-moded programs. For every skeleton of such a program take as S_1 the equations originating from the nodes labeled by clauses with non-co-linear input positions, and as S_2 the equations originating from the other nodes. The ordering of equation solving imposed by the standard SLD-resolution fulfills then the compatibility condition.

The approaches to the occur-check problem based on the abstract interpretation techniques are also designed with the purpose of including sufficient occur-checks in the analyzed programs [Søn86, Cor89, Cod89].

Thus, there exists a broad spectrum of methods which make it possible either to show that a program is NSTO or NSTO w.r.t. a given resolution scheme, or to identify program points where the occur-check can be omitted without violating soundness of the resolution scheme.

Bibliography

[AB90]   K. R. Apt and M. Bezem. Acyclic programs. In Warren
           and Szeredi [WS90], pages 617–633.

[ABK89]   K. R. Apt, R. N. Bol, and J. W. Klop. On the safe ter-
           mination of Prolog programs. In G. Levi and M. Martelli,
           editors, *Proceedings of the Sixth International Conference
           on Logic Programming*, pages 353–368, Lisbon, 1989. The
           MIT Press.

[ACG92]   I. Attali, J. Chazarain, and S. Gilette. Incremental eval-
           uation of natural semantics specifications. In Wirsing and
           Bruynooghe [WB92], pages 87–99.

[AFZ88]   I. Attali and P. Franchi-Zanettaci. Unification-free execu-
           tion of TYPOL programs by semantic attribute evaluation.
           In Deransart et al. [DLM88], pages 252–272.

[AM91]   H. Alblas and B. Melichar, editors. *Attribute Grammars,
           Applications and Systems, Prague Summer School*, volume
           545 of *Lecture Notes in Computer Science*. Springer-Verlag,
           1991.

[AP90]   K. R. Apt and D. Pedreschi. Studies in pure Prolog: termi-
           nation. In J.W. Lloyd, editor, *Symposium on Compution al
           Logic*, pages 150–176, Berlin, 1990. Springer-Verlag.

[AP92a]   K. R. Apt and A. Pellegrini. On the occur-check free Prolog
           programs. TR CS-R9238, CSD, Center for Mathematics
           and Computer Science, Amsterdam, October 1992.

[AP92b]   K. R. Apt and A. Pellegrini. Why the occur-check is not a
           problem. In Wirsing and Bruynooghe [WB92], pages 69–86.

[Apt90]   K. R. Apt. Introduction to logic programming. In J. van
           Leeuwen, editor, *Handbook of Theoretical Computer Sci-
           ence: Formal Models and Semantics*, volume B, chapter 10,
           pages 493–574. Elsevier, 1990.

[Apt92]   K. R. Apt, editor. *Joint International Conference and Sym-
           posium on Logic Programming, JICSLP'92*. ALP, The MIT
           Press, November 1992.

[Arb86]   B. Arbab. Compiling circular attribute grammars into Pro-
           log. *IBM Journal of Research and Development*, 30(3):294–
           309, 1986.

[BC89]   A. Bossi and N. Cocco. Verifying correctness of logic pro-
            grams. In *Proceedings of the Tapsoft'89*, volume 352 of *Lec-
            ture Notes in Computer Science*, pages 96–110, Barcelona,
            Spain, 1989.

[BD75]   R.M. Burstall and J. Darlington. Some transformations for
            developing recursive programs. In *Proceedings of the Inter-
            national Conference on Reliable Software*, pages 465–472,
            Los Angeles, USA, 1975.

[Bee88]   J. Beer. The occur-check problem revisited. *Journal of
            Logic Programming*, 5(3):243–262, 1988.

[Bid81]   M. Bidoit. *A method of presentation of the abstract data
            types*. PhD thesis, University of Paris-Sud, France, 1981.
            (in French).

[Bid82]   M. Bidoit. Automatic transformation of abstract data types
            "fair" presentations. In *Proceedings of the First European
            Conference on Artificial Intelligence (ECAI)*, pages 91–95,
            Orsay, France, july 1982.

[BM75]   J. W. de Bakker and L.G.L.T Meertens. On the complete-
            ness of the inductive assertion method. *Journal of Com-
            puter and System Sciences*, 11:323–357, 1975.

[BM88]   R. Barbutti and M. Martelli. A tool to check the non-
            floundering of logic programs and goals. In Deransart et al.
            [DLM88], pages 58–67.

[Bor86]   Borland, Int., Scotts Valley. *Turbo Prolog owner's handbook*,
            1986.

[Bou92a]   J.-F. Boulicaut. *Vers une programmation grammaticale à
            large spectre- Application à la construction de programmes
            avec le Métacompilateur STARLET*. PhD thesis, INSA de
            Lyon, France, 1992.

[Bou92b]   J.-L. Bouquard. *Etude des rapports entre grammaires at-
            tribuées et programmation en logique: application au test
            d'occurrence et à l'analyse statique*. PhD thesis, University
            of Orléans, France, January 1992.

[Boy91]   J. Boye. S-SLD-resolution – an operational semantics for
            logic programs. In Małuszyński and Wirsing [MW91], pages
            383–394.

[BS69]   J.W. de Bakker and D. Scott. A theory of programs. IBM
           Seminar, unpublished notes, 1969.

[CC79]   P. Cousot and R. Cousot. Systematic design of program
           analysis frameworks. In *Conference Record of 6th ACM
           Symposium on POPL*, pages 269–282, San Antonio, Texas,
           1979.

[CD88]   D. Courcelle and P. Deransart. Proofs of partial correct-
           ness for attribute grammars with application to recursive
           procedures and logic programming. *Information and Com-
           putation*, 78(1), 1988.

[CFZ82]   B. Courcelle and P. Franchi-Zannettacci. Attribute gram-
           mars and recursive program schemes (I and II). *Theoretical
           Computer Science*, 17(2 and 3):163–191 and 235–257, 1982.

[CH87]   J. Cohen and T. Hickey. Parsing and compiling using Pro-
           log. *ACM Transactions on Programming Languages and
           Systems*, 9(2):125–163, 1987.

[CL88]   H. Comon and P. Lescanne. Equational problems and dis-
           unification. RR 904, INRIA, 1988.

[Cla79]   K. L. Clark. Predicate logic as a computational formalism.
           Technical Report 79/59, Imperial College, London, Decem-
           ber 1979.

[CM91]   L. Colussi and E. Marchiori. Proving correctness of logic
           programs using axiomatic semantics. In K. Furukawa, ed-
           itor, *Logic Programming, Proceedings of the Eighth Inter-
           national Conference*, pages 629–642, Paris, 1991. The MIT
           Press.

[Cod89]   P. Codognet. *Backtracking intelligent en programmation en
           logique: de la théorie à l'implantation et à l'application au
           parallélisme*. PhD thesis, University of Bordeaux I, January
           1989.

[Coh88]   J. Cohen. A view of the origins and development of Prolog.
           Communications of the ACM, 31(1):26–43, 1988.

[Col78]   A. Colmerauer. Metamorphosis grammars. In L. Bolc, edi-
           tor, *Natural Language Communication with Computers*, vol-
           ume 63 of *Lecture Notes in Computer Science*, pages 133–
           189. Springer-Verlag, 1978.

[Com86]   The Computer Society of the IEEE. *Proceedings of the 1986 IEEE Symposium on Logic Programming*, Salt Lake City, November 1986. The IEEE Computer Society Press.

[Coo78]   S. A. Cook. Soundness and completeness of an axiom system for programs verification. *SIAM*, 7(1):70–90, 1978.

[Cor89]   M.-M. Corsini. *Interprétation abstraite en programmation logique, théorie et applications*. PhD thesis, LABRI, Université de Bordeaux I, 1989.

[Cou84]   B. Courcelle. Attribute grammars: definitions, analysis of dependencies, proof methods. In B. Lorho, editor, *Methods and Tools for Compiler Construction*, pages 81–102. Cambridge University Press, 1984.

[CU77]   J. C. Claeveland and R. C. Uzgalis. *Grammars for Programming Languages*. Elsevier, 1977.

[DA89]   V. Dahl and H. Abramson. *Logic Grammars*. Springer-Verlag, 1989.

[Dal83]   D. van Dalen. *Logic and Structure*. Springer-Verlag, second edition, 1983.

[Der83]   P. Deransart. Logical attribute grammars. In North-Holland, editor, *IFIP 83*, pages 463–469, 1983.

[Der84]   P. Deransart. Validation des grammaires d'attribut. Doctoral Dissertation N 822, University of Bordeaux I, October 1984.

[Der88]   P. Deransart. On the multiplicity of operational semantics for logic programming and their modelling by attribute grammars. Technical Report RR 916, INRIA, October 1988.

[Der93]   P. Deransart. Proof methods of declarative properties of definite programs. *Theoretical Computer Science*, 1993.

[Dev90a] Y. Deville. Generalized Herbrand interpretations. Research Report 88/21, University of Namur, 1990.

[Dev90b] Y. Deville. *Logic Programming – Systematic Program Development*. Addison-Wesley, 1990.

[DF86]   P. Deransart and G. Ferrand. Programmation en logique avec négation (présentation formelle). Publication du Laboratoire d'Informatique RR 87-3, University of Orléans, June 1986.

[DF88]   P. Deransart and G. Ferrand. Logic programming, methodology and teaching. In K. Fuchi and L. Kott, editors, *Proceedings of French Japan Symposium*. North Holland, August 1988.

[DJL88]   P. Deransart, M. Jourdan, and B. Lorho. *Attribute Grammars: Definitions, Systems and Bibliography*, volume 323 of *Lecture Notes in Computer Science*. Springer-Verlag, 1988.

[DLM88]   P. Deransart, B. Lorho, and J. Małuszyński, editors. *Proceedings of the first international workshop on Programming Language Implementation and Logic Programming, PLILP'88, Orléans, France*, volume 348 of *Lecture Notes in Computer Science*. Springer Verlag, May 1988.

[DM84]   P. Deransart and J. Małuszyński. Modelling data dependencies in logic programs by attribute grammars. Technical Report RR 323, INRIA, 1984.

[DM85a]   P. Dembiński and J. Małuszyński. AND-parallelism with intelligent backtracking for annotated logic programs. In *Symposium on Logic Programming*, pages 29–39. The Computer Society of the IEEE, The IEEE Computer Society Press, July 1985.

[DM85b]   P. Deransart and J. Małuszyński. Relating logic programs and attribute grammars. *Journal of Logic Programming*, 2(2):119–156, 1985.

[DM87]   W. Drabent and J. Małuszyński. Inductive assertion method for logic programs. In *TAPSOFT*, volume 250 of *Lecture Notes in Computer Science*, pages 167–181. Springer-Verlag, 1987.

[DM88]   W. Drabent and J. Małuszyński. Inductive assertion method for logic programs. *Theoretical Computer Science*, 59:133–155, 1988.

[DM89]   P. Deransart and J. Małuszyński. A grammatical view of
            logic programming. In Deransart et al. [DLM88], pages 219–
            251.

[DM90]   P. Deransart and J. Małuszyński. What kind of gram-
            mars are logic programs? In Saint-Dizier and Szpakowicz
            [SDS90], chapter 2, pages 29–55.

[Dra87]   W. Drabent. Do logic programs resemble programs in con-
            ventional languages? In *Proceedings of the 1986 IEEE Sym-
            posium on Logic Programming* [Com86], pages 389–396.

[Dum92]   B. Dumant Checking the soundness of resolution schemes.
            In Apt [Apt92], pages 37–51.

[Fag89]   F. Fages. Le théorem le plus général. In *Seventeenth school
            of the LITP*. LITP, Paris 7, April 1989.

[Fer87]   G. Ferrand. Error diagnosis in logic programming, an adap-
            tation of E.Y. Shapiro's method. *Journal of Logic Program-
            ming*, 4(3):177–198, 1987.

[Fer92]   G. Ferrand and P. Deransart. Proof method of partial cor-
            rectness and weak completeness for normal logic programs.
            In Apt [Apt92], pages 161–176.

[Fil83]   G. Filé. *Theory of attribute grammars*. PhD thesis, TH
            Twente, 1983.

[FLMP88]   M. Falaschi, G. Levi, M. Martelli, and C. Palamidessi. A
            new declarative semantics for logic languages. In Kowalski
            and Bowen [KB88], pages 993–1005.

[FLMP89]   M. Falaschi, G. Levi, M. Martelli, and C. Palamidessi.
            Declarative modeling of the operational behaviour of logic
            languages. *Theoretical Computer Science*, 69(3):289–318,
            1989.

[Flo67]   R.W. Floyd. Assigning meanings to programs. In J.T.
            Schwartz, editor, *Mathematical Aspects of Computer Sci-
            ence, Proceedings of Symposia in Applied Mathematics*, vol-
            ume 19, pages 19–32. American Mathematical Society, 1967.

[Fri88]   L. Fribourg. Equivalence-preserving transformations of in-
            ductive properties of Prolog programs. In Kowalski and
            Bowen [KB88], pages 893–908.

[Fri90]   L. Fribourg. Extracting logic programs from proofs that
            use extended prolog execution and induction. In Warren
            and Szeredi [WS90], pages 685–699.

[GM89]   G. Gazdar and C. Mellish. *Natural Language Processing in
            Prolog*. Addison-Wesley, 1989.

[GRJ91]   A. van Gelder, K.A. Ross, and Schlipf J.S. The well-founded
            semantics for general logic programs. *Journal of ACM*,
            38(3):620–650, July 1991.

[GS89]   H. Gaifman and E.Y. Shapiro. Fully abstract compositional
            semantics for logic programs. In *Proceedings of the Six-
            teenth Annual ACM Symposium on Principles of Program-
            ming Languages, POPL'89*, pages 134–142, January 1989.

[Hen89]   P. van Hentenryck. *Constraint Satisfaction in Logic Pro-
            gramming*. The MIT Press, 1989.

[HH80]   G. Huet and J.-M. Hullot. Proofs by induction in equational
            theories with constructors. Technical Report 28, INRIA,
            1980.

[Hoa69]   C.A.R. Hoare. An axiomatic basis for computer program-
            ming. *Communications of the ACM*, 12(10):576–580, 1969.

[Hog81]   C.J. Hogger. Derivation of logic programs. *Journal of ACM*,
            28(2):372–392, April 1981.

[Hog84]   C.J. Hogger. *Introduction to Logic Programming*. London:
            Academic Press, 1984.

[HS84]   J. Hsiang and M. Srivas. On proving first order inductive
            properties in Horn clauses. Technical Report 84/075, New
            York University, April 1984.

[HU79]   J. Hopcroft and J. Ullman. *Introduction to Automata The-
            ory, Language, and Computation*. Addison Wesley, 1979.

[Hue88]   G. Huet. A uniform approach to type theory. In Huet,
            G., editor, *Logical Foundations of Functional Programming*.
            Addison Wesley also INRIA RR 795, 1988.

[Hun90]   C.K. Hung. Equivalent logic programs. *Journal of Logic
            Programming*, 9(8):187–199, 1990.

[Isa85]   T. Isakowitz. *On the relationship between logic programs and attribute grammars*. Master's thesis, University of Pennsylvania, December 1985.

[Jaz81]   M. Jazayeri. A simpler construction for showing the intrinsically exponential complexity of the circularity problem for attribute grammars. *Journal of ACM*, 28(4):715–720, October 1981.

[JL87]   J. Jaffar and J.-L. Lassez. Constraint logic programming. In *Conference Record of 14th Annual ACM Symposium on POPL*, pages 111–119, 1987.

[Kan86]   T. Kanamori. Soundness and completeness of extended execution of proving properties of Prolog programs. Technical Report TR 175, ICOT, May 1986.

[KB88]   R. A. Kowalski and K. A. Bowen, editors. *Proceedings of the Fifth International Conference and Symposium on Logic Programming*, Seattle, 1988. The MIT Press.

[KB91]   C. H. A. Koster and J. G. Beney. On the borderline between grammars and programs. In Małuszyński and Wirsing [MW91], pages 219–230.

[KFHM86]   T. Kanamori, H. Fujita, K. Horiuchi, and M. Maeji. Argus/v : a system for verification of Prolog programs. Technical Report 176, ICOT, May 1986.

[KH81]   T. Katayama and Y. Hoshino. Verification of attribute grammars. In *Conference Record of the 8th ACM Symposium on POPL*, pages 177–186, Williamsburg, VA, 1981.

[KNPS86]   K. Koskimies, J. Nurmi, J. Paakki, and S. Sippu. The design of the language processor generator HLP84. Technical Report A-1986-4, Department of Computer Science, University of Helsinki, Helsinki, 1986.

[Knu68a]   D. E. Knuth. Semantics of context-free languages. *Mathematical Systems Theory*, 2(2):127–145, 1968.

[Knu68b]   D. E. Knuth. Semantics of context-free languages, correction. *Mathematical Systems Theory*, 5(1):95–96, 1968.

[Kos71]   C. H. A. Koster. Affix grammars. In J. E. L. Peck, editor, *Algol 68 Implementation*. North-Holland, 1971.

[Kos91]   C. H. A. Koster. Affix grammars for programming languages. In Alblas and Melichar [AM91], pages 358–373.

[KS86]   T. Kanamori and H. Seki. Verification of Prolog programs using an extension of execution. In E Shapiro, editor, *Proceedings of the Third International Conference on Logic Programming*, volume 225 of *Lecture Notes in Computer Science*, pages 475–489, London, 1986. Springer-Verlag.

[KW76]   K. Kennedy and S. K. Warren. Automatic generation of efficient evaluators for attribute grammars. In *Conference Record of the 3rd ACM Symposium on POPL*, pages 32–49, Atlanta, 1976.

[Llo87]   J. W. Lloyd. *Foundations of Logic Programming*. Springer-Verlag, Berlin, second edition, 1987.

[LS87]   J. Loeckx and K. Sieber. *The Foundations of Program Verification*. John Wiley and Sons, second edition, 1987.

[Mał84]   J. Małuszyński. Towards a programming language based on the notion of two-level grammars. *Journal of Theoretical Computer Science*, 28:13–43, 1984.

[Mał91]   J. Małuszyński. Attribute grammars and logic programs: a comparison of concepts. In Alblas and Melichar [AM91], pages 330–357.

[Man74]   Z. Manna. *Mathematical Theory of Computation*. McGraw Hill, NY, 1974.

[MBB+93]   J. Małuszyński, S. Bonnier, J. Boye, A. Kågedal, F. Kluźniak, and U. Nilsson. Logic programs with external procedures. In K. R. Apt, J. W. de Bakker, and J. J. M. M. Rutten, editors, *Logic Programming Languages, Constraints Functions, and Objects*, pages 21–48. The MIT Press, 1993.

[Mei90]   H. Meijer. The project on extended affix grammars in nijmegen. In P. Deransart and M. Jourdan, editors, *Proceedings of the International Conference on Attribute Grammars and their Applications, WAGA'90*, volume 461 of *Lecture Notes in Computer Science*, pages 130–142, Paris, 1990. Springer-Verlag.

[MN82]   J. Małuszyński and J. F. Nilsson. A comparison of the logic
            programming language Prolog with two-levels grammars. In
            M. van Caneghem, editor, *Proceedings of the First Interna-
            tional Logic Programming Conference*, pages 193–199, Mar-
            seille, France, 1982. ADDP-GIA.

[MTH+83]   Y. Matsumoto, H. Tanaka, H. Hirakawa, H. Miyoshi, and
            H. Yasukawa. BUP: A bottom-up parser embedded in Pro-
            log. *Journal of New Generation Computing*, 1(1):145–158,
            1983.

[MW91]   J. Małuszyński and M. Wirsing, editors. *Proceedings of
            the 3rd International Symposium on Programming Language
            Implementation and Logic Programming, PLILP'91, Pas-
            sau, Germany*, volume 528 of *Lecture Notes in Computer
            Science*. Springer Verlag, August 1991.

[Nil83]   J. F. Nilsson. On the compilation of domain-based Prolog.
            In R. E. A. Mason, editor, *Information Processing 83*, pages
            293–298. North Holland, 1983.

[Nil86]   U. Nilsson. AID: an alternative implementation of DCG's.
            New Generation Computing, 4(4):383–399, 1986.

[NM90]   U. Nilsson and J. Małuszyński. *Logic, Programming and
            Prolog*. John Wiley & Sons, 1990.

[Paa90]   J. Paakki. A logic-based modification of attribute gram-
            mars for practical compiler writing. In Warren and Szeredi
            [WS90], pages 203–217.

[Paa91]   J. Paaki. PROFIT: A system integrating logic program-
            ming and attribute grammars. In Małuszyński and Wirsing
            [MW91], pages 243–254.

[Pag81]   F. G. Pagan. *Formal specification of programming lan-
            guages: a panoramic primer*. Prentice Hall, 1981.

[PAN76]   C. Pair, M. Amirchahy, and D. Néel. Correctness proofs of
            syntax-directed processing descriptions by attributes. *Jour-
            nal of Computer and System Science*, 19:1–17, 1976.

[Par69]   D. Park. Fixpoint induction and proofs of program proper-
            ties. In B. Meltzer and D. Michie, editors, *Machine Intelli-
            gence*, volume 5, pages 59–78. Edinburgh University Press,
            1969.

[Pla84]   D. A. Plaisted. The occur-check problem in Prolog. *Journal of Logic Programming*, 2:309–322, 1984.

[Plü89]   L. Plümer. *Termination proofs for logic programs*. PhD thesis, University of Dortmund, 1989.

[Plü90]   L. Plümer. Termination proofs for logic programs based on predicate inequalities. In Warren and Szeredi [WS90], pages 634–648.

[Plü91]   L. Plümer. Automatic termination proofs for Prolog programs operating on nonground terms. In V. Saraswat and K. Ueda, editors, *Logic Programming, Proceedings of the 1991 International Symposium, ILPS'91*, San Diego, pages 503–517. ALP, The MIT Press, November 1991.

[Tég90]   M. Téguia. *Construction de grammaires attribuées associées à un programme logique et application au test d'occurrence*. PhD thesis, University of Orléans, France, February 1990.

[PW80]   F. C. N. Pereira and D. H. D. Warren. Definite clause grammars for language analysis— a survey of the formalism and a comparison with augmented transision networks. *Artificial Intelligence*, 13:231–278, 1980.

[RL88]   G. Riedewald and U. Lammel. Using an attribute grammar as a logic program. In Deransart et al. [DLM88], pages 161–179.

[Ros90]   D. A. Rosenblueth. Using program transformation to obtain methods for eliminating backtracking in fixed-mode logic programs. TR 7, Universidad Nacional Autonoma de Mexico, Instituto de Investigaciones en Matematicas aplicadas y en Systemas, Mexico, 1990.

[Saï92]   S. Saïdi. *Extensions grammaticales de la programmation en logique, application á la validation de grammaires affixes*. PhD thesis, Ecole Centrale de Lyon, 1992.

[SB92]   S. Saïdi and J.-F. Boulicaut. Checking and debugging of two-level grammars. In Wirsing and Bruynooghe [WB92], pages 158–171.

[SDS90]   P. Saint-Dizier and S. Szpakowicz, editors. *Logic and Logic Grammars for Language Processing*. Ellis Horwood, 1990.

[Sim81]   M. Simonet. *W-grammaires et logique du premier ordre pour la définition et l'implantation des langages.* PhD thesis, University of Grenoble, 1981.

[Sin67]   M. Sintzoff. Existence of a Van Wijngaarden syntax for every recursively enumerable set. *Ann. Soc. Science Bruxelles,* 81:115–118, 1967.

[SISN85]   M. Sassa, H. Ishizuka, M. Sawatani, and I. Nakata. Introduction and user's manual for RIE. Technical report, University of Tsukuba, 1985.

[Søn86]   H. Søndergaard. An application of abstract interpretation of logic programs: occur-check reduction. In *Proceedings of ESOP'86,* Saarbrücken, volume 213 of *Lecture Notes in Computer Science,* pages 327–338. Springer-Verlag, 1986.

[SS86]   L. Sterling and E. Shapiro. *The Art of Prolog.* The MIT Press, 1986.

[Tär77]   S.-Å. Tärnlund. Horn clause computability. *BIT,* 17:215–226, 1977.

[VP86]   T. Vasak and J. Potter. Characterization of terminating logic programs. In *Proceedings of the 1986 IEEE Symposium on Logic Programming* [Com86], pages 140–147.

[Wan78]   M. Wand. A new incompleteness result for Hoare's system. *Journal of ACM,* 25(1):168–175, 1978.

[Wat74]   D. A. Watt. *Analysis-oriented two-level grammars.* PhD thesis, University of Glasgow, 1974.

[WB92]   M. Wirsing and M. Bruynooghe, editors. *Proceedings of the 4th International Symposium on Programming Language Implementation and Logic Programming, PLILP'92, Leuven, Belgium,* volume 631 of *Lecture Notes in Computer Science.* Springer Verlag, August 1992.

[Wij65]   A. van Wijngaarden. Orthogonal design and description of a formal language. MR 76, Matematisch Centrum, Amsterdam, 1965.

[WML84]   D. A. Wolfram, M. J. Maher, and J.-L. Lassez. A unified treatment of resolution strategies for logic programs. In S-Å Tärnlund, editor, *Second International Logic Programming Conference,* pages 263–276, Uppsala, 1984.

[WMP+75] A. van Wijngaarden, B. J. Mailloux, J. E. L. Peck, C. H. A. Koster, M. Sintzoff, C. H. Lindsey, L. G. L. T. Meertens, and R. G. Fisher. Revised report on the algorithmic language ALGOL 68. *Acta Informatica*, 5:1–236, 1975.

[WRC+76] R. Wilhelm, H. Ripken, H. Ciesinger, W. Lahner, and R. D. Nollmann. Design evaluation of the compiler generating system MUG1. In *Proceedings of the 2nd International Conference on Software Engineering*, pages 571–576, 1976.

[WS90]   D. H. D. Warren and P. Szeredi, editors. *Proceedings of the Seventh International Conference on Logic Programming*, Jerusalem, 1990. The MIT Press.

Index

Logic Programming

Ehud Shapiro, editor
Koichi Furukawa, Jean-Louis Lassez, Fernando Pereira, and David H. D. Warren, associate editors

The Art of Prolog: Advanced Programming Techniques, Leon Sterling and Ehud Shapiro, 1986

Logic Programming: Proceedings of the Fourth International Conference (volumes 1 and 2), edited by Jean-Louis Lassez, 1987

Concurrent Prolog: Collected Papers (volumes 1 and 2), edited by Ehud Shapiro, 1987

Logic Programming: Proceedings of the Fifth International Conference and Symposium (volumes 1 and 2), edited by Robert A. Kowalski and Kenneth A. Bowen, 1988

Constraint Satisfaction in Logic Programming, Pascal Van Hentenryck, 1989

Logic-Based Knowledge Representation, edited by Peter Jackson, Han Reichgelt, and Frank van Harmelen, 1989

Logic Programming: Proceedings of the Sixth International Conference, edited by Giorgio Levi and Maurizio Martelli, 1989

Meta-Programming in Logic Programming, edited by Harvey Abramson and M. H. Rogers, 1989

Logic Programming: Proceedings of the North American Conference 1989 (volumes 1 and 2), edited by Ewing L. Lusk and Ross A. Overbeek, 1989

Logic Programming: Proceedings of the 1990 North American Conference, edited by Saumya Debray and Manuel Hermenegildo, 1990

Logic Programming: Proceedings of the Seventh International Conference, edited by David H. D. Warren and Peter Szeredi, 1990

The Craft of Prolog, Richard A. O'Keefe, 1990

The Practice of Prolog, edited by Leon S. Sterling, 1990

Eco-Logic: Logic-Based Approaches to Ecological Modelling, David Robertson, Alan Bundy, Robert Muetzelfeldt, Mandy Haggith, and Michael Uschold, 1991

Warren's Abstract Machine: A Tutorial Reconstruction, Hassan Aït-Kaci, 1991

Parallel Logic Programming, Evan Tick, 1991

Logic Programming: Proceedings of the Eighth International Conference, edited by Koichi Furukawa, 1991

Logic Programming: Proceedings of the 1991 International Symposium, edited by Vijay Saraswat and Kazunori Ueda, 1991

Foundations of Disjunctive Logic Programming, Jorge Lobo, Jack Minker, and Arcot Rajasekar, 1992

Types in Logic Programming, edited by Frank Pfenning, 1992

Logic Programming: Proceedings of the Joint International Conference and Symposium on Logic Programming, edited by Krzysztof Apt, 1992

Concurrent Constraint Programming, Vijay A. Saraswat, 1993

Logic Programming Languages: Constraints, Functions, and Objects, edited by K. R. Apt, J. W. de Bakker, and J. J. M. M. Rutten, 1993

Logic Programming: Proceedings of the Tenth International Conference on Logic Programming, edited by David S. Warren, 1993

Constraint Logic Programming: Selected Research, edited by Frédéric Benhamou and Alain Colmerauer, 1993

Logic Programming: Proceedings of the 1993 International Symposium, edited by Dale Miller, 1993

A Grammatical View of Logic Programming, Pierre Deransart and Jan Małuszyński, 1993